MW00791357

FROM BAYOU TO ABYSS

EXAMINING JOHN CONSTANTINE, HELLBLAZER

FROM BAYOU TO ABYSS

EXAMINING JOHN CONSTANTINE, HELLBLAZER

EDITED BY

RICH HANDLEY

LOU TAMBONE

SEQUART ORGANIZATION   EDWARDSVILLE, ILLINOIS

From Bayou to Abyss: Examining John Constantine, Hellblazer
edited by Rich Handley and Lou Tambone

Copyright © 2020 by the respective authors. Characters and works mentioned herein are trademarked by various owners.

First edition, June 2020, ISBN 978-1-9405-8922-0.

All rights reserved. Except for brief excerpts used for review or scholarly purposes, no part of this book may be reproduced in any manner whatsoever, including electronic, without express consent of the publisher.

Cover art by Leah Battle. Book design by Julian Darius. Interior art is © by various respective rights holders.

Published by Sequart Organization. Edited by Rich Handley and Lou Tambone.

For more information about other titles in this series, visit Sequart.org/books.

Contents

John Constantine's very first solo issue, *Hellblazer* #1.

No Hard Feelings: A Foreword

by Jamie Delano

Constantine. John fucking Constantine. You changed my life, you bastard. How the Devil are you?

We were close for a while there, weren't we, back in the day? Got a bit messy together and enjoyed some weird sport on the dark side. But I guess I didn't have the stamina or share your addiction to the angst of supernatural contest. So, after a few years screwing around in Hell's lowest dives and leaving a trail of corpses and deranged casualties behind us, I had to quit the game and leave you to it. Cash in my stack of souls. Enjoy a breath of air and a bit of daylight.

I'm amazed you've lasted so long, if I'm honest – the way you burn through shit like a drunk fucking sailor on payday. You picked some good creative pals to soldier on with and energize you, though. And, as far as I know, they all survived their acquaintance with you, too. None were sucked completely dry. But if they're not scarred on the inside, they're not human...

I guess mostly they must have believed in you, tried sincerely to do their best to stick alongside through the psychic mayhem, or else you'd have left them twitchy and gibbering incoherent in the filthy ruins of their sordid imaginations. I applaud their loyalty and dedication. You may take your immortality for granted, but you didn't get where you are today all on your fucking own, mate, did you?

I remember – it must have been '86 – when Alan Moore introduced me to you. That sly glint in the beardy old bugger's eye when he said, "Jamie, here's a bloke you might get along with."

Moore rolled a few of his six-skin spliffs to grease the conversation (although, come to think of it, you just looked slightly amused at our narcotic indulgence and stuck to chaining Silk Cuts), pointed out some common ground, and then slipped away about some other dodgy business, leaving us together in that grubby smoke-filled backroom to chatter on in the eerie flickering half-light of my old Amstrad green screen.

Or maybe that's poetic license. Thinking about it, the first jaunts we went on together were hammered out, without the new-fangled aid of word processing, on my old portable Remington, weren't they? With carbon copies. And Tippex. And FedEx to pick the scripts up. FedEx was the cutting edge of intercontinental comms then. Email was still sci-fi. Makes me feel old, if I'm honest.

But you needn't fucking laugh, mate. You're going on bloody seventy, in case you'd fucking forgotten.

Oh, sorry, were you trying to keep that quiet? Maybe Keanu Reeves wouldn't be so keen to have another go playing you in the movies if he knew you were practically geriatric. And there's the TV franchise to think of. And the cartoon incarnation. You're a multimedia icon now; I hear people even write essays about you...

Oh well, never mind, mate – you shouldn't join if you can't take a joke, eh?

Maybe you think I sound bitter, regret not staying committed longer, claiming a larger share of your growing occult fortune?

Honestly, that's not the case, mate. I'm grateful. Really. Those first few years were exhausting but a hell of an education. They earned me a lot of insight (not to mention a smoker's cough that still persists ten years after I quit that filthy, dangerous habit) that served me well in my other wordy experimentations. Although – being a self-centred, arrogant prick – you probably didn't notice.

Plus, you'd started necking Guinness within five minutes of our parting. And that shit will deaden your senses. Should have stuck with the mothers' ruin, mate. You were well ahead of the curve there. Gin's all the rage with 21st-century hipsters. Could've had a nice fat endorsement deal from Gordon's if you'd played your cards right...

And it was genuinely a pleasure to hook up with you and that musty old trenchcoat again on the odd occasion. I still chuckle from time to time when I remember Slag the monkey. And the trip to Iraq was a proper blast of catharsis. Although, a decade after we turned the djinn loose in Whitehall, I'm not certain we really helped advance the Middle East situation...

Fine times. All water under the bridge now, though. And what was jolly japes all those upstream years ago would likely be more tedious now that we're oozing out stale into the delta. Good luck keeping it all afloat for as long you can, John. Toddle on about your mucky business. You've got new generations of eager, young minds to corrupt. And I've got my five grandkids...

So, no hard feelings, mate. But if you see me on the street one day, maybe just move on and pretend you didn't.

— Jamie Delano: somewhere in England, 2019

Give 'em Hell, John: An Introduction

by Rich Handley

"What the heck is *Hellblazer*?"

That's a question I asked my friend Joe Bongiorno sometime around 1998, and it's one that would have a profound effect on my comic book collecting habits and, ultimately, would lead me on the path to co-editing this anthology. But I'm getting ahead of myself here. Let's step back a few months prior, to a time before I had reason to ask this question. It's a Hell of a story.

Joe had recently finished tracking down every issue of DC Comics' *Swamp Thing* up to that point, from Len Wein's first muck-encrusted tale, published in *House of Secrets* #92, to the end of Mark Millar's sweeping storyline that concluded *Swamp Thing*'s second monthly series with issue #171. After reading the entirety of the saga and loving most of it, Joe had forced me, on threat of pain, to borrow his comics so I could read them, too. Despite my stubborn kicking and screaming and protesting, I begrudgingly picked up the first issue and began reading it, fully expecting to hand it back to him and say, "See? Told ya'. This just isn't my thing."

Why was I so reluctant? Well, I'd never actually read an issue of *Swamp Thing* before, so my dismissal was admittedly not an informed one, but I *had* watched the movies and some of the television series starring Dick Durock, and thus had an idea (a very inaccurate one, as it happened) of what the character and his world were all about: cheesy monsters, gratuitous titillation, and painfully goofy dialogue, presented in hackneyed tales which went nowhere that countless superior stories had not already gone. So reading more than 200 *Swamp Thing* comic books wasn't something I could picture myself enjoying at all.

Within only one or two issues, however, I realized how embarrassingly wrong I'd been. Such wonderfully macabre storytelling from Wein, simultaneously evoking classic horror motifs and contemporary comic book tropes – and accompanied by such extraordinary Bernie Wrightson artwork, to boot. I was hooked by the plight of scientist-turned-bog-beast Alec Holland in a way I had most definitely not been with either the *Swamp Thing* movies or TV shows, and I had to keep reading one issue after the next, like a strung-out heroin junkie jonesing for his next fix, so I could find out what happened to Alec and his friends.

"You aint' seen nothin' yet, Pilgrim," Joe told me (which most certainly was *not* his actual wording, since Joe pretty much never talks like John Wayne). "Just wait 'til you get to Alan Moore, Rick Veitch, and Nancy A. Collins. They'll blow your mind."

I took such hyperbole with a grain of salt, of course. Everyone says *everything* they want you to watch, read, or experience will blow your mind. I'm just as guilty of this as anyone else; I am not above over-hyping the things I'm passionate about if it will convince others to give them a try, so I recognize that trait in others.[1] If even a fraction of the "blow your mind" claims people made were true, we'd all be walking around looking like Toht and Belloq from *Raiders of the Lost Ark*'s head-melting climax, or Darryl Revok in *Scanners*.

As it happens, though, Joe was dead-on in his praise, with not an ounce of overstated hyperbole. Moore's poetic and incredibly literate reworking of the *Swamp Thing* mythos was nothing short of revelatory, and the accompanying artwork by Stephen R. Bissette, John Totleben, and Rick Veitch did incredible justice not only to Alan Moore's scripting, but to Wrightson's initial designs. My mind was, indeed, blown. Later storylines from Veitch, Collins, and Millar would continue that trend (not so much the meant-well-but-tried-too-hard Doug Wheeler run, wedged between Veitch and Collins), and Millar's final issue brought a genuine tear to my eye as <<spoiler alert!>> Swamp Thing united every mind on Earth in an exquisitely satisfying moment of planetwide

---

[1] Now go read all my other books! They will blow your mind!

harmony.

I'd never guessed *this* was what *Swamp Thing* was like – a mythology in the truest sense – and I'd missed out on a good thing for more than 25 years due to dismissiveness borne of ignorance. I was fully prepared to make up for this grievous oversight, though. How? By reading it all a second time, naturally.

Constantine had me hooked from his first speaking appearance, way back in *Swamp Thing* #37.

Now, I didn't want to bother Joe by asking him to lend me his *Swamp Thing* comics again. There's a limit to how much you can ask of your friends, after all. Thus, I did what any collector with far more obsessive-compulsiveness than common sense and impulse control would do: I went online, and to every comic book store I could find, and I completed my *own* set. Then I sat down and marathoned it all yet again, starting with that *House of Secrets* mini-story. By the time I'd reached Millar's concluding chapter a month later, I didn't want it to end.

It would still be another two years before Brian K. Vaughan would revive *Swamp Thing* for a third monthly series, so I needed a more immediate fix. "You gotta gimme *somethin'*, man! I gotta have *more!*", I begged, clinging desperately to Joe's arm while trying to ignore the withdrawal symptoms taking shaky hold of my soul as insects crawled over my skin,[2] prompting me to scratch and bite myself uncontrollably. "Just a little somethin' to take the edge off, ya' know? Come on, man, you know I'm good for it!"

Joe detached my unsteady hand from his elbow with distaste, then asked me a question that would change everything: "Have you tried reading *Hellblazer*?"

:::blink blink:::

"What the heck is *Hellblazer*?" I asked, thus ending the above flashback and bringing the fully caught-up reader back to the present.

"It's a *Swamp Thing* spinoff comic starring John Constantine," Joe told me. My eyes grew wide with wonder. "It's been going for about a decade now. It's all about John's life as an occultist in Britain, and it's excellent. I highly recommend reading it. It'll blow your mind!" (Once again, I've shamelessly made up Joe's wording, as 20 years have passed since then, so I couldn't possibly have any idea what he really said – plus, Joe has never even read *Hellblazer*, which means I'm blatantly attributing opinions to him that he couldn't possibly have had.)

An entire series starring John Constantine? How had I overlooked this?[3] More to the point, how quickly could I find every issue? The British mage had ranked among my favorite recurring *Swamp Thing* cast members, alongside Abby Cable-Holland, Chester Williams, Liz Tremayne, Matthew Cable, Lady Jane, and Anton Arcane. If he had his own long-running comic, then I was duty-bound to read it.

Whereas Alec's allies spoke to him with respect bordering on reverence, John mocked his slow speech patterns and ridiculed his failure to discover his elemental abilities without a teacher. While Abby and Chester supported Alec's

---

[2] Not unlike *Hellblazer*'s Gary Lester.

[3] This is especially embarrassing since *Swamp Thing* and *Hellblazer* crossed over on several occasions – and *Hellblazer* was mentioned multiple times in the letters pages, so I really have no excuse here.

journey of self-discovery, John led him around by the nose, on the vague promise of information that the mage withheld to further his own agenda. Although the series regulars were decent people who meant well and tried to do the right thing, Constantine seemed to resent involving himself in others' dangerous affairs. He came off as selfish, rude, crude, and arrogant beyond belief – but his scenes in *Swamp Thing* elevated storylines. If any character deserved a spinoff, it was John Constantine.

Naturally, my search began anew, and it wasn't long before I'd compiled a complete set of *Hellblazer* up to that point, to go along with its parent title. When I sat down to read it all, I was floored by how much I enjoyed it – possibly even more so than *Swamp Thing*. This was a worthy successor in every sense, thanks to the complex character into whom Constantine had evolved under the guidance of such gifted writers as Jamie Delano, Neil Gaiman, Garth Ennis, Paul Jenkins, and Warren Ellis, and such wonderful artists as John Ridgway, Mark Buckingham, Sean Phillips, Will Simpson, Steve Dillon, Warren Pleece, John Higgins, and so many others (too many to name here, for sure).

I had already been a major fan of John from his interactions with Swamp Thing and Abby. While catching up on the first decade of *Hellblazer*'s storyline, however, I came to adore the bastard as I got to know his sister Cheryl and niece Gemma; his best mate, Chas Chandler; his many lovers, such as Zed, Marj, Kit Ryan, and Dani Wright; his gallery of friends past and present, dead or alive, like Gary Lester, Ray Monde, Jerry O'Flynn, Brendan Finn, Rick Nilsen, Chantinelle, Straff, and Rich Eldridge; and recurring nemeses who made Constantine's life a living Hell, like Nergal, the First of the Fallen, and John's demon doppelgänger.

Moreover, I came to understand England a lot better than I had, since *Hellblazer*'s DNA is steeped in the politics, history, culture, literature, and essence of London; the city (all of Great Britain, really) is just as vital a component of the comic as its varied cast members are. As a person of English descent who can trace his heritage back to the *Mayflower*,[4] I found that gratifying. Each time I've reread *Hellblazer*, the experience has made me want to visit the land of my ancestors even more.[5]

---

[4] Admittedly, this is not as impressive as it may sound, since an estimated 35 million individuals worldwide are *Mayflower* descendants.

[5] Which I finally did in 2018, when my wife and I spent two weeks touring the area. It was exhilarating. I would move there tomorrow.

Throughout the next two decades, I remained a loyal reader. Writers Brian Azzarello, Mike Carey, Denise Mina, Andy Diggle, and Peter Milligan rounded out the comic's publication history, along with other scribes on various miniseries (*Bad Blood, Hellblazer/Books of Magic, The Horrorist, Love Street, Lady Constantine, The Trenchcoat Brigade, Papa Midnite, Chas: The Knowledge, City of Demons*); one-shots (*Heartland, Death Talks About Life, Totems, Vertigo Secret Files, Shoot*, two annuals, and a special); anthologies (*Vertigo Jam, Winter's Edge, 9-11, The House of Mystery*); graphic novels (*All His Engines, Pandemonium, Dark Entries*); prose novels (*War Lord, Subterranean*); and the *DC Heroes Role-Playing Game*'s *Swamp Thing Sourcebook/Adventure*. John was featured in several other comic books as well, notably *The Sandman, The Books of Magic, Shade the Changing Man, Zatanna*, and *Mobfire*. I, of course, chased down and read them all.

My personal favorites were the stories and characters from *Hellblazer*'s first three ongoing writers: Jamie Delano, Garth Ennis, and Paul Jenkins. That doesn't mean I didn't enjoy the other writers' work, because I did – everyone who worked on the original *Hellblazer* added something worthy, and I love it all. But the Delano, Ennis, and Jenkins runs, in particular, are what I think of first when I have a hankerin' for *Hellblazer*. They epitomize the title and its lead character. That's why I'm overjoyed that Jamie Delano kindly penned the foreword to this anthology. Jamie not only turned in something wonderfully witty and wistful, but he did so within a matter of days. It would be a grave understatement to say Lou Tambone and I are excited about having *Hellblazer*'s creator aboard – we're positively ecstatic. Our thanks to Jamie for adding the final, perfectly fitting piece to the puzzle, and to contributors James Wilkinson and Draško Roganović for helping us to make that happen.

Collectively, *Hellblazer*'s writers vastly fleshed out John Constantine's history and world by the time the series left the stands with issue #300. Sure, it wasn't a smooth, even ride – what decades-long comic series is? – but even with the occasional road bumps and cringeworthy moments, it was one well worth taking. Sadly, all of that storytelling build-up was swept away with the 2011 rebooting of the entire DC Universe in the pages of the *Flashpoint* crossover and subsequent New 52 revamp, which de-aged John and other DC characters, placing them in a new timeline.

I must admit I found that heartbreaking to witness. Unlike most comic characters, John had aged in real time since his debut. Batman and Superman have remained young thanks to multiple reboots, but Constantine had continued to grow older. He'd been in his thirties during Moore's *Swamp Thing* saga and was nearing his senior years by the time Milligan's *Hellblazer* run had concluded. He'd grown immensely as a character – and we, as the audience, had eagerly accompanied him in this growth. We'd reveled in his successes; cheered him on as he defeated demons, devils, and death; empathized as he dealt with middle age and the loss of his family; and shook our heads every time the poor sod's self-destructive nature inevitably resulted in yet another tragedy, yet another downfall, yet another stain on his already blood-soaked and nicotine-blemished soul.

Though it was easy to miss, John had previously had a Sting-like cameo in *Swamp Thing* #25.

So to see him return to a man in his thirties during the New 52 era, with all that we knew of the mage wiped clean, was difficult. Younger John's story has since continued and has told some solid tales along the way, but I can't help (with no disrespect intended to any of the current creators) but miss that earlier continuity and the vast tapestry the writers had woven for three decades. That was my *Hellblazer*, my John Constantine, and it still is.

In 2018, I had the privilege of working on a DC Comics hardcover collection, *John Constantine, Hellblazer: 30th Anniversary Celebration*, thanks to editor Alex

Galer, who'd invited me to write four essays discussing *Hellblazer*'s long history, as well as a detailed timeline of Constantine's entire life and family history. Amazingly, Sting – lead singer of The Police and the very person on whose image Constantine had originally been based – provided a foreword to that volume. When I first suggested that Sting write the foreword, I did so half-jokingly, assuming neither DC Comics nor the singer would go for it. To my amazement, not only did the publisher wholeheartedly endorse the idea, but Sting said "yes" and turned in a wonderful intro within only a week or two – written in-universe as John's murdered twin, the Golden Boy, no less! I still can't believe that actually happened.

In a universe populated by heroes and villains clad in colorful, tight-fitting outfits, you might not expect a chain-smoking ex-punk rocker wearing slacks, a tie, and a trenchcoat to stand out among the rest. Yet when the occultist showed up in Moore's *Swamp Thing*, that's exactly what happened. John became a fan favorite and has arguably emerged as DC Comics' most popular mystical character. In one of my essays for that collection, I summed up Constantine as a character:

> Handy with a sharp wisecrack, reluctant to help others yet often forced to solve their problems, he has an affinity for the occult, a tendency toward heavy drinking and narcotics use, questionable hygiene, a single jacket and necktie, and a lengthy list of ex-girlfriends (and occasional ex-boyfriends) whom he has loved, lost, used, and betrayed. He's flipped the bird at the Devil, murdered his twin brother in the womb, come back from the dead, fathered an elemental, and bested angels and demons alike. He'll do whatever it takes to come out on top, even if it means getting his friends killed.
>
> Who is this depraved individual? He's Aleister Crowley, the Winchester brothers from *Supernatural*, and Spike from *Buffy the Vampire Slayer*, all rolled up into one, with Sting's face, Sid Vicious's lifestyle, and James Bond's libido. He's John Constantine. He can be a right bastard, and he'll hurt you if you let him in… but in his own way, he's a hero.

Well, a Byronic hero, in any case.

One aspect of Constantine's psyche that I find fascinating and heartbreaking is how self-destructive he can be in every area of his life, from booze and drug abuse to sex, magic, and interpersonal relationships. I suspect John may even suffer from borderline personality disorder. If you've ever watched *Crazy Ex-Girlfriend*, then you're familiar with BPD, since Rachel Bloom's character, Rebecca Bunch, had the disorder, causing her to repeatedly destroy her own life. Those with BPD tend to make astoundingly poor decisions, and those around them often pay the price. Sounds like John, doesn't it? Consider Constantine's history as a conman, blackmailer, cheat, thief, mob associate, and occasional murderer. Recall his multiple prison and asylum incarcerations. Look back at how many lovers, friends, and family members he's damaged – and how often he's knowingly hurt himself. Perhaps *Hellblazer* should have been called *Crazy Ex-Boyfriend*.

Every writer who spends a significant amount of time on a series leaves an indelible mark on the title and its characters. This was certainly true of the original *Hellblazer*. Moore made Constantine a sarcastic yet well-meaning mystery man. Delano molded him into a self-doubting, self-medicating ex-musician who hung out with hippies. Ennis transformed John into a reckless, cancer-ridden, pub-crawling alcoholic prone to playing with fire and ending up burned (most people have their own personal demons, but John has personal *demons*). Campbell taught him Aboriginal magic, while Jenkins and Ellis each gave him a much-needed boost of optimism, only to smack him down again.

Then things *really* got crazy.

Azzarello sent John to prison for murder and launched him on a trek across the seedy, redneck underbelly of the United States. Carey gave John three demonic children and killed off most of his remaining friends. Mina subjected the world to a deadly empathy plague and introduced a new afterlife, while Diggle brought back the Golden Boy and revisited John's painful asylum stint. Finally, Milligan married the aging mage to a woman almost 40 years his junior and offered closure to John's self-destructive path. Since then, other writers have been charting a new course for a more youthful, continuity-rebooted John, including a disturbing team-up between Constantine and Batman, courtesy once more of Azzarello, in the penis-dangling *Batman: Damned*.

Through all of this, no matter how much pain Constantine has endured, he has somehow managed to come out on top, typically at the expense of everyone around him. John has saved the world countless times, yet he's done so without recognition and the cost to his own happiness has frequently broken him. His story is ultimately one of tragedy and pain, without fairy-tale endings, and it's usually his own fault. *Hellblazer*'s writers have gone to great lengths to remind Constantine – and readers – that the magician's place is not in a happy, safe, and secure comfort zone, but in the dark shadows among occultists, necromancers, demons, ghosts, and other supernatural denizens. I wouldn't have it any other way, for a happy, contented Constantine would be a *boring* Constantine.

If you've ever wondered what every *Swamp Thing*, *Hellblazer*, and *Books of Magic* comic and novel (pre-New 52) would look like on a shelf in chronological order, now you know. (Photo courtesy Josh Handley.)

This volume examines the mage's history from his earliest appearances to the present – not only in the pages of *Swamp Thing* and *Hellblazer*, but also on film and television.[6] I've been an avid *Hellblazer* fan for the past 20 years of its 30-year run, and I'm thrilled at the opportunity to helm (with Lou) another celebration of Constantine and his hellish history. I couldn't be happier with the contributors' essays – even those with which I might not fully agree, because they still gave me new viewpoints to consider – and I'm grateful that Sequart invited us to take this journey. I hope you enjoy reading this anthology as much as I, Lou, the writers, and cover artist Leah Battle all enjoyed creating it.

Maybe I should force my friend Joe to borrow my *Hellblazer* collection so I can finally return the favor. It would blow his mind.

---

[6] Sadly, no one is covering *The Mystery of the Meanest Teacher: A Johnny Constantine Graphic Novel*. This young-adult book, written by Ryan North and illustrated by Derek Charm, was announced just as this anthology's manuscript was being completed, and it has not yet been released as of press-time. That title alone would have justified an essay.

Mad, Bad, and Dangerous to Know: Alan Moore's John Constantine

by John Trumbull

I just missed John Constantine. And a part of me still misses him.

I should explain. Stay with me for a bit, though, because, like Constantine, I'm not going to tell you everything right up front.

In 1982, I was a 10-year-old comic book fanatic and a DC Comics kid to my core. I dreamed of someday drawing comics for DC. So an ad in my subscription copy of *Justice League of America* #207 (October 1982, the first part of the "Crisis on Earth-Prime" crossover with the Justice Society), announcing the Great *Swamp Thing* Movie Contest, really caught my attention.

Now, I'd never read *Swamp Thing*, so I wasn't too interested in the fact that someone had made a movie about it. But I sure was interested in the grand prize of that contest: a free trip to New York City and a tour of the DC Comics offices! Wow! I'd get to visit the place where they actually *made* the comics? Seeing inside Willy Wonka's Chocolate Factory paled in comparison. All I had to do was send in a postcard with my name, address, and phone number to DC Comics. What could be easier?

I *really* wanted to win this thing, so I sent in ten postcards. That seemed like a lot to 10-year-old me. Filling all of them out took forever, but the effort was worth it. Surely, one of the ten would win me the grand prize.

As it turned out, I wasn't the grand-prize winner. But I *was* one of the 100 second-prize winners, and I received... a free one-year subscription to *The Saga of the Swamp Thing,* a comic that I never would've read under normal circumstances.

My subscription began with issue #17 (October 1983), one month after a couple of young turks by the names of Stephen R. Bissette and John Totleben took over the art chores. Three issues after that, a Brit by the name of Alan Moore started writing the series.

Now, understand something: I was not then, nor am I now, a horror guy. I never got into slasher movies and I'm not much for jump scares, or for gore in general. The periodic Alfred Hitchcock film is about as far as I ever went in that direction. Kid me was a superhero guy through and through, and 47-year-old me is still one at heart. I find the real world frightening and horrific enough. I don't really need to seek out any additional scares in my fiction. But I still faithfully read *Swamp Thing* when it arrived in that USPS Second Class brown paper wrapper every month because, hey, free comic.

I was a little too young to truly appreciate what Moore, Bissette, and Totleben were doing, but the book was still good enough for me to keep reading. I was as startled by the revelation in *The Saga of the Swamp Thing* #21 ("The Anatomy Lesson") as everyone else: Swamp Thing wasn't ever really scientist Alec Holland, but was instead just a plant creature that only *thought* he was Alec Holland? Whoa! And, hey, the Justice League of America and the Floronic Man from the Secret Society of Super-Villains showed up in the first half-dozen issues, so that was cool. Overall, though, I still regarded *Swamp Thing* as that weird book in which Monkey Kings ate children's parents or obnoxious husbands were unexpectedly impaled by swordfish. So when my renewal notice came in the mail, I thought, "Why would I pay to keep on reading this when there are cooler books like *All-Star Squadron* or *Batman and the Outsiders* out there?"

I let my subscription lapse. In retrospect, this was undoubtedly one of the Top Ten Stupidest Things I've Done in My Life, right up there with not asking Leigh L. out in high school.

The last issue of my subscription was *The Saga of the Swamp Thing* #28 ("The Burial"). It was a good story, one of my favorites, and it even called back to Swampy's origin as he finally laid to rest Alec Holland's spirit. The issue was a nice epilogue to my one-year sojourn into the Louisiana bayou.

Eventually, I wised up and started buying the rest of the Alan Moore *Swamp Thing* run as back issues, and bit by bit, I filled in the gaps. I watched Swamp Thing travel through the mystical realms of the DC Universe to rescue his beloved Abby's spirit from Hell, chilled at the horrific return of Anton Arcane, smiled as Alec and Abby finally consummated their love in issue #34, gasped as a vengeful Swamp Thing transformed Gotham City into a new Garden of Eden in issues #52-53, and followed his travels through outer space in issues #55-63. But there was one issue I could never get my hands on: *Swamp Thing* #37, the ultra-expensive first appearance of John Constantine.[1]

Constantine arrived in Swamp Thing via a circuitous route – one that, surprisingly enough, involves Gumby. I had occasion to hear the full story from Stephen Bissette himself, so I'll let him tell it from here:

> John Totleben and I often had running jokes going between us. The running joke we had going for the first few issues that we did with [editor] Len Wein, is we would sneak Gumby into every issue of *Swamp Thing*. There's a Gumby in the early two or three issues we did of *Swamp Thing*, and Len Wein spotted it, and he got really pissed. I'll never forget the day the phone rang. Len would always say hello, even if he was mad at me about something. He didn't say hello. I picked up the phone, and Len went, "...You are playing a very dangerous game, young man." [laughs] He had spotted the upside-down Gumby I had snuck into a panel. So I had to promise Len that I wasn't going to draw any more Gumbys in.
>
> So John and I were like, "Well, what are we going to do [instead]?" So we decided, all right, [let's do Sting]. John really liked the band The Police. He had sent me their first album, I enjoyed them, and we liked the look of Sting. I liked the look of Sting in the movie *Quadrophenia*, The Who rock album. And John really liked the look of Sting in *Brimstone and Treacle,* which had just played in theaters. So we decided, okay, let's put Sting in the backgrounds. We weren't going to tell [new editor] Karen Berger, and we *sure* weren't going to tell Len Wein [laughs], but we did tell Alan, "We're going to keep doing this. You're going to have to make him a character, 'cause we're not going to stop." And much to everyone's benefit, Alan did. But it started with Gumby. It all started with Gumby.[2]

---

[1] I still don't have that issue. I had to rely on a digital copy to write this essay.

[2] If you're curious about which issues contain those Gumbys, Bissette explains: "You will find Gumby in *Saga of the Swamp Thing* #16, which was the kind of *Twilight Zone* story that Marty Pasko wrote ['Stopover in a Place of Secret Truths']. And then Gumby is visible... there's like this giant annelid, this huge sort of worm monster, in

As good as their word, Bissette and Totleben began sneaking The Police's frontman into the backgrounds of panels. (Indeed, you can clearly see a striped-shirted Gordon Sumner in a crowd scene in issue #25, as one of the witnesses to the aforementioned swordfish impaling.)

Sting as Ace Face in *Quadrophenia*. In another time and place, Sting could have very well played Constantine on television or in a film.

Acceding to the good-natured blackmail of his art team, Moore began thinking about what sort of character this new Sting doppelgänger should be. As he later told William A. Christensen and Mark Seifert in a 1993 interview in

Swamp Thing #17, and there's one panel where he's coming down in silhouette on top of his prey, and if you turn the panel upside down, you'll recognize that the silhouette in the worm is a Gumby face. And I don't remember what the third attempt was, but the third attempt was the one that Len caught, and he made us remove it. So those first two Gumbys are the only two that made it into print."

Wizard magazine:[3]

> I have an idea that most of the mystics in comics are generally older people, very austere, very proper, very middle class in a lot of ways. They are not at all functional on the street. It struck me that it might be interesting for once to do an almost blue-collar warlock. Somebody who was streetwise, working class, and from a different background than the standard run of comic book mystics. Constantine started to grow out of that.

Moore drew further inspiration from a couple of Sting's movie roles: the posh mod Ace Face in 1979's *Quadrophenia,* who nonchalantly pays a £75 fine in the middle of his trial, rolling his eyes all the way, and the sinister Martin Taylor in 1982's *Brimstone and Treacle,* a trenchcoated con man who worms his way into the household of a middle-aged British couple and rapes their invalid daughter.

Ironically, while Constantine owes his existence to Bissette's and Totleben's fondness for drawing Sting, John's first appearance in *Swamp Thing* #37 was penciled by the comic's regular fill-in artist, Rick Veitch. But Constantine still arrived on the scene almost fully formed, his tan trenchcoat draped over his shoulders in a distinctly Ace Face-like manner. He had the air of someone who'd already lived a life outside the four-color confines of the DC Universe, with contacts ranging from disaffected punk rocker Judith to stuttering Lovecraftian scholar Benjamin Cox, to stern nun Sister Anne-Marie. And like Bissette and Totleben, he wasn't above using coercion to get what he wanted, as he threatened to expose Abby's romantic relationship with Swamp Thing to her employers at the Elysium Lawns school for autistic children.[4]

Manipulating Swamp Thing into following him around the country, Constantine promised to reveal the secrets of the elemental's true nature. He even saw his girlfriend Emma killed by mysterious forces before the end of the issue. By the end of his 23-page debut, all of John Constantine's major tropes were in place: dark, devious, double-crossing, and above all, dangerous to know.

During the next several months of Moore's "American Gothic" saga (*Saga of the Swamp Thing* #37-50), Constantine led Swamp Thing across the United

---

[3] Christensen, William A., and Seifert, Mark. "The Unexplored Medium: Alan Moore speaks on what makes working as a comic writer so appealing." *Wizard*, November 1993: http://www.qusoor.com/hellblazer/Sting.htm.

[4] In hindsight, threatening an all-powerful earth elemental might not be the smartest thing for a mere mortal to do. You'd think Constantine would know better. Then again, he rarely does.

States on a tour of hoary horror clichés with new twists: the vampire, the werewolf, the ghost story, the haunted house. He gave Swamp Thing tips on how to utilize his new abilities as "the last plant elemental in the bloody world," pushing him to feats he didn't realize were possible. Constantine kept his promise, leading Swamp Thing to the Parliament of Trees, a community of former swamp creatures in Brazil. It all came to a stunning climax in *Saga of the Swamp Thing* #50, as Constantine manipulated the mystic characters of the DC Universe into fighting a war to save Heaven itself from the Primordial Shadow.

Along the way, Moore dropped tantalizing hints to Constantine's past: *He knew the Phantom Stranger, who hated his guts! He'd led an exorcism in Newcastle that had killed a child and left him in an insane asylum! He'd attended a tantric studies group with Zatanna in San Francisco!* These teases were as effective and intriguing as any of Sir Arthur Conan Doyle's references to the untold cases of Sherlock Holmes.

(Incidentally, while the Newcastle reference was yet another Sting connection – it's the singer's hometown – the tantric sex with Zatanna was not. The oft-told urban myth about Sting's hours-long marathon tantric sex sessions originated in a drunken interview Sting gave to *Q* magazine with his friend Bob Geldof in March 1993.[5] That is, unless the tales of Alan Moore, Jamie Delano, and Brian Azzarello all having fleeting encounters with a real-life John Constantine are to be believed, and the fictional Constantine began influencing his real-life counterpart in the same way that Sting had inspired his creation. But I digress.)

Impressively, Moore kept Constantine consistently tight-lipped about himself. When Swamp Thing asks John "Who are you?" in *Swamp Thing* #51, the mysterious Englishman replies, "Me? I'm just an ordinary person with ordinary needs: food, shelter, sleep, sex, recreation, and a safe world to enjoy it all in. That's all most ordinary people want, all us poor, uncomplicated buggers. We're harmless." Then, with an abrupt disappearance that would put Batman to shame, John Constantine is gone.

Eventually, Constantine proved popular enough to be spun off into his own

---

[5] You can read quotes from the *Q* interview at
https://calendar.songfacts.com/march/1/17791, and listen to Sting discussing that interview during a later interview with *Inside the Actor's Studio* here:
https://www.bravotv.com/inside-the-actors-studio-season-20/episode-4/videos/sting-talks-tantric-sex.

comic book, *Hellblazer* (hastily renamed from *Hellraiser* when Clive Barker's horror film of the same name was released in September 1987). Alan Moore, busy with *Watchmen, V for Vendetta*, and other projects, turned down the writing job, so the task fell to Jamie Delano, a fellow Englishman who injected his own passions and politics into the character of Constantine. Inevitably, we learned more about John: He'd been in a punk band called Mucous Membrane in the 1970s. He had a sister, a niece, and a twin brother whom he'd killed in the womb. There were even a few retcons: That botched Newcastle exorcism now had happened in 1978 instead of "last winter," as was said in *Swamp Thing* #46, and John had now been left in a mental asylum for years, not weeks.

Hellblazer became part of DC's Vertigo imprint with issue #63, ultimately running 300 issues before the character of John Constantine was reintegrated into the DC Universe. Along the way, Constantine has been written by Garth Ennis, Paul Jenkins, Warren Ellis, Brian Azzarello, and others. He's been adapted into a major motion picture, *Constantine*, starring Keanu Reeves, and as of this writing, he's been featured in three primetime television series on two different networks, as well as a few animated versions.[6] He's also, oddly enough, inspired the creation of *three* different counterparts in the DC Universe when other creators weren't allowed to use Constantine himself: Gregori Eilovotich Rasputin in *Firestorm,* Willoughby Kipling in *Doom Patrol,* and Ambrose Bierce in *Stanley and his Monster*.[7]

Suffice it to say, John Constantine's gotten pretty big.

But it could have gone a different way. In a 1986 proposal for a company crossover series called *Twilight of the Superheroes,* Alan Moore gave us an alternate vision of a John Constantine who was even more strongly integrated into the DC Universe.

I won't get too bogged down explaining the ins and outs of *Twilight of the Superheroes'* plot, or why it ultimately didn't happen. That's an entire essay in itself.[8] You can easily find Moore's full proposal online, with a little magic

---

[6] All of which are covered in greater detail elsewhere in this volume.

[7] In fact, as soon as I finish this essay, I'm submitting a proposal to DC to assemble all of these *Hellblazer* doppelgängers together into one book called *John Constantine and His Covert Cabal of Mysterious, Chain-Smoking, Trenchcoated Magicians.* Wish me luck.

[8] In fact, it's one of the subjects of another essay in this very anthology: "The Hell They Weren't: *Hellblazer*'s Lost Lore," by Rich Handley.

incantation via Google.[9] Long story short: it concerns a grim future for the DC Universe, not unlike the one later depicted in Mark Waid and Alex Ross's 1996 miniseries *Kingdom Come,* with all of the heroes of 20 years hence divided into various warring houses. It's a fascinating look at where Moore's head was at in the mid-1980s, before he became disenchanted with mainstream comics in general and DC Comics in particular. The Alan Moore of 1986 was trying his damnedest to make a superhero company crossover work, even to the point of asking if DC still had the rights to Tarzan and the Shadow, and suggesting possible merchandising tie-ins. The plot outline is quite odd at times, with some great ideas side-by-side with utterly bizarre ones, like speculation on the sex life of Billy Batson, the boy who changes into Captain Marvel with the magic word "Shazam."

Flitting in and out of the chaos of this future world, playing all sides against the others, is an older, craftier John Constantine, still manipulating everyone the way he did in Moore's *Swamp Thing,* only on a grander scale. As Moore's proposal describes the John Constantine of 20 years from now:

> [I]n the whole story of *Twilight*[,] he seems to be the only character who has his finger upon all the pulses and knows exactly what's going on in this maze of plot and counterplot between the various factions involved. He thus becomes a central character in the story, and it strikes me that Constantine would probably be a logical choice to launch into his own title off the back of this crossover, if you're looking for characters to do that with.

As you read Moore's *Twilight of the Superheroes* proposal, it becomes apparent just how central John Constantine would have been to the whole crossover. It's a shame it never happened, because even though *Twilight* was never scripted, drawn, or published, it still contains my all-time favorite scene with Constantine.

Twilight begins and ends with the present-day (1987) John Constantine in a New York City bar, a crumpled letter in one hand and a drink in the other, as a beautiful woman comes up to him and asks him for a light. During the course of the series, we learn that this crumpled letter was written by the older Constantine to his past self, with instructions on how he can prevent the horrible future that awaits. The woman who asks him for a light (possibly Fever

---

[9] Or you can save some time by simply going to https://archive.org/stream/TwilightOfTheSuperheroes/TwilightOfTheSuperheroes_djvu.txt.

from Moore's two-part story in *Vigilante* #17-18) will be the great love of John Constantine's life. She will heal his heart and make all the grief he endures worth it. But Constantine is such a trickster that he can't be honest with anyone, not even himself. As John reads the letter from his future self at the end of *Twilight,* he learns that the future he's been trying to prevent is actually inevitable. He's been strung along for the entire series by the one person he'd never suspected: his own future self.

Moore sets the scene perfectly:

> Reading the letter, the younger Constantine is furious. It has turned out that there is someone craftier than John Constantine... namely, John Constantine twenty years older and smarter. Constantine has been conned by himself. Worse, since the person who tricked him is twenty years away in an unreachable future, Constantine has no way of getting vengeance upon the person who did this to him. Angered and enraged, he goes into a bar and sits with the crumpled letter in his hand, getting drunk.

> This is the end of the story, and we only have a final one-page epilogue that takes us back to the beginning, now that we've come full circle. The woman enters the bar and notices John, asking him for a light. He looks up and their eyes meet. She is beautiful. He knows instantly that he could love this woman forever. Knows who she is, knows how happy him and all his future selves are going to be with her... and finally, perversely, he understands how he can have his revenge against his future self, how he can avert the circumstances that lead to *Twilight* by throwing a small but important spanner into the workings of destiny.

> "Excuse me, have you got a light?"

> Constantine looks at her and blinks twice before replying.

> "No. I'm sorry. I don't smoke."

> The woman shrugs, and after a while leaves the bar without speaking to Constantine any further. After she's gone he sits, dead drunk at a dimly lit corner table, and cries his cold and cynical heart out.

I don't know how artistically successful *Twilight* would have been as a whole, but that ending would've worked like gangbusters. Constantine intentionally throwing away his one chance at true love just to take revenge on his own future self? What could be more clever, more cynical, more definitively John Constantine than that?

But *Twilight* also would've put John Constantine on a vastly different path from the one we know. To give you an idea of just how huge and nutty the story of *Twilight* gets by the end, here's another excerpt from Moore's proposal, this one from the climax of the story:

It is at this point that Constantine plays his trump card. Using the Moebius chair of Metron, Constantine has visited the antimatter universe of Qward. In return for a firm promise of immunity for the planet Earth and its immediate system, Constantine has then sold them the secret of the Boom Tube, which he has also managed to wheedle from Metron. Thus, while the assembled aliens are preparing to pour into Earth via Zeta Beam, Thanagar, new Mars, Rann and Oa are currently being overrun by a vast army of Qwardian weaponeers.

Now, I'm not a big prognosticator, but I think it's a safe bet that any John Constantine series that spun out of *that* storyline would've been a tad different from the one we ultimately got – and I genuinely don't know if that's a good thing or not. Because *Twilight of the Superheroes* wasn't just a look into a world where Alan Moore wrote a big company crossover for DC Comics; it was also the last hurrah of the classic John Constantine. As Rick Veitch explained to me last year:

> When they spun off Constantine, they kind of changed him and made him more of a sorcerer kind of thing. Where he was originally, the way Alan saw him, and the way Alan explained him to me, is that he was more like a Houdini where he could slip out of any kind of weird scrape. He was involved with occult things, but not as a player, not like he is in the *Hellblazer* books. It was [a] much, much smaller part of his character and who and what he was. Because the character of Constantine was being changed in the DC Universe by *Hellblazer*.
>
> He was such a great foil for the superheroes. That's how he was originally conceived. And you'd see in *Swamp Thing,* Alan would have him run into somebody like Batman, and in a page or two, he would just eviscerate Batman [laughs] with his wiseass dialogue and that was the value with him, as a foil for these characters. And then once he got into *Hellblazer,* they dropped all the superhero stuff.
>
> He was originally designed it to be part of the DC Universe. To kind of infiltrate it with a certain way of thinking about what it was. I mean, the *Hellblazer* thing was great, and it sold really well, and you've a lot of great creative stuff [in that series], but I think Constantine as a foil for the DC superhero universe was where it worked really well.

I don't know about you, but I find that intriguing as hell. I mean, sure, I like the *Hellblazer* John Constantine who tricked his way out of dying from lung cancer by simultaneously selling his soul to three different Devils. You're going to read a lot about him in this book. But I also like the original DC Universe Constantine, the one who was old pals with Mento from the Doom Patrol and who escorted Swamp Thing around the Monitor's satellite so they could have a private pow-wow with Alexander Luthor from Earth-Three. That's the guy we would've seen in *Twilight of the Superheroes,* and as cool as the Vertigo version is, I still miss that first guy, the one who lived squarely in the DC Universe, with all of the goofiness and madness that that implies. I wonder who that Constantine might be today.

But, hey, DC Comics brought back their multiple Earths a few years ago. There have got to be at least a couple of them where Alan Moore never became disenchanted with DC Comics, and *Twilight of the Superheroes* came to pass. Surely, the original John Constantine still exists on one of those worlds, rubbing shoulders with 'Mazing Man, the Linda Lee Supergirl, and Captain Carrot and his Amazing Zoo Crew. And maybe somewhere, on yet another parallel Earth, there's an alternate John Trumbull writing about the John Constantine of the mainstream DC Universe, wondering what would've happened if DC had instead done a "Mature Readers" book called *Hellblazer* that was only tangentially connected to the rest of the DCU.

At least, I hope there is, because I want there to be *some* version of me who got to read about John Constantine taking Metron's Moebius Chair to the antimatter universe of Qward, dammit.

Gordon "Sting" Sumner, the inspiration for John Constantine's look, cosplaying as Constantine while announcing his involvement with a DC Comics project celebrating *Hellblazer*'s 30th anniversary.

The Sum of His Parts

by Tony Simmons

John Constantine didn't manifest out of nowhere when he appeared in comics.[1] Even his creator, Alan Moore, has said he was a culmination of older ideas — namely, the comic book trope of the occult investigator — with a decidedly street-level spin. As Moore told *Wizard* magazine in an oft-quoted[2] 1993 interview:[3]

> I have an idea that most of the mystics in comics are generally older people, very austere, very proper, very middle class in a lot of ways. They are not at all functional on the street. It struck me that it might be interesting for once to do an almost blue-collar warlock. Somebody who was streetwise, working class, and from a different background than the standard run of comic book mystics.

Moore wasn't wrong about the more respectable socio-economic levels at which most comic book mystics lived. In fact, an inordinate number of them claimed advanced degrees, many unverified, as if to give them some sort of legitimacy. See Doctors Fate, Occult, Spektor, Strange, and Thirteen, for example. (The less said about Dr. Droom,[4] who eventually became Dr. Druid, the better.)

---

[1] *Swamp Thing* Vol. 2 #37 (June 1985).
[2] In fact, the previous essay quoted it as well.
[3] Christensen, William A. and Seifert, Mark. "The Unexplored Medium: Alan Moore speaks on what makes working as a comic writer so appealing." *Wizard*, November 1993: http://www.qusoor.com/hellblazer/Sting.htm.
[4] *Amazing Adventures* #1 (June 1961).

But Moore is also known for his deep dives into fantastic literature, as his *League of Extraordinary Gentlemen* series would prove in 1999.[5] No doubt, he was well aware of the literary antecedents of Constantine, characters like Dr. Martin Hesselius, created by Joseph Sheridan Le Fanu to stitch his shorter tales (including "Carmilla") into the 1872 book, *In a Glass Darkly*.[6]

Hesselius is often noted as the first confirmed "occult detective" in modern literature. Many others followed, including the pagan scientist Dr. Raymond, in Arthur Machen's *The Great God Pan* (1894);[7] Professor Abraham van Helsing, in Bram Stoker's *Dracula* (1897); occult psychologist Flaxman Low, created by E. Heron and H. Heron and first appearing in an 1898 short story;[8] Dr. John Silence,[9] Algernon Blackwood's "physician extraordinary," who debuted in 1909; and Thomas Carnacki, who first appeared in the short story "The Gateway of the Monster," by William Hope Hodgson, in 1910.[10]

The infamous Aleister Crowley, under the pseudonym Edward Kelly, wrote stories about magician and detective Simon Iff, who was viewed by some as a wiser form of the real-world magician himself. The stories were originally sold to *The International* in 1917-1918.[11] Crowley, of course, would become John Constantine's recurring ally and adversary (depending on the writer) in various issues of *Hellblazer*.

The pulp magazines of the early 1900s were a breeding ground for tales of characters caught up in supernatural events. One of the few who had more than one outing was Robert E. Howard's Steve Harrison, who appeared in several stories fighting graveyard rats, the Lord of the Undead, and voodoo

---

[5] See the excellent annotations of the series here:
http://enjolrasworld.com/Jess%20Nevins/League%20of%20Extraordinary%20Gentl emen/LoEG%20index.htm.
[6] Read *In a Glass Darkly* at
https://web.archive.org/web/20070212034823/http://gaslight.mtroyal.ca/lfanume n.htm.
[7] Read *The Great God Pan* at http://www.gutenberg.org/ebooks/389.
[8] Read *Flaxman Low, Occult Psychologist* at
http://gutenberg.net.au/ebooks06/0605811.txt.
[9] Read *John Silence, Physician Extraordinary* at
https://www.gutenberg.org/files/49222/49222-h/49222-h.htm.
[10] Read the Carnacki stories at
http://www.forgottenfutures.com/game/ff4/carnacki.htm.
[11] https://hermetic.com/crowley/simon-iff/index

cultists in the pages of *Strange Detective* and other magazines.[12] Sax Rohmer's Dr. Morris Klaw was a "dream detective" who used his supernatural power to solve mundane mysteries in a series of tales.[13] And Seabury Quinn's Dr. Jules de Grandin, both a physician and a former French agent, appeared in more than 90 adventures in *Weird Tales* throughout a 25-year period.[14]

Manly Wade Wellman[15] introduced two well-liked occult detectives, Judge Pursivant and John Thunstone, in the pages of *Weird Tales*. Thunstone even fought a character called Rowley Thorne, who was based on Crowley. There are many others, including the redoubtable Sherlock Holmes himself, who investigated the mystery of *The Hound of the Baskervilles* in a serial that began in 1901 in *The Strand* magazine. However, like the Scooby Gang's weekly unmasking of the bitter old man behind the mask, the hound was determined to be non-supernatural – which is not the area we're looking into when it comes to John Constantine.

Certainly, not all who investigate weird occurrences are detecting occult activity. Many of the investigations spearheaded by the Hardy Boys and Nancy Drew, back in their day, had elements that appeared on the surface to be paranormal, but again their ghosts and witches were revealed as crooks, spies, or smugglers – and they never had to employ occult powers to close their cases. That's why the Hardys and Nancy – and, for that matter, Fred, Velma, Daphne, Shaggy, and Scooby-Doo – don't make the list.

When you're dealing with a mystery, the process of elimination is an effective tool. I'm using it here to narrow the field of investigators, or else we'd be here all day. That's why we won't delve into all magic users in comics and literature, and why we'll eschew most of those on television and in movies – which are, let's face it, probably more well-known parts of the pop psyche anyway. (I'll touch on the TV occult detectives when we get to the 1970s, which is when a glut of them filled the airwaves, but let's not go down the rabbit hole that is film. Discussing the investigators and monster fighters found in Hammer horror productions alone would require a whole book.)

What follows is a brief chronology of the standout genre characters.

---

[12] http://www.rehfoundation.org/the-works-of-reh/detective-stories/
[13] See some of Rohmer's work here:
http://www.gutenberg.org/ebooks/author/110.
[14] https://archive.is/20130415012132/http://www.gwthomas.org/degrandin.htm
[15] http://www.gutenberg.org/ebooks/author/25394

In comics, the four-color successor to the pulp magazines, the trope of the trenchcoat-wearing occult detective got its start in the pages of *New Fun Comics* #6 in 1935, with the lazily named Dr. Richard Occult[16] – who, in later adventures, sometimes was switched out with the female Rose Psychic. (It's very comic booky-complex, as one would transform into the other, and ahead of its time considering today's ongoing transgender social debates in the United States.) Created by Superman's two dads, Jerry Siegel and Joe Schuster (under the pen names of Leger and Reuths), Dr. Occult was most often found clutching a mystic disc, the Symbol of Seven. He was resurrected from obscurity in DC's 1991 miniseries *The Books of Magic* by Neil Gaiman, in which he was specifically declared part of the "Trenchcoat Brigade" (so nicknamed by Constantine), which also included Mister E and the Phantom Stranger.

Let's take a second to admire the man's name: Dr. Occult, the occult detective – he who can find himself. "Occult detective" is a nicely redundant job description, as "occult" means "hidden" and a "detective" is one who seeks to uncover that which is hidden. By definition, then, every detective is an occult detective. It's only in the modern sense of "occult," referring to the supernatural realm, that the term works – and Dr. Occult doubles down on it.

Occult was preceded on the comics "stage" by Mandrake the Magician, who debuted in a newspaper comic strip syndicated by King Features beginning in June 1934.[17] Created by writer-artist Lee Falk, who soon turned over the art to Phil Davis, Mandrake was one of the first "super heroes," according to many comic historians, though he didn't wear a skin-tight suit (the first to do that would be the Phantom, also created by Falk). His enemies ran the gamut from gangsters to aliens and would-be world conquerors, which he initially defeated by way of hypnotic illusions (later, actual magic powers). But he fit the adventurer model, rather than the detective model.

Mandrake's shtick was soon picked up by another magic user, Giovanni "John" Zatara (whose daughter, Zatanna, would become Constantine's on-again/off-again girlfriend). He came on the scene at the same time as Superman, in *Action Comics* #1 (June 1938), created by writer-artist Fred

---

[16] Read more about Occult here: http://techland.time.com/2010/07/05/75-years-of-the-first-comic book-superhero-its-not-who-you-think/.

[17] Check out Mandrake at http://kingfeatures.com/comics/comics-a-z/?id=Mandrake.

Guardineer.[18] Zatara passed his trademark backward-speaking spells down to his daughter in later years, but again, he was less of a detective and more of a crime-fighting hero.

An actual cop who became an occult powerhouse, the Spectre – created by Jerry Seigel and Bernard Baily – manifested in *More Fun Comics* #52 (February 1940), when policeman Jim Corrigan was killed.[19] Denied entry into Heaven, he was returned to life infused with the spirit of God's vengeance. The Spectre's power has grown to be depicted as vast, nearly omnipotent. His early adventures were focused more on street-level crime, but he did things like turning thugs into skeletons or inanimate objects.

John leads a séance with deadly consequences in *Swamp Thing* #50.

As part of Constantine's effort to halt the Ultimate Darkness, the Spectre grows to mammoth proportions in *Swamp Thing* #50 (July 1986), and is soundly defeated when he attempts to wrestle the creature that predates Creation itself. During the battle at the outskirts of Hell, the Darkness has enough strength to reach into the realm of humanity and destroy both Sargon the

---

[18] More about Zatara is available at https://www.webcitation.org/mainframe.php.

[19] See more details at https://dc.fandom.com/wiki/More_Fun_Comics_Vol_1_52.

Sorcerer and Zatara, who are locked in a séance on Earth, supporting the supernatural battle.[20]

Ibis the Invincible first appeared in Fawcett Comics' *Whiz Comics* #2 (February 1940), the same issue in which Captain Marvel debuted. Created by Bob Kingett, he's another who got his fashion sense from Mandrake, though he added a turban to top off his black tuxedo, and he wielded an Ibis stick rather than a wand.[21] Ibis was originally an Egyptian prince, Amentep, who awakened in 1940 to seek his beloved Taia – and fight bank robbers.

Doctor Fate, who turned up in *More Fun Comics* #55 (May 1940), was created by writer Gardner Fox and artist Howard Sherman. He didn't get an origin story for 12 more issues, despite being a member of the Justice Society of America. Less of an investigator and more of a superhero, he flew about in his blue tights, showing off his muscles and shooting beams of light at evil-doers.

Doctor Terrence Thirteen, "The Ghost Breaker," first appeared in *Star-Spangled Comics* #122 (November 1951), which was created by an uncredited writer and artist Leonard Starr. (Dig the duster on that first cover image!)[22] Also known as "Dr. 13," he was convinced that the supernatural had rational explanations, and he came from a long line of scientists who had been executed or tormented by the superstitious people of their times. In later adventures, he ran afoul of the Phantom Stranger and other supernatural creatures, but somehow never believed in their origins. Thirteen appeared in *The Books of Magic*, and even gave hitchhikers John Constantine and Tim Hunter a ride, ironically telling future master magician Hunter that magic isn't real. In modern continuity, his daughter Traci is a sorceress.

The Phantom Stranger first appeared in *Phantom Stranger* #1 (August–September 1952), created by writer John Broome and artist Carmine Infantino. Initially appearing to debunk supposed supernatural occurrences, similar to Doctor Thirteen, he soon began facing occult characters, demons, and ghosts. His origins (pre-New 52) were never revealed, though several possibilities were put forward in a *Secret Origins* collection, in which Alan Moore suggested the Stranger was a fallen angel rejected by both Heaven and Hell because he'd

---

[20] Read more about this epic battle at http://sequart.org/magazine/27384/"the-end"-alan-moore's-swamp-thing-50/50-1/.

[21] The NBC series *Constantine* showed the Ibis stick and the helmet of Doctor Fate as two of the items in John's collection of mystic artifacts.

[22] https://dc.fandom.com/wiki/Star-Spangled_Comics_Vol_1_122

refused to take sides in Lucifer's rebellion.[23] He exists as a guide to those in supernatural peril, but is seldom allowed to intervene directly in the fate of mortals. Although a member of the Trenchcoat Brigade, he was more often depicted in a cloak or opera cape.

After the Phantom Stranger, there was a bit of a dry spell for the introduction of new magic users or occult investigators to comics during the 1950s, as the horror genre died off in the wake of the Comics Code Authority. Established in 1954, the Code was the industry's attempt to police itself rather than submit to government censorship. It prohibited, among other aspects common to stories of the supernatural, anything associated with "walking dead, torture, vampires and vampirism, ghouls, cannibalism, and werewolfism."[24] Publishers replaced tales of ghosts and magic with space adventures, extraterrestrials, and super technology. The explosion of heroics in the so-called Silver Age of the 1960s brought a resurgence of weirdness that hit its peak with the birth of Doctor Strange in Marvel Comics' *Strange Tales* #110 (July 1963).

There are a number of comic book doctors with the last name Strange, but the one we're interested in is Stephen, created by Stan Lee and Steve Ditko. Dr. Stephen Strange was a brilliant – if egocentric and rude – surgeon until a car accident gave him permanent nerve damage, and he set out on a quest to heal himself. He ended up in Tibet, studying magic under the Ancient One, whom he eventually replaced as the Sorcerer Supreme of this dimension.

Strange employs magic objects and calls on extra-dimensional beings to lend him power to cast spells, binding charms, hexes, and bolts of energy as he fights to protect Earth from cosmic invasion. In the age of LSD, Ditko's trippy visuals found a home on college campuses, but the Doc has had some trouble maintaining a steady series over time. Again, he's less of a street-level detective and more of a god-fighter and superhero.

Zatara's daughter Zatanna, created by writer Gardner Fox and artist Murphy Anderson, first appeared in *Hawkman* #4 (November 1964). She has spent most of her career questing after her missing father or the Books of Magic, and was a member of the Justice League of America before the "Crisis on Infinite Earths" (which was right around the time John Constantine got involved with Swamp Thing). She most assuredly did not frequent a trenchcoat, as it

---

[23] *Secret Origins* Vol. 2 #10 (January 1987).
[24] Read the whole 1954 Code here:
https://en.wikisource.org/wiki/Comic_book_code_of_1954.

would obscure the view of her fishnet stockings, preferring instead to sport a tuxedo jacket with tails.

A Word from Our Sponsors

The 1970s saw another explosion of titles from the big comic companies (followed by an implosion, as sales didn't demand that many books). While on television, the occult detective came into a sort of renaissance. Let's take a brief intermission from comics to glance at the telly.

Dan Curtis was a big part of this trend. His ABC soap *Dark Shadows* (1966-1971) employed gothic horror tropes aplenty, including the investigator Professor Timothy Eliot Stokes, portrayed by Thayer David. After the series ended, Curtis produced a TV movie called *The Night Stalker* (1972, written by Richard Matheson, based on the unpublished novel by Jeff Rice), starring Darren McGavin as intrepid reporter Carl Kolchak. Curtis both produced and directed its sequel, *The Night Strangler* (1973, written again by Matheson).

The success of those telefilms led to the *Kolchak: The Night Stalker* series (1974), with which Curtis was not involved. Rather, Curtis produced and directed *The Norliss Tapes*[25] (1973, written by William F. Nolan), with Roy Thinnes as a reporter who disappeared while investigating a vampire; the tapes of his journal indicate he had many more adventures, which would have supported a series if the pilot had been picked up.

Several *Star Trek* names got into the act as well. Leonard Nimoy starred in *Baffled!* (1973), in which he played a groovy race car driver who began experiencing prophetic visions after a near-death experience. Gene Roddenberry tried his hand with *Spectre* (1977), starring Robert Culp and Gig Young as an occult version of Holmes and Watson in modern times. None of these pilots went to series.

There were earlier attempts as well. Leslie Nielsen starred in *Dark Intruder* (1965),[26] a black-and-white pilot in which he played an occult expert trying to solve the murders of women in San Francisco at the turn of the century. Louis Jordan starred as psychologist David Sorrell in a pair of TV films, *Fear No Evil*

---

[25] Watch *The Norliss Tapes* here: https://www.youtube.com/watch?v=crNstutYXik.
[26] Watch the *Dark Intruder* trailer:
https://www.youtube.com/watch?v=goFKNx1DkSA.

(1969) and *Ritual of Evil*[27] (1970), which were intended to continue into a weekly series that never materialized.

And Now, Back to Our Stories

The first major occult detective to surface in the 1970s, Doctor Adam Spektor, debuted in *Mystery Comics Digest* #5 (July 1972), from Western Publishing's Gold Key imprint. As envisioned by writer Donald F. Glut (author of the novelization of *The Empire Strikes Back* in 1980) and artist Dan Spiegle, Spektor fought all the big monsters: vampires, mummies, and werewolves, among others. He even became a werewolf himself for a while, which was rough on his trenchcoat.[28]

Jason Blood, the human counterpart to Etrigan the Demon, first appeared in *The Demon* #1 (August 1972), created by Jack Kirby. An immortal demonologist based in Gotham City, Blood has a vested interest in learning how to defeat demons, as he longs to be freed from his dual existence with Etrigan. Both of them appeared in Moore's run on *Swamp Thing*, and Etrigan led a demonic charge during the war with the Great Darkness.

Madame Xanadu is a tarot reader and clairvoyant created by writer David Michelinie and artist Val Mayerik (with character designs by Michael William Kaluta) for DC's *Doorway to Nightmare* #1 (February 1978). Often, however, she served more as a catalyst for stories, rather than as a main character.[29]

Like these next couple of blokes, Mister E barely predates John Constantine, having first appeared in *Secrets of Haunted House* #31 (December 1980), created by Bob Rozakis and Jack C. Harris. Known only by his first name, Erik, he got a makeover in *The Books of Magic* and its first sequel, the *Mister E* miniseries, from writer K.W. Jeter and artists John K. Snyder III and Jay Geldhof – including a cool, if smudged, white trenchcoat. E also starred, along with Constantine, Occult, and the Phantom Stranger, in *The Trenchcoat Brigade*, a miniseries by John Ney Rieber and John Ridgway, which brought back Lovecraftian *Swamp Thing* deity M'Nagalah the Eternal. The character has been reintroduced in recent years as Constantine's enemy.

---

[27] Watch *Ritual of Evil* here: https://www.youtube.com/watch?v=TkAHjjPIdlk.
[28] Issues 11-13 of his own title, *The Occult Files of Doctor Spektor* (on the Great Comics Database at http://www.comics.org/series/2140/)
[29] More on Madame Xanadu is available at http://comicbookdb.com/character.php?ID=1047.

The Trenchcoat Brigade: The Phantom Stranger, Dr. Occult, Mister E, and John Constantine.

Baron Winters made his first appearance in an insert in *New Teen Titans* #21 (July 1982) before showing up the next month in *Night Force* #1, created by writer Marv Wolfman and artist Gene Colan. A sorcerer of unknown age, Winters gathered a team to send against evil in the world; he had to send a team because he was trapped inside his manor house in Washington, D.C. Like Mr. E, Winters sported a white longcoat.[30]

Alan Moore has said specifically that he didn't draw on Baron Winters when imagining John Constantine, though he added, "I suppose there is a similarity with Baron Winters in that he is another manipulative character who has a bunch of agents working with him."[31] And there was no love between the two characters: Under Moore's pen, when Constantine approaches Winters to request the use of his magical home for the séance that took place in *Swamp Thing* #50, Winters calls his young visitor "a jumped-up London street thug."[32] This brings us full-circle, with Winters speaking for Moore, describing his first concept of the character with typical brass.

The twist here is that Constantine created something of a new trope in the genre, with trenchcoat- or duster-wearing, magic-using, cynical detectives or

---

[30] A great look at Baron Winters and *Night Force* can be found at https://ifanboy.com/articles/dc-histories-night-force/.

[31] "Alan Moore On (Just About) Everything," *The Comics Journal* #106 (March 1986), page 42.

[32] *Swamp Thing* Vol. 2 #49 (1986).

demon fighters all over the place, such as John Taylor in the *Nightside* novels and Eddie Drood in the *Secret History* novels, both by Simon R. Green; Harry Dresden, from the novels by Jim Butcher; and even Castiel, the angel featured in the *Supernatural* TV series.[33]

 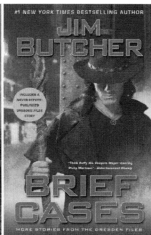 

Who would have imagined that Constantine's trenchcoat would inspire a legion of spell-casters, such as Simon Green's John Taylor and Eddie Drood, Jim Butcher's Harry Dresden, and the angel Castiel from TV's *Supernatural?*

Through John Constantine, Alan Moore helped to tip the scale toward the common man, rather than the doctors, superheroes, and stage magicians. Here was a kind of deeply flawed and achingly human investigator that any schmuck could aspire to become – no advanced degree, pedigree, or colorful tights required.

---

[33] *Supernatural*'s creator, Eric Kripke, even based Castiel's look on Constantine.

The Birth of a Mark: Swamp Thing Puts Revenge Behind

by John E Boylan

While en route to Houma, Louisiana, John Constantine's airplane has a layover in Washington, D.C. After having been seated next to the talkative Funky Flashman for the duration of a nine-hour flight from London, John leaves the airport looking to clear his head and kill some time. He prowls downtown with revenge on his mind and makes his way to the Tattoos While U Wait tattoo shop, where he awaits his turn to receive some ink. The tattoo he chooses is of a tree.

The placement: John Constantine's arse.

At the time, Constantine is in the midst of an out-of-body experience, possessed by the Swamp Thing, Alec Holland. John won't remember the events that unfold on this evening. He won't even be aware of the tree tattoo that has been permanently emblazoned on his rear end for another four months, until learning about it in *Hellblazer* #14 (published in the summer of 1988).

Writer Rick Veitch is to thank for orchestrating Constantine's secret butt tattoo. I contacted Veitch to ask what had inspired him to give John such a tattoo in the first place. The writer's brief but concise response was: "It felt right character-wise. John had been such a manipulating pain in the butt to Swampy, it seemed obvious that Swampy would exact a little revenge once he had the chance." It did, indeed, feel right, but continuity has not always been kind to the tree tattoo.

Since its inception, various artists and writers have ignored the tree's existence. Garth Ennis and John Higgins left the tattoo out of *Hellblazer* #134 ("Haunted") in 1999. On pages 3 and 4, John walks across his flat naked as a jaybird, and the illustration is missing from his rear end. The lack of consistency in tattoo sightings makes the appearances entertaining, and readers aware of the tree can't help but wonder what significance it might play in a particular story.

Constantine's tattoo represents an aspect of comic books that I hold dear: the connective tissue. It spans time, tying together stories, fans, writers, and artists, and further develops the narrative for the characters involved. Moreover, it provides a glimpse into Swamp Thing's character, showing that he is capable of a mischievous sense of humor.

The spiteful gag was a minor event during Veitch's transformative "Infernal Triangles" story arc.[1] In that multi-part tale, a new plant elemental is being ushered into the world to replace Swamp Thing, who entrusts Constantine with finding options for a host ("the Sprout"). None, however, prove successful. After a myriad of failed attempts, Swamp Thing comes to realize that he and his human wife, Abigail Holland, can provide the Sprout with a safe vessel – namely, the two must have a child in order to bring the Sprout to the Earthly plane.

Veitch presents an entertaining and perverse conundrum: namely, how will Swamp Thing (an earth elemental) and Abby (a mortal) produce their child? It's a case of plant meets human, with a seed and an egg not quite compatible. This requires a little help from a friend, John Constantine – whether he likes it or not. In *Swamp Thing* #76 ("L'Adoration de la Terre"), Swamp Thing violently enters John's body through what seems like every orifice in his face, pondering, "...Wasn't it worth... any slight unpleasantness... just to see... the look on his face? ...Didn't I enjoy his shock... when he realized... how helpless he was before me?"

John has dealt with possession aplenty, but it's a rare moment to see Swamp Thing in control of Constantine's body. Wrestling with a great deal of resentment, the elemental finds pleasure in having the upper hand for once in

---

[1] Presented in *Swamp Thing Annual* #3 and monthly issues #77-81.

his dealings with the con man. He takes time to observe John's flat, and this brief moment provides insight into the duo's relationship. While gazing in the mirror at the Brit's face, Swamp Thing muses, "After all these years... of twisting me around his finger...." In that moment, Swamp Thing reconsiders his feelings about Constantine. He wants to see the humanity within John, but history has taught him better. With such an important task at hand, Swamp Thing knows he can't be bogged down by sympathy for the mage.

Revenge of the Swamp Thing.

In John's body, the elemental makes his way to the airport to catch a flight to Houma and reunite with Abby. Flashman greets him at the British Airways ticket counter and, throughout the flight to D.C., annoys him with his hair-brained schemes. His connecting flight to Louisiana does not depart for some time, so he takes to the street. Without Flashman in his ear, Swamp Thing continues to ruminate. The angst and animosity he feels about using John's body to have sex with his wife, paired with his being fed up by the twisted capers into which Constantine keeps roping him, makes the elemental do some scheming of his own, and he stops at Tattoos While U Wait to get John a gift.

A tattoo as an unwitting gift seems excessive, but great frustration typically comes from working with John Constantine. Within *Swamp Thing* continuity, John's relationship with the bog god has been a consistent bother for both. Constantine comes off as a prankster, reckless, wanton, and self-serving, while Swamp Thing generally takes himself too seriously. The two often face grave consequences and great responsibilities, but each handle such tensions very differently, making Swampy's visit to the tattoo parlor all the more surprising.

John has played an integral role in helping Swamp Thing harness his powers, but this often comes with a price. Swampy feels a great deal of responsibility as a plant god, wearing his frustrations on his muck-encrusted sleeve. He carries with him the memories and emotions of a human, often feels pulled between two worlds – tethered to the Green, yet drawn to humanity. By exploiting this vulnerability, John Constantine is able to manipulate his mossy friend. Swamp Thing typically comes when called upon, begrudgingly going along with the other's elaborate schemes. But in this scenario, the elemental is in complete control, and he uses the symbol of the tree tattoo to unify those two worlds. Perhaps Swamp Thing was inspired by an old college prank orchestrated by his human template, Alec Holland.

With fresh ink on his rear end, Swamp Thing / John finally arrives in Houma to be with Abby. The couple tries to get comfortable, and when Abby admits her hatred for Constantine and her dismay at having to share a bed with him, Alec follows her to the balcony of their bayou home. In all its glory, the tree tattoo emblazoned on John's posterior can now be viewed for the first time. Constantine's bare butt cheeks are illuminated in the moonlight, and the tattoo is a simple, elongated triangle atop a small half-circle. The tree appears in only two panels of *Swamp Thing* #76, situated opposite each other on pages 19 and 20.

Amid the chaos involved in Swamp Thing abducting Constantine's physical form and ushering the new plant elemental into the world, John's tattoo is almost overshadowed. The Devil is in the details, though, and the tree is on John's arse. Perhaps that's why it's so intriguing.

Dominic Fouseca, of Newark, New Jersey, was the first reader to mention the "revenge" tattoo in *Swamp Thing* #80, in that issue's "Swamp Things" letters column. Fouseca concluded his letter to editor Karen Berger with this comment: "Before I go: the artwork keeps getting better and I especially liked Swampy's 'revenge' on John." The discreet tattoo makes for an entertaining inside joke, one too good to be contained in a single issue. Glimpsing John's tattoo requires a look at his naked body, so you'd think this would limit the number of appearances or mentions. However, *Hellblazer* rarely shies away from nudity, and the tattoo would make another appearance four months later, when Constantine at last learned that it existed.

John's tree tattoo has a more triangular shape in *Swamp Thing* #76.

After eluding police in *Hellblazer* #14 ("The Fear Machine, Part I: Touching the Earth"), John ends up soaking his outfit and belongings while hiding out in a culvert. In an attempt to dry himself, John strips and wrings out his clothes. As he changes outfits, he is startled to hear a young woman's voice saying "Hullo." The girl, Mercury, comments, "I like your tattoo. It's really cool," to which John replies, "Huh... what tattoo?" Mercury responds, "The tree – on your bum, silly." John looks away, feeling defeated and finally aware of Swamp Thing's derrière calling card.

The ever-observant Mercury spies John's arse art in *Hellblazer* #14.

The fun spirit of the prank captured the imagination of later writers and artists who would chronicle John Constantine's adventures. Throughout the next three decades, the tattoo would make its way into a few *Hellblazer*-related books, most recently in *Constantine: The Hellblazer* #1 ("The Poison Truth, Part One," published in 2016). The tattoo can also be spotted on page 18 of 2002's *Hellblazer* #168 ("A Fresh Coat of Red Paint"), from creative team Brian Azzarello, Giuseppe Camuncoli, and Cameron Stewart. In the latter tale, John is shown standing in front of an FBI pal, Agent Frank Turro, with his pants around his ankles. Sure enough, the Swamp Thing tree mark is partially visible on John's pale, right butt cheek.

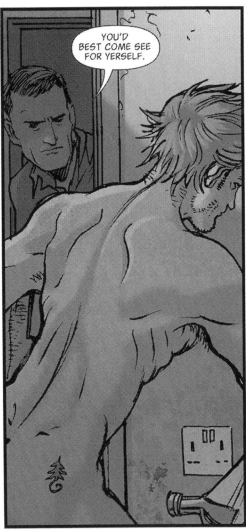

John's cheeky tattoo returns in *The Hellblazer* #1.

In 2007, *Hellblazer* writer Andy Diggle took a focused interest in the arse tattoo. On 27 February 2007, Diggle posted the following on the Voices From Beyond *Hellblazer* message board:[2]

> Right then, I want to lay the whole 'does Constantine or does he not still have a tree tattooed on his arse cheek' question to rest once and for all. He *probably* no longer has the tattoo, as his body was destroyed and re-created at the end of 'Dangerous Habits' (*Hellblazer* #45). Now, we might well be seeing Constantine's lily-white arse in issue 232 – and unless

---

[2] http://hellblazer.ipbhost.com/topic/5122-the-arse-tattoo/

someone can give me an exact issue-and-page reference for an image of the tree tattoo seen *since* issue 45, I will assume it's gone. Off you go then!

Diggle's query was answered in the affirmative, and come *Hellblazer* #232 ("Wheels of Chance, Systems of Control"), the tattoo made yet another appearance. The tree takes center stage on the second page as John stands in front of a mirror getting ready in the morning. The mage's inner dialogue, paired with the butt tattoo, alludes to Alec's possession of his body in *Swamp Thing* #76. "Except this time," he notes, "I'm the one who's in control. And that's what it's all about, ennit? Control." He comments that he's "just surfing the synchronicity[3] wave," mirroring Abby's comment, in issue #76, that "it's all part of the synchronicity storm...."

The tree tattoo establishes a connection between the two characters and symbolizes their complex, permanent relationship – their struggles, as well as what they are willing to do for each other. It highlights a bond between two individuals who could not be more different, yet who are brought together time and again under highly unusual circumstances. The tattoo makes for a more textured storytelling, reminding long-time readers that the series is, first and foremost, a source of fun and adventure. Those new to the title, meanwhile, have a clue to explore. The tattoo appeals to fans who relish being in on a prank played on John Constantine, the mage who can con his way past any obstacle. It's an inside joke that the reader is in on long before Constantine is.

Two years ago, to commemorate the existence of John Constantine's tree tattoo, I visited a tattoo artist friend. I didn't go to Tattoos While U Wait, of course, but I can happily say that I now have a tree emblazoned on my own arse. On the off chance someone sees it, I'm often delighted in realizing that I have forgotten it's there – and, as in John's case, a fun explanation ensues.

---

[3] The term "synchronicity" has sometimes been used to describe John Constantine's powers. As a magic user, he can travel the "synchronicity highway," for instance. This could be a sly reference to *Synchronicity*, the fifth and final studio album by The Police, released in 1983.

What Do You Do with an Undead Sailor? The Creation of "Dark Conrad" Constantine

by Nancy A. Collins

I've always been into monsters. For as far back as I can remember, ghosts, ghouls, and things that go bump in the night have been my jam. It had a lot to do with my maternal grandfather being a huge fan of Boris Karloff and taking me to see the classic Universal monster movies when they would play the revival circuit. I loved them all, but one of my favorites was the Wolf Man — which is how I ended up becoming a fan (and writer) of *Swamp Thing*.

It was the cover of *Swamp Thing* #4 ("Monster on the Moors"), drawn by the late and greatest Bernie Wrightson, that first attracted me to the muck-encrusted mockery of a man once known as Alec Holland. Bernie's version of a werewolf was unlike anything I'd ever seen before, and I eagerly surrendered my sticky dimes. I've been a fan of *Swamp Thing* ever since.

Ten years later, I was residing in New Orleans, living the student lifestyle and scraping to get by. I met a guy who had basically turned the living room of his apartment into an unofficial comic book store specializing in independent comics and titles from overseas. One of these was a black-and-white magazine called *Warrior*, which featured serialized stories about characters like

Marvelman, V, Axel Pressbutton, The Bojeffries, Zirk, and Warpsmith. Although I enjoyed all the series in *Warrior*, the ones written by some guy called Alan Moore really stood out.

So when it was announced in 1984 that the writer of *V for Vendetta* would be taking over the writing chores on *The Saga of the Swamp Thing*, I had high hopes for the title. And I was not disappointed. The reinvention of the character by Moore, Stephen Bissette, and John Totleben was pivotal in jumpstarting my own creative juices as a struggling writer. How pivotal, you might ask? Well, the character of Geoffrey "Chaz" Chastain in my first novel, *Sunglasses After Dark* – a treacherous alcoholic Cockney psychic with a drug problem, a nicotine habit, and an inability to stay dead – was very much influenced by a particular ne'er-do-well warlock, and his nickname was a tribute to Constantine's ill-fated best friend, Chas Chandler, in the pages of *Hellblazer.*

In a roundabout way, *Sunglasses After Dark* is what led me to being signed to write *Swamp Thing* following the departure of Doug Wheeler. You see, DC Comics was looking for a horror novelist to take over the title in mid- to late 1990. The book's sales were – by the metrics of the time – abysmal. Back then, monthly sales of fewer than 40,000 issues were the kiss of death, and Swampy had fallen well below that. The only reason it was still being published was that the live-action cable TV show, as well as the syndicated cartoon series and associated toy line, were still in production.

The new editor on the title, Stuart Moore, had recently arrived from St. Martin's Press and was the one to suggest bringing in a novelist to revive the flagging sales on the book. He contacted a short list of authors he had worked with as an editor over at St. Martin's, one of whom was me. I like to think I landed the job because of my talent, but I suspect the fact I had actually lived in Louisiana at the time – and had inserted a lot of local color into my proposal – helped me to land the gig.

Around the time I was working on the proposal for my first year of *Swamp Thing*, I read Neil Gaiman's *The Sandman* #29, in which he introduced John Constantine's ancestress, the Lady Johanna.[1] The idea of expanding on the Constantine family tree intrigued me. My personal take on the Constantine bloodline is that the men tend to be easily drawn to the dark arts, while the

---

[1] After being first mentioned in *Hellblazer* #40 and then featured in *The Sandman*, Johanna later returned in *The Dreaming*, as well as in her own miniseries, *Hellblazer Special: Lady Constantine.*

women lean toward neutral good and are inherently more powerful than their male relatives. Given that John Constantine is definitely "mad, bad, and dangerous to know,"[2] his having an aristocratic relative with a penchant for necromancy seemed a likely bet.

The decision to make this relative a pirate was inspired, in part, by Alan Moore's "Tales of the *Black Freighter*" backup story from *Watchmen* (which was, itself, based on the legend of the ghost ship *Flying Dutchman*), as well as by my own genealogy. One of my ancestors, who was of Scots-Native American heritage, spent most of his life as a privateer in the Caribbean during the early 1800s, before retiring to Kentucky to open a dry goods store with his Jamaican wife and ultimately becoming the richest man in the valley. If anyone didn't like the fact that he was married to a "woman of color," they could go kiss his ass.

I also drew on a number of other threads to weave together the shadiest member of a family famous for its black sheep. In fact, one of my references was the 1982 nonfiction work *Black Sheep: Bad Boys, Villains, Cheats and Spendthrifts*, by Christopher Simon Sykes, described by the publisher as "an entertaining history of rogues who disgraced their families." In particular, I referenced the story of Captain John Graham Knatchbull (1793-1844), the disgraced son of a nobleman who went on to become a murdering bandit in Australia.

I also mined the histories of Gilles de Rais (a French nobleman who was both a friend of Joan of Arc and one of the worst serial killers in human history) and Stede Bonnet (a.k.a. "The Gentleman Pirate") to create the story of Conrad Constantine ("Dark Conrad"), a cruel and depraved Regency-era English nobleman who became a servant of the Old Ones after obtaining a copy of the *Necronomicon.*

I'm not 100 percent certain of Dark Conrad's exact relationship to John Constantine. I had him being born around 1750 and "dying" in 1811, which would have made him ten years old when Lady Johanna was born. My guess is that he is a first or second cousin on Lady Johanna's father's side – or, given how often mothers died in childbirth before the advent of modern medicine, he could very well be her half-uncle by her grandfather's second or third wife.

---

[2] A phrase originally used by Anglo-Irish aristocrat and novelist Lady Caroline Lamb to describe her lover, British poet and politician Lord Byron; also the title of John Trumble's essay, elsewhere in this anthology.

The pirate "Dark Conrad" Constantine.

The decision to make the real-life pirate Jean Lafitte a character in the story – and the enemy of Dark Conrad – had everything to do with where I resided at the time. From 1982 to 1992, I lived in New Orleans, a city rich in history and legends. One of its most prominent historical figures is Jean Lafitte, whose base of operations was Barataria Bay, a network of bayous and tributaries on the Gulf Coast, in what is now Jefferson and Plaquemines parishes. Lafitte's camp, The Temple – a prehistoric earthwork mound located halfway between Grande Terre and New Orleans – also served as the inspiration for the ancient temple Dark Conrad summons from the bayou's depths in *Swamp Thing* #115.

The physical appearance of Dark Conrad and his pirate gang, as well as the mentions of the *Necronomicon* and the Old Ones, are a tribute to the Cthulhu Mythos of author H.P. Lovecraft. In true Lovecraftian tradition, Baron Constantine committed nameless crimes serious enough to be stripped of his title and sentenced to death. However, thanks to his diabolical masters, he was able to escape the Tower of London, become a pirate, and continue his murderous ways. It's obvious that when Dark Conrad opened the dimensional portal to escape Jean Lafitte, he and his shipmates underwent a "sea change" into the Deep Ones mentioned in the Mythos stories "The Shadow Over Innsmouth" and "Dagon."

For those unfamiliar with the works of H. P. Lovecraft, he was a pulp horror writer from the early 20th century who created the concepts of both "cosmic horror" and the shared universe, as he encouraged numerous writers – including Robert E. Howard (the creator of Conan the Barbarian) and Robert Bloch (the author of *Psycho*) – to write stories utilizing elements and characters from his Cthulhu tales. Cthulhu was a giant, ancient god/demon with wings, and an octopus-like head with a dangling beard of tentacles. For a man who died in poverty and relative obscurity during the Great Depression, Lovecraft has become one of the most influential American horror writers since Edgar Allan Poe.[3]

As for the name "Dark Conrad," that had existed long before I made him a member of one of the DC Universe's more questionable magical families. The moniker was originally created for a character in a series of heroic fantasy stories I wrote while in college that were inspired by Fritz Leiber's *Fafhrd and Gray Mouser* series and Michael Moorcock's *Eternal Champion* saga. The stories involved a pair of female adventurers – an Amazonian barbarian named Ra Hastur and a diminutive witch-thief called Scratch – and their archenemy, Dark Conrad, a wizard-lord who was so evil that part of his soul solidified. He also happened to be Scratch's biological father.

Although these characters have never appeared anywhere outside of a handful of fanzines and an aborted black-and-white indie comics story drawn by *Teenage Mutant Ninja Turtles* artist Rick McCollum, elements of their universe have worked their way into a lot of my professional work – in particular, the authorized Elric short story "The Heart of the Dragon," the *Golgotham* urban fantasy series (*Right Hand Magic, Left Hand Magic*, and *Magic and Loss*), and the Red Sonja comic "Eyes of the Howling God," which appeared in *Legends of Red Sonja* #1. Oh, and *Swamp Thing* #111, 114, and 115, of course.

Although there is foreshadowing of Dark Conrad's return in Abby Holland's dream sequence in "Les Perdu" – my debut story in 1991's *Swamp Thing Annual* #5 – he is not mentioned by name until *Swamp Thing* #111 ("Zydeco Ya-Ya"), in which Swamp Thing hears the tale of the archenemy of pirate king Jean Lafitte

---

[3] He was also more than a little racist by today's standards – and had a neurotic fear of seafood and penguins. I'm not making any of that up.

from friendly zydeco player Augustine "Ya-Ya" Dupin. When the warlock-pirate murdered his wife, Lafitte swore he'd "make Dark Conrad pay for his evil deeds and that he'd never rest until he saw him dead, once an' for all."

In order to escape the pirate king, Dark Conrad struck a bloody bargain with his masters and sailed his ship, the *Cockatrice*, into Black Bayou, never to be seen again. However, Lafitte knew Dark Conrad would return one day, "and when he did, he'd find Jean Lafitte waiting for him!" At the end of the issue, Ya-Ya reveals himself to be a ghost and warns Swamp Thing of a coming storm. He then gives the elemental a doubloon from Jean Lafitte's lost treasure and tells him, "When the time comes, take the coin and call for Lafitte!"

In *Swamp Thing* #114 ("Pirate's Alley"), Dark Conrad and the crew of the *Cockatrice* finally return – although much has changed. Conrad now resembles a humanoid aquatic iguana with tentacles growing from his torso and a cuttlefish-like beak in the center of his chest. The long fingernails/claws on Dark Conrad's left hand were inspired by a character in the 1976 pirate movie *Swashbuckler*, starring Robert Shaw, who wore long metal fingertips as a torture device/weapon. As for his shipmates, they look like everything from humanoid frogs to angler fish, and one even has an octopus for a head, like Cthulhu.

This is also when John Constantine makes his first appearance in my run. Appropriately enough, he's awakened from a drunken stupor by a vision of demon pirates taking Cajuns prisoner. Constantine travels to Louisiana to warn Swamp Thing of the danger, though the bog god isn't particularly happy to see him. They return to Swamp Thing's home in time to see Abby and daughter Tefé being kidnapped by Dark Conrad and his crew. John recognizes the Hell-pirate as one of his ancestors. When Swampy makes a derogatory comment about the occultist and his relatives being unsavory, Constantine reminds him that Tefé (John's biological daughter) is "kin t'the blighter, too," which shuts down any more snark.

The story continues in *Swamp Thing* #115 ("Rum, Necromancy, and the Lash"),[4] in which Dark Conrad reveals that the sacrifice of a human-elemental hybrid will not only open a doorway for the Old Ones to enter into this world,

---

[4] The title "Rum, Necromancy, and the Lash" paraphrases the title of the second album by London punk band The Pogues – who had stolen it from former U.K. Prime Minister Winston Churchill, who famously said, "Don't talk to me about naval tradition. It's nothing but rum, sodomy, and the lash."

but also make it impossible to shut, thereby returning Earth to the control of its first masters. Swamp Thing uses the doubloon Ya-Ya gave him to summon forth Jean Lafitte and his gang – who emerge from the swamp as rotting zombie pirates.

Lafitte and his crew battle Dark Conrad and his Hell-pirates while Constantine and Swamp Thing try to rescue Tefé. It is the first time that Constantine actually touches his biological daughter, who – puzzled and frightened by what's going on – senses their relationship and calls him "Daddy."

Although Lafitte tries valiantly, the resurrected pirate is defeated by Dark Conrad – who then finds himself facing a very, very, *very* pissed-off Swamp Thing, who goes on to rid the swamp of his evil. However, the elemental admits to Abby that he does not know "if one like Dark Conrad is capable of dying." He then tries to make amends with Constantine, in his own way, by presenting the occultist with the tattered Jolly Roger that flew on Dark Conrad's ship to serve as a souvenir "for the family album."

Dark Conrad and his crew resemble characters later appearing in a certain Disney pirate franchise.

The return of Jean Lafitte and his crew was originally intended as a tribute to John Carpenter's *The Fog*, but in the years since the Dark Conrad story arc was first published, it now seems to bear a far closer resemblance to Disney's

Pirates of the Caribbean franchise, what with the magic gold doubloon, undead pirates, tentacled pirate captains, and disreputable, quasi-sober wisecracking Englishman. Shortly after the trailer for *Pirates of the Caribbean: Dead Man's Chest* aired during 2006's Super Bowl XL, I called up DC Comics' legal department and said, "You might want to talk to Disney about this." Whether or not they ever did, I have no idea.

So, there you have it: the story of how Dark Conrad Constantine came into being. As far as I know, the character has yet to return in the DC Universe (or whatever pocket dimension in which DC's Vertigo Comics imprint exists). I was fortunate to have had the Dark Conrad arc illustrated by the talented Tom Mandrake and Kim DeMulder, both of whom knocked it out of the park, and I consider myself damn lucky to have had the chance to add to the stories of characters whom I had read about and enjoyed in the past.

Swamp Thing scribe Nancy A. Collins and *Constantine* star Matt Ryan.

Author's Note: Since I first wrote this essay, DC / Black Label has released my entire run – including the Dark Conrad story arc – in a hardcover format, titled *The Swamp Thing by Nancy A. Collins Omnibus.*

Going for It: The Personal Is Political in Jamie Delano's *Hellblazer*

by Ross Johnson

When Alan Moore, Stephen R. Bissette, and John Totleben created the antihero John Constantine for *Swamp Thing* in 1985, their real-world concerns were largely environmental, both in terms of stewardship of natural resources (swamps, specifically) and in the sense of reflecting a broader interest in the interconnectivity of nature. Though Constantine walked in this world, he really didn't have much to say about any of that, serving instead as the mildly amoral mystical advisor and aid to Alec Holland (or, rather, to the swamp-creature who'd thought it had been formerly known as Alec Holland – it's complicated). The environment can obviously be political, as can Moore's work (just look at the near-future neo-fascist state of *V for Vendetta*, or the indictment of social inequality in *From Hell*), but just as often his themes are rather too esoteric (i.e. weird) to be pinned down to any strict political platform.

So we come to 1988. We're nine years into the government of Prime Minister Margaret Thatcher (to whom we, and Constantine, will return with a vengeance) and about 10 years after the peak of punk rock. *Never Mind the Bollocks, Here's the Sex Pistols,* the *only* studio album from the Sex Pistols, came out in 1977, and the band's charismatic co-front man, Sid Vicious, was dead by 1979. Those certainly aren't the only two dates you need to know when considering the British punk scene of the 1970s, but they were twin sonic booms emblematic of the peak of punk, and then of the beginning of its decline as a cultural force.

It's no coincidence, perhaps, that Conservative Party leader Thatcher became Prime Minister with her party's takeover of Parliament in (you guessed it) 1979. There's no single punk aesthetic (conformity being the antithesis of the punk ideal), and it's much too simple to suggest that a punk-rock ethos is the strict antithesis of the Thatcher program of deregulation, privatization, and cuts to social programs... but it's hard to picture the later Baroness Thatcher in a leather jacket and mohawk.[1] Likewise, we don't tend to associate safety pins and ripped jeans with right-wing governance. What hasn't disappeared from the cultural conversation has been absorbed: tattoos and dyed hair might still be slightly daring in certain contexts, but no longer signal much other than a style preference.

The hippies of the 1960s and the punks of the late '70s and early '80s wouldn't seem, at first blush, to have much in common, but both were counter-cultural movements that flourished for a time before being swallowed by the larger culture (tie-dyed shirts, once a sure signal of revolt against conventional values, are now conveniently available in any mall). Uncoordinated and often apolitical movements struggled against the likes of President Richard Nixon in the United States and Thatcher in the United Kingdom, high-minded ideals being insufficient to counter single-minded and well-organized opponents who presumably got up much earlier than their liberal opponents.

In many ways, and perhaps intentionally, Constantine himself parallels the trajectory of punk as a cultural force. When we meet John at the beginning of *Hellblazer*, he's on the downside of that curve: (perpetually) rumpled and disillusioned, having already learned some very hard lessons (what those lessons were, exactly, we'll learn throughout the course of the series). His beliefs haven't changed, but life and almost a decade of conservative government have left him deeply cynical about his own ability to change the world.

---

[1] Amusingly, the TV show *Legends of Tomorrow* portrayed Queen Elizabeth II (or, rather, a magical creature pretending to be her) embracing the punk style in the episode "Dancing Queen."

Harry Wambach wastes away while simultaneously eating everything in sight in a New York restaurant.

The first couple of issues introduce some interesting, if over-crowded ideas about imperialism and greed. In "Hunger" and "A Feast of Friends," from writer Jamie Delano and artist John Ridgway, an American named Harry Wambach develops an insatiable appetite that leads to a gruesome scene in a New York restaurant: he finds himself wasting away even as he eats everything in sight, and before long, he's not limiting himself to food, per se. The woman on whose leg he gnaws isn't any happier about the situation than he is, but Harry soon dies, a withered husk who'd just been witnessed devouring many thousands of calories.

Harry, a supervisor at a local post office, had opened an undelivered package that he shouldn't have. Fairly or not, his Alfred Hitchcock-like build, balding head, and business suit, as well as the Manhattan location, all tend to mark him as an uninteresting middle-management type. Despite his job at the post office, he reads as a cog in the machinery of big-city business who ought not to have stuck his hands into something that wasn't his.

From there we travel to London, where we meet Constantine again, now for the first time as the star of his own book. Coming home after an absence, he finds his old friend and former bandmate, Gary Lester, in the bathtub. As if coming home to find an old acquaintance in your bathroom wouldn't be horrific enough, the heroin-addicted Gary insists that he's *hallucinating* that he's covered in insects; Constantine can see quite clearly, however, that the bugs are very real. Gary, it seems, had been in Tangiers, where he'd attempted an exorcism on a Sudanese child. It sounds noble at first, but Delano and company are generally too canny to fall into white savior narratives: Gary was mostly doing it for kicks, to recapture the feel of his youthful dalliances with magic and for the thrill of battling a demon.

That's bad enough, but it's even worse given what we'll learn later in the series. When they were younger, Gary and John were both nearly destroyed by incautiously toying with demons – others weren't even that lucky – so Gary should have known better. He kidnapped the boy and trapped the possessing hunger-demon, Mnemoth, but the boy died in the process and Gary became concerned that the bottle in which he'd trapped Mnemoth wouldn't be sufficient. When he couldn't find Constantine, he mailed it to a friend of John's in the United States, where it was intercepted by none other than Harry Wambach, bringing us back to the beginning. If it's not entirely clear, none of this was in any way a good idea.

In pursuit of a solution, Constantine visits first a Dinka shaman in Sudan, and then the Haitian voodoo practitioner (and crime boss) Papa Midnight. As they look for ways to stave off Mnemoth, the hunger plague spreads throughout New York City. Ultimately, Gary is sacrificed in order to trap the demon, with John at last offering him the heroin fix he'd been begging for by way of comfort.

As a kick-off to the series, it's a busy but otherwise excellent taste of what's to come: the horror elements are firmly in place, hand in hand with some genuinely gruesome moments (a bit of attempted cannibalism, as well as lots of gross insect bits). There are also plenty of exotic locations, and magic grounded in the real-world history and mythology of several different cultures. John's anti-heroic status is credibly established: he's entirely reluctant to become involved, yet commits himself fully once he sees no other choice. We'll go on to learn that his own past is an anchor that draws him down into these types of situations; even though we don't yet understand that fully, it dovetails perfectly into what's to come.

Though none of it is particularly on-the-nose, there are also hints of the more political *Hellblazer* to come: Sudan had been part of the British Empire until 1956, and while it's probably going a bit far to infer that there's a *strong* message in the choice of that location, Gary Lester's careless and callous treatment of a Sudanese child is the sin that begets his own eventual downfall. (Looking for clues, John makes a trip to the British Museum, which he describes as the "treasure house of the empire.") And it's probably no accident that the demon's ravenous hunger plague begins among the skyscrapers and big money of Manhattan. Just a year earlier, Gordon Gecko had informed moviegoers, via the film *Wall Street*, that "Greed is good." *Hellblazer*'s Manhattanites, some of whom eat their own flesh out of sheer rapacity, might well re-think the maxim.

Just as Wambach's insatiable greed for food kicks off the story, it's Lester's greed for drugs, and then for callous and cheap thrills, that incites the entire story – and, one could just as easily say, the entire long-running comic series. If there's a clear moral here, it has to do with the kind of rapaciousness that leads us to shove someone out of the way in favor of the thing we want. Being anti-greed isn't necessarily a political statement, but in the hyper-capitalist, "greed is good" 1980s, it could certainly have been read as a statement against the prevailing orthodoxy.

So issues #1 and 2 tell a single story with hints about what's to come. It wouldn't take Delano and company long, though, to offer up a more concrete mission statement. "Going For It," in #3, takes sharp and wildly unsubtle aim at Britain's Conservative leadership. This is the issue in which Delano declares that he's no longer playing around, which is a bold move just a couple of issues in. Given 21st-century reactions to politics in pop culture, it would have been interesting, to say the least, had there been an Internet back in 1988.

Vertigo was a "Mature Readers" imprint of DC Comics that offered more adult material and themes, usually in horror or dark fantasy, and *Hellblazer* was among the first books to carry the banner. That would be five years away from this issue, though (in #63, to be precise – an issue celebrating Constantine's 40th birthday). At this point, *Hellblazer* was technically a mainstream DC book. The character had already appeared in a couple of superhero books, even popping up in 1986's *Crisis on Infinite Earths* mega-crossover. I'm hard-pressed to think of a single example of one of the present-day big-two publishers going anywhere *near* as far as Delano does here.

It's no coincidence that Delano begins the story in the Spitalfields neighborhood of London. By the Victorian era, the working-class region came to such a low pass that Queen Victoria staged a particularly elaborate Bal Costumé in support of the neighborhood's silk merchants, who had come under increasing pressure from Chinese competitors producing good quality silk at lower prices.[2] So notable was the ball as an example of both Victoria's (somewhat fickle) largesse and changing fortunes, brought about by industrialization and globalization, that ITV's *Victoria* series (featuring actress Jenna Coleman) dedicated almost an entire episode to it during its second season.

In modern-day London, Spitalfields is a much trendier neighborhood, something that Delano anticipates and takes an interest in.[3] At the outset of the story, an investment banker-type dies while jogging, having been pursued by a pair of mysterious figures who wouldn't let him stop. The narration refers to the all-important "rat-race" by way of making things crystal-clear. Spitalfields serves a dual purpose in the story: yuppies are interested in it both for its impending gentrification, and also because it's still poor enough to offer up some good old-fashioned poverty tourism, a place where the adventurous can see exactly how the other half live.

Though the book came out in early 1988, our story is set on 11 June 1987 – Election Day in the U.K. This is the election that would see another landslide victory for the Conservative Party under Thatcher, the party's third in a row. In just a couple of pages, so early in the series' history, Delano makes clear that magic and demon hunting are not, for either himself or John, exclusive from events in the real world. As we move into central London, Tory papers in the street decry the scourge of "loony lefty lesbos," while beggars line the streets of London as drawn by John Ridgway. In Spitalfields, or London proper, the social and class divide is very much present. The difference is only in degree.

As the election heats up, John is unhappy but largely resigned. For others, though, there's money to be made. Demons are running a market in souls that parallels our real-world stock market, and business is gangbusters (once again, we're solidly in the "greed is good" '80s here). Souls are up for sale in greater quantities than ever before, and business is expected to remain brisk given the prospect of a third Thatcher term. The demons are in ecstasy.

As is so often the case, John, not looking for trouble, stumbles into the demonic stock market. By the story's conclusion, Constantine has beaten the demons at their own game: by riskily offering to sell his own soul at market

---

[2] Gray, Annie. "The Wider World of Food." *The Greedy Queen: Eating with Victoria,* by Annie Gray, Profile Books LTD, 2018, p. 255.
[3] Cruickshank, Dan. *Spitalfields: The History of a Nation in a Handful of Streets.* Windmill Books, 2017.

rate, he spooks the demonic investors into believing that he has insider knowledge of a forthcoming Labour Party victory in the election, and that a crash in the market for souls is imminent. Blathoxi, the flatulence demon running the whole show, thinks he's trying to sell while the value is high. Knowing enough to recognize that John is no fool, the fart monster refuses to buy, and John escapes with his life and soul, having done immeasurable (if temporary) damage to Hell's market in souls.

Of course, it's not an entirely happy ending for John, the story concluding with the night's election results and another appearance by Thatcher herself proclaiming victory. None of it is particularly subtle at this stage, but Delano and Ridgway do skittish readers a big favor here by letting them know what they're in for early on. The series would run for 300 monthly issues, after all, as well as numerous one-shots and miniseries, so readers with no stomach for jabs at consumerism and unfettered capitalism here had an opportunity to jump ship before becoming too committed.

Margaret Thatcher is re-elected in *Hellblazer* #3. According to issues #63 and #122, she had demonic help from the First of the Fallen.

Everyone still here? Good. Because very shortly thereafter, we briefly meet the British Boys. The neo-Nazi youths had made a couple of cameos before their proper debut in "Extreme Prejudice," at which point they are slaughtered by the demon Nergal and his Damnation Army, after having followed a man they believe to be gay into a public restroom, as well as having set fire to a newsstand run by a person of color (probably not the description they would use). Nergal isn't standing up for anyone's rights, merely enjoying using the corpses of a few bigots to get under John's skin.

Delano and Ridgway introduce gay antique dealer Ray Monde in this issue – a groundbreaking character in some regards who hasn't aged flawlessly. There had been very (*very*) few explicitly queer characters in mainstream comics by this point, so his introduction here as a friend of John's, and as a sympathetic character in his own right, is positive. His camp attitude and attire, alongside his AIDS diagnosis, could be viewed as stereotypical attributes, but could just as easily be seen as the creative team's refusal to soft-peddle Ray's queerness.

More troubling, certainly from a modern perspective, is the fact that Ray is beaten to death by thugs in the following issue. It's treated sympathetically, and he dies helping to protect a woman in John's care, but it still reads as an early example of the "Bury Your Gays" trope, in which queer characters are frequently seen as more expendable than their heterosexual counterparts, particularly in stories full of straight characters, with the suggestion being that tragedy is the homosexual's natural fate. Ray is killed by a gang who justifies his death by his homosexuality, while he is *already* dying of AIDS and thus is doubly doomed. Of course, sometimes characters die, and this *is* a *Hellblazer* comic, after all – but the death of Ray feels like a misstep in an otherwise progressive book.

Of course, these particular issues came out at almost exactly the same time as the Thatcher government's infamous "Section 28" amendment, which banned the "promoting" of homosexuality by local authorities, leading to a de facto 15-year ban on positive representations of queer people in British schools.[4] So Delano and Ridgway still deserve a fair bit of credit for Ray Monde, even though they might've had him stick around a bit longer.

---

[4] Sommerlad, Joe. "Section 28: What Was Margaret Thatcher's Controversial Law and How Did It Affect the Lives of LGBT+ People?" *The Independent*, Independent Digital News and Media, 25 May 2018:

John Constantine visits his dear and doomed friend Ray Monde.

The Conservatives and suits weren't the only ones under the microscope of Delano and company, however. Even from the beginning, there is the sense with Constantine of a person trying to atone for past sins. Issue #11, "Newcastle: A Taste of Things to Come," reveals why, and is, as a result, one of the most consequential stories of *Hellblazer*'s entire run. Here we meet John's old crew: Frank North, Judith, Anne Marie, Ritchie Simpson, Ben Cox, and the particularly ill-fated Gary in a flashback to events 10 years in the past. They're a band of occult enthusiasts, while John and Gary are also part of a *literal* band: Mucous Membrane, best known for their poorly performing single, "Venus of

http://www.independent.co.uk/news/uk/politics/section-28-explained-lgbt-education-schools-homosexuality-gay-queer-margaret-thatcher-a8366741.html.

the Hardsell," for the 'Snot Music label. Good luck getting your hands on a copy.[5] The band lasted for just two years, from 1977 to 1979 – the same two years which began with Sid Vicious joining the Sex Pistols and ended with his fatal heroin overdose, a murder allegation, an assault, and a suicide attempt in between.

John revisits the site of the old Casanova Club, where a past incident set some key events in motion.

For punk music fans, those two years are either legendary or horrific – and probably a bit of both. It was similarly the best and worst of times for John Constantine, all leading up to events at the Casanova Club that we visit in the issue. The once-popular club was run by Alex Logue, a magician of some ability who also had no compunctions about using his own daughter in any number of

---

[5] Though you can find the song covered by the band Spiderlegs: https://www.youtube.com/watch?v=lV6SI_u1s3M.

truly repugnant ways. In the abandoned club, the band discovers that young Astra Logue has used her own natural abilities to call forth a demonic entity to end her father's abuses, and that the murderous being is out of control. John summons a bigger demon to put a stop to Astra's demon... an idea as dumb as it sounds. John's demon does the job, but then claims Astra's soul as payment, promising to claim the rest of the group in his own sweet time.

Here is an instance in which John and his friends have no one to blame but themselves for the damage done; the road to Hell well and truly having been paved with their good, but ill-considered, intentions. Likewise, those neo-Nazi British Boys from a few issues back represent another split in the punk movement that occurred in the '80s, as West German pro-fascist groups began recruiting disaffected youths by co-opting particular aspects of the punk aesthetic in such a way that "skinhead" came to be almost synonymous with "racist."[6] It's another way in which the rule-bending ideals of the punk movement came under fire not from without, but from within.

In Delano's longest arc, the nine-part "The Fear Machine" (with artists Mike Hoffman, Mark Buckingham, and Alfredo Alcala), Constantine joins up with a group of new-age travelers who eventually run afoul of the appropriately named Geotroniks company, as well as Members of Parliament working together to create the titular machine using ley lines and a demon named Jallakuntilliokan. The travelers are a nod to, and make reference to, what was called the Battle of the Beanfield: in 1985, courts prohibited what had been an annual free cultural festival at Stonehenge. Police officers came out in force to block several hundred travelers from approaching the monument.[7] Though accounts vary, violence ensued, with authorities having been held legally liable for at least some of the chaos. From one perspective, it was yet another way in which the 1980s were pushing back against alternative and counter-cultural ways of living that had emerged in the 1960s and '70s.

"The Fear Machine" involves not just new-age travelers, MPs, and shadowy corporations, but Masons as well, with a lodge inside of Parliament itself. Freemasonry here can stand in for any secret organization believed to

---

[6] Knopper, Steve. "How Black Flag, Bad Brains, and More Reclaimed Punk from White Supremacists." *GQ*, 16 January 2018: http://www.gq.com/story/punks-and-nazis-oral-history.

[7] Hallett, Emma. "Summer Solstice: How the Stonehenge Battles Faded." *BBC News*, BBC, 20 June 2014: http://www.bbc.com/news/uk-england-27405147.

manipulate global events and pull on the reins of power from the highest levels. Think of the Illuminati (whose influence is mostly limited to pop culture) or real-life groups like Yale's Skull and Bones (whose membership boasts at least three U.S. Presidents)[8] or Oxford's Bullingdon Club (which counts London politicians Boris Johnson and David Cameron among its members).

The Freemasons seem to have fallen out of favor in more recent stories of secret societies, given current examples in the news. With their secretive natures, there's always debate about how much influence these groups have but, for example, the 2004 U.S. Presidential election was a choice between one or another member of Skull and Bones, a statistically suspect lineup. Even without resorting to conspiracy theories, a bit of paranoia is *probably* justified. Delano, obviously, goes to the more extreme end of what such an organization might seek to accomplish, at least in terms of demon-raising. Dramatic license and all that.

There's not a lot of ambiguity around the purpose of the device being created. (The story arc *is*, after all, called "The Fear Machine.") But fear can have many sources and many purposes. Political fear is a very particular thing, though – crime, immigration, queer equality – and bringing up specific modern examples can be fraught, since what looks like fear-mongering to one voter might feel like a legitimate source of concern to another. But certainly, we can look at examples from throughout history: Adolf Hitler was a far greater threat to peace and prosperity than were the Jewish citizens he scapegoated. Franklin D. Roosevelt summarized things pretty well when he famously warned of there being no greater fear than fear itself.

Remove the horror elements, and it's not hard to see Delano making a fairly straightforward critique of then-current (and, by extension, current-current) politics, specifically but not exclusively directed at the Thatcher government at a time when corporations were being allowed to hold greater and greater sway over British life (and not just Britain: certainly Thatcher and U.S. President Ronald Reagan were very much on the same page in their desire to deregulate and denationalize institutions). Members of Parliament working behind the scenes with a mundane-sounding corporation and getting a nudge from a secretive group of elites doesn't even sound particularly far-fetched if you skim past the bit about the demons. Not everyone would agree that there's anything

---

[8] William Howard Taft, George H. W. Bush, and George W. Bush.

nefarious about such arrangements, but Delano certainly does, and he pushes the metaphor to horrific limits.

Toward the end of Delano's run, the writer revisits some of the characters who've been important throughout his three years, as well as some of the ideas he'd put forth. He also comes back to the idea of John as a man perpetually in twilight, having wasted his youth, even though he's not yet 40 years old. In the uncharacteristic "Sundays Are Different," illustrated by Dean Motter and Mark Pennington, John welcomes the new decade of the 1990s by buying a bag of apples rather than his usual cigarettes, and runs into an old acquaintance from back in the punk days, Patrick McDonell,[9] who's now developing eco-friendly housing in Northern Ireland.

Patrick and his wife are into clean living and wine bars, and he even wants to pay John back for scamming him back in the day. It's all meant to seem very suspicious and borderline insufferable, but John's enjoying the example before him of a man who put his past behind him. Of course, it can't last – the story ends on a slightly psychedelic and ambiguous note, but, essentially, John's body and soul reject the idea of moving on. It winds up not really mattering how sincere Patrick and his wife are, since John will not be moving forward. It could be a critique of anyone of any generation for whom the pull of past mistakes is stronger than the hope of the future.

In "The Undiscovered Country..." with artist Sean Philips, Delano introduces John to a version of himself at the age of 80 years old. The elderly Constantine is alone in a nursing home that no longer wants to put up with his reckless behavior (and refusal to give up smoking, naturally). In his escape from the home, his fear of damnation leads John to stumble off a bridge, to drown in the water below. It's only John's imagined version of his own fate, but it's a sadly plausible end for a man who can't embrace his humanity and heroism because he's trapped in his own dark past. Though few of us have run afoul of literal demons, it's not hard to relate in greater or lesser ways.

John's fears, at the end of Delano's run, reflect the fears of many who live even slightly outside of the cultural mainstream: he's afraid of control, and of a broader culture that wants to squash the things that make him unique and special, and that even wants to take away his precious smokes. That's all very punk. But he's also afraid of being alone, of watching his one-time way of life

---

[9] A.k.a. Martin Peters, a.k.a. Destructo Vermin Gobsmack.

slowly melt away as his friends age, overdose, or take up time-shares. Suddenly, he's alone on the stage and the once-rowdy club is empty. Any counter-cultural movement is going to come under tremendous pressure from mainstream society (see also: hippies); that's the unfortunate but unavoidable cost of doing something different.

John's life during the decade between his Mucous Membrane stint and the beginning of his solo book follows a course that tracks with the sidelining of the punk scene and the rise of a modern style of conservative politics in both the United Kingdom and the United States. Whether one leads to the other is debatable, but there are certainly connections, with John representing someone who seemed to thrive for a time under one broad cultural force and has struggled under another. That's why the politics in *Hellblazer* aren't merely incidental, certainly to the mind of Jamie Delano and company – they're essential. When the character's stories have moved away from politics, as has been the case in the years since the conclusion of the original *Hellblazer* book, his hard-living ways and curmudgeonly nature read more as charming quirks than as signs of deep pain. A John Constantine untethered from his times isn't quite the same character.

Jamie Delano's last issue came out just as Margaret Thatcher was on her way out the door – not exactly a bookend, but symbolic, nonetheless. When we first meet John, he's rumpled and disillusioned, having already learned hard lessons. His beliefs haven't changed, but life and almost a decade of conservative government have left him deeply cynical about his own ability to change the world for the better. So he doesn't try to change the world – he changes the lives of individuals, perhaps never realizing how much good he's capable of doing. Other writers would tackle Constantine, each with his or her own individual concerns, but none would ever be quite as overtly and fearlessly political as Delano.

The Making of a Forgotten Hit: Putting *Constantine* into Context

by Alex Galer

Part I: A Comic Book Movie

The year 2005 was a unique one for comic book movies.

For Marvel Comics, it felt like the beginning of the end. After the critical and commercial success of *Spider-Man 2* in 2004, Marvel films suddenly took a turn for the worse. *Blade: Trinity* ended the year (and the *Blade* franchise), then 2005 swept theaters with such classics as *Elektra* (killing the possibility of a *Daredevil* franchise) and *Fantastic Four* – not to mention *Man-Thing*, which was intended for theaters but landed on the Sci-Fi Channel. The years to follow wouldn't be any kinder to Marvel, with *X-Men: The Last Stand* in 2006 and *Fantastic Four: Rise of the Silver Surfer, Ghost Rider*, and *Spider-Man 3* in 2007.

Oddly enough, for the first time in more than a decade, DC Comics was back in the game and making movies. In 2004, Warner Bros. released *Catwoman,* DC's first feature since 1997 – the year of *Batman & Robin* and *Steel*. But just a year later, in 2005, *Batman Begins, V for Vendetta*, and the Academy Award-nominated masterpiece *A History of Violence* hit theaters and changed everything.

This was the beginning of the end for superhero movies as we knew them. Camp, comedy, and B-movie ethos were on the out, and dark, gritty realism was sweeping the nation by storm.

So where does *Constantine* fit into all of this?

Well, the movie was a hit financially. While *Constantine*'s total domestic gross ended up being only a little higher than those of *V for Vendetta* and *Sin City* (also released in 2005), coming in at just under $76 million,[1] its numbers overseas brought its total worldwide gross to more than $230 million.[2] Regardless, the movie has largely been forgotten by the public and remains hated by the comic book community. At best, it has garnered a slow-rising cult status online. *V for Vendetta*'s cultural influence, on the other hand, has become immeasurable.

At the time, PG-13 horror was on the way out. Remember, 2004 was the year of *The Grudge*, *Van Helsing*, and *Alien vs. Predator.* While these movies were hits, they were also the end of a trend. Something that started strong with *The Sixth Sense*, *The Ring,* and *The Others* would die in a slog of terrible features marketed toward high schoolers on dates. Once more, it was the dark, serious, and gritty films that were trending. In 2004, we saw *Dawn of the Dead* and *Saw* hit big on small budgets. Then 2005 came out swinging even harder, with *Saw II, Hostel, The Devil's Rejects*, and *The Descent.*

Ironically, the pendulum has swung back. Looking at the trends of today, DC's tendency to ruminate on darkness has taken a hard hit, and the success of comic book films (that are not part of the Marvel Cinematic Universe) has been paved by features like *Deadpool 2, Kingsman: The Secret Service*, *Venom*, *Aquaman*, and *Shazam!.* Even more shocking, PG-13 horror has been embraced by the public more than ever before, with franchises spawning out of *The Conjuring, Insidious,* and *A Quiet Place.*

But we're not there yet. This is 2005, and in an age trending toward the dark and gritty, *Constantine* took its NC-17 source material and made a PG-13 film for the masses. It may have gotten the R in the end, but *Constantine* was made for a PG-13 rating. At the end of the day, the Motion Picture Association of America's decision to brand it as such would doubly damn this feature's future (more on that later).

Batman Begins gave its characters greater realism and maturity than ever

---

[1] https://www.boxofficemojo.com/movies/?id=vforvendetta.htm
[2] https://www.boxofficemojo.com/movies/?id=constantine.htm

before; *V for Vendetta* represented its source material faithfully and used its narrative to say something about the world; and *Constantine* tried to appeal to the American audience at large by simplifying Garth Ennis's "Dangerous Habits" story arc (*Hellblazer* #41-46) with Keanu Reeves in the leading role. John Constantine was now an American living in the uncharacteristically dark, rainy, and empty streets of Los Angeles. Spouting one-liners to anyone who would listen, Constantine spent his days searching for his golden ticket into Heaven.

Despite all of this, I would argue that none of these decisions damned the movie to the point of no return. There could easily be a fantastic PG-13 *Hellblazer* movie about an American John Constantine that has next to nothing to do with the comics. As proven by the films of today, PG-13 horror isn't always a bad thing – and loose adaptations can be incredible.

An adaptation doesn't need to be faithful to be quality. I'm going to put aside examples like *Blade Runner*, *Apocalypse Now*, and the Marvel Cinematic Universe to speak to non-superhero comic book adaptations. Arguably, some of the best comic adaptations took their source material and made it entirely their own. *A History of Violence*, *The End of the F***cking World*, *Josie and the Pussycats*, *We Are the Best!*, *Oldboy*, *Legion*, and *The Death of Stalin* all come to mind. Obviously, *Constantine* is not on the same level as those, but it does find a place somewhere among the *Hellboy*, *Men in Black*, and *Blade* films, which also pull away from their comic origins.

Yes, *Constantine* was out of step with 2005. This likely hindered its cultural longevity, despite its initial success. That being said, the most important thing people forget about fiction is how much our culture shapes the way we enjoy our entertainment. What audiences crave from the big or small screen is constantly evolving. It's why so many classics and cult hits failed to find an audience at the time of their release. When something is presented in a new context, revisited years later, or given an entirely new audience, it can achieve a second life. Hell, look at how many countless movies have become iconic thanks to reruns and cable television. Our surroundings, frame of mind, and frame of reference for things affect how we perceive them. It's why Rotten Tomatoes can damn a film before it has even been released. It's why we bring something new to the table every time we revisit a narrative.

This same logic can be applied to the making of a movie. When a film studio invests a lot of money into a feature, it expects a big return on investment. The problem is that our culture is constantly shifting, and what studios expect out of a hit changes just as fast. Warner Bros.' *Constantine* began development during the year of *Batman and Robin* and came to theaters just months before *Batman Begins*. What started as a movie became a product of years of revision. This was more than a cultural shift – this was a sea change.

Part II: The Making of a Movie

Development on *Constantine* began in 1997 under the guidance of producer Laura Shuler Donner, with writer Kevin Brodbin. By the time of its release in 2005, it had passed through three directors, four screenwriters (that we know of), and two leading actors. This means that the final product had been tooled and repurposed for years behind the scenes, with expectations and visions likely shifting every step of the way as movie audiences grew and changed. This puts *Constantine* into an important context. Across years of development hell, it took many changes along the way before it could receive the full green light.

What we know about the production of *Constantine* comes from the tidbits let loose in the world by those who have worked on the project, the lawsuits that unfolded, and the various reporting done on the film throughout its eight years of production. It should be noted that many of the original articles, interviews, and Hollywood reports covering the production of this film are no longer available on the Web.

The story of *Constantine* begins with Kevin Brodbin. While helping to publish *Empire* magazine in England, Brodbin discovered the comic book series *Hellblazer* – or, more importantly, he discovered John Constantine. "He's one of the more reluctant heroes I had ever come across," he said during an interview with *Screenwriter's Utopia*.[3] "He's really kind of an asshole. He doesn't want to give a shit, but he realizes it's part of his nature." Brodbin was clearly in love with the character.

Brodbin's true passion had always been writing, so he left for the United States to sell screenplays. Not long after he sold his first two specs (*The Glimmer Man* and *Tick-Tock*), an executive asked him to pitch his dream project.[4] He replied "*Hellblazer*," and just like that, Brodbin was put in contact

---

[3] Wehner, Chris. "Ten Questions with Kevin Brodbin co-writer of CONSTANTINE" *Screenwriter's Utopia,* March 2005:
http://www.screenwritersutopia.com/article/d19a6c5a.
[4] Ibid.

with Michael E. Uslan and Ben Melniker, who owned the rights.[5] *Constantine* would be Brodbin's third script.

In late 1997, producer Lauren Shuler Donner (who would go on to produce the *X-Men* franchise) acquired the John Constantine property from Uslan.[6] When asked in 2005 about what drew her to *Constantine,* Donner replied, "It's the same thing that attracted me to *X-Men*. It's all about the characters for me. [Constantine] walks both sides. He's good and he's bad. Then this wonderful writer, Kevin Brodbin, had this whole take on how to do it – how to bring 'Dangerous Habits,' which is the comic we focused on, to life."[7]

Brodbin remembered those early days of development just as fondly:

> The way I pitched him to the producers was as a kind of rock-n-roll star of the occult. He didn't do it for religious reasons but almost as an extreme sport. To bedevil the devil, you know. I've always seen him as a hero with an evil soul. I originally pitched him as English, no one really knew the comic book. He wasn't like Batman or X-Men, where part of the deal is that the character already has a fanbase. This was the opposite. No one knew about the comic book, especially here. So, as you can imagine, an English character [the producers] never heard of and a comic book they never heard of, I decided to make him American. As long as his voice worked it wouldn't matter how his accent worked.[8]

Donner, on the other hand, stated that it was the studio's decision to make Constantine an American. "If we had done the English version, I would've wanted Paul Bettany," she once said.[9] As development on the project continued, more compromises were made to target a wider audience. "He was a dark character at first and has become more sympathetic towards the final version," Brodbin recalled.[10]

[5] Biodrowski, Steve. "To Hell and Back." *Cinefantastique*, February 2005: http://www.whoaisnotme.net/articles/2005_02xx_toh.htm.
[6] Hindes, Andrew. "Aguilar moving to Donner." *Variety*, 9 October 1997: https://variety.com/1997/film/news/aguilar-moving-to-donner-111662407/.
[7] Donner, Lauren Shuler (March 2005). Personal interview with Mark Wheaton for *Starburst.*
[8] Wehner, Chris. "Ten Questions with Kevin Brodbin co-writer of CONSTANTINE" *Screenwriter's Utopia,* March 2005: http://www.screenwritersutopia.com/article/d19a6c5a.
[9] Donner, Lauren Shuler (March 2005). Personal interview with Mark Wheaton for *Starburst.*
[10] Wehner, Chris. "Ten Questions with Kevin Brodbin co-writer of CONSTANTINE" *Screenwriter's Utopia,* March 2005: http://www.screenwritersutopia.com/article/d19a6c5a.

In the original drafts of the film, Brodbin told *Cinefantastique*, "I had Constantine discovering that he's dying... He was more of a con man than he is in this film, and he had stopped doing exorcisms because he'd lost the soul of a little girl – it was called the 'Newcastle incident' in the comics, and he'd stopped doing exorcisms by this point and he was kind of dragged back into it."[11] As he explained to *Screenwriter's Utopia*, "[John] knows because he lost her soul he is going to Hell... It was very involved in my original script because the female cop, the character I created, Angela,[12] turned out to be that girl. So there was a twist at the end where the person he's working with turned out to be the soul of the little girl he lost."[13] But he was asked to change it. All references to the Newcastle incident were removed and the storyline was simplified.

"We went through another writer," Donner told *Starburst*, "and then Frank Cappello came on and did a really good draft and the studio said, 'Okay, you can make the movie.' Akiva [Goldsman] came on and did a polish, too."[14] Cappello came on board *Constantine* without any knowledge of the source material,[15] but his strength in storytelling helped to get the movie into production. Without *Hellblazer* as a guide, he was able to streamline overly convoluted plotlines and introduce more humanity and visual flair to the piece.

> I thought that it should be a very serious tone, it should be a guy who hates both Heaven and Hell and his only allegiance is to himself. Screw anybody else. [Constantine] has friends he will sacrifice to complete a job, he has ghosts that follow him around – he's a tortured soul but he's always got this dry wit...[16]

By this time, the story's location had changed from New York City to Los Angeles. Unlike many comic fans, Capello didn't see the Americanization of Constantine as a departure from the source material. If anything, he felt, it was

---

[11] Biodrowski, Steve. "To Hell and Back." *Cinefantastique*, February 2005.

[12] Editors' note: Interestingly, *Hellblazer*'s Constantine had a girlfriend named Angela "Angie" Spatchcock, introduced in issue #175 in 2002. He has also known at least three other Angies: a pub owner (issue #67), a fellow punk-rocker (issue #99), and another fellow punk, Angie White (issues #162-163).

[13] Wehner, Chris. "Ten Questions with Kevin Brodbin co-writer of CONSTANTINE" *Screenwriter's Utopia,* March 2005:
http://www.screenwritersutopia.com/article/d19a6c5a.

[14] Donner, Lauren Shuler (March 2005). Personal interview with Mark Wheaton for *Starburst.*

[15] Brodbin, Kevin and Cappello, Frank (February 2005). Personal interview with Hannibal Tabu for CBR.com.

[16] Biodrowski, Steve. "To Hell and Back." *Cinefantastique*, February 2005.

only a surface-level change:

> Constantine is multinational – he has houses all over and stays all over the world,[17] so the original character in the screenplay could have been British. LA is not actually a bunch of people in Beverly Hills drinking lattes all day – it's a huge multicultural, multiclass place that can ignite over the littlest thing. There's a lot of anger, resentment and envy, which are things Constantine deals with in London and Liverpool. A lot of people who reject an American version of him say that England is his character – he grew up in England, he hates the Queen and the society of class structures, but I say, 'How is that any different from LA?' I've been to premieres where you see homeless people standing next to the limos pulling up and letting out the stars – you have people with no money next to people who have millions and millions.[18]

Rachel Weisz plays both Angela and Isabel in the movie *Constantine*.

The plotline involving Detective Angela Dodson's twin sister was all Capello's doing and would become the driving storyline of the feature. When Isabel Dodson kills herself, it becomes Angela's mission to prove it was a murder and to find the killer responsible. It seems impossible to Angela that a

---

[17] Editors' note: In truth, this is an inaccurate description of Constantine, who has always been shown living in a single, squalid apartment, then moving to another equally awful flat – and pretty much always in England.

[18] Biodrowski, Steve. "To Hell and Back." *Cinefantastique,* February 2005.

devout Catholic like Isabel would take her own life. Angela's mission beautifully parallels Constantine's own journey. After an attempt at suicide as a teenager, Constantine damned himself to Hell and has since spent every waking minute trying to earn his way into Heaven. When their paths converge and the forces of evil lead them to unite, a kinship develops into something greater and Constantine abandons his own cause for hers. At the end of the day, though, Capello would argue that it was, in fact, Angela who was changed by John Constantine.

> Constantine should not change, really – you should not make a soft Constantine at the end of the movie or you fail. You have to have him basically be [James] Bond – he stays the same and you have to have him affect other people, so I really built up the Angela story so she's the one that changes.[19]

Cappello would also pull Hell further from the comics in an effort to go more cinematic and draw the narrative closer to its allegorical ties.

> In the comics, Constantine just sits on the floor and puts some candles down and suddenly he's in Hell. I came up with this idea that water is actually the medium between two planes, so he has this baptism for Angela during which he puts her in this bathtub and actually drowns her to the point where she's almost dead so she'll see the other side and go in that realm she wants to see so badly – it scares the hell out of her but it's like she is being born again.[20]

Brodbin watched as the story continued to stray further from his vision. "In my version... there was [sic] three Devils, kind of a reflection of the Catholic notion of three Gods and one God. One of the Devils betrayed the others to walk the Earth."[21] This was streamlined in the feature film so that Mammon, Lucifer's son, schemed behind his father's back to break into the human plane and rule. Originally, the Devil used one of the nine-inch nails from Jesus's crucifixion to escape Hell, but writer Mark Bomback changed it so that Mammon utilized the Spear of Destiny.[22] Also, guns would be added to the mix. Americans love guns. "In my version," Brodbin recalled, "there were no guns,

---

[19] Ibid.

[20] Ibid.

[21] Wehner, Chris. "Ten Questions with Kevin Brodbin co-writer of CONSTANTINE" *Screenwriter's Utopia,* March 2005:
http://www.screenwritersutopia.com/article/d19a6c5a. In *Hellblazer* continuity, Hell is ruled by the trinity of the First, Second, and Third of the Fallen, until the First slays his brothers and assumes full control.

[22] Lawrence, Francis (March 2005). Personal interview by Chris Wehner for *Screenwriter's Utopia.*

and John Constantine was never a big fan of guns, be they holy or not, so there was gunplay with other people, but Constantine never had a gun."[23]

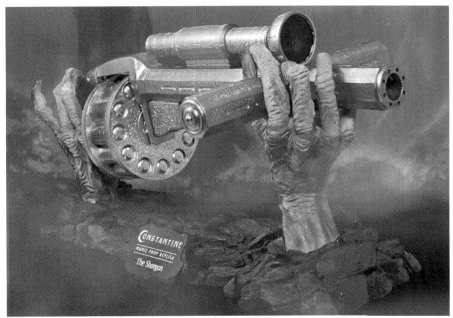

"The Shotgun," a movie prop replica released by DC Direct in 2005.

Of all these changes, probably the least surprising is the change in title. *John Constantine: Hellblazer* was being confused with Clive Barker's *Hellraiser* franchise, and was thus shortened to *Constantine*.[24]

Even on the press tour, the three writers would admit that the extensive changes were creating problems. In an interview with Comic Book Resources, they pointed to the handling of the archangel Gabriel as a prime example.[25] While Gabriel was originally intended to be the Biblical character of the same name, the film would repeatedly claim that neither angel nor demon could manifest on Earth – only half-breeds were capable of this. In an attempt to course-correct, a reference is made to Gabriel being a half-breed, but the character's origins are still clearly that of the biblical character.

---

[23] Biodrowski, Steve. "To Hell and Back." *Cinefantastique,* February 2005.
[24] Wehner, Chris. "Ten Questions with Kevin Brodbin co-writer of CONSTANTINE" *Screenwriter's Utopia,* March 2005:
http://www.screenwritersutopia.com/article/d19a6c5a.
[25] Brodbin, Kevin and Cappello, Frank (February 2005). Personal interview with Hannibal Tabu for CBR.com.

"When I left the project, [Warner's] wanted to make it more of a PG-13 film and wanted it to be a character that everybody could get into," Brodbin explained.[26] "The studio is not going to put $100 million into a story if it's depressing, so he's not going to be that drastic at any point."[27] He told *Cinefantastique*, "To be honest, I don't know how you could do that with this character. My version was a hard R, close to NC-17, and they progressively made it a little lighter, but Francis's version is very true to the character and Frank Cappello honored that very well also."[28]

Cappello would later point out that with the character made American, adhering to the PG-13 mandate became all the more difficult. "If you're going to shoot for PG-13, then a British character can say so much more colorful language, cussing really, than we could get away with otherwise – 'bloody' and 'wanker' are not cuss words in our (U.S.) vocabulary, so we can get away with their cuss words. At least that way he sounds like a real guy."[29]

Finally, the necessary changes were made and *Constantine* was ready to go into production. Nicholas Cage was cast in the leading role, but co-creator Alan Moore was not happy. "No offense to Nicholas Cage, but they should've gotten Sting," Moore told reporters at the time. A statement was then given by a Warner Bros. spokesperson in response: "No offense to Sting or disrespect to Mr. Moore, Sting is not the appropriate age for the role, nor is he as accomplished an actor."[30]

By 1999, music video director Paul Hunter (of Will Smith's "Wild Wild West" music video fame) was attached to direct the movie. Variety reported that his *Constantine* film would be "an action-adventure thriller."[31] Hunter, at the time,

---

[26] Biodrowski, Steve. "To Hell and Back." *Cinefantastique,* February 2005.
[27] Wehner, Chris. "Ten Questions with Kevin Brodbin co-writer of CONSTANTINE" *Screenwriter's Utopia,* March 2005:
http://www.screenwritersutopia.com/article/d19a6c5a.
[28] Biodrowski, Steve. "To Hell and Back." *Cinefantastique,* February 2005.
[29] Ibid.
[30] Hiatt, Brian. "Nicholas Cage Goes To 'Hell'." *Entertainment Weekly,* 4 January 2002: https://ew.com/article/2002/01/04/nicolas-cage-goes-hell/. Sting was the inspiration for Constantine's creation in *Hellblazer*, and he was 53 years old in 2005; Keanu Reeves was 40 years old at the time, so the two were actually close in age.
[31] Archerd, Army. "Callner goes from TV specs to film." *Variety*, 1 July 1999: https://variety.com/1999/voices/columns/callner-goes-from-tv-specs-to-film-1117503651/.

said the studio was giving him "incredible support."[32] By 2001, however, he would be replaced by Tarsem Singh (the director of *The Cell*).

Some say Cage saw Constantine as more of an action hero, while Singh was looking to invoke an experimental take closer to his work on *The Cell*.[33] Regardless, a clear divide began to form between Singh and the studio as he commenced work on the film. As Capello put it:

> It was a legal issue, but I can say that for once it wasn't the studio's fault. The script was starting to turn into *The Cell 2* – it was going places nobody wanted it to go to and there were scenes with Jesus on a surfboard with blood coming out of his eyes. That can sound pretty provocative, but in the context of the film it didn't make any sense, and we were throwing out all these great character moments for just some weird thing.[34]

Singh would be less open about his time on the film. In a 2008 interview with AVClub, he stated, "*Constantine* would have been a good fun one, I think. I'm not allowed to talk about that."[35] Cage and Singh would exit the project during production, leading to Warner Bros. and Singh filing lawsuits against each other.[36] Warner Bros. alleged that Singh had violated his contract, while Singh claimed their agreement was verbal, and that he'd never signed a contract. He also stated that Warner Bros. "baited [him] with false promises, usurped his creative rights (rights guaranteed under the DGA Agreement), and then, in an ultimate irony, sued him for millions for allegedly failing to do exactly that which they prevented him from doing."

As reported by CBR, Singh also claimed "The studio prevented him from meeting with the film's writers and ignored his script changes, and pushed a script on him that could not be performed at a cost the studio was willing to accept."[37] Oddly enough, all reports on this lawsuit seem to have been wiped from the *Hollywood Reporter*'s website, although citations directed toward their reporting on the matter still exist.

Writer-producer Avika Goldsman tasked Capello with returning the script to its darker pre-Singh state. Now, this $80 to 90 million production required a star

---

[32] Ibid.

[33] Biodrowski, Steve. "To Hell and Back." *Cinefantastique*, February 2005.

[34] Ibid.

[35] Singh, Tarsem (May 2008). Personal interview with Tasha Robinson for *The A.V. Club*.

[36] Harris, Dana. "WB: fewer pics, more punch." *Variety*, 30 June 2002: https://variety.com/2002/film/news/wb-fewer-pix-more-punch-1117869140/.

[37] Worley, Rob. CBR.com, 1 May 2002.

capable of ensuring a return on investment.[38] "You know that thing about creative differences? We literally had creative differences and the budget grew too big. So, that whole incarnation [with Singh] ended and then Keanu came on," Donner told *Starburst*.[39] Reeves was working on *The Matrix Revolutions* when he came across the script for *Constantine*. He had no familiarity with the comic, but immediately took to the screenplay.

After signing onto the picture, Reeves and Cappello began discussing directors. "Keanu and I had talked in Australia and we agreed: No music video directors," Capello told *Cinefantastique*. "We were looking for a Francis Coppola – a guy that really understands character and doesn't worry so much about where the camera was going to be as he does about what the guy was feeling. We didn't want a 'shooter' but someone that really believes in the characters because Constantine is a pretty complex character."[40]

It would seem that Donner had other plans. She would tap Francis Lawrence to direct the film as his first feature. "Because he's been a music video and commercial director, he's very visual," she told *Starburst*. "When he came in to talk about the script, he talked about character and story, which most of the video directors we met with didn't. He focused on content and we were very impressed with what he said."[41] From Paul Hunter to Tarsem Singh to Francis Lawrence, it seemed Donner was keen on utilizing visual directors new to the world of big-budget, feature-length films.

Once Lawrence began talks with Warner Bros., it was clear to him the studio was heading down the wrong path. As Lawrence put it, "They never really understood the tone of this movie. They thought this movie should be like *Ghostbusters* or *Men in Black*. But to their credit, we put together this 25-minute package of clips and they got really excited about it."[42] As he told *Cinefantastique*:

> I was trying to not make a comic book movie. Even though it's based on a series of comics, I didn't want to set this in a city that we've seen before – a lot of comic book movies create these Gotham-like cities and I didn't

---

[38] Biodrowski, Steve. "To Hell and Back." *Cinefantastique,* February 2005.

[39] Donner, Lauren Shuler (March 2005). Personal interview with Mark Wheaton for *Starburst.*

[40] Biodrowski, Steve. "To Hell and Back." *Cinefantastique,* February 2005.

[41] Donner, Lauren Shuler (March 2005). Personal interview with Mark Wheaton for *Starburst.*

[42] Lawrence, Francis (February 2005). Personal interview with Staci Layne Wilson for Horror.com.

want to deal with that. The script took place in Los Angeles and I wanted to show the city in a very realistic way. There's definitely a hard-boiled film-noir side to *Constantine* and LA is perfect for that – it's a classic noir city. I was trying to base it in reality and sell the environment as a real place in which these strange things happen.[43]

At this time, the movie developed into its final form under the guidance of three people. "Once I came on board," Lawrence told Horror.com, "we were probably working on the film for I don't know, nine months or a year before. We worked with Akiva Goldsman, who was one of the producers of the movie. He did the last draft. And the three of us [Francis Lawrence, Avika Goldsman, and Keanu Reeves] worked really hard together, working on the script, working on the character, and just sort of creating a language we could talk about Constantine with. He's a very dedicated actor."[44]

Constantine's Hell.

Lawrence made his mark on the film by creating greater definition to the world's relationship with Heaven and Hell. Originally, the script featured Hell as a black void, but under Lawrence's direction, it became something wholly original with visual flair.

> I came up with this idea which goes along with some of the philosophies in the movie, which is that wherever you are there's a Heaven version of the place and a Hell version of the place, so if you're in some person's

---

[43] Biodrowski, Steve. "To Hell and Back." *Cinefantastique,* February 2005.

[44] Lawrence, Francis (February 2005). Personal interview with Staci Layne Wilson for Horror.com.

apartment, when you go to Hell you're in that person's apartment in Hell. It gave Hell a geography that people could relate to but it was just a different version of that place. Then working with the visual effects supervisor and production designer we came up with what the environment looked like – that there was a strange biological growth on everything and that Hell was kind of like an eternal nuclear blast, and so we referenced those old test films from the 1940s where they're testing nuclear bombs, watching what happens to the buildings right before they get pulverized – you have this intense impact and this heat and smoke whipping off them in this high wind and things being eaten away and eroding except they never completely get eaten away because Hell is eternal.[45]

He also cast Tilda Swinton in the role of Gabriel, playing into the androgyny she brought to her role in *Orlando*. "...I was sort of shocked and surprised... that the studio let me go that route," Lawrence told *Cinefantastique*. "There were certain things in this movie like Hell and Gabriel and Satan where you had to try to find unique ways of presenting them so that it's not something we've seen before, and I thought she has this kind of grace that no one else has and she also has such an interesting take on everything she does. Angels to me are the highest levels of priesthood in a weird way in being asexual, and I thought that was interesting."[46]

There was a line, though, that Lawrence couldn't cross. This was something he would discover early on in the process.

My first idea, which was honestly the only one that got nixed by the studio, was I thought: 'Okay, so Satan is the Antichrist so I'm going to make him be the dark version of Christ.' He was going to look like Christ except with all this black blood and this crown of thorns made out of bugs and the studio were just like, 'No fucking way!' You know? So that didn't happen. I came up with the idea that Satan doesn't necessarily have to get angry, maybe he's just really nonchalant. He's so powerful he doesn't have to yell or scream. Maybe he's the kind of guy who wants to fuck every man, woman, child, elderly person and animal on the planet. So he's got that sick perversity. Then I thought of Fagin from *Oliver Twist* and mixed all those things up.[47]

In a 2005 interview conducted prior to *Constantine*'s release, Brodbin defended the film's final vision, saying that despite it being a redemption story,

---

[45] Biodrowski, Steve. "To Hell and Back." *Cinefantastique,* February 2005.
[46] Ibid.
[47] Lawrence, Francis. (March 2005). Personal interview with Stella Papamicheal for *BBC*.

John Constantine would be true to the comics and remain the asshole viewers had met at the beginning of the movie:

> With a character like this you have to break him down to his core: for me he's like James Dean spliced with Humphrey Bogart. He's not amoral, but has his own morality. He's a mouthy, chain-smoking, hard drinking agonist who only reluctantly becomes a hero... It's not like he becomes a totally different person at the end. He's not gonna stop smoking or drinking, or stop taking on the Devils.[48]

In the final version of the film, John would give up smoking. To top it all off, despite the filmmakers' best efforts to get a PG-13 rating, the movie received an R from the MPAA.

Francis Lawrence has gone on to become a successful director with films like *The Hunger Games* sequels and *I Am Legend* under his belt. In a recent interview with *Coming Soon*, Lawrence spoke about the regrets he has about his debut picture:

> Now I've made seven movies, that was my first. I think there's definite story issues, I would change some things there. I would definitely give it more levity, things like that. It's tricky because if I'm starting from scratch I would have had him, like in the material, be blonde and English. Right? I wasn't the first one hired on the movie, so it's a whole different thing, but it's tricky because I love Keanu and I think he did a great job in the movie and all of that, but it's a tough tough thing. I think the biggest things I would change are in the story, I think it gets too bogged down in supernatural gobbledygook at the end of the movie. If I'd known we were getting an R, I would have really made an R-rated movie. We followed all the PG-13 rules, but still got an R so it's not really an R. That's what I would suggest.[49]

Part III: The PG-13 Rules

Though *Constantine* will never be considered a great film, it is, at the very least, a decent one. It tells an effective story with well-developed characters in a fully imagined world. Though it may have more in common with the show *Angel* than the comic *Hellblazer*, it is a competently made and cohesive journey, which is more than can be said of many comic book movies these days – i.e. *Venom, Suicide Squad, Justice League*, etc.

---

[48] Wehner, Chris. "Ten Questions with Kevin Brodbin co-writer of CONSTANTINE" *Screenwriter's Utopia,* March 2005:
http://www.screenwritersutopia.com/article/d19a6c5a.
[49] Lawrence, Francis. (February 2018). Personal interview with Max Evry for *ComingSoon.*

Despite this, its failures seem to be derived by the studio's desire to do what is perceived as most profitable and accessible. Whether this was a case of death by a thousand cuts, or simply adhering to the needs of a big-budget American feature, the fault does not seem to lie with the creative minds behind the film. All evidence points to the writers' and directors' intelligence, thoughtfulness, and overall ability to tell a quality story.

Following the development of the film from beginning to end, we see an endless array of compromises being made to make *Hellblazer* more marketable. And while *Constantine* makes for an imperfect final product, it's hard to say the movie didn't succeed by these studio standards. A sequel never got off the ground (though Reeves has expressed interest in reprising the role),[50] but it scored big financially and launched the career of a Hollywood director.

What this film could have been is impossible to say, but what we got is the result of Hollywood spending nearly a decade trying to figure out how to sell a foul-mouthed, self-loathing, chain-smoking, supernatural con man bastard to everyday Americans. Ironically, this would be a harbinger of things to come. DC Comics would strive toward the same goal with its 2011 reincarnation of the character in the New 52, killing its "Mature Readers" title *Hellblazer* by 2013.

Until the end of 2018, John Constantine seemed destined to spend an eternity poked and prodded with endless adjustments and reinventions to his character, all in the spirit of marketability. What began in film cemented its way into the culture of television. Since the release of *Constantine*, John has starred in a short-lived NBC television series, guest-starred on *Arrow*, and even joined the *Legends of Tomorrow* cast for more campy, fun adventures.

Since the character's reboot in the comics, we have seen John move to New York City, form his own Justice League, and even fight Darkseid. It took until December 2018, with the release of *The Sandman Presents: The Books of Magic* #1 – and October 2019, with the release of *The Sandman Presents: Hellblazer* #1 – for John to return to form in all his "Mature Readers" glory. But how long can a nostalgia-fueled change like this last? Inevitably, there will come a time when the pendulum swings back and the character is retooled once more for a new age of readers.

While John's ultimate fate remains unknown, Garth Ennis's sanitized prediction for the character, showcased in *Sixpack & Dogwelder: Hard Travelin'*

---

[50] https://bloody-disgusting.com/movie/3562067/pretty-please-keanu-reeves-wants-play-john-constantine/

Heroz, feels more likely than ever. In issue #2, John Constantine, "The Heckblazer," flies in on a silver hoverboard with a laser blaster in hand and touts his sad fate to those who will listen:

> Time goes by. Fings follow their natural course. An' someone says summink about *sales*. An' someone says summink about *change*, an' before you know it some ****'s gone an had a ******' *bright idea*, ain't they...?...An' next fing yer know — well, tell you what, 'ave a butchers! See for yourself! Look what they *done to me*, son — *Look what they bleedin' done to me...!*
>
> I used to *be* someone, yer know? *John Constantine*, that name used to mean summink. Bloke o' mystery... feared an' respected... all the birds I could handle... an' now I'm just a **** in a space 'elmet.

"Look what they bleedin' done to me...!" exclaims John in issue #2 of Garth Ennis's *Sixpack and Dogwelder: Hard Travelin' Heroz.*

Chas Chandler: The Left Side of the Road

by Martín A. Pérez

Out of the shadows he comes, all British accent and blue-collar looks, the smell of a crusty London pub billowing around him like a cape. It's not what you'd expect from a magician, is it?

Well, good, because I'm not talking about John Constantine. This is about his best mate, Francis William "Chas" Chandler.[1]

First appearing in *Hellblazer* #1, published in 1988, Chas was co-created by writer Jamie Delano and artist John Ridgway. While not part of Constantine's earlier debut in *Swamp Thing*'s "American Gothic" storyline, Chas is the oldest aspect of *Hellblazer*'s ongoing mythology. In fact, besides John, Chas is quite likely the character with the most appearances throughout the series.

The first time we see him, Chas behaves a bit differently than what we would grow used to. Revisiting that first *Hellblazer* arc after reading later stories is thus a bit shocking. Chas is already John's henchman by this point, doing his bidding even though he complains about it. That much is consistent with his later evolution, but what is *not* is that he doesn't seem to have many scruples. One expects Constantine to be dismissive of poor Gary Lester's life, but Chas? Not Chas!

---

[1] *Hellblazer* #120 and #196 erroneously call Chas by the birth name Charles, but his first name is actually Francis. According to issue #58, his nickname was based on Chas Chandler, the former bassist of English rhythm and blues band The Animals.

And yet, Chas wants to dump Gaz somewhere and forget about him.

Starting with Delano's run on the title, let's take a look at what Chas has gone through, and what we can conclude about him and his relationship with John. We'll focus only on the original *Hellblazer*, and on those writers who had actual ongoing runs, not those who filled in for one or two issues, mainly because the former were the ones who actually paid attention to Chas. For that same reason, writers Warren Ellis, Brian Azzarello, and Andy Diggle are excluded from this discussion, as they each did very little with Chas during their tenures. He shows up in two of Azzarello's issues, three of Diggle's, and five of Ellis's, doing little more than driving John around and providing some muscle.

What made Delano change his mind about Chas? Without asking him, we might never know, but I have a theory. Delano establishes that Chas owes Constantine a big favor, and also that all of John's other friends end up dead and/or in Hell. So why is Chas still helping him?

It seems that Delano set up Chas to be the common-man foil to John, someone with whom readers can identify. For all the talk about John being a blue-collar magician, a working-class magus, he's anything but. Sure, he dresses like a regular bloke, but he doesn't hold an actual job, nor does he have a family, much less a normal life – not even during the few periods of "normalcy" John undergoes, those times when he is involved in a relationship with one of his (male or female) paramours who are not part of his "business."

Delano quite possibly realized that a ruthless Chas would not be a sympathetic character to the audience, who already had John to love and loathe. Chas would keep his seedier side, as befitting a big-city cab driver, but he'd mellow out and become more of a normal sidekick to John, driving him around, keeping his magical supplies safe, and joining him for a pint or two.

Chas is not, however, a sounding board for the reader's benefit or an excuse for John to sputter off exposition. As a matter of fact, during his first appearances, Chas doesn't even seem to be aware that John practices magic. He might think his mate has his fingers in some shady pies, but there is no evidence that he knows what is actually going on. Whether or not that was Delano's intention, it can all be made sense of, or retconned, in a certain way. By *Hellblazer* #21, it's clear the writer intended that Chas *did* know about John's mystical inclinations, and by issue #28, he's fluently talking about magic and John pissing off demons.

One can infer that Constantine wants to keep Chas safe, somewhat apart from the more involved facets of his work. That's why John relegates him to being his driver and refuses to discuss his work with him. Chas, having been around that stuff before (as readers later learn), is fine with pretending it doesn't exist, but he still owes John, and they're still friends.

Chas's last appearance during Delano's run involves him getting his ass kicked by the Family Man, a rather mundane villain. It's almost as though the writer was acknowledging that no one was off-limits, not even good old Chas Chandler. He does, however, make a point of establishing that Chas has a backbone, that he has agency, and that he's not just John's flunky. This very thing is what gets him beaten up by the elderly serial killer, in fact, and perhaps it gives credence to the idea that John should leave him out of things.

In 1994, several years after his original run, Delano returned to *Hellblazer* for a fill-in story (*Hellblazer* #84), which revealed exactly why Chas owed John the favor that kept the cab-driving companion around for so long. In so doing, the author confirmed that Chas had been aware of magic since his teenage years. His mother Queenie was a witch who held séances, and she had a chimpanzee familiar named Slag. Together, ape and mother treated Chas like a slave; the poor lad was even fingered by Slag. When John moved in as a lodger, he became aware of this situation and agreed to help out his friend, even if he had to do it behind Chas's back.

This all sounds quite altruistic, but we *are* talking about John Constantine. Young and ambitious, he's only ever used his magic on unsuspecting targets and humdrum antagonists. Queenie is his first magical adversary, and thus poses a challenge. By getting rid of her, John might have expected to have Chas's gratitude for life.

The subject of magic never comes up, and barring specific instances, Chas seems to prefer not to discuss the mystical arts with John. He is content paying off his "debt" in mundane ways, and is comfortable having an old friend who understands him, even if his wife Renee hates Constantine.

Garth Ennis kicked off his run with the acclaimed "Dangerous Habits" story arc, in which John learns he has lung cancer. Distraught, he criticizes Chas's life choices, and the cab driver blows up at him because some of his woes (money issues, in particular) are John's fault. Once more, Constantine leaves Chas in the dark regarding the serious issues, but thinking he's going to die, John leaves him money and a letter in which he even admits he's proud to call Chas a mate.

You would think that with Chas as his best friend, John would want his support in these times of hardship. But no, he finds it easier to relax with other friends (Brendan Finn and Katherine "Kit" Ryan), and commiserates with fellow cancer patient Matt Higgins, someone he has only recently met. This reinforces the impression that John cares about Chas more than he's willing to admit, and that he doesn't want to burden him with his problems.

That, of course, blows up in John's face, because after he's beaten cancer with the help of some deals with devils, he forgets to tell Chas that he's alive. Chas is mad at being treated like a child, although he soon forgives John. But beating cancer gives John a new outlook in life, and – together with starting a steady relationship with Kit following Brendan's passing – he enters a period of normalcy. Or, at least, what most people would consider normalcy, since for John this is abnormal.

Even the best of mates disagree sometimes.

Chas's preeminence is low, but he's around much of the time – not just driving John from one place to another, but being his mate. They drink, they joke, and they give each other a shoulder to cry on, so to speak. In *Hellblazer* #57, it's even John's turn to help Chas again after the latter's Uncle Tom dies and his body is stolen from his coffin. Readers see a darker side of Chas here, as he ends up killing the man responsible for stealing his uncle's corpse. We knew he wasn't an innocent babe (one obviously would have to be a tough bastard to be a cab driver in London, after all), but this Chas is a bit different. We don't even blink, in issue #78, when John asks Chas to hire some guys to beat up a pimp – and, of course, Chas knows the right people for the job.

At the same time, Chas has his feet on the ground, and he helps keep Constantine grounded, too. He's there for him when John breaks up with Kit, and when his friend starts behaving like an asshole again, Chas is more than willing to beat some sense into him. He might seem like John's flunky, but he's not afraid to stand up to Constantine and make him see how much of a jerk he is.

In addition to being his regular driver, Chas also acts as John's occasional bodyguard, dealing with flesh-and-bone threats that John (who isn't much of a fighter) is less prepared or willing to face. But even then, when dealing with some crooked cops and mobsters giving Chas a hard time, John still helps. It's like he learns from Chas... and Chas learns from John, because they face a demon together, and Chas stands up to it.

Chas doesn't show up in every single issue of Ennis's run,[2] but he appears in a substantial number of stories. Not only that, but Ennis makes great use of the character, firmly establishing him as part of John's life, after Delano only utilized him in a handful of tales. Chas grows during this seminal period of the original *Hellblazer* comic, and many of the basics of his future developments seem to stem from this run.

Paul Jenkins doesn't do much with Chas, as he introduces another period of semi-normalcy for John, along with other regular friends. Jenkins has a lengthy run (around 30 issues), but Chas only shows up in a handful. There are a couple of moments when he tries to keep Constantine grounded and steer him in the right direction. He identifies himself as John's best friend to other people, and in one story, he even asks John to help his wife's uncle – but that's about it. Chas is usually relegated to driving John around, not even drinking with him, despite many of Jenkins' stories beginning or ending in pubs with other friends.

In what we might consider a tradition by this point, Chas's last appearance during Jenkins' run (in the second-to-last issue) ends with him being fed up with John. Chas complains about having to drive Constantine out of town, and goes

---

[2] The second longest by any writer, at more than 40 issues, plus five more some years later.

on to explain that he wants out of their arrangement. John reacts negatively and lashes out at Chas, accusing him of being a slave and saying he has a shitty life. Chas predictably punches John and strands him in the middle of nowhere.

Mike Carey's run, only slightly shorter than Ennis's, doesn't feature Chas heavily. That would change, much to Mr. Chandler's misfortune. One of John's enemies, Peter Gill, kidnaps Chas and all his family, and almost kills his granddaughter Tricia. The danger by association with Constantine is never far away, and in the graphic novel *All His Engines*, Trish falls into a coma. Despite being on the outs with John, Chas calls on him for help. He doesn't care that magic always comes at a cost. Of course, the demon responsible for the coma has targeted Chas's grandkid to blackmail John. This story is perhaps Chas's biggest moment up to that point. With the stakes never higher, the cabbie rejects his sidekick status and takes a more active role during the quest, despite John's desire to keep him sidelined.

Chas's granddaughter comes out of the ordeal safe and sound, but Carey's attention to the character doesn't stop there. He's almost killed by John's demon-children (family is always a theme in *Hellblazer*), and even though John rescues him, Chas rightfully blows up at his mate for all the chaos that always surrounds John and endangers those close to him. To top things off, he is possessed by the demon Nergal, John's archenemy. Using Chas's body, in fact, Nergal beats up his wife, Renee, profoundly damaging their marriage.

Toward the end of Carey's run, John tries to commiserate with Chas about his supernatural ordeal with real-life consequences, as his family is now broken. Chas won't have any of that, accusing John of putting everyone at risk because of his addiction to magic, and adding that whatever Constantine did for him all those years ago, he's paid for it over and over. Then, as is often the case, a *Hellblazer* run ends with Chas beating the shit out of John.

Denise Mina, the first woman to write *Hellblazer*,[3] is the writer who seems to have brought John and Chas closer together than ever. Chas is not present during most of her run, but he plays an important part during the climax and conclusion to her overarching storyline. The story revolves around Constantine trying to stop a plot that forces people to empathize with each other, and which has driven many people to commit suicide after being overwhelmed by others'

---

[3] Nancy Collins had previously written John into several stories during her run on *Swamp Thing*.

burdens. Chas is part of a group of John's friends and family members who rush to his aid.

When he first appears on the scene, Chas once again punches John and threatens to kill him for his fault in what's happening. Embittered by having lost his family after Nergal's meddling, he takes it out on his mate, physically and verbally. But when the spell protecting Constantine's friends from the "empathy machine" starts to wear off, Chas is hit with all the guilt and remorse John has ever felt during his misadventures.

Before that happens, Chas tells John that he plans to get as far away from him as possible while the spell is still in effect, because when it faltered slightly, he saw all the things John had ever seen and felt all he had ever felt. He can't forget those things – the pain, the terror, the horrors beyond his imagination. He says it's as though they were branded onto his mind.

That's the burden of being John Constantine, for all his mistakes, for all his flaws. Chas admits it's easier to paint someone as the bad guy without hearing his or her side of the story. He can empathize with John now, even if John is responsible for what happened to him. Chas apologizes and promises to never talk about it again.

This results in an uncharacteristic lack of an ass-kicking at the end of Mina's run.

Peter Milligan wrote the longest and final run of the title: issues #251 to 300.[4] Sadly, he's one of the writers who did little with the character of Chas Chandler – barely more than the writers excluded from this essay's focus, in fact. On a positive note, Chas does little driving during this era of *Hellblazer*, as Milligan utilizes him more as John's best friend than as his chauffeur and bodyguard.

Milligan has John undergo one of his "domestic bliss" periods with a woman (Phoebe Clifton-Avery), who, not surprisingly, is murdered by one of his enemies, Julian.[5] Wanted by the police for her murder, John is on the run, but Chas knows he's innocent... of *that* crime, at least.

Chas ends up captured by mobsters and tortured to lure in Constantine, who tries to abandon him to his luck. However, John finds that he can't do it – not because of his conscience, but because legal issues prevent him from

---

[4] Or *Hellblazer* #250 to 300, depending on how you count it, since Milligan is one of several authors who contributed to issue #250.

[5] An ekimmu, or shapeshifting Sumerian spirit demon.

leaving the country. Chas never learns of this, and he continues to be John's mate for the rest of the series. When Constantine becomes engaged to his latest partner, Epiphany "Piffy" Greaves, he naturally asks Chas to be his best man. Their wedding may be the only time we don't see Renee angry at John.

Milligan's *Hellblazer* tenure ends with Constantine certain he will die (for real this time), and Chas is there with him, his friend until the end. He cries at John's funeral, defending his mate's honor after he's gone. It's a fitting end to their saga.[6]

Is John Constantine taking advantage of Chas Chandler? He certainly is, but not in the way you'd think – or, at least, not *only* in that way. As mentioned at the beginning of this essay, Delano seems to have created Chas to serve as the common-man foil to John, in order to keep him grounded and give the reader someone to see John's madness through, even if Chas doesn't voice his opinions about mystical subjects very often.

Thus, while it's obvious that John enjoys having a lackey and whipping boy to drive him around London and beyond, that's not the main reason for his dependency on Chas. If he wanted, Constantine could use magic to come up with the money for his own car (he knows how to drive),[7] to pay for other cabs, or to hire a private driver. Hell, he could have a mansion and a staff of servants at his beck and call. He just doesn't want to. John wants to feel like he's still part of the working class, and doesn't want to betray his roots.

Constantine is a junkie, addicted to magic and to the thrills it brings. But those thrills would mean nothing to him if he were to set himself apart from the rest of the world, living in a gargoyle-infested stone tower on a hill. His low opinion of mystics like Baron Winters and the Phantom Stranger makes that clear. Chas is his link to the streets. He doesn't want in on Chas's family life (it doesn't help that Renee hates him), but he's content to drink with him and, on rare occasions, share his feelings with him. He needs Chas because he doesn't want to become the kind of magic user he has often told to get stuffed throughout the course of his career.

This is almost literally alluded to in *Swamp Thing* #169, written by Mark Millar. John is attempting to join a lodge of haughty magicians, and is

---

[6] But not a permanent one, since younger versions of the two friends had already been reunited in the *New 52* rebooting of the DC Universe.

[7] Constantine drives a car in *The Books of Magic* Book II, as well as in *Hellblazer* issues #298 and 300.

Constantine's conscience gets the best of him in *Swamp Thing* #169.

undergoing several trials to prove his worth. His last one, however, is to kill Chas, thereby severing his link with the common man. Even though something big is on the line, John can't do it. He can't kill Chas. Part of it is because he's his best mate, but that's not all, is it? Chas is as important to John's "street magician" persona as his crumpled trenchcoat and Scouse accent.

But, again, this isn't about John Constantine — it's about Chas Chandler. What part does Chas play in all of this? On the surface, it seems pretty clear. We all have a friend who demands more than he or she gives in return. If not, then perhaps we have observed a friend of a friend or a spouse's friend who acts in such a manner. They leech off our food and booze, they overstay their welcome on a work night, and when we need them, they vanish on us. They say they'll go with us to the movies or help us move to a new home, but they don't show up. Hopefully, none of these friends get our families killed.

Many of us get a kick out of hanging out with that friend who never grew up because that person makes us feel a bit younger. In that same vein, Chas gets something out of associating with Constantine. Yes, it might be dangerous, but John helps him escape the toil of his daily routine. When Chas beats John up at the end of Jenkins' run, it's because he knows John is a bit right when he calls Chas a "slave." He knows his life is somewhat "shitty." John recognizes what Chas is getting out of their association, and it's not just the occasional betting tips.

In 2008, Chas was given his own spinoff miniseries, *Chas: The Knowledge*, by writer Simon Oliver — who, in my opinion, should have been hired to pen a *Hellblazer* run of his own. In this book, we learn that cab drivers are much more important to London's survival than we might have thought, and magically so. Chas faces a dangerous demon, saves London, and even gets to practice some magic of his own, even if it is with John's help via phone and fax.

What caught my attention in *The Knowledge* was Chas finally admitting that he uses John to break his ordinary routine. Without a bit of danger in his life, every day would seem the same. It seems that Chas is as much an addict as Constantine is, though he's what one might call a high-functioning addict. Chas manages to keep (or at least recover) his job, house, and family, but he's always waiting for that next hit, that next call from John Constantine — even if he complains and curses while driving on the left side of the road.

And occasionally punches John.

The Birth and Death of John Constantine: A Critical Analysis of *Hellblazer* #4 and #40

by James Chambers

Waiting for the Man

> Forbid away, chum. And don't give me that 'Dennis Wheatley' black arts crap!
> — John Constantine, *Hellblazer* #4

John Constantine – the Constant One – has lived multiple lives, past, present, and future.

Many writers explored this bedrock aspect of the character during *Hellblazer*'s 300-issue run and various miniseries, such as Andy Diggle's gender-swapping *Lady Constantine* and Jamie Delano's futuristic *Bad Blood (A Restoration Comedy)*. Then there are the incarnations of Constantine from DC Comic's New 52 relaunch and onward, which returned him to his roots in the larger DC Universe but presented conceptions of the character substantively or, at least, tonally quite different from the original pre-Vertigo and Vertigo continuity.

Within that original continuity, in *Hellblazer* #40 ("The Magus"), while speaking to one of his alter-egos – the Magus Constantine – John states: "We've got at least two emperors to our name. One was a black African and the other a Christian stooge. And then there's the psychic assassin, born sometime on the moon. There was a priest in Clapham. Another a woman called Johanna, nasty piece of work." Of course, most Constantine readers best know old Con-Job, the con-man street-magician who first appeared officially in *Swamp Thing* #37. Woven into the 1980s DC Comics continuity and a longtime partner/adversary to the Swamp Thing, this version of Constantine launched and secured the character's legacy as one of the most interesting and popular characters to arise from post-Bronze-Age comics.

By a quirk of fate, I encountered Constantine in his own comic book before I read the issues of *Swamp Thing* that had introduced him. A faithful reader of *The Saga of the Swamp Thing* from issue #1, I'd followed Martin Pasko and Tom Yeates' 13-issue Antichrist epic and felt let down by the less ambitious stories that followed it. I dropped the book ahead of Alan Moore's stint as writer and didn't return until Rick Veitch's run. When *Hellblazer* #1 hit the racks at my local comic shop, I snatched it up having no idea what to expect, thinking it marked the first appearance of a new character. I found myself immediately obsessed with the book, the stories, the world it presented, and, of course, old Con-Job himself. But it was #4 ("Waiting for the Man") in which Constantine first truly came to life as a fully formed character.

Classic superhero comics often followed a standard formula of presenting an action-packed first issue that established the new hero, his or her world, supporting cast, and main conflicts. The second issue, traditionally, told the hero's origin and back story. In many ways, *Hellblazer* #4 stands as John's second-issue origin story. A case may be made that #11 ("Newcastle: A Taste of Things to Come") better fits this role, but the crucial difference is that "Waiting for the Man" provides readers with their first insight into Constantine before Newcastle left him broken and haunted. The events of *Hellblazer* #11, which so damaged and derailed John's path, only resonate so deeply because regular readers possessed a sense of who John was before they occurred.

The surprisingly dark and intimate story in *Hellblazer* #4 followed the two-issue opening tale, which had brought Constantine to New York, introduced Papa Midnite, and told the fate of Gary Lester. Those issues hinted at Constantine's history, but much less at his future, and in them, John wore a very different face from the one now most associated with the occultist. Slick.

Polished. Double-breasted blue suit. Natty coif. The poised air of an English gentleman. Reminiscent more of mobsters Reggie and Ronnie Kray than of occultist Aleister Crowley in attitude. A far cry from Constantine's iconic rumpled, trenchcoat-wearing, drunken, chain-smoking rake, he kept his tie neatly knotted at his collar and his suit jacket buttoned.[1]

Issue #3 ("Going For It") had presented a dark piece of sociopolitical satire about the U.K. elections and gentrifying yuppies selling souls to a devil. Excellent, surprising, disturbing stories of the kind I'd never before read in a comic book, these illustrated the potential of Constantine as a character and simultaneously set the very broad boundaries of the horror stories for which he provided a platform. In contrast, #4 humanized Constantine, brought him down to earth, and quietly marked the path ahead for much to come through the end of Jamie Delano's run in #40, and beyond.

The landmark "Waiting for the Man" introduced John's sister and niece, Cheryl and Gemma Masters; Gemma's stepdad, Tony Masters, and the sinister religious multi-level marketing scheme to which he belonged; and the mysterious, artistic psychic, Zed. It also gave *Hellblazer* readers their first prolonged view into John's personal life and told a perfect, sequential art horror story that pushed the boundaries of horror comics at that time.

"Waiting for the Man" is a masterpiece of comic book horror fiction. While Clive Barker, Stephen King, Dean Koontz, Anne Rice, and Whitley Strieber dominated horror literature in the 1980s and 1990s, some of the absolute best, most original, and most incisive horror of the decade appeared in comics, especially in the pages of *Hellblazer*, under the pen of Jamie Delano – much of it sadly overlooked at the time by readers outside the comics audience.

After the shocking, over-the-top stories of *Hellblazer*'s first three issues, "Waiting for the Man" begins with a fantastically quiet page: Gemma Masters broods on an empty playground at dusk. This sharp visual shifts readers smoothly from the previous issue's tongue-in-cheek satire to a darker, more personal place. Next, we catch up with a jaunty, *smiling* Constantine enjoying such a run of good luck that he gifts Chas with the jackpot from a pub gambling machine. He then turns a corner – both literally, as he steps down an alley, and figuratively, as he comes upon Zed for the first time and steps into a brilliant splash page that foreshadows not only what's to come in the issue ahead, but

---

[1] This, of course, matched his depiction in Alan Moore's "American Gothic" *Swamp Thing* epic.

Zed's first appearance in *Hellblazer* #4.

much of what is in store for John several issue down the road.

John – and readers – first meet Zed sitting cross-legged, facing the camera, in front of graffiti she has painted on the wall behind her: the silhouette of a large man looking down at a young girl who mirrors Zed, cross-legged with her back to us (presumably Gemma, but given Zed's history and her fate in *Hellblazer* #8, perhaps also a representation of young Zed herself). Zed's spray-paint cans lie at her side. Her psychic abilities, we will later learn, manifest in her art. She regards John (off panel) with a raised eyebrow. It's easy enough to interpret the title "Waiting for the Man" as a reference to Zed, whose psychic powers have led her to wait in Constantine's path, but that represents only one layer of the title's meaning.

On the next page, we return to Gemma. Unhappy about her family's recent move and her stepfather's faith in the Pyramid of Prayer, whose videos he sells, she's thinking of all the things she hates, resenting her parents' choices, wishing for her voice to be heard – when three odd girls approach her on the swings and invite her to the house they share with their husband. Gemma's naïveté, curiosity, and longing for a different life lead her to go with them and wait to see if their husband might marry her, too, introducing a second meaning to the title, hinted at in Zed's splash-page graffiti.

Back in London, John and Zed become acquainted and then head to Zed's apartment, where John sees her art and finds his own face amidst a wall of sketches of people Zed has seen around town – a subtle touch back to her "waiting" for him to come along. There, the news reaches them that Gemma Masters has been reported missing. In a surprising moment, John reveals that Gemma is his niece, ending his run of good luck, which culminated in his meeting Zed. In Constantine's world, good luck only serves to move John into position for the worst to come. The two borrow long-suffering Chas's car and head for Liverpool, adding a third layer of meaning to the title as Gemma now unknowingly waits to be saved by her uncle from a threat not yet fully revealed.

When John and Zed reach the Masters' home, Cheryl welcomes her brother, while Tony and his colleagues from the Resurrection Crusade spurn John. They hope prayer will bring Gemma home, and are waiting for God to intervene – yet another subtle nod to the story's title and theme. John brushes aside their objections with the memorable line quoted above. He and Zed use their magical and psychic abilities, respectively, to narrow down Gemma's location. At the abandoned house, Gemma finds herself under the influence of magic that clouds her judgement as her new friends prepare her for her wedding to "the Man." One girl shows Gemma her "wedding ring," a bruise around her neck. The threads come together, hinting at a truly horrific end for John's niece.

The balance of the story follows John and Zed's search for the house. They find it and make a terrible discovery: the corpses of three young girls, the bodies of Gemma's ghostly new friends. In the cellar, John confronts the Man in the act of ritualistically asphyxiating Gemma with a rope round her neck in front of a Satanic altar, intending to add her to his ghost girl harem. Gemma, losing consciousness, senses a sinister entity in the darkness, waiting to tell her its name and bind her spirit to the Man. John impulsively attacks the brutish killer. The altercation leaves John beaten and bloodied and at the Man's mercy – until Zed steps in and takes out the psychopath with a bottle. The words "Damnation Army" are then revealed branded into the Man's chest.

Zed saving John is a remarkable twist. In a story called "Waiting for the Man," a woman ultimately saves the day. The moment marks the introduction of a recurring theme throughout other *Hellblazer* stories: John relying on women for salvation from his own reckless self.

John then returns Gemma to Cheryl as the Resurrection Crusade arrives with a group of God's Warriors, who burn down the house with the Man still inside. No one remarks on the reality of Satan's involvement in what happened, giving some substance to the zealots' claims that Gemma's sins invited the Devil into her life. John and Zed slip away to avoid the authorities. Later, in a motel, John asks Zed if she had ever encountered "any of these bozos before," meaning the Resurrection Crusade. Zed, lying, says she hasn't.

As a single story, "Waiting for the Man" excels in telling a tightly plotted, suspenseful, and emotionally engaging tale. Despite Gemma's survival, the darkness runs deep because the Man had already claimed three other girls' lives. It's a surprisingly grim tale for comics in 1988, one with thematic echoes to 1982's *The Saga of the Swamp Thing* #4 ("The White Room"), a milestone story that ventured into similar territory.

From its brilliantly conceptualized splash page to pages filled with panels that hone in on key moments and emotions to provide the perfect emphasis, "Waiting for the Man" makes masterful use of the comic book form. John Ridgway's confident and powerful grasp of the characters ensures that Gemma's girlish sadness on the swings, John's contempt for the Resurrection Crusade, Cheryl's grief, Zed's wry cynicism, and even the dull evil of the Man are all expertly depicted. The Man spends little time on panel, yet Ridgway's drawings convey all the reader needs to envision him as hulking and dull-witted, faithful to Satan simply because the Devil gives him what he wants.

The story unfolds in parallel, switching from John in London to Gemma in Liverpool, with page and panel designs that reflect the changing moods. Cluttered, busy pages showcase John in London, capturing the bustle of the city. Pages of ten or more panels bring the reader's focus into the tension and anxiety of the Masters family. For John and Zed's rush to Liverpool, Ridgway switches to widescreen panels and sharp angles. A five-panel page as the Man prepares to marry Gemma draws the reader inexorably from the killer's diabolic altar into Gemma's sudden realization of pure terror.

The horror here begins small. It's hinted at early, but the story progresses in one direction long enough for the twist revelation of John's niece to jolt the reader. In this aspect lies the real birth of John Constantine. The reader is plunged from the grand scope and sociopolitical nature of the previous issues into a starkly personal horror for a character who has previously been depicted as impersonal and indifferent – a con man and a user. Here, though, John is off-balance. The stakes are personal. His anger rises from a different, less calculated part of his psyche. This is a brawl, not a chess game, a crucial fact that belies the calm, cool, con-man attitude seen prior, and it leads him to foolishly rush the Man without thinking, and without a weapon.

Much of what follows through Jamie Delano's run on *Hellblazer* begins in "Waiting for the Man." This story introduces a major supporting character in Gemma and opens the door to the stories involving John's father and his dead twin brother that define Constantine's life and character. It shifts *Hellblazer* firmly out of the superhero universe that had birthed John and into his own personal and deeply troubled world. John, of course, would return to interact alongside Swamp Thing, the Spectre, the Phantom Stranger, and even Superman and Batman at times, but those stories became exceptions to the rule.

We begin to understand what motivates John, to see that he is not only a rakish bastard out to save his own skin at all costs, but a man with a decent heart polluted by darkness, both personal and existential – a man still capable of love and compassion, who hasn't yet learned to fully hate himself as he does in later stories. "Waiting for the Man" sets up the emotional and psychological aspects of Constantine needed for the stories that come later. We truly meet him for the first time, in what is perhaps our last glimpse of John with a bit of shine still on his soul before his long and constant descent. Strong-willed and smart, Zed prefaces John's later romantic interest, Kit Ryan – and one wonders how things might have turned out for this brighter John had Zed not lied, or had he gotten together with Kit before all the awful things that came after.

The Magus

> Now we've both been 'round the track again and fetched up at the start.
> — John Constantine, *Hellblazer* #40

When Jamie Delano departed the ongoing *Hellblazer* series, he did so having completed the creation of John Constantine begun by Stephen Bissette, Alan Moore, and John Totleben in the pages of *Swamp Thing*. Constantine's mythos took on a life of its own and grew to maturity during Delano's run. Readers learned what had happened in Newcastle (in *Hellblazer* #11) and had followed John on dark journeys into fear (*Hellblazer* #14-22), into past lives, both distant and recent (*Hellblazer Annual* #1), to confront the circumstances of his birth and his relationship with his father, and ultimately to his seeming death after an encounter with one of his alternate selves, the Magus Constantine from one of John's possible futures. In *Hellblazer* #40, Delano committed one of the boldest acts of comics writing: He killed off the series' lead character before handing the book to new writers – who then kept it going for another 260 issues.

By the close of Delano's *Hellblazer* run, John had struggled through horrors great and small, tainted himself with demon blood, confronted darkness out of history and government, led a pastoral life in the countryside where he found an ersatz family in the Freedom Mob (with Marj, Mercury, Errol, and others), ended the evil of the serial killer known as the Family Man, lost and regained Zed, and came to fully believe in the inherently guilty and tortured nature of his own existence. He believed this so much, in fact, that he rejected any hope of living a good life with Marj and her friends, considering himself too damaged and fearing that he'd only spoil it as he had every other relationship. A recurring theme, John has often saved himself at the expense of others, starting with his own birth which killed his twin and their mother. Delano ends his time on *Hellblazer* with John struggling to come to grips with that.

In *Hellblazer* #39 ("The Hanged Man"), John walks away from his friends following an ominous tarot reading from Zed. In recent times, he has seen the Golden Boy, a spectral vision of his dead twin, the son his father wished had survived instead of John, the son who would've been born strong and good unlike John, born weak and craven. John ingests psychedelic mushrooms and enters a cave near the ruins of a church, wherein he undertakes a symbolic return to his mother's womb and passes into an unearthly place outside reality.

There, John confronts the Golden Boy in utero. He relives the accident of birth that led to him choking his twin with the latter's umbilical cord, but chooses this time to sacrifice himself to gift his lost brother with life, saying: "Greater love hath no man, don't they say – so while he flourishes, bask in reflected glory, accept this peace of righteousness... fade into the forgiveness of this silently submissive dark." The issue ends when Errol goes looking for John but finds only his footprints entering into a subterranean pool, with no sign of him returning.

Hellblazer #40, drawn by frequent cover artist Dave McKean, opens with an older and very different Constantine. Much of "The Magus" tells the story of an alternate world in which Constantine had stayed with Marj, Zed, and the rest of the Freedom Mob, lived to old age, fathered children (by Marj's great-granddaughter, no less!), and led his extended family to survival on a dying Earth in the refuge of Ravenscar (the asylum to which he'd fled following the events in Newcastle).

Mirroring the other Constantine's self-doubt, the Magus views his life as a lie. He, too, struggles with guilt over the fate of his lost twin, the "poor crippled thing," as his father describes him, sitting *this* John upon his lap and calling him "Golden Boy." The Magus experienced his own visions of his dead brother, the negative of John's "Golden Boy," a child whose "hollow eyes sucked with an emptiness that would never be filled," one he chooses to dismiss with "a vicious glance." The Magus mirrors Constantine, a what-if incarnation if old Con-Job had perished in the womb and his twin had lived. Troubled by his choices, the Magus leaves Zed and enters the same otherworldly realm John had entered at the end of the previous issue.

Constantine and the Magus meet and discuss their existential crises. The Magus offers to make the sacrifice he once refused and grant his life to heal John. He asks for forgiveness, which John grants glibly, while suggesting that's not the point of their meeting. In John's view, they haven't come together to heal or forgive the damage each brother did the other, but rather the greater damage they did to their mother. John describes his opposite's offer of self-sacrifice (a sacrifice John himself made in the past issue) as "self-obsessed," suggesting a growth in self-awareness for our Con-Job. Here, Ravenscar – which has offered the Magus shelter and John healing – stands in for their lost mother. The pair approach a massive fertility icon out of pagan lore – a *sheela na gig* – carved into a cliff side, an enormous crack representing the torn womb of their dead mother, an image echoing panels from John's vision in the previous issue.

In a pivotal moment, John rises above the narcissistic tendencies the two Constantines share and states: "It isn't you who's right or me the one who's injured. We're two halves of the problem – symptoms of the same disease. I think the Earth's the victim of the crime we're both guilty of." This brings full-circle the journey Constantine began in *Hellblazer* #4, the journey toward becoming both a self-aware human being and a fully realized fictional character.

In "Waiting for the Man," readers meet John, the man, and get their first look at his tortured family history. In "The Magus," they meet John, the older, wiser man, who has sought to be the man he thought he should be – and finally comes to understand the man he actually is. The two halves of the disease named Constantine both reach enlightenment about the nature of their existence – or existences – and choose to return *together* to the womb in the hope of achieving something better. The Magus says, "There's always hope," and John answers, "But just as much *despair*." Then, in typical Constantine fashion, he decides to gamble and take his chances. "Still, like they say in magic circles, everything goes round. So come on, then, you golden *bastard* – let's have a laugh and give it one last *whirl*."

The last we see of either Constantine, they regress to embryonic form, twisting together in the classic ying-yang symbol, floating back into the womb, melding into the single cell from which they both sprang. Later, Errol rouses Zed, and they search for John, finding the cave he entered now closed by a pile of rocks. Inexplicably, footsteps lead out from the stones and a startling message has been carved into a large boulder. The message, inscribed beneath the image of a tower, reads (on page 33):

> In Memoriam
> John Constantine
> From Womb to Tomb
> And Back Again
> The Journey Wobbles On

In the sand beside the boulder, Zed finds a single tarot card: The Magus. Errol complains that if the stones and engraving are a joke, it isn't funny, and how he hates magic because it makes him feel stupid. Zed, comforting, says: "Nobody understands everything. We just get momentary glimpses of something massive going on."

Zed finds a tarot card near the cavern where Constantine "died."

Although much symbolism is at work throughout this issue, a literal reading of the art suggests that only one Constantine emerged from the cavern and that one did, indeed, die there — and it's left to the reader's speculation regarding which exactly is which. Did Con-Job finally best the Golden Boy, make his peace, and move on? Did the two incarnations perish to be reborn as a single new Constantine? Or, in a darker vein, did John con the Magus and walk out, having absorbed the Golden Boy? Perhaps John staged all of this as an elaborate charade to make it easier for him to part with Marj, Errol, Zed, and the others.

Or possibly John sank back into the madness that first brought him to Ravenscar and experienced events entirely within his own mind.[2]

Regardless, the memorial marker informs us that Constantine (or some aspect of him) died. After midwifing John's birth as an iconic character in his own independent regard apart from DC Comics' larger continuity, Delano now elegantly concludes the process – and closes the many themes he introduced – with the literal and symbolic death of John Constantine. In a quirk of synchronicity with the twin theme of the story, "The Magus" closes not only an era in Constantine's fictional life, but one in his representation in comics as well. The Constantine introduced in *Hellblazer* #41, the first issue of writer Garth Ennis's run and part one of the famous "Dangerous Habits" storyline, is a very different man.

Ironically, after "dying" at the end of *Hellblazer* #40, John tells us on page one of the next issue that he is dying yet again, this time from lung cancer due to smoking rather than from a metaphysical and mystical crisis. This development telegraphs the more down-to-earth version of Constantine of Ennis's stint on the series. With that soft rebirth, many of the pagan and occult elements of Delano's stories are swept aside in favor of a Judeo-Christian-inflected mythology, a more black-and-white universe, one governed by angels and devils rather than Earth forces, past lives, and primal emotions.

Given the Satanic influences at work in "Waiting for the Man," this change marks an interesting return, a loop of sorts back to the well from which Delano's vision of Constantine sprang – as if his death in *Hellblazer* #40 only paved the way for his rebirth in #41. Or, as John might put it, "round the track again and fetched up at the start."

---

[2] The Golden Boy later returns during Andy Diggle's run. In *Hellblazer* #247-249, John learns his twin has been secretly sabotaging his happiness for decades (ever since their fusion in issue #40), causing John to repeatedly ruin his own life, thereby weakening John and enabling the Golden Boy to replace him.

"The Odd Boyfriend": John Constantine's Bisexuality in *Hellblazer* and Beyond

by James Wilkinson

A dog-eared Englishman sits in a New Orleans bar, nursing his pint amid the revels. A handsome bartender hands him his food. They make eye contact. Cut to: clothes peeling off, warm flesh being groped, lips locked by lamplight. The footage, shot through a hazy, woozy filter, lasts less than a minute, but the moment is significant: John Constantine has had a sexual encounter with a man on screen for the first time.

The episode – "Hell No, Dolly!", the seventh installment of the fourth season of *Legends of Tomorrow*[1] – is ostensibly about Constantine (played by Matt Ryan, star of the canceled *Constantine* show on NBC)[2] and the titular time-travelers hunting a murderous doll. But it's John's doomed relationship with this man, Oliver, that is the real focus of both the episode and much of the season. The LGBTQ-friendly press was delighted – and the overtone of many of the articles was "at last!" In the run-up to the show, Out.com announced,

---

[1] Airdate: 3 December 2018.

[2] While The CW Network's *Legends of Tomorrow* is substantially wackier than *Constantine*, they appear to exist in the same world.

"Constantine Returning to TV, This Time With Bisexuality Intact,"[3] while *The Mary Sue* went with "It Sounds Like TV John Constantine Will Finally Be Canonically Bisexual,"[4] and – following the broadcast of "Hell No, Dolly!" – *Queerty* noted, "'Legends of Tomorrow' Finally Showed John Constantine Hooking Up With a Dude."[5]

To the layman reading these articles, it might seem as though John had always been portrayed as bisexual, even in his comic book days – indeed, that his bisexuality was one of his primary characteristics. But as with everything concerning John Constantine, the truth is more slippery and complex than it first seems.

Part One: Waiting for the Man

In his earliest appearances, there is no doubt that Constantine likes women. During his first speaking role, in *Swamp Thing* #37, he's shown getting out of bed with his lover, Emma; then, in *Hellblazer* #4, he sleeps with street magician Zed, and ten issues later he shacks up with Marj, a traveling hippie. He also has intense, feverish dreams in which he seduces women.[6] As these earliest issues, by regular writer Jamie Delano and guest authors Neil Gaiman and Grant Morrison, continue, the reader encounters more of his romantic entanglements: ex-girlfriends, one-night-stands, and even a sordid knee-trembler with a prostitute.[7] Constantine is clearly devoted to women in general, if rarely to any of them in particular.

What we don't see are his relationships with men. However, for those

---

[3] Hinzmann, Dennis. "Constantine Returning to TV, This Time With Bisexuality Intact." Out.com, 13 October 2017: https://www.out.com/entertainment/2017/10/13/constantine-returning-tv-time-bisexuality-intact.

[4] Jasper, Marykate. "It Sounds Like TV John Constantine Will Finally Be Canonically Bisexual on *Legends of Tomorrow*." *The Mary Sue*, 11 October 2017: https://www.themarysue.com/constantine-bisexual-legends-of-tomorrow/.

[5] Villarreal, Daniel. "'Legends of Tomorrow' Finally Showed John Constantine Hooking Up With a Dude." *Queerty*, 10 December 2018: https://www.queerty.com/legends-tomorrow-finally-showed-john-constantine-hooking-dude-20181210.

[6] In *Hellblazer* #7 (July 1988), by Jamie Delano, John Ridgway, Brett Ewins, and Jim McCarthy, and #13 (cover undated), by Delano, Richard Piers Rayner, Mark Buckingham, and Mike Hoffman.

[7] Norma, the cousin of John's long-suffering pal Francis "Chas" Chandler, in *Hellblazer* #29 (May 1990), by Delano, Ron Tiner, and Kevin Walker.

hunting early hints at John's queer leanings, there is a seemingly ambiguous scene in issue #7, in which Zed talks to Ray Monde, an elderly gay man and one of Constantine's oldest friends, about their history together:

Jamie Delano may have planted the seeds of John's sexual complexity in *Hellblazer* #7.

> **Ray:** I met him when he first came to London. Such a strange young man...
> **Zed:** Did you...? Were you and he...?
> **Ray:** Do you think I'd kiss and tell? You're right, I probably would. But, fortunately, my heart belongs to another – and I'm an old-fashioned, monogamous sort of a chap.

What's said here isn't quite as interesting as what's *not* said. Ray doesn't say that John isn't gay or bisexual, and he doesn't say that John never expressed an interest in him. The only impediment to a spot of Constantine-Monde slap and tickle, it would seem, is that Ray was already attached to another man – which is all well and good, but doesn't get us anywhere, does it? The musings of this one fella don't prove anything concrete about the author's intentions. Happily, the author in question was happy to answer inquiries by email for this essay. Over to Jamie Delano for his thoughts on this scene:

> It's a long time ago now, but I don't think I ever had any particular vision regarding Constantine's sexuality. Obviously, his occasional behaviors suggest a basic heterosexuality, but I think you'd have to assume that his intrinsic nature means he could always be open to persuasion, given the right time, place, and company. As far as any sexual relationship with Ray

Monde is concerned, I personally don't think there was one. But Constantine is a contrary sort, and if he thought someone was trying to use an "accusation" to the contrary against him (or Ray), he might well be unconcerned – even proud – to let it stand.

[...] While I still maintain it was not an objective decision to imply a bisexual facet to Constantine's personality, I'd have to concede that the mere fact his lover, Zed, asks the question in the first place suggests she does not question that possibility. Women's instincts in these intimate matters can generally be trusted, I think. Couple that with Ray's response and I'd have to acknowledge [that argument].

I'm not an analytical sort of writer. I rarely plot intensely, or cold-bloodedly design characters to make points. My approach is to try and understand the people unlucky enough to find themselves in my stories on a subconscious level – to trust them to reveal truths and discover the drama in their reactions to one another, and usually they come through.

Still, Delano says he *did* contemplate having John kiss a gay man in a later storyline – the nine-part epic "The Fear Machine," which ran from late 1988 to September 1989 – though it wasn't exactly romantic. In that tale, Constantine, who is on the trail of a kidnapped child, stumbles across a journalist named Simon whose parallel investigation has gotten him tangled up in something nasty (literally – sinister agents have trussed him up in a wardrobe with a plastic bag on his head, hoping to make his death look like autoerotic asphyxiation gone tragically wrong). John rescues him, comforts him over booze, and holds the man's hand while he falls asleep. When writing this scene, Delano says, he "faintly" recalls considering having John kiss Simon:

[I'm] pretty sure I contemplated the kiss as a genuine expression of deep compassion for someone traumatized by powers beyond their comprehension. But with Constantine, there's always a percentage in any otherwise sincere, human, altruistic act: part of him is thinking here that he's earning useful information through his understanding and kindness. And, I think, part of me as the writer is probably thinking: How deep do we want to go here? Can I be bothered to ask the questions and work through all the answers? Or swerve the kiss and keep it lower key – and just a little bit less complicated a characterization than I'd already started to uncover?

If I'm honest, I was probably also tempted to do it as a way of pushing the creative envelope in a direction that would eventually become Vertigo,[8] but then decided that such a gesture was a maybe a little bit cynical and didn't really serve the story.

---

[8] Vertigo Comics was a DC Comics imprint launched to house the company's "Mature Readers" line of comics in March 1993. In June 2019, it was announced that DC was shutting down its Vertigo label, only a year after re-launching it.

So in these earliest stories, then, it's fair to say that Constantine was not consciously being written as explicitly bisexual. And that certainly didn't change with the next regular writer, Garth Ennis, who wasted little time in setting up what would become one of Constantine's most defining romances – with a woman, the hard-nosed Irish artist Katherine "Kit" Ryan.

More importantly, Ennis took a sharp turn away from the previous writers in his depiction of LGBTQ individuals. Delano's and Gaiman's stories are dotted with supporting characters who just happen to be gay, lesbian, or bisexual, most of whom are allies or acquaintances of Constantine. But in Ennis's run – with the exception of a brief appearance by Ray in a flashback – they are unanimously dubious: a pedophile priest (*Hellblazer Special* #1), depraved bisexual vampires and a rent boy with AIDS[9] (*Hellblazer* #68-69), and a group of homeless rapists (*Hellblazer* #75).

The Ennis run is certainly not an LGBTQ haven, that's for sure.[10] It's surprising, then, that it was in the midst of all this that the first true mention of John Constantine's bisexuality actually emerged. It came in issue #51, a one-shot fill-in story by guest writer John Smith[11] and recurring *Hellblazer* artist Sean Phillips. Largely taking place in a claustrophobic laundromat following an exorcism gone awry, the yarn relies heavily on Constantine's inner monologue – which at one point features the line "Girlfriends, the odd boyfriend... they all have a nasty habit of walking out on me. A couple of weeks and they've had enough. The mystique gets shabby, the jokes turn into digs, the sex goes stale."

That Smith should have introduced this aspect to John's character isn't much of a surprise – he himself is gay, and a couple of months later, in May 1992, Smith and Philips would debut Devlin Waugh, a homosexual exorcist, in the *2000AD* spin-off *Judge Dredd Megazine.* However, perhaps because of this, the manner in which John's bisexuality is introduced is admirably casual and matter-of-fact. For comparison, look at *Alpha Flight* #106 – published the same month as *Hellblazer* #51 (March 1992) – in which Northstar becomes Marvel

---

[9] To be fair to Ennis, Ray Monde was also HIV-positive, and mainstream stories concerning gay characters at the time commonly tied in with the then-headline-dominating AIDS crisis.

[10] Many Ennis comics from around this time are similarly unforgiving in their depictions of LGBTQ individuals, including the otherwise excellent *Preacher*, which was published by Vertigo from 1995 to 2000. Since the mid-2000s, Ennis has depicted LGBTQ characters in a more positive light.

[11] Efforts were made to contact Smith for this essay, but he proved unreachable.

Comics' first-ever openly gay superhero, but not before adopting an HIV-positive baby, fighting a superpowered Mountie whose son died of AIDS, and proclaiming, mid-fight: "Do not presume to lecture me on the hardship homosexuals must bear! No one knows them better than I. For while I am not inclined to discuss my sexuality with people for whom it is none of their business – I am gay!"[12]

John Constantine's inner monologue in *Hellblazer* #51 is the earliest reference to John's bisexuality.

However, the differences between the revelations of the characters' sexualities go beyond basic authorial competence. Northstar had, since his creation in 1979, been coded as a gay character (even if Marvel was reluctant to make that explicit for 13 years), whereas Constantine, as we have seen, had been consistently shown in heterosexual encounters up until that point. It was a switch that could have proved controversial. But that didn't bother then-editor Stuart Moore – or DC itself. In an emailed interview, Moore recalled:

> I was aware that the line could be provocative, but I had no problem with it. Constantine, as established, was an experienced chaos magician. That implies – to me, anyway – a level of sexual experimentation, especially during one's training. [...] DC made no comment about the line to me, before or after publication. [...] I can't remember whether I flagged it internally or not. I probably mentioned it to [editor and later Vertigo founder] Karen Berger, but I can't swear to that. We were publishing books with openly gay characters, so it wasn't that big a stretch, and as a single

---

[12] It was super dumb.

line of dialogue it wasn't going to draw the sort of fire that scenes in *The Invisibles* or *Preacher* did a few years later.[13]

Indeed, only one reader letter printed in the pages of *Hellblazer* even referred to the line, with the letter writer approvingly noting, "It just adds to John's already fascinating character." Moore said he couldn't recall any particular reader feedback and declined to comment on the depiction of LGBTQ characters in Ennis's run, but added, "If [Smith's] one line did open up the character in an inclusive way, I'm very happy about that."

It would indeed open up Constantine – but not for a long time. In fact, this newly carved facet of his character wouldn't see the light of day again for another 10 years, when it was dug up by writer Brian Azzarello for his final *Hellblazer* arc, "Ashes and Dust in the City of Angels" (*Hellblazer* #170-174). The story is split into two halves, one with the villainous billionaire Stanley "S.W." Manor giving a sinister confession to a priest, and the other following an FBI agent investigating Constantine's apparent death in an S&M club by interviewing its workers and patrons, *Rashomon*-style. At the midpoint of the yarn, John approaches Manor in the club and kisses him; in the next issue, one of the witnesses to John's death describes Constantine as Manor's boyfriend. Elsewhere, Manor recalls how Constantine kissed, masturbated, and whipped him – with the scenes depicted for the reader in softcore fashion as he speaks.

The "relationship," it turns out, is just part of a con being played by John as revenge for Manor's own meddling in his life.[14] Still, the fact that John was willing to get so hands-on (as it were) suggests a certain amount of sexual fluidity in the character, and – according to Azzarello in an emailed interview for this essay – was written to evoke Smith's earlier blink-and-you'll-miss-it characterization, but not to set any solid definition on Constantine's preferences:

> I did know about [Smith's mention of Constantine's old boyfriends] and thought it should be explored. I chose to do it in a way not many readers who wanted it explored wanted to see it. Character sexuality is the stuff of

---

[13] *The Invisibles*, written by Grant Morrison and published by Vertigo, included a transgender shaman, while storylines included the characters being trapped in a psychic reenactment of the Marquis de Sade's *120 Days of Sodom*. *Preacher*, meanwhile, was joyously blasphemous, with characters including the inbred, mentally disabled descendant of Jesus Christ.

[14] Previous issues showed how John had ripped off Manor in the 1970s, sparking his anger and leading to the complex web of lies and betrayal that would be slowly uncovered across Azzarello's run.

fan fiction, a wish fulfillment if you will. Well, no one should ever want to get close to John. His legion of dead 'friends' is all the proof you need. [...] I don't consider Constantine straight, gay, or bi; John is always working a con, and if sex can be used to further it, he'll use it. Writing that just now, it makes him both meaner and sadder to me.

Brian Azzarello was anything but vague when it came to Constantine's sexuality, as shown in this S&M scene with "boyfriend" S.W. Manor.

The story led to consternation and controversy on both the long-dead DC message boards and on the Straight to Hell fansite,[15] with some fans repelled by the kinky man-on-man action, and others digging up Smith's issue as precedent for the scenes – conversations that would continue to repeat for years

---

[15] Sadly, the messages on both boards from 2002 have long since been lost in the digital dustbin, so you'll have to rely on the memory of the author here. Then again, if we learned anything from "Ashes and Dust in the City of Angels," it's that memories are fallible – and that all the women who go to S&M clubs have gravity-defying 34FF breasts.

afterwards.[16] It was something Azzarello himself had predicted. "Did I think it might stir up some conversation? Make some folks uncomfortable? Absolutely – and all the better," he said. "I don't want to say I understand John; I think that would be presumptuous. But we do have an affinity."

Part Two: Bye Bi Baby

For a while, that was about it for Constantine's bisexuality; a brief mention in issue #51, a couple of issues in which it was used as a tool to mess with a mark's head, and we were done. None of the writers who would touch Constantine in *Hellblazer* or any other comic for the next 11 years would broach the subject of John's same-sex dalliances. A missed opportunity? Perhaps, but not really surprising, given that after Delano left the title, *Hellblazer* became a decidedly unfriendly place for LGBTQ characters and storylines.

That's right – although John himself is very much a left-wing, "do what you will" sort of chap, and despite most of the book's authors being socially progressive themselves, much of *Hellblazer* is dismissive of LGBTQ people at best, and at worst actively demonizes them.

There's the Ennis run, as outlined above, but the next writer, Paul Jenkins, had his share of troubling queer representation, too. In issue #92, we're introduced to Buer, the demon in charge of all the souls of children who were ever sent to Hell. In just three pages, he's established as having "once been drawn to the children himself," having flirted with Lucifer, and being in love with the First of the Fallen.[17] In fact, it's his love for the First – who had been defeated by Constantine at the end of Ennis's run – that motivates him to seek revenge on John.

In issue #108, we're introduced to Simon Harcourt, MP, who has organized an orgy; he's later seen wearing a pink tutu while holding hands with another man in leather fetish gear. Not that there's anything wrong with an orgy, of course, so long as you remember to wash your hands before you go to the buffet – but it's not exactly a casual, normalized depiction. In the same issue, an

---

[16] Straight to Hell message board search:
http://hellblazer.ipbhost.com/search/?&q=bisexual&page=9&search_and_or=or&sortby=relevancy
[17] Lucifer Morningstar was the lord of Hell introduced in Neil Gaiman's *The Sandman* comics; the First of the Fallen was a substitute Devil character introduced by Ennis in *Hellblazer* #42 (June 1991), because Gaiman had Lucifer abdicate his throne in *The Sandman* #22 (January 1991).

apparently heterosexual woman at the orgy becomes possessed by a spirit and wreaks vengeance on a (heterosexual) child abuser – but then kisses the little girl he was abusing on the lips in a transference of magical energy.

In issue #114, John is depicted on the cover recoiling comically in surprise as he's kissed on the lips by King Arthur; the same scene occurs in the issue itself, and John wipes his mouth in apparent disgust afterwards. Two issues later, a short-haired woman is shown buying child pornography featuring young girls and boys alike. The only issue in this run (and one of only a couple in post-Delano *Hellblazer*) to depict a normal gay relationship is issue #106, in which a pair of young men with brightly colored hair are seen living together in a small house, as part of a gentrified neighborhood loathed by a petty, right-wing local official – although their exact relationship is not confirmed on-panel.

Things get substantially nastier in "Son of Man" (issues #129-133), a broadly cartoony five-issue fill-in story that followed Jenkins' run, in which returning writer Garth Ennis pits Constantine and the ever-suffering Chas against a pair of gangland thugs inspired by the real-life Kray twins,[18] as well as the corpse of a little boy that has been possessed by a demon. In the climax to the story, the demon – an incubus known as a "Fuckpig," representing the act of rape – bursts out of the child's body to reveal that it has an enormous, three-foot-long penis. It then calls Norman (who is gay, presumably in reference to the bisexual Ronnie Kray) "a horrible old poofter," promises that he'll spend eternity being raped in Hell, and then sends him there by anally violating him until he explodes.

The next permanent writer, Warren Ellis, included relatively few LGBTQ characters. In issue #140, however, Constantine investigates a serial killer, possibly inspired by Jeffrey Dahmer, who is so lonely that he murders both men and women so he can sleep next to their corpses.

Azzarello followed, and while he was responsible for reviving interest in Constantine's bisexuality – it's hard not to imagine that it would have been forgotten altogether had "Ashes and Dust" not brought it back – depictions of gay and transgender people in his run weren't generally positive. His first issue (*Hellblazer* #146) opens on a man being raped at a prison in which Constantine is serving time. At the end of the issue, Constantine himself is almost gang-raped in the showers because he owes cigarettes to a bunch of inmates, but he

---

[18] Brothers Ronald "Ronnie" Kray and Reginald "Reggie" Kray, who perpetrated a great deal of organized crime in London throughout the 1950s and 1960s.

uses magic to render them all catatonic. As he leaves the shower, he tells the man who was being raped at the start of the issue, "We're all out of fags." Azzarello confirmed in an email for this essay that this was a pun on both the British slang for cigarette and the homophobic slur.

That slur pops up again in issue #152, when a creepy old man asks Constantine "Are you a faggot? Because I am." And in his final arc, the LGBTQ members of the S&M club include a fat man who identifies as bisexual and likes to be pissed on (issue #170), as well as a transgender sex worker who likes to show off her penis (issue #172). Then there's S.W. Manor, a gay psychopath (and Bruce Wayne analogue) who boasts about killing Jason, a boy with a "hot ass" (issue #169), and also feeds orphans to ravenous vampire bats for fun (issue #174). He's hardly the poster boy for positive queer representation.

The next writer, Mike Carey, seemed like he might tip the scales in favor of the angels early on when he depicted two gay man on a date in issue #177, but they were gruesomely killed by villains two pages later.[19] Denise Mina, who followed Carey, didn't include any LGBTQ characters at all, but the next writer, Andy Diggle, did in issue #248 – revealing that his primary villain, a decrepit and evil aristocrat, had arranged for his own personal afterlife to be filled with semi-sentient sex slaves. Most were women, but one was a bald, overweight man and two others appeared to be young boys.

Hellblazer's final author, Peter Milligan, went light on LGBTQ characters, though he did feature Julian, an evil spirit whose gender is unclear but who takes the form of a schoolgirl despite having a traditionally male name. On a slightly more positive note, Milligan introduced the woman who would become Constantine's first and (so far) only wife – Epiphany Greaves. She's revealed to be bisexual, having previously had relationships with other women, including a supernatural being, and is generally portrayed as a smart and resourceful alchemist. On the other hand, she's also less than half Constantine's age by that point, being in her twenties, and arguably comes across as a bit of a middle-aged fantasy.

Now, none of this is to suggest that any of these writers are homophobic, biphobic, transphobic, or generally opposed in any way to LGBTQ people. Most

---

[19] They were also shown in bed in a flashback in the following issue, making this the only depiction of fully consensual male-on-male sexual activity in the original *Hellblazer* comic – compared with *two* depictions of sex between a dog and a man, in issues #154 (November 2000, by Azzarello and Frusin) and #245 (August 2008, by Jason Aaron and Sean Murphy).

of them have written great, nuanced queer characters elsewhere, after all. But for whatever reason, *Hellblazer* under their tenure was largely a queer-free zone – and that was about to make things a lot more complicated.

Part Three: Bi-Furious

In 2005, John Constantine made the leap from the four-color page to the silver screen, courtesy of the Keanu Reeves vehicle *Constantine*, which loosely adapted stories by Delano and Ennis to middling reception. In the film, John is barely portrayed as a sexual being at all, largely because his enemies-with-benefits relationship with the succubus Ellie (played by Michelle Monaghan) was almost entirely cut out. He's certainly not portrayed as having any interest in men – which shouldn't be too much of a surprise. This was a mainstream Hollywood action film in the mid-2000s, after all. *Brokeback Mountain* might have cleaned up at the Oscars that year, but *Constantine* was in the market for video game adaptations, merchandise, and maybe even a full-on franchise down the line.[20] Would the studio execs have trusted America's teenage boys and young men to have gotten wholeheartedly behind a bisexual male hero? That's highly doubtful.

Then again, they probably had no idea about that aspect of the character, what with it having been, up to that point, an extremely minor element of a relatively obscure comic book. And they weren't alone. Aside from the odd comment on the nerdier parts of the internet, almost nobody noticed that movie John had ditched an entire gender altogether; the world was oblivious.

But it wouldn't stay that way.

With the bump in profile that the movie brought and a concurrent run of tie-ins from DC/Vertigo, more people jumped aboard the *Hellblazer* train, and the news about John's sexual history began to spread. A Google search for *"John Constantine" bisexual* with the dates restricted to single years brings up an increasing number of hits as time goes by, from a scant three in 2005 (of which only one concerns the actual character) up to several pages of results in 2013, including articles lauding Constantine as an LGBTQ icon. Of course, some older sites will have been lost to the mists of time, but the growth of interest in John's bisexuality is obvious – even though it was restricted at the time to just

---

[20] In fact, Keanu Reeves was talking up a possible *Constantine* sequel as late as May 2019: https://variety.com/2019/film/news/keanu-reeves-speed-3-john-wick-chapter-3-1203216561/.

those two *Hellblazer* stories. Indeed, one gets the feeling that many of the articles were based on other articles saying the same thing, rather than the original (negligible) content of *Hellblazer* itself.

Which explains why the shit really hit the fan in July 2014, when Daniel Cerone, the executive producer of the soon-to-air NBC television adaptation *Constantine*, told the press that John-on-man sex was off the table: "In those comic books, John Constantine aged in real time. Within this tome of three decades [of comics] there might have been one or two issues where he's seen getting out of bed with a man. So [maybe we'll show that] 20 years from now? But there are no immediate plans."[21]

As promised, *Constantine* only involved its lead character with women – whether as exes, one-night stands, or an ongoing will-they-won't-they relationship with the TV version of Zed. The reactions to Cerone's early announcement were… not happy. On Twitter, the hashtag #BiBlazer was launched to demand the character not be "straightwashed." *Advocate*, an LGBTQ news site, ran an article titled "Op-ed: NBC's Straight-Washing of John Constantine Is Bi Erasure."[22] Tumblr posts called for people to contact NBC to share their displeasure.

Things got worse the following month at the San Diego Comic Convention, when Lindsey Cepak, of *When Nerds Attack*, asked Cerone and fellow executive producer David S. Goyer on video[23] about the adaptation.

>**Cepak:** In the comics, Constantine is known as a bisexual –
>
>**Cerone:** [laughs]
>
>**Cepak:** I know, I know…
>
>**Cerone:** You're the first person to ask us today!
>
>**Goyer:** I have a question for you: When, in the comics, was he introduced as being bisexual?
>
>**Cepak:** It was back in Image. Back before it was owned by DC.
>
>**Goyer:** Yes, but my point is, it was about 12 years into the character's history. It's not like he was introduced in the first comic… it happened 12

---

[21] Hibberd, James. "'Constantine' team on why NBC character isn't bisexual, smoking cigarettes." *Entertainment Weekly*, 13 July 2014: https://ew.com/article/2014/07/13/constantine-bisexual-smoking/.

[22] Cruz, Eliel. "Op-ed: NBC's Straight-Washing of John Constantine Is Bi Erasure." *Advocate*, 28 July 2014: https://www.advocate.com/commentary/2014/07/28/op-ed-nbcs-straight-washing-john-constantine-bi-erasure.

[23] "Roundtable with Constantine Producers @ SDCC." YouTube, 30 July 2014: https://youtu.be/DSMORYN6tOc.

years later. … By the way, we didn't say he wasn't [bisexual]. We just don't show him getting in bed with a man in the pilot.

As it happens, they're *both* wrong here. Cepak appears to have confused Image Comics (which never published *Hellblazer*) with DC Comics, and DC with its Vertigo imprint (which was never owned by any company other than DC, and which published *Hellblazer* years *after* the comic's debut in mainstream DC). Meanwhile, *Hellblazer* #51 was published seven years after Constantine's first appearance, not 12.[24]

The video sparked more furor, with LGBTQ site *Back2Stonewall* posting an article titled "Constantine Producer Gets Defensive Over Bi-Erasure of Title Character – Is David S. Goyer A Queer Culture Leech?",[25] which concluded: "Back2Stonewall.com will not promote or watch any program that erases the sexuality of any character either gay, lesbian or bisexual and we ask that everyone join us in the boycotting of this show."

It's easy to see the frustration on both sides here. While Goyer's questioning of Cepak's geek credentials was aggressive and unnecessary, the show *had* become a cause célèbre for LGBTQ sites that were clearly unfamiliar with the comic itself, but had decided to weigh in anyway, as demonstrated in the *Advocate* op-ed on bi erasure:

> Although his sexuality isn't the main plot point, it's pretty clear after reading a few issues that Constantine has had both girlfriends and boyfriends, and that he has been in some kinky man-on-man situations, à la *Fifty Shades of Grey*. But instead of staying true to the character, producers of the show have decided his sexuality isn't that big of a deal. Or at least, representing his sexuality accurately isn't that important to him.

However, Constantine's bisexuality *wasn't* that big of a deal in *Hellblazer*. Indeed, beyond a single mention in a single issue and an ambiguously motivated sexual relationship (that's described by a string of unreliable narrators) ten years later, it was never really a character trait of his at all throughout the entire 300-issue run. Constantine, as seen in *Hellblazer* and its contemporaneous spinoffs, was *canonically* bisexual, but not *materially*

---

[24] Cepak later admitted to *Back2Stonewall* that she had been "flustered" because she "was not expecting to be accused of being a fake geek girl and condescended to." (Kohler, Will. "Constantine Producer Gets Defensive Over Bi-Erasure of Title Character – Is David S. Goyer A Queer Culture Leech?" *Back2Stonewall*, 3 August 2014: http://www.back2stonewall.com/2014/08/constantine-producer-gets-defensive-over-bi-erasure-of-title-character-is-david-s-goyer-a-queer-culture-leech.html.)
[25] Ibid.

bisexual. Of all the traits essential to his character – cunning, manipulativeness, deadly pragmatism, a hatred of authority, loyalty to friends, compassion for the oppressed, and a compulsion to investigate the uncanny – being bisexual just didn't rank.[26] Contrary to what *Advocate* claims, if Cerone and Goyer actually had waited several (though not 12) years to show John hooking up with a guy, they actually *would* have been representing his sexuality accurately.

As the previously mentioned Google search suggests, the perception in 2014 that Constantine was a major bi icon came largely from articles based on articles based on articles based on the comics, rather than on the comics themselves. This demand simultaneously grew out of and fed upon itself, and publications such as *Advocate* were ironically contributing to it.

More pressingly, until *Constantine* pushed the issue into the wider public sphere, the awareness of John as a bisexual comic book character was mostly limited to a disparate selection of "Top 10 LGBTQ comic book heroes"-type articles and a relatively tiny number of *Hellblazer* geeks. So was he legitimately part of queer culture before most LGBTQ people had even heard of him?

The question, ultimately, is whether queer culture is passive or enacted. Does it exist as some kind of entity separate from the people within it, such that any LGBTQ character or story, no matter how obscure, is automatically folded into the culture upon publication? Or is queer culture defined by what is actively embraced and promoted by a wide swathe of those within the culture? And either way, does the claim that queer culture has over *Hellblazer* trump Cerone's and Goyer's stated desire to accurately adapt Constantine's love life as depicted in the original stories?

On the other hand, why should "it's not comics-accurate" be the metric for what appears in the show? God knows *Constantine* takes enough liberties with the source material. Most of the British supporting cast are made into Americans, for example. John has a magical map that shows him where the monster of the week will turn up, changing him into a crusading hero seeking out trouble rather than a magnet for it, the better to fit it into NBC's worn-out procedural format. His time in the mental asylum is shaken off within minutes and treated like a slightly shitty holiday. He's given a cottage that's bigger on the inside, like a bucolic version of *Doctor Who*'s TARDIS, for some mad reason.

---

[26] Neither John nor anyone else even identifies him specifically *as* bisexual in the comics; I'm only doing so in this essay for convenience.

And – most egregiously of all – in the adaptation of "A Feast of Friends,"[27] Gary Lester offers himself up as a sacrifice against John's protestations, rather than John manipulating him into it.

With all that in mind, sticking to some arbitrary rule about John's sexuality is small potatoes indeed. They were adapting *Hellblazer*, after all, not re-enacting it – and John *is* canonically bisexual, and bi erasure is a bad thing, so including the full range of his sexuality in the show wouldn't be out of character, nor would it interfere with whatever story needed telling.

More importantly, while John's bisexuality might not matter to *Hellblazer*, it matters to queer TV viewers – whether they were familiar with the character before watching *Constantine* or not. Bisexual characters don't always get much play on television, and when they do, they're often the sexy young women who appeal to straight male writers and audiences, and not the sexy young men who potentially make them feel threatened. So having John Constantine – a sexy bisexual man who's also well-rounded, complex and, well, *cool* – is an absolute win for bi viewers looking for representation. Hell, the fact that his sexuality isn't his most prominent characteristic helps: instead of being The Bisexual Guy, he's a fascinating human being who happens to be queer.

Of course, the main factor behind the "straighwashed" Constantine was likely a fear – on the parts of Cerone, Goyer, NBC, or all of the above – of alienating mainstream audiences. A show about a chain-smoking demonologist who accidentally sent a little girl to Hell is one thing, but having him kiss a fella? That's a little too spicy for the conservative U.S. network television viewership that exists only in the imagination of TV execs, and for the hordes of imaginary squirming straight fanboys.

That latter demographic might not have been as much of a problem as expected, though. By the summer of 2014, when Cerone and Goyer were defending their stance by appealing to the now-defunct *Hellblazer* series, Constantine was starring in other comic books – and had already been shown shacking up with a man.

Part Four: Another Guy, Another Planet

In August 2011, the same month in which *Hellblazer* #280 was released, a second John Constantine appeared in comic shops around the globe. This younger, less sweary version – first glimpsed in *The Search for Swamp Thing* #1

---

[27] The storyline presented in *Hellblazer* #1 (January 1988) and #2 (February 1988).

– was the character's grand re-introduction to the DC Universe after decades spent in a Vertigo Comics bubble. He then became a lead player in the first issue of *Justice League Dark* in November 2011 before getting his own solo comic, *Constantine*, in May 2013.

In *Justice League Dark* #0,[28] readers are introduced to Constantine's one-time mentor Nick Necro via flashback. Despite sounding like a 13-year-old who's just started his first black metal band, Nick is a New York-based warlock and the top dog of the magical pile,[29] so a young Constantine, clad in punk leathers, seeks him out for magical training. Nick accepts and he, Constantine, and future magical superhero Zatanna Zatara – who is dating Nick – form a magical triumvirate. Sometime later, John and Zatanna hook up, and a furious Nick turns on them. But Constantine has outgrown his master, and he sends Nick to Hell – then steals Nick's trenchcoat-suit-and-tie combo to boot.[30]

Although John makes a sarcastic remark about a threesome in the issue, there's no suggestion that he and Nick are interested in one another. And when Nick comes back in later *Justice League Dark* issues to wreak his revenge, it's all played as two heterosexual guys fighting over a girl. But when Nick pops up again in *Constantine* #12, their relationship is retconned by writer Ray Fawkes into something more sensual. In flashback, we see the trio performing a ritual to link their fates – which requires them to all kiss one another. In a further retcon, his anger now is not just at Constantine for hooking up with Zatanna, but with both of them, as he screams: "We were all in love. And you two shut me out!" Shortly afterward, he refers to Constantine as "a blood brother... or a lover."

That was in May 2014, two months before Cerone and Goyer would spark anger over their plans for their own *Constantine*. Another glimpse is offered in *Constantine* #21, when John enters a doomed parallel universe, encounters

---

[28] Published in November 2012, a year after issue #1, it was a craftily numbered flashback story.

[29] His real name is Nicolas Nolan, by the way – which means he *chose* to call himself "Nick Necro." This, in turn, makes him the world's most prominent magician *and* twat.

[30] Whereas in *Hellblazer*, John taught himself and made his own dubious fashion choices, here in the rebooted continuity, he basically takes everything – including his iconic look – from Nick. Narratively, Nick's job seems to be doing Constantine better than Constantine does himself, so that Constantine can out-Constantine the guy who out-Constantined Constantine. And if you don't understand why this is a terrible idea, I don't think we can be friends.

another version of himself, and muses, "You ever wonder what you'd do if you met yourself? I always said I'd shag the handsome bastard." He doesn't screw his other self, though he does screw him *over* – by giving him a Judas kiss as he fatally stabs him, using the killing to power a portal that will allow him and others to escape the doomed dimension and travel to his own. In *Constantine* #23, John has a flashback to the happiest moments in his life, which includes himself and Nick in a topless embrace.

In an interview with *Den of Geek* in September 2014, Fawkes was asked about the furor surrounding the *Constantine* TV show, and responded:

> Well, John's bisexuality has already been mentioned in the pages of *Constantine* – and made nary a ripple in the fan base, as far as I can tell. I'm not sure how much of the demand comes of a desire for diversity and how much is down to a respect for the canon – but I do know that the choice to reveal his sexual preferences should, if it happens at all, be relevant to the story above all. I can't speak for the people involved with the TV show, but I know that my intent, in the comic book, is to explore more of John's relationships in the future, but never to sensationalize, never for a headline grab. Always for the story.

The lack of a response by the fanbase might just have been down to the relative subtlety of the depictions of John's time with Nick – a few snatches of topless intimacy – and the fact that Constantine's love for Zatanna was a major plot point throughout that run. But perhaps not, as times had been changing in the world of American comics.

When Constantine "came out" to the readers in 1992, queer characters were still largely on the fringes of mainstream U.S. comic books. *Hellblazer* and its future Vertigo stablemates, such as *The Sandman* and *Shade the Changing Man*, were putting forward nuanced depictions of LGBTQ people, but in the world of superheroics, things were a little cagier. The "Comics Code," a series of rules used by comic companies to self-regulate their content (which was eschewed by DC for its "Mature Readers" titles, but applied to most of its superhero fare), had prohibited depictions of LGBTQ relationships and characters until 1989.[31] While both DC and Marvel embraced that for

---

[31] Though not directly; among the various commands were the following: "Illicit sex relations are neither to be hinted at or portrayed. Violent love scenes, as well as sexual abnormalities, are unacceptable," "The treatment of love-romance stories shall emphasize the value of home and the sanctity of marriage," and "Sex perversion or any inference to same is strictly forbidden." Add them up and put them in a 20th-century context and you get a prohibition against LGBTQ characters. (Kistler, Alan. "A Little History: LGBT Representation in Mainstream American

prominent characters on occasion – such as Northstar coming out – for the most part, queer characters were given only minor or supporting roles. Even when they were depicted openly, they were often tied to the AIDS crisis or portrayed as flamboyant caricatures – or both, in the case of DC's Extraño, who was essentially one part Doctor Strange to a thousand parts Liberace,[32] and who became HIV-positive after being attacked by a Nazi vampire named "The Hemo-Goblin."[33]

However, things improved markedly as the years went on, and by the mid-2010s both Marvel and DC had a slew of gay and lesbian heroes under their belts,[34] with DC's roster including – among many others – the Midnighter and Apollo, an ersatz Batman and Superman who had superhero comics' first gay wedding;[35] Renee Montoya, a lesbian police detective who would later take on the mantle of the superhero the Question;[36] and Kate Kane, a lesbian who was the new Batwoman.[37] Several pre-existing characters were also revealed as bisexual, including Catwoman,[38] Catman,[39] Harley Quinn, and Poison Ivy.[40]

Comics, Part 1." *The Mary Sue*, 15 May 2014: https://www.themarysue.com/lgbt-history-in-mainstream-comics-part-1/.)

[32] In fact, *extraño* is Spanish for "strange," so he was almost certainly a direct parody of Doctor Strange himself.

[33] *The New Guardians* #1 (September 1988), by Steve Englehart, Joe Staton, and Mark Farmer. In the next issue, they fought Snowflame, a Colombian who got his super-powers from snorting cocaine.

[34] Transgender heroes, as of the time of writing in June 2019, are still a relative rarity. Vertigo introduced one of the first trans superheroes in the form of Kate Godwin, a.k.a. Coagula, in *Doom Patrol* #70 (September 1993, by Rachel Pollack, Scott Eaton, and Tom Sutton).

[35] *The Authority* #29 (July 2002), by Mark Millar, Gary Erskine, and Tim Townsend; Northstar got hitched ten years later, and his wedding would be wrongly identified as the first gay superhero marriage by some in the media.

[36] In *52* #48 (4 April 2007), by Morrison, Geoff Johns, Greg Rucka, Mark Waid, Keith Giffen, and Darick Robertson. Then she spent some time dead, because this is still comic books. As of 2015, she was both alive and a cop once more – because, again, comics.

[37] Introduced in *52* #7 (21 June 2006), by Millar, Johns, Rucka, Waid, Giffen, Ken Lashley, and Draxhall Jump Studios.

[38] In *Catwoman* vol. 4 #39 (April 2015), by Genevieve Valentine and Garry Brown.

[39] In *Secret Six* vol. 4 #1 (February 2015), by Gail Simone, Lashley, and Drew Geraci.

[40] This had been a long-running implied joke since the pair appeared together in "Harley and Ivy," the 47th episode aired in the first season of *Batman: The Animated Series* (airdate: 18 January 1993). It was confirmed in a tweet by DC Comics' official account on 12 June 2015: "Yes, [Harley and Ivy] are girlfriends

So when *Constantine* ended with issue #23 in July 2015 (outliving its TV namesake by three months), it probably seemed like the right time to bring his bisexuality to the fore. In August 2015, *Constantine: The Hellblazer* was launched, with the new creative team of writers Ming Doyle and James Tynion IV,[41] along with regular artist Riley Rossmo, and it wasted no time in setting out its stall. In the first issue, Constantine meets Oliver, a handsome, buff New York restaurant owner, and happily flirts with him. In issue #6, they become a couple.

The series was canceled with issue #13, so Tynion and Doyle didn't have much time to get into the details of the relationship before Constantine was forced to go to Hell in order to save Oliver, Oliver's ex-wife, and their daughters. However, the pair are written with the same natural chemistry that John had with his girlfriends in the original *Hellblazer*, and their story explores some familiar ground as John tries to balance the normality of Oliver's world with the madness of his own.

In an interview with the *Chicago Review of Books*,[42] Doyle said that John's sexuality was a key focus for the series:

> There still aren't a lot of same-sex romances present in mainstream entertainment, and to gloss over that with one of the few historically bisexual characters in modern comics would've been ridiculous. The representation simply matters. And it's a big part of Constantine's life and personality, besides. We had no interest in denying him that. It's one thing to say that a character has hooked up with guys, or dated men, but we wanted to realize that part of him, not just allude to it. Some readers have commented that they felt we were bringing his sexuality too much to the fore, but John has always been really good bad-idea sex poured into tight pants, so I don't agree with that.[43]

---

without the jealousy of monogamy." Twitter: https://twitter.com/DCComics/status/609458213197606912.

[41] Attempts were made to contact Doyle and Tynion for this essay, but neither responded.

[42] Morgan, Adam. "'Resetting' Constantine: Ming Doyle at C2E2 2016." *Chicago Review of Books*, 16 March 2016: https://chireviewofbooks.com/2016/03/16/ming-doyle-constantine-interview-c2e2/.

[43] Doyle admits she was only familiar with the *Constantine* movie before signing on to write the comic, which may explain why John's characterization is so egregiously off early in their run; see "A Nasty Piece of Work? The Mercurial Morality of John Constantine," by this same author, elsewhere in this volume.

John's ill-fated boyfriend Oliver, from *Constantine: The Hellblazer* #6.

When asked by *Comics Alliance* whether it was difficult to "acknowledge a character's queerness,"[44] Tynion responded:

> [T]here are a few small stories over the course of [John]'s history that acknowledge his bisexuality, but there are a lot more where it just never comes up. Therefore, when you're constructing a John out of all of those favorite stories, you have to deliberately approach it. You have to deliberately name it. And that was important to me. And, frankly, it's also the simple fact that as a bi creator, the stories that mattered to me the

---

[44] Christianson, Jon Erik. "Bi the Books: James Tynion Pulls Back the Curtain on Erasure and Queer Haircuts." *Comics Alliance*, 31 August 2016: https://comicsalliance.com/james-tynion-flame-con-interview/.

most, that went to influence my take on the character, were the stories that did acknowledge. I can understand from the perspective of – it can be difficult, especially in a story that does have John with a female love interest, which, there have been many of those stories, and many of them are great. I understand the difficulty, in that story, of finding a place to call out something that isn't relevant to that story, but I would push that creator to be creative in a way to acknowledge it. In a very simple way, I think it's important for people to know.

Constantine: The Hellblazer was canceled in June 2016 with issue #13, which is a shame, because – John's horrendous characterization aside – it's better than its immediate predecessors by a country mile, and a worthy book in its own right. John then returned in a new comic in October 2016, simply titled *The Hellblazer*. New writer Simon Oliver told *Comics Alliance* that he'd been given a brief "to take John Constantine back to his roots,"[45] which he interpreted as removing John from the United States, where he'd spent most of his time since the reboot, and putting him back in the U.K., surrounded by a supporting cast of old familiar faces like Mercury, Marj, Ken "Map" Ondaatie, Clarice Sackville, and Albert Case from the old *Hellblazer* run, as well as Swamp Thing.

However, the new series swings back to the old school in another way: by downplaying Constantine's bisexuality. John is exclusively interested in women in all of the issues – including those by Tim Seeley, who took over as writer with issue #13. There's a moment in *The Hellblazer* #13 when he kisses a man on the lips, but it's just part of a spell to reclaim his lost memory; there's no romantic or sexual impulse involved. Instead, Constantine is – for the last half of the run – tangled up in the life of a female British police detective whom he once knew from his punk days and whose life rapidly goes downhill after they meet again.

There's no suggestion that this was a conscious decision on the parts of Oliver, Seely, or the DC editorial team, but it comes as something of a surprise following the apparent embracing of John's bisexuality in the previous comic. Was that partially why *Constantine: The Hellblazer* struggled? Whatever the intention, the move looked decidedly retrograde. *The Hellblazer* was canceled with issue #24 in September 2018; Constantine wouldn't get his own series again until the end of the following year, beginning with the desperately titled

[45] Shiach, Kieran. "More Conman Than Magician: Simon Oliver and Moritat on 'The Hellblazer'." *Comics Alliance*, 7 July 2016: https://comicsalliance.com/simon-oliver-moritat-hellblazer-interview/.

The Sandman Universe Presents: John Constantine: Hellblazer.[46] That continued into a resurrected *John Constantine: Hellblazer* title in 2020 that once again promised a back-to-basics approach. However, author Simon Spurrier largely delivered on that vow in its early issues[47] – and as a bonus for bi-spotters, had Constantine having "a thing with a deaf bloke in the nineties... he had no idea how noisy he was in the sack." However, that line came as John was apparently being set up with Nat, a surly female bouncer. That issue came out in 2020, but fans of bisexual Constantine hadn't been lacking for John-on-man action all that time. No, he'd already returned to a starring role, man-swaying powers fully intact, two years previously – it just wasn't in the comics.

Part Five: It's About Time

Following the cancelation of the *Constantine* television series, star Matt Ryan had enjoyed a nice side-gig playing the character in other live-action shows, first in an episode of the CW's Green Arrow vehicle *Arrow* in 2015, then in three episodes of its time-traveling spinoff, *Legends of Tomorrow*, in 2017. The appearances proved so popular with both the audience and writers that Ryan was brought back for a regular role in *Legends'* fourth season in 2018 – and this time, unlike on his own show, John would be portrayed as fully bisexual.

While that was a new development for TV Constantine, it was hardly new ground for *Legends*, which had featured a wide roster of gay, lesbian, and bisexual heroes and anti-heroes during its first three seasons, including team leader Sara Lance. Nor was it unusual in a TV and film landscape that was increasingly embracing non-straight, non-white, non-male, non-cisgender audiences, with the success of *Wonder Woman* (2017; $821 million box office) and *Black Panther* (2018; $1.3 billion box office) showing that big, big money could be made by going off the beaten track. In 2019, midway through *Legends'*

---

[46] DC decided in mid-2019 that it would discontinue Vertigo and a number of other imprints so that it could simplify and unify its range under the DC name, with three lines separated by age: DC Kids for those aged 8-12, plain old DC for the 13+ audience, and DC Black Label for readers aged 17+. Then it announced *The Sandman Presents* as yet another line, this one dedicated to its occult-focused mature-readers brands *The Sandman Universe*, *The Dreaming*, *The House of Whispers*, *Lucifer*, *The Books of Magic*, and *Hellblazer*. You know, like Vertigo was created to be in the first place. Nice one, lads.

[47] At the time of writing, the latest issue was #3, with art by Aaron Campbell. It went on sale in January 2020 and was cover-dated March 2020.

season four, *Captain Marvel* made $1.1 billion and spurred talk by Marvel that an LGBTQ cinematic hero was on the horizon.[48]

To justify Constantine's presence among the time-traveling Legends, the fourth season had the team hunting magical creatures that had been scattered throughout time – a unicorn at Woodstock, for example, or an evil fairy godmother causing chaos during the Salem witch trials – but Constantine's own character arc was much darker. In flashbacks glimpsed throughout the first half of the season, we discover that he had been happily involved in a relationship with Desmond,[49] who was a handsome bartender in New Orleans until a demon named Neron tricked Constantine into sending the unfortunate man to Hell.

Unlike pretty much every other element of the increasingly campy and absurd show, this is played absolutely dead straight, with Constantine as angst-ridden as one might expect. It also takes John's relationship with Desmond seriously, with flashbacks showing it to be passionate and physical, while also loving and emotionally connected. In the season's ninth episode, Constantine steals some time-travel technology and pretends to be his past self in order to break up with Desmond and scare him off before Neron can get his claws in. We get to see two sides of their relationship – past Constantine happily cooking a full English breakfast for his boyfriend, and the future mage torn up by what has happened, breaking the heart of the man he loves to save his soul.

Sadly, John realizes that there's no way for him to change the past without screwing up the space-time continuum and getting a lot more people killed in the process, so he undoes his meddling by getting his past self to reconcile with Desmond. That results in a kiss that sends a shockwave of time energy throughout the universe, restoring things to how they ought to be. That delighted writer S.E. Fleenor of *SyfyWire*, whose article "A Queer Kiss Saves the World on Legends of Tomorrow"[50] stated:

---

[48] Sposato, Sean. "Marvel Studios Plans to Reveal One of its Superhero Characters is Gay." *Inside the Magic*, 9 May 2019: https://insidethemagic.net/2019/05/mcu-to-have-a-gay-character/.

[49] Who bears an uncanny resemblance to Oliver, the love interest in *Constantine: The Hellblazer*, right down to meeting John while serving him some food. John has two friends named Desmond in the original *Hellblazer* – Desmond "Dez" Foster / Ridley (his surname changes from issue #64 to #78 for some reason), and another Dez in issue #111 – but neither is his lover.

[50] Fleenor, S.E. "A Queer Kiss Saves the World on Legends of Tomorrow." *SyfyWire*, 27 December 2018: https://www.syfy.com/syfywire/a-queer-kiss-saves-the-world-on-legends-of-tomorrow.

In our reality, a tide of evil, a tide of hatred and discrimination and fear, is trying to erase and destroy the lives of queer people right now, right here. Queer folks are fired from jobs, stabbed while walking home from the club, legislated against, and mercilessly murdered just because of who we are. And what do we have to fight back with? We're not a large voting bloc. We don't tend to patrol in packs to defend everyone under our rainbow. We're really just a loosely affiliated group filled with people who dare to live and love outside the norm. And that love, queer love, defines us.

Queer love is our superpower. Queer love strengthens us. Queer love can save the world, even if just for a moment, even if we will have to save it again later. The impact of that love is revolutionary. Just ask Constantine.

Ultimately, Constantine *is* able to rescue Desmond through other means – but their relationship is over. John offers him the chance to forget everything that happened, but Desmond refuses. He has changed, and to go back on that would be a denial of the truth.

On *Legends of Tomorrow*, the mage's lover Desmond (played by Christian Keyes) sold his soul to Neron in exchange for John's life.

The same can be said of our John. Yes, the origins of his sexuality comprise just a handful of issues from throughout 25 years of *Hellblazer*. And yes, his bisexuality came to the fore seemingly because of a critical mass of online misperception about a comic with a dire history of queer representation. But the path we've walked isn't as important as where we stand – and Constantine now takes pride of place in the pantheon of bisexual anti-heroes, an exemplar of a complex, fascinating character who happens to be queer.

Just whatever you do, don't call him a role model.

What's Love Got to Do with It? John Constantine, Kit Ryan, and the Women of *Hellblazer*

by Julianne Clancy

As any devotee of *Hellblazer* knows, there's something irresistible about John Constantine. Sure, he may be a "useless wanker in a trenchcoat,"[1] but he's also smart, sly, wry, and alluringly mysterious. With a quick smile, roguish good looks, and a prowess between the sheets that's won over good girls, bad boys, and demons alike, our beloved antihero is the very definition of a devil dressed up in angel wings. It's no wonder so many have fallen under Constantine's spell – and it's no secret that, when it comes to women, John is nothing but disaster.

Mingling with the fairer sex might not be the only area of life in which Constantine is unlucky, but it sure does seem to be the one in which he causes the most wreckage. From his family to his magical career to his (mis)adventures in romance, John continually destroys relationships and, most often, the lives of the women with whom he comes in contact. In fact, only one woman ever

---

[1] Jenkins, Paul (writer), Al Davison (pencils), and Pamela Rambo (inks). "Football: It's a Funny Old Game." *Hellblazer* #101 (May 1996).

seems up to the task of surviving the curse of being adored by Constantine relatively intact – and both she and John are too damaged to make it work.

With that in mind, let's take a stroll down the primrose path of the ladies who love, lust after, and lose themselves to our favorite mage.

From the day he was born, Constantine seemed destined to rain misery down on women. His entrance into the world, through no fault of his own, was a harrowing event, deadly for his mother, precipitated by his father, and leading to a life (and afterlife)-long struggle between the two Constantine men. The only female role model in his early life is his sister, Cheryl, and even she eventually grows to have complicated if not downright antagonistic feelings toward her dear little brother. It probably doesn't help that John keeps up his pattern of corrupting the Constantine women through Cheryl's daughter, Gemma, who, despite John's best efforts to keep her from the world of magic, ends up following in her wayward uncle's footsteps.

It's no wonder Cheryl grows to dislike her brother. He harbored incestuous thoughts for her, which he fueled by secretly watching her undress (in *Hellblazer* #7). He pranks Gary Lester into taking honey from a wasps' nest on the (broken) promise that Cheryl would let him feel her up beneath her skirt ("All Those Little Boys and Girls," in *Vertigo Winter's Edge* #2). When Cheryl does try to hang out with young John, he refuses and taunts her, calling her "Beryl the Peril" (*Hellblazer* #213). John even turns his big sister away, with baby Gemma in tow, when she tries to stay with him after leaving her mentally unstable husband Tony (*Hellblazer* #273). By the time John's actions led to Cheryl being murdered and ending up in Hell (*Hellblazer* #212), readers were almost immune to Cheryl suffering due her brother's actions.

Given his conflicted connections to the women in his family, it shouldn't come as a surprise that Constantine's struggles with the ladies in his life continue after he leaves home and breaks out on his own. As a young man, he stumbles into a tragic incident involving a young girl which colors the rest of his long, notable, and fraught magical career. In Newcastle, John boldly believes he can save Astra Logue from the demons that thirst for her. But his attempt to lead the little girl from Hell only precipitates her fall into damnation. This failure haunts him throughout his days, no matter how much he tries to distance himself from the event or atone for it, leading him to constantly seek redemption through more and more mystical meddling – a penance which, ironically, damages even more innocents in the process.

Loaded with baggage from both his relatives and his lethal mistake in Newcastle, John does what any respectable, red-blooded man would do: he returns to his promiscuous ways with a vengeance, trying to sleep with as many women as humanly possible in order to forget his gnawing guilt. His partners are many. His sexual health is questionable.[2] His aptitude as a reliable partner is dismal. Frankly, his ventures into the land of love and lust are unfortunate at best and downright despicable at worst.

Zed, Marj, and John break some love taboos in *Hellblazer* #22.

One of his earliest entanglements in the series is with Zed, a beautiful, edgy woman avoiding a foretold fate with the religious cult called the Resurrection Crusaders. John is immediately drawn to her enigmatic charisma and knowledge of the occult, while Zed falls for John's charm and the prospect of him being her salvation: "She needs him – needs a friend to help her cheat her destiny."[3] But Constantine is, obviously, the worst friend she could pick. His selfish need to be at the center of any mystical event ("I don't like secrets I'm not a part of"[4]) leads him to hunt her down after she's reunited with the Crusaders. Playing the lonely, hangdog victim, he convinces her to have one last tryst with him, corrupting her chances of becoming the Chalice. While his

[2] Is demon blood considered a sexually transmitted disease?

[3] Delano, Jamie (w), John Ridgway (p), and Lovern Kindzierski (i). "Ghosts in the Machine." *Hellblazer* #7 (July 1988).

[4] Delano, Jamie (w), John Ridgway (p), and Lovern Kindzierski (i). "Extreme Prejudice." *Hellblazer* #6 (June 1988).

intervention does save her from the cult, he abandons her afterwards, heading off on an admittedly necessary quest to stop the Antichrist but ultimately also leaving her to languish in Glastonbury. Zed would later come back in the series as a powerful mage in her own right, embracing the all-mighty girl-powers of earth and motherhood, and using John for her own magical rites, but her path had been forever twisted from what it once was because of John.

When Constantine tries to fight his own tendencies and orchestrate an average romantic life, he makes an even worse mess of the entire scenario. He becomes obsessed with Doctor Phoebe Clifton-Avery – a beautiful, smart, educated, professional woman with little to no interest in John's nasty habits. John wants her because of how different she is from the occult life he knows: "She's normal and tame compared to the vixens and damaged goods I usually go after."[5] The two date for two years, until she ultimately leaves him. So obviously, to win her back, John only has one option: try to magically compel her to want him again.

Much to his annoyance, John's love potion doesn't work on Phoebe. She sniffs out his scheme when he comes over with an apology and a bottle of wine, then turns him down once and for all (after letting him scratch a certain itch for her one more time). Unfortunately, it's not that easy to escape the curse of Constantine. Despite rebuffing his magical advances, Phoebe still winds up on the wrong side of a demon with a vendetta against John – and is killed.

Phoebe isn't the only fatality to come out of John's quest for connection. One of John's longest-lasting girlfriends, Emma, fights the Brujería at Constantine's side, only to be murdered by the cult they were investigating. Constantine's on-again-off-again relationship with Zatanna Zatara spans years, series, and timelines. But their romantic and magical partnership ultimately ends up killing her beloved father, the consequence of a séance that saves the world but destroys some of its members.[6]

Even when John's dalliances aren't deadly or damning, they rarely end on a positive note. Some relationships succumb to supernatural irreconcilable differences. Marj, the sweet hippie who helps John while he's on the lam from the law, can't resist Constantine's rough charm. But after her daughter,

---

[5] Milligan, Peter (w), Giuseppe Camuncoli and Stefano Landini (p), and Jamie Grant(i). "Hooked: Part One of Three." *Hellblazer* #256 (August 2009).
[6] It is worth noting that Zatara dies in order to save Zatanna, who would have been killed by the séance were it not for her father's intervention (*Swamp Thing* #50).

Mercury, is kidnapped and used for her psychic powers (through no fault of Constantine's), Marj leaves John, turning instead to Zed's sisterhood of shamans for aid and fulfillment. And Chantinelle, a succubus who enlists Constantine's aid when she finds herself impregnated by an angel, winds up eternally in John's thrall due to a nasty trick he pulls while appearing to save her.[7] The demon and demon hunter keep becoming entangled in each other's lives, such as when John manipulates her into sleeping with him so he can regain his demon blood, but the outcome of their interactions is never very pleasant.

Dani Wright gets the upper hand on John Constantine.

Other trysts come to much more mundane, if still painful, ends. Much of John's relationship with Angie Spatchcock, a fellow mage who helps defeat both the Shadow Dog and The Beast, revolves around dark magic and demons. But their breakup isn't because of magic meddling: John blames himself – and Angie – for losing Cheryl and simply walks away.[8] Meanwhile, Danita "Dani" Wright,

---

[7] John later reveals that the masking spell he placed on Chantinelle (whom he nicknames "Ellie") to protect her contained a little bit of his blood, thus making the spell linked to his life. In other words, she can never exact deadly revenge on John without putting her own being in mortal peril (*Hellblazer* #104).

[8] Angie's reaction to the breakup also is rather ordinary. She reappears at John's wedding, comforting herself with a candy bar and bemoaning the fact that he's with Plffy (*Hellblazer* #275).

an American reporter with whom John has one of his most normal relationships, ends up with a broken heart after finding John in bed with Chantinelle. It isn't her succubus nature that's the problem – it's a simple case of assumed infidelity.

John does eventually settle down and find a partner willing to submit to the bonds of (un)holy matrimony, but his relationship with his bride, Epiphany "Piffy" Greaves, lasts in part because she's willing to be drawn into the darkness which Constantine inhabits. Before they even couple up, Piffy allows herself to become entangled in the whole Phoebe disaster, providing John with the fateful potion and then helping him attempt to resurrect his lost obsession – a macabre plot which does nothing to bring Phoebe back and leaves Piffy in a coma. Even with such an inauspicious start, Piffy agrees to be John's wife.[9]

Piffy Greaves and John tie the knot amid a cast of unsavory characters.

On the eve of their wedding, John boasts about how comfortable Piffy is with the unsavory elements of his life.[10] Their actual nuptials are almost thwarted when Constantine's demonic other half and his perpetual nemesis Nergal attempt to trick Piffy into a different kind of ceremony. Yet still, Piffy ultimately says, "I do," instead of pulling a runaway bride or trying to get an annulment due to irreconcilable demons. In the end, she's as deep into John's

---

[9] According to *Hellblazer* #295, Piffy has loved John and has known she would marry him since meeting him when she was only *nine years old*... even though John was forty-two at the time.
[10] To be fair, a succubus head in the fridge isn't *that* much more harrowing than two-week-old Chinese take-out.

damage as he is – the only way she can actually make it work with the morose mage.

Despite all of these catastrophic interactions with women, John remains relatively unfazed by the wreckage he continually leaves in his wake. He may whine and mope about the unfairness of what happens to him, but when push comes to shove, he maintains an edge of righteousness about his actions. Before Astra is devoured, he gloats that "They should make me a bloody saint for this."[11] And when Zed takes him to task for leaving her high-and-dry in Glastonbury, his weak rebuttal is that "It doesn't mean I don't still lo..."[12] – a half-hearted apology that Zed cuts off before he can fully get it out. Phoebe gets the stirring and emotional eulogy of "I'm sorry for not feeling more. This is just the way I'm made."[13] Constantine even bookends his marriage to Piffy with a triumphant declaration of his unchanging ways: "I'm now officially a married man. And you know what? I'm still John Constantine."[14]

More so, Constantine often seems to view the women in his life as no more than set pieces in his personal Greek tragedy.[15] In his mind, he is a tormented hero who faces unbelievable odds and tests to his unique skill – as in his episodes with Astra, Zed, Gemma, and Zatanna. Other times, he wallows in his identity as a scoundrel, a broken man who brings nothing but doom and gloom to those around him – as he does to his mother, Cheryl, Phoebe, and Dani. His relationships with other women give him the opportunity to flex his muscles as a legendary mage whose exploits earn him fame and infamy – such as with Piffy, as well as with Marj, Chantinelle, Emma, and Angie. To these women, John is life-changing and earth-shattering. To John, they're just more evidence supporting the portrait he paints of his own existence.

---

[11] Delano, Jamie (w), John Ridgway (p), and Lovern Kindzierski (i). "Newcastle: A Taste of Things to Come." *Hellblazer* #1 (November 1988).

[12] Delano, Jamie (w), Mark Buckingham and Alfredo Alcala (p), and Lovern Kindzierski (i). "The Fear Machine, Part IX: Balance." *Hellblazer* #22 (September 1989).

[13] Milligan, Peter (w), Giuseppe Camuncoli and Stefano Landini (p), and Jamie Grant(i). "Hooked: Part Three of Three." *Hellblazer* #258 (October 2009).

[14] Milligan, Peter (w), Giuseppe Camuncoli and Stefano Landini (p), and Trish Mulvihill (i). "Bloody Carnations, Part 5: Confetti and Brimstone." *Hellblazer* #275 (March 2011).

[15] This could explain the indefensible sexual relationship he apparently had with 12-year-old Katrina Bogdonovich before her first menstruation (per *Hellblazer* #157), which seems wholly out of character for John, considering his reaction to Astra Logue's molestation in issue #11.

Among all the women in Constantine's life, Kit Ryan was something special.

In fact, only one woman appears to actually get under Constantine's thick, cancer-riddled skin, refusing to become merely a footnote in his long line of conquests. Katherine "Kit" Ryan, the raven-haired, flashing-eyed beauty from Belfast, goes toe-to-toe with Constantine time and again before escaping his gravitational pull with only a few emotional scars to show for it (which, in John's world, is basically unscathed). Even though Piffy is John's eventual life partner, it's Kit who seems truly to be his soulmate – or, at least, the soulmate he *should* have had were he able to actually dump some of the baggage he'd accumulated throughout years of demonic entanglement.

Kit's backstory isn't exactly sunshine and rainbows. Raised in a poor Belfast home by an alcoholic father and the love-lost mother who couldn't leave him,

Kit becomes a woman who doesn't "take shit off anyone"[16] from a young age. Her no-nonsense attitude and innate ability to defend herself, both physically and mentally, make her a match for the brooding and unbelievably damaged Constantine. His wicked ways just don't intimidate her in the slightest, as she demonstrates by continually threatening to "beat the shite out of [him],"[17] "kick [his] arse,"[18] and "give [him] the ballacking of his life."[19] Her assertions aren't just talk or a colorful demonstration that the writers understand an Irish accent, either. Kit manages to hold her own through several frays, brutally battering the family jewels of not one but two attackers without a second thought, then admonishing John after a scuffle, "What've I told you about getting into bother without me to help?"[20]

This straightforward, strong attitude puts John in the unfamiliar situation of being back on his heels. Kit isn't a prop in anyone's story. She controls her own narrative, as well as the stories of most people she meets. John's left feeling cautious, even scared, of embarking on a romantic relationship. Even though John often notes that people who get close to him wind up being hurt, his whinging doesn't actually keep him from charging ahead anyway. But something about Kit – his admiration for her or his awe of her, or maybe both – stops him from even attempting to woo her at first, as he declares, "I need to know for certain, right before the very first kiss."[21] And, in fact, it's Kit who eventually has to make the first move.

Once the ice is broken, Kit's strength keeps John interested for longer than most woman are able.[22] Instead of having a quick shag before heading off on his

[16] Ennis, Garth (w), Steve Dillon (p&i). "Heartland." *Hellblazer* #70 (October 1993). Ennis and Dillon further spotlight Kit's background and family life in the same-named one-shot *Heartland* (March 1997), in which John does not appear.

[17] Ennis, Garth (w), Steve Dillon (p), and Tom Ziuko (i). "Lord of the Dance." *Hellblazer* #49 (January 1992).

[18] Ennis, Garth (w), William Simpson (p), and Tom Ziuko (i). "Royal Blood: Part One." *Hellblazer* #52 (April 1992).

[19] Ennis, Garth (w), Steve Dillon (p), and Tom Ziuko (i). "Fear and Loathing, Part 2: London Kills Me." *Hellblazer* #65 (May 1993).

[20] Ennis, Garth (w), Steve Dillon (p), and Tom Ziuko (i). "Mortal Clay." *Hellblazer* #57 (September 1992).

[21] Ennis, Garth (w), Steve Dillon (p), and Tom Ziuko (i). "Lord of the Dance." *Hellblazer* #49 (January 1992).

[22] In fact, John had already been in love with Kit for years before they'd dated, ever since being introduced to her by his close mate (and her boyfriend at the time), Brendan Finn.

next adventure, John comes back for more time and again. With Kit, John's more open and honest, sheepishly so, than with anyone else, noting that he "never could keep anything from [her]"[23] and that "there's no fooling Kit, no smart looks and wisecracks and slipping into the shadows."[24] Kit also stubbornly refuses to fit neatly into one of the boxes he's set up for the rest. She doesn't need saving, has no time for his scoundrel antics, and is thoroughly unimpressed by his supposedly extraordinary magical conquests. Kit forces Constantine to be just John – a stripped-down identity that is at once appealing and frightening in its simplicity.

For her part, Kit isn't oblivious to the fact that she's special in getting John to open up to her. As she tells Gemma, "He doesn't put up a front or try to be clever."[25] But she's also not blind to the fact that her paramour is bad news when it comes to the battle of good and evil. While she's not frightened by John's occult occupations, she (wisely) wants nothing to do with the more dangerous elements of John's existence: "I wouldn't mind if John Constantine moved in... I'm just not sure if I want all the baggage that comes with him."[26] She knows him well enough not to ask him to give up his dark magics completely, but she does demand that he keep that part of his life separate from her, telling him more than once, "Don't bring it here with you, okay?"[27]

But even that is too much to ask of John. His magic and mayhem are as much a part of his being as his trenchcoat, cigarettes, blonde hair, and flashing smile. Even if he wanted to, Constantine couldn't keep the "ghoulies, ghosties, and things that go bump in the night"[28] from invading every aspect of his life. Unsurprisingly, his Irish lass eventually winds up on the wrong side of some baddies – and, true to her word, Kit immediately packs her bags and heads back

---

[23] Ennis, Garth (w), Will Simpson (p), and Mark Pennington, Mark McKenna, Kim DeMulder, and Stan Woch (i). "Dangerous Habits – Epilogue: Falling into Hell." *Hellblazer* #46 (October 1991).

[24] Ennis, Garth (w), Will Simpson (p), Stan Woch (i), Tom Ziuko (c). "The Pub Where I Was Born." *Hellblazer* #47 (November 1991).

[25] Ennis, Garth (w), Steve Dillon (p), and Tom Ziuko (i). "End of the Line." *Hellblazer* #62 (February 1993).

[26] Ennis, Garth (w), William Simpson (p), and Tom Ziuko (i). "Royal Blood: Part One." *Hellblazer* #52 (April 1992).

[27] Ennis, Garth (w), William Simpson (p), and Tom Ziuko (i). "Royal Blood: Part Two." *Hellblazer* #53 (May 1992).

[28] Ennis, Garth (w), William Simpson (p), and Tom Ziuko (i). "Royal Blood: Part One." *Hellblazer* #52 (April 1992).

to the relative peace of Belfast.

The failure of his relationship with Kit is, like Newcastle, another defining moment in Constantine's narrative. For the first time, John is the one who is nearly destroyed by love. He winds up drunk in the streets, lamenting what he lost for months on end, and wondering: "How'd I get to this...? ...But I know... I did my usual trick... took something good and made it rotten."[29] Even after he pulls himself out of the gutter, takes a shower, and shaves his beard (a hygienic choice to which the modern millennial reader may object), he is haunted by the shadow of Kit, so much so that when he splits himself into two entities, banishing his vices to Hell as a demonic doppelgänger, he leaves his feelings for Kit with his Hell-bound half. ("You love her, I don't, she's yours.")[30] Kit is as damaging to him as cancer, cigarettes, self-destruction, and demon blood – a weakness that he cannot shake, cannot despise, and cannot abide.

The timeline of causes and effects seems pretty clear here: John and Kit meet, John loves her from afar, Kit eventually reciprocates his feelings, John nearly gets Kit killed, and Kit peaces out before she actually dies. But the failure of Kit and Constantine goes deeper than a hitman with a switchblade. As mentally and emotionally well-matched as they are in most ways, and as deeply as they open up to each other, there are two indestructible hurdles standing in the way of them ever finding a "happily ever after": fear and addiction.

John Constantine is an addict. He cures his lung cancer, pissing off not one but three powerful dark forces in the process, and proceeds to continue smoking like a chimney. He's a man who knowingly has dangerous habits and refuses to quit them – and he cannot and will not stop chasing the high of interfering in demonic, occult, and magical chaos. Of course, he continually promises Kit that he'll give up his dangerous lifestyle for her if she asks. When he first moves in with her, he swears, "I wouldn't ever let any of this shit hurt you, y'know. Soon as I even got a hint you could be tangled up, I'd drop it like a stone."[31] But when Kit *does* get tangled up in it, John's back to his old excuses: "You know what I get up to! You can't expect to be left out of it forever.

---

[29] Ennis, Garth (w), Steve Dillon (p), and Tom Ziuko (i). "Down All the Days." *Hellblazer* #68 (August 1993).

[30] Jenkins, Paul (w), Sean Phillips (p), and Matt Hollingsworth (i). "Critical Mass 5: Hook Line & Sinker." *Hellblazer* #96 (December 1995).

[31] Ennis, Garth (w), William Simpson (p), and Tom Ziuko (i). "Royal Blood: Part Two." *Hellblazer* #53 (May 1992).

Nobody's perfect, luv."[32]

When Kit once again appears back in his life in "Rake at the Gates of Hell," this time for one last night out and a goodbye shag, Constantine pleads with her to stay, vowing to leave his old life behind: "You want me to leave London and give up magic and even knock off the soddin' Silk Cut, no problem. Anything. Anything at all. I'm yours."[33] But, at the end of the day, Kit and John both know he will never let go of the cigs or the spells. His promises could all be lies, but, more likely, they're just weak attempts to break yet another addiction of which he has no will, or desire, to shed himself.

Constantine has some level of awareness, or fear, of his shortcomings that keeps him from ever fully committing to Kit. Despite the length and intensity of their relationship (perhaps short for many people, but epically long in Constantine's terms), he never once tells her he loves her. When Kit and Constantine reunite briefly, years after the end of their romance, in John Shirley's prose novel *Hellblazer: Subterranean*,[34] John is moved by his immediate re-infatuation to pen Kit a letter promising to leave the "Hidden World" (his frequent description of magic in Shirley's novels) behind and find a steady job if she'll take him back. But, per usual, he chickens out at the last minute, tossing his letter in a stream instead of giving it to her.

In fact, the only time he even utters the phrase in her presence is during Peter Milligan's run, when Constantine invites Kit to his wedding to Piffy (and she begrudgingly attends). Even then, he's only able to say it in comparison to his future bride, when Kit pointedly asks why John is marrying someone other than her, and he bluntly says that he can be himself with Piffy, without having to hide his occult side. He argues to himself that his inability to tell Kit he loves her, out loud and without couching it in an insult, is because he's afraid of the word, but that's just another comforting lie to protect his own unbreakable image of himself.

John tells Zed he loves her during their last dalliance before she's supposed to give herself over to the Crusaders. He says he loves Phoebe, though he does acknowledge that his feelings are more akin to obsession. He even declares his love for the demon Chantinelle, convincing her of the veracity of his claim

---

[32] Ennis, Garth (w), Steve Dillon (p), and Tom Ziuko (i). "Dear John." *Hellblazer* #67 (July 1993).

[33] Ennis, Garth (w), Steve Dillon (p), and Tom Ziuko (i). "Rake at the Gates of Hell: Part Five." *Hellblazer* #82 (October 1994).

[34] Shirley, John. *Hellblazer: Subterranean*. Pocket Star, 2006.

despite it only being a ploy to use her for his own purposes. Only with Kit do the words stick in his throat, closing it up before he can make a statement of devotion nearing his actual depth of feeling. John isn't afraid of love, either the word or the emotion. He's afraid of Kit – the woman strong enough to strip him down to his essential elements and make him face himself. He's afraid of what he would become if he were truly allowed to let himself love her, and what he might have to lose or give up in the process.

Lest we go too far down the John-bashing rabbit hole, let's not ignore the fact that Kit is far from blameless in this scenario. She has her own addiction which helps lead to the failure of the Constantine/Kit coupling: broken men. John meets Kit when she is eighteen years old and living with his long-time friend, Brendan Finn, an unrepentant alcoholic who eventually drinks himself into an early grave. Kit leaves Brendan before his inevitable destruction, going to see him one last time and recoiling at his unwillingness or inability to give up the vice which is devouring him. Sound familiar? During her farewell trip to London, she openly acknowledges the similarity between her two great loves – that John is allowing his demonic dabbling to endanger his life and that she cannot stay to watch him do so – but falls short of facing the fact that she should have seen this coming a long time ago.

Kit has always known about Constantine's activities. She knew before they were lovers. She knew when they moved in together. She must have known that despite her protestations and ultimatums, she would become involved in something nasty. Her attraction to Constantine persisted not necessarily in spite of, but perhaps *because* of his literal and figurative demons. As Kit tells Gemma, "Sometimes people are just themselves, not what other people hope they'll be."[35] There's an openness and honesty about damaged men that draws Kit in and gives her the freedom to let her emotional-freak flag fly as well. It's unfair for her to expect them to magically heal when their baggage no longer suits her.

Ultimately, though, Kit is just as unable to bear witness to the destruction of the people she loves as John is to quit destroying himself. She watched alcohol consume her father and her mother's love for her dad consume them all. She then watched Brendan descend into alcoholism. She has no interest in continuing the cycle, even if she keeps starting it over and over again. When Kit

---

[35] Ennis, Garth (w), Steve Dillon (p), and Tom Ziuko (i). "End of the Line." *Hellblazer* #62 (February 1993).

leaves London, she claims it's because "I'm fed up with this town. It smells rotten, so it does. And the people carry on like – I dunno. It's like they're beaten. They've got nothing left in them."[36] But it's not the city itself she fears is sinking into defeat – it's the man with whom she so closely associates it.

All good stories must come full-circle, and so it is with John and Kit. Eventually, Kit and Piffy have their momentous meeting as two of the most important women in John's life, though the fireworks aren't quite as spectacular as the more voyeuristic reader might hope. Piffy calls Kit "the love of John's life,"[37] and Kit graciously demurs. Yet there is truth to Piffy's statement. Constantine and Kit are two sides of the same coin: strong, proud, and unapologetic; haunted by their pasts; estranged from their families; desperate for someone with whom they can fully be themselves; tormented by addictions they cannot shake. But while Constantine leans in to his issues, wrapping them around himself like a shield, Kit runs from hers, constantly trying to keep one step ahead of the grief that's just below the surface. Like any other coin, the two faces are made of the same stuff but will simply never see eye to eye – no matter how much they might each benefit from taking in the world from the other's point of view.

When reflecting on the numerous women in his life, Constantine says, "I miss 'em all, me. Even the ones who hated me."[38] In his own way, John loves each of them, laments the damage he causes them, and mourns for something he's never had and never will: a normal relationship. But at the same time, he knows that "all that fucking insanity is a big part of who I am."[39] No matter what he does, John Constantine will always be John Constantine: our lovable and hate-able rogue mage, traveling on, lonely but never alone, surrounded by the ghosts of the women he's adored, lost, used, and abused – especially one dark-haired lass from the Emerald Isle.

---

[36] Ennis, Garth (w), Steve Dillon (p), and Tom Ziuko (i). "Dear John." *Hellblazer* #67 (July 1993).

[37] Milligan, Peter (w), Giuseppe Camuncoli and Stefano Landini (p), and Trish Mulvihill (i). "Bloody Carnations, Part 5: Confetti and Brimstone." *Hellblazer* #275 (March 2011).

[38] Ellis, Warren (w), James Romberger (p), and James Sinclair (i). "One Last Love Song." *Hellblazer* #142 (November 1999).

[39] Milligan, Peter (w), Giuseppe Camuncoli and Stefano Landini (p), and Trish Mulvihill (i). "Bloody Carnations, Part 5: Confetti and Brimstone." *Hellblazer* #275 (March 2011).

Manifest Magic: John Constantine on Television

by Joseph Dilworth

From his first appearance in 1985, John Constantine has left an almost runic mark on comic books. Given primordial form by Alan Moore, Stephen R. Bissette, John Totleben, and Rick Veitch in the pages of *Swamp Thing*, then later fully evolved by Jamie Delano and John Ridgeway in *Hellblazer*, Constantine was a character who initially worked behind the scenes, but readers increasingly demanded to know more about him. While eventually getting his own comic book series, which ran for a staggering 300 issues, he also popped up in other comics as well, even if sparingly.

Moreover, Constantine and his stories have gone on to influence and inform nearly every shady occult character of the last 30 years. On the long-running series *Supernatural*, the look and initial attitude of the angel Castiel were based on John. The literary private investigators Harry Dresden and Felix Castor are obvious spiritual cousins. There are also nearly a dozen comic book characters inspired by him, or that are direct rip-offs. Not bad for a one-note character originally created, according to Moore, "purely to get Sting into the story."[1]

---

[1] Moore, Alan. "Alan Moore on (Just About) Everything." *Comics Journal* #106 (March 1986).

Naturally, fans began to wonder if there would ever be a theatrical or television adaptation featuring Constantine. In 2005, the occult detective was brought to life in a feature film starring Keanu Reeves. This was met with a decidedly mixed reaction, although it has been viewed more favorably in recent years. I always thought it was a decent attempt, capturing the essence of the character and his world, and was unfairly treated at the time. Its less-than-stellar performance seemed to put a halt to any more live-action adventures for John for nearly a decade.

Transmogrified to Television

In 2014, NBC announced plans to bring John Constantine to TV as part of its fall 2015 lineup. This was provisionally good news. On one hand, with *Constantine* airing on one of the major broadcast networks, there was concern that the content would be watered down, particularly regarding the main character. On the other hand, the show was being developed by Daniel Cerone and David S. Goyer. Goyer was favorable to comic book sensibilities, having written many comics himself and having been previously involved with bringing comics characters to the screen. Then again, *Constantine* was relegated to late Fridays, which didn't speak well about the network's confidence in the series.

Then the show debuted, and the grumbling from the fans began. The horror aspects were front and center, certainly. Gore and violence were not taboo on network TV. It was the finer details of the character that were troublesome, as they'd largely been shorn away. John no longer smoked, since that couldn't be depicted on primetime TV. Also, there was no more swearing, though this being American television, they could get away with a fair amount of explicit British slang epithets. Particularly egregious was the erasure of Constantine's bisexuality. Now he was a lady's man, through and through.

I know what you're thinking, and any other time you would be right. These seem like minor changes made to a character to make him more palatable to a wider audience. In John's case, however, these are all aspects that inform later parts of his life, while the self-medicating and foul language are deeply entrenched coping mechanisms for someone who lives most of his life on the dark side. Anyone who has read the original *Hellblazer* comics will know that the chain-smoking, drinking, swearing, and sleeping with anything with a pulse are as much the framework of John Constantine as the trenchcoat, disheveled tie, and Scouse accent. To strip most of that away was to essentially neuter the character into a barely recognizable ghost of what he used to be.

The cast of the CW's *Constantine* (left to right): Harold Perrineau, Matt Ryan, Angélica Celaya, and Charles Halford.

A more minor change was the accent. Matt Ryan, cast as the titular character, affected a Welsh accent. Overall, given all the other restructuring, this was less of a grievance and more necessitated by how the actor approached the role. Ryan himself is from Swansea, so the accent wasn't a reach for him. Moreover, Welsh and Liverpudlian (Constantine's described accent) are not too dissimilar, so it kind of fit.

What of Matt Ryan, chosen to bring the madcap magician to life? In this regard, the production struck gold. There are a few actors who are forever intrinsically linked with characters they've played. William Shatner will always be James Tiberius Kirk. Christopher Reeve is Superman. Certainly, Hugh Jackman and Wolverine are forever entwined. And anyone who isn't Val Kilmer or George Clooney is Batman. Matt Ryan *is* John Constantine. It certainly helps that, apart from the previous, forgettable "Americanized" film, no one else has portrayed the character on the large or small screen.

But more than that, Ryan found the heart and soul of a character who frequently seems to lack both. This is a rare case of an actor not just portraying a fictional person but inhabiting the role. Ryan absolutely brought forth the complete essence of Constantine, while at the same time adding his own swagger and punctuation that gave a sublime dimension to his performance. This would be the silver lining of the whole endeavor, but also its greatest tragedy. Here was an actor who was note-perfect in a role that was betrayed by a production that didn't seem to want that character to be a part of it.

In and of itself, the show isn't really that bad. Perhaps the most frustrating aspect is that you can tell they're holding back and trying to soften up both the character and the storylines. Herein lies the biggest issue with the series – and most likely its undoing. It's almost as though the writers came up with the premise and framework of the series first, along with their idea for the main character, and then tried to shoehorn Constantine in after the fact.

For fans, the episodes walk right up to the front door of the house that the comic books built, then steadfastly refuse to open it and walk in, especially with John's defining vices either tempered or eliminated. It's to Matt Ryan's credit that all the rough edges aren't worn away. It's his nuanced performance that prevents Constantine from becoming a run-of-the-mill antihero with a heart of gold.

That's the problem for the viewer who is unfamiliar with the character. It's difficult to see anything unique about him and his world, apart from the few flashes that Ryan forces through, or that the writers sneak by the censors. However, there are enough of those moments that make the show off-putting to those who are expecting a by-the-numbers supernatural procedural with a romantic flair.

Refusing to fully embrace the *Hellblazer* source material, while simultaneously not falling into the trap of being a harder-edged *Angel*, leaves a confusing mess. Interestingly, several months later, along came *Lucifer*, which struck the perfect balance between the two. John Constantine and Lucifer Morningstar inhabited the same comic book universe and seemingly tried to tread the same path on TV, but only the latter series would figure out the formula for success.

To be fair, later episodes of *Constantine* did move more in the direction that was expected by hardcore fans, but this was a lesson in "too little, too late." It also likely further alienated the general audience as well, since it started to veer away from the show to which they had grown accustomed. It was a welcome move, but it should have been the path from the first episode onward, instead of a late-hour recalibration.

Constantine failed to click with its audience and the show was summarily dismissed from NBC's lineup. There was a brief spark of hope as the production company tried to find a new home for the series, but those efforts failed. Usually, that would have been the end. Constantine, both the character and the series, should have slouched off into obscurity, semi-fondly remembered as a misguided attempt at a Hell-blazing TV show.

Enter the Arrowverse

The month that *Constantine* was officially canceled, rumors immediately began to fly that the mage would appear on one of the so-called "Arrowverse" series (the DC superhero shows airing on The CW, beginning with *Arrow*). This was all sparked by a comment from *Arrow* star Stephen Amell, who stated that he had pushed to guest-star on *Constantine* in order to indirectly bring that show into the world of his series, despite their airing on different networks.

Matt Ryan reprises his role as John Constantine on the CW's *Arrow*.

Hope was heightened when *Arrow* showrunners Marc Guggenheim and Wendy Mericle revealed their desire to have Constantine appear on their series, and that they had been having talks with the Powers That Be to that end.

Fortunately, fans wouldn't have to wait long for the sorcerer's supreme resurrection. In August 2015, just three months after his show was canceled, it was announced that Matt Ryan would reprise the role of John Constantine in the fifth episode of *Arrow*'s fourth season. As it turned out, that episode's director, John Badham, had previously directed the fifth episode of *Constantine*. All the ingredients were in place to cast an amazing spell over the whole affair.

Indeed, the episode in question, "Haunted," was magical. A flashback revealed that Oliver Queen and John Constantine had initially met five years before the present-day storyline, thus establishing a pre-existing relationship. As such, Oliver turning to Constantine for mystical help wasn't a gimmick, since he was relying on a known ally with information pertinent to the plot.

The writers treated the team-up as though John's show was still going somewhere, with this episode simply serving as a crossover. It worked brilliantly and increased requests for the character's return. However, this once again seemed to be the final page in John Constantine's spell book. While everyone involved spoke highly of Ryan and his participation, he was heavily involved in a Broadway play, and that seemed to put an end to his time as the naughty necromancer.

Animated Necromancy

Rumors of Constantine's eternal exile to purgatory were greatly exaggerated. In the summer of 2016, DC announced a straight-to-video film version of *Justice League Dark* as part of its line of animated films. The comic of the same name features a branch of the Justice League whose members are characters who dabble in the occult, including one Mr. John Constantine.

Yes, Constantine was an actual member of the Justice League until quite recently. For anyone wondering how well he does in group situations, let's just say the results were mixed. The important thing is that John was a part of the animated film and Matt Ryan was reprising the role, albeit in voice only. The movie was well-received, and soon after its debut, The CW announced a Constantine-centric animated spinoff for CW Seed, its online hub. Once again, Ryan would provide the voice of John.

The animated adventure of John Constantine is more or less its own thing. It doesn't follow the continuity of the NBC series, doesn't provide a direct thread to John's subsequent appearances, and doesn't necessarily contradict anything that follows. In fact, it somewhat cleans the slate for his later appearances.

Constantine gets to be a little bit more himself in animated form. The solo outing, *Constantine: City of Demons*, was written by veteran comic book writer J. M. DeMatteis. While he has never directly written John Constantine before, DeMatteis has dipped his toe in DC Comics' supernatural world. The writer's script is itself an adaptation of the standalone graphic novel *Hellblazer: All His Engines*, by Mike Carey and Leonardo Manco, and is very faithful to the source material.

Legendary Spellbinder

John Constantine's next resurrection happened in a few stages, but they all seemed to occur in rapid succession. While *City of Demons* was in production, it was announced that Constantine would also appear in the flesh on The CW's *Legends of Tomorrow*, to help the time-traveling team with a mystical problem. Due to the positive response to that appearance, John was slated to appear again toward the end of the then-current season. Completing the trifecta, when season four of *Legends* was announced, Matt Ryan's Constantine was added to the cast as a series regular.

And so it was, nearly four years after his series was canceled, that Ryan was back starring as John Constantine in a regular capacity. This time, the actor and the writers would push the envelope with the character. Smoking is part of John's persona once more, even if there have been creative ways to avoid showing him actively doing so. His bisexuality is front and center, with a past male lover providing a crucial plot point to the season overall and a reason for John's willingness to join up with a team.

Constantine is adamant in his assertion that he doesn't play nice with others, and he even turns down the initial offer to join the team on their timeship, the *Waverider*. Once he's reminded that the demon Neron – who has taken his lover Desmond to Hell – is after him, however, John becomes very Constantine-ish. Instead of initially asking for help outright with Neron, John ostensibly joins the team in order to help them with *their* magical problem. He recognizes their abilities would be useful to him and, hey, cannon fodder is good as a shield while trying to work out a permanent solution. The trouble is, against his better judgement, Constantine has come to like the folks on the team, even if he dislikes their code names and outfits.

Sara Lance, the team leader, has herself died and been resurrected by mystical means. In fact, John was called upon in that episode of *Arrow* to save her soul after her revival. Their lives are intertwined in many ways at this point, and now that he has revealed the full story to her, Lance is onboard with vanquishing Neron. Mick Rory is never one to back down from an impossible-to-win fight, but everyone else is more or less innocent and unprepared to face the horrors and make the sacrifices that John Constantine usually needs to in order to save the day. Yet, they will stand by his side because it's the right thing to do.

This is ultimately why John Constantine prefers to be a solo artist, as opposed to guitar thrashing in a band. He isn't afraid to make the hard choices or sacrifice friends – he'd just rather not have to be in that position to begin with. Ultimately, though, John has learned the value of friendships, relying on others and being a team player. In particular, the punk rock, Devil-may-fear John Constantine has taken a particular shine to the hapless Gary Green. All of this is as if The Police had reunited, but with Sting realizing he could still also have a vibrant solo career.

Conjuring the Future

So, where does John Constantine go from here? As of this writing, *Legends of Tomorrow* was renewed for a fifth season, with Ryan remaining in the main cast as Constantine. John had initially joined the crew of the *Waverider* to combat and contain the magical menaces that formed that season-long storyline, but the writers were quick to find a reason for John to stick around after the finale, because his character was too great to lose. Additionally, the writers returned to the nightmare scenario of the child Astra Logue being taken to Hell, which had haunted John in his solo series. On *Legends*, Astra is now grown and seeking revenge on the man she thinks abandoned her to eternal torment. The show is returning for another season, and it is reasonable to assume John Constantine will remain a member of the crew. What fate awaits Astra will probably be revealed by the time you've read this, so the drama will be in how this affects John going forward.

A rumored solo TV series is once again a very real possibility. The audience response to the character's presence on *Legends* certainly garners enough support for him to spin off on his own. There would be delicious irony in a new *Constantine* series, especially if it were to succeed on The CW. However, the full tone of the stories that John is a part of would be better suited to DC's streaming service. Shows like *Titans* and *Doom Patrol* aren't censored for explicit content. A *Constantine* show that wasn't watered down and didn't have to pull any of its punches would be very welcome.

Speaking of streaming services, a new *Swamp Thing* television series premiered in May 2019. Considering that it was based on the comic book in which John Constantine got his start, there was naturally a huge fan expectation that the occultist would appear at some point. Ryan was asked about this possibility at a convention appearance and, while he didn't indicate any plans were afoot, he didn't rule out the possibility. Sadly, the question was rendered moot when *Swamp Thing* was prematurely canceled after only ten episodes.

Great hands of fire! Many feel Matt Ryan was born to play John Constantine.

For now, Matt Ryan continues to delight audiences on *Legends of Tomorrow*. But even if that were to end after the current season, I don't think it would take dark magic to bring back our favorite down-on-his-luck sorcerer. Ryan seems content to keep playing John Constantine, and both the audience and the writers seem happy to have him stick around. Whether it's as part of an ensemble or headlining his own show once again, I'm inclined to believe we'll keep seeing him involved in new adventures on our home screens for quite some time.

Dirty, Dirty Hands: Touring the Underbelly of America with Azzarello

by Robert Jeschonek

What's a comic book road trip without prison brutality, bestiality, serial killers, neo-Nazis, and an S&M sex club? Oh, and the incineration of the comic's title character?

In the case of John Constantine's tour of the United States at the hands of writer Brian Azzarello, documented in *Hellblazer* #146-174, all those hardcore highlights and more are on the map. Constantine, who pretty much *always* goes through the wringer, does so in *spades* in these harrowing adventures.

It's not exactly a *relaxing* vacation.

Hard-Traveling Antihero

Long before Azzarello – who made his bones as the acclaimed writer of the Vertigo crime epic *100 Bullets* – stepped into the frame, Constantine had taken another trip across the USA in a much different capacity. In the mid-1980s, he had served as sarcastic guide and provocateur extraordinaire in Alan Moore's "American Gothic" arc of *Swamp Thing*.[1] From toxic waste dumps in

---

[1] *Swamp Thing* #35-42, DC Comics, April to November 1985.

Pennsylvania to a zombie-haunted plantation in Louisiana, Constantine led Swamp Thing through the underbelly of America, forcing him to see the true horrors at its heart.

John Constantine learns that he's taken the phrase "man's best friend" to a new level.

When Azzarello gets hold of him 15 years later, however, Constantine ends up on a much darker and more personal journey. First, he serves time behind bars, experiencing some of the most vicious and dehumanizing behavior mankind has to offer. Next, he dives deep into an impoverished Appalachian community where pornography (of the human *and* bestial varieties) is a means of survival. After that, he embeds himself among stranded travelers at a snowbound saloon where the legend of an ice-wielding serial killer strikes fear in the hearts of sheep and wolves alike. Then, he infiltrates a brigade of neo-

Nazis just begging for a golem to show them the error of their racist ways. Finally, he explores the ways of the flesh at an extreme sadomasochism (S&M) club – in flashbacks recounting his erotic adventures and death by fire, engineered by his jilted gay lover.

Not exactly a light-hearted tour of fun roadside attractions, is it? More like topping – or *bottoming* – every other writer who'd thought they'd taken Constantine as low as he could possibly go. And that, at least in part, is the point. "I just want to get filthy with him. Let him get his hands dirty."[2] That is what Azzarello said at the time when discussing his plans for Constantine. Looking back at his run of stories, the words "Mission Accomplished" come to mind in giant flashing letters.

But there's more to it than that, in the end. Wallowing in filth is just one aspect of Azzarello's challenging run. Jailhouse horrors, puppy love gone wrong, white supremacist atrocities, and orgies with a flambé finish might shock and even disturb, but a bigger game's afoot than at first appears to be.

Which, actually, is much like Constantine himself.

This is America

Leave it to an Englishman to shine a light on America's dark side even as it threatens to consume him.

Taking a hard look at the United States' darkest sins is one of the most powerful elements of Azzarello's *Hellblazer* run. It parallels *Swamp Thing*'s "American Gothic" in this regard, with various monsters personifying particular facets of evil (and its victims). The monsters along Constantine's road have decidedly *human*, non-supernatural origins... though it's not always easy to pick who the *true* monsters are in these stories.

Some of the most memorable villains take center stage right from the start, during Constantine's spell in the slammer in the "Hard Time" arc. Mob boss Ray Stark, who pretty much runs the place and takes a liking to Constantine that borders on the carnal, is a violent thug who lives by the code of organized crime. He rules by brutality and intimidation, meting out harsh punishments to keep his enemies (and friends) in line – even murdering a guard and pinning the crime on Constantine to ensure his loyalty and keep him around.

---

[2] "Hellblazer: The Hard Time to Come." *Vertigo Subculture, Hellblazer* #149, DC Comics, June 2000.

Constantine's tenure in prison during Brian Azzarello's run finds him at the mercy of mob boss Ray Stark. Or is Stark at John's mercy?

By the end of "Hard Time," though, Ray and his fellow inmates aren't the only monsters in sight. The corrupt system that lets them treat each other like animals looms over everything – and Constantine is revealed as the greatest dark force of all. Using tricks, psychological warfare, and subtle magicks, he turns the prison into a true horror show that reflects his guilty conscience over the death of his friend, Richard "Lucky" Fermin, which had landed him in jail. "I *am* a bastard," he tells Lucky's ghost. "The *worst* you'd ever want to meet."[3]

The worst bastard is harder to find in the next arc, "Good Intentions," though there are plenty to go around. Lucky's brothers Richie and Dickie[4] are nasty enough, running a pornography ring in the aptly named Appalachian town of Doglick. They drug Constantine and film him in action with their too-affectionate canine, Cerberus (a.k.a. "Puppy Love"). Dickie's wife, John's ex-lover Rose, isn't such a sweetheart either, going along with their unsavory business without batting an eyelash. The whole town's in on it, everyone doing their part to survive the only way they've managed to since the closing of the mines – by degrading themselves sexually for the pleasure of strangers. Though a giant wild boar kills Puppy Love and Dickie, the townspeople have a darker agenda than the murderous beast... but it's hard to condemn them as evil since their actions are desperate acts of survival.

Are the monsters any more clearly set apart in the "Freezes Over" arc, in which a legendary killer stalks snowbound victims in an isolated saloon? Well... yes and no.

The gang of ruthless fugitives who take the occupants hostage are certainly monstrous and wreak their share of bloody havoc. The Iceman serial killer who helps thwart them is cruel and twisted, following in the footsteps of other bogeymen before him. But the truest monster, it seems, is not man or beast at all; it's the chain of violence that propagates itself from person to person and generation to generation. One savage act begets another, ad infinitum, in a microcosm of the cycle of violence that takes place across the United States. One bullet leads to another, and one serial killer gives birth to another. In the end, however good and decent some of the players might be, there are dead bodies everywhere.

In contrast, the "Highwater" arc is less ambiguous about its villainy. The squad of neo-Nazis, their hate-spewing leader Major Ellison Gage, and his disciple Marjorie Fermin (dead Lucky's wife) are all monsters through and through. So is the Major's racist daughter and the Nazis' backer, Stanley "S.W." Manor. In fact, "Highwater" isn't so much about who *is* a monster, but who *isn't*.

---

[3] "Hard Time, Part Four," *Hellblazer* #149, DC Comics, June 2000.
[4] All three Fermin brothers are named Richard, you see.

S.W. Manor expresses his true feelings for Constantine.

Finally, in "Ashes & Dust," S.W. Manor reigns supreme as the monster-in-chief of the entire Azzarello run. He's revealed as the engineer of Constantine's murder frame-up and prison stay, as well as his apparent execution in a wild S&M club. Manor, an orphaned psycho with more than a passing resemblance to Bruce "Batman" Wayne (who *lives* in a manor, after all), even threatens to feed a child to a flock of ravenous vampire bats.[5]

---

[5] Stanley Manor serves as an evil analogue to Bruce Wayne. The name "S.W." Manor references "stately Wayne Manor," a descriptor often mentioned on the 1960s *Batman* television series, while his butler Fredo is a stand-in for Alfred, and his lavish lifestyle masks a darker side and a secret desire for vengeance stemming from the murders of his parents. Manor even keeps vampire bats in his underground game room, which resembles Batman's own Batcave trophy collection. What's more, he has a ward named Tim (Tim Drake was one of several

By the end of Azzarello's run, we see a real cross-section of American evil in all its awful complexity – from jailhouse brutality to extreme pornography, from serial killers to violent racists to sexual deviance and the corruption of the super-rich. But as with so many stories set in Constantine's world, additional complexities lurk within that framework. As revealed in the two-part "Lapdogs and Englishmen," this parade of horrors was set in motion years earlier, when a young Constantine had pulled off a brash con at Manor's expense. Without that triggering incident, things would not have escalated the way that they do in the present-day storyline; the body count would be much lower or nonexistent. And that's all on Constantine for inciting the whole mess in the first place.

So in his way, Constantine himself can be viewed as the true monster of the Brian Azzarello run – the ultimate Big Bad – though his actions in cleaning up the aftermath of his crime are sometimes heroic in spite of himself.

Hellblazer, by John Constantine

What would a comic be like if John Constantine wrote it?

It's a safe bet it wouldn't be bland or shallow, unless intended that way as a goof. The subject matter would probably be challenging, to say the least. Everything about it would be seriously *in your face,* from the incidents depicted to the dialogue to the structure itself... because that's just how Constantine rolls, innit?

Azzarello seems to capture this very sensibility in writing his run of *Hellblazer*, and it makes for a unique reading experience. The stories are full of tricks and surprises, both narratively and structurally – and they rarely turn out the way you might expect, except that Constantine walks away in the end (until the events of "Ashes & Dust").

When Stark frames Constantine for murder in "Hard Time," it's shocking – as it is when John drives all the prisoners insane and sets himself up as "king" of the madhouse, with the electric chair as his throne. There's a bigger shock in "Good Intentions," when Constantine watches a video playback and realizes he made a "doggie-style" mistake while drugged by Lucky's brothers. The flashbacks to Constantine's wild performance at an S&M club in "Ashes & Dust"

---

youths to be called Robin) and arranges the death of a former employee named Jason (Jason Todd, another Robin, was killed by the Joker). Given Constantine's leering grin throughout Azzarello's *Hellblazer* run, plus the fact that Manor views John as his arch-nemesis, the mage thus becomes this evil Batman's metaphorical Joker.

are cumulatively just as shocking. So is the big revelation that he had a sexual affair with S.W. Manor.[6]

But perhaps the biggest surprise is how the overarching story comes together from start to finish. During the first half of the run, especially, the individual arcs feel somewhat haphazard, without much connective tissue to link them up. But little by little, as the bigger story unwinds, we begin to glimpse the author's grand plan.

The reason for Constantine's imprisonment, for example, is held back until the last chapter of "Hard Time." Until then, we're left to swim in the deep end, wondering exactly how John wound up in jail. Even then, however, we don't know all the crucial facts. It's not until part two of "Highwater" that Constantine reveals he could have stopped Lucky from killing himself but chose not to. Delayed as it is for so long, this revelation is more powerful than it would have been had it been provided at the start, putting all of Constantine's cards on the table.

Delayed revelations also keep us wondering about the villain behind Constantine's descent, S.W. Manor, and the motivations for his actions. Manor first appears as "Stanley" in "Lapdogs and Englishmen" in *Hellblazer* #162-163, more than halfway through the run. He steps back into the story in part three of "Highwater" (#166) and in "Chasing Demons" (#169), but we don't realize his true significance until the later stages of "Ashes & Dust." By then, hints have been dropped and threads woven through ten issues of *Hellblazer*, suggesting Manor's role in the greater narrative without spelling it out.

It's a risky approach, keeping us guessing for so long about the forces orchestrating Constantine's downfall. How long will the reader continue to care about John's plight if the driving forces behind it are unclear?

Azzarello makes it even *more* challenging to keep the rooting interest strong by essentially putting a *wall* between Constantine and the reader. The perspective of the narrator and primary point-of-view character moves *away from* Constantine for the first time in the series. Azzarello explained his technique like this:[7]

> When I wrote John in *Hellblazer*, I intentionally took a different approach than the previous writers on his book. John had been, up until my run, the

---

[6] Not due to John being bisexual, of course, which had been established by previous authors (though some readers might not have been aware of Constantine's orientation), but rather because his fling with Manor comes out of nowhere.

[7] "Back in Black," *DC Nation* #3, DC Comics, October 2018.

narrator of the stories. We were in John's head. And I thought, after over 150 issues – all this time – let's get out of his head and make him the wild card in his stories. Play him like the con man that he was. When he'd show up in *Swamp Thing,* when Alan Moore was writing it, you didn't know what to expect. I wanted to bring that into it.

It's a gutsy approach, effectively making Constantine more distant, while still expecting the reader to invest deeply in the outcome of his struggles. Would it have worked so well if the character hadn't already had a well of reader sympathy and interest from previous stories by other writers? It's hard to say, but the strategy certainly works well enough to keep us engaged throughout "Azzarello Gothic." The surprise of it alone might be enough to earn our admiration – and that of Constantine, too, if he existed beyond the printed page.

What would a comic be like if John Constantine wrote it? Much like Brian Azzarello's run, perhaps... though maybe not the part where Constantine isn't the narrator anymore. Honestly, can you imagine John himself willingly reducing that distinctive voice of his from front and center to background noise?[8]

Sub-Genre Smorgasbord

The originality of Azzarello's take on Constantine is undeniable. The surface narrative is shocking, the thematic elements are presented in surprising ways, and the structure of the stories is innovative. Truly, his Constantine is like no other. Even so, the author looks to the past in weaving his tapestry. He taps rich fiction traditions to create his tale – and lovingly pays homage to them throughout.

Most notably, as might be expected from the author of *100 Bullets*, he tours a range of crime fiction sub-genres. "Hard Time" is a jailhouse thriller, complete with a protagonist who's unjustly imprisoned and forced to rely on his wits (and magic) to survive. "Good Intentions" is hillbilly noir crossed with seedy sexploitation (and black humor that would be right at home in Garth Ennis' *Preacher*, another Vertigo series). "Freezes Over" is a classic snowbound crime story, *à la* Quentin Tarantino's film *The Hateful Eight*. "Lapdogs and Englishmen" is a high-energy caper tale, and "Highwater" is a hate group infiltration thriller. As for "Ashes & Dust," it's part S&M noir, part post-mortem

---

[8] Constantine gets his revenge when he serves as the narrator in *Batman: Damned*, the 2018-2019 DC Black Label miniseries, written by Azzarello.

procedural, as Constantine's federal handler, Agent Turro, investigates his charge's murder (and loses a hand for his trouble).

The overarching story linking all these arcs together is firmly rooted in the tropes and traditions of crime fiction and suffused with a strong noir component throughout. We have a very flawed hero at the mercy of dark forces, fighting for some semblance of justice in a cold, cruel world. Haunted by the ghosts of his past and a tragic love gone wrong, he tries to redeem himself but is doomed to disappointment in the end. Even then, the outcome of his journey remains uncertain, his future ambiguous, his very existence tenuous or terminated.

By the end of Azzarello's run, Constantine is more fully a noir protagonist. He has been one almost from the start of his life in comics, presented as an antihero of murky morals and motives who often comes up a loser even when he wins a small victory. He is rarely recognized by the world at large for the good he achieves; more often than not, he receives some kind of pain for his efforts.

Thanks to Azzarello, this noir image becomes more indelible than ever – with a hard-boiled overlay that makes *Hellblazer* more crime story than ghost story. The abundance of extreme violence, profanity, and sexuality grounds the stories in a dark and very down-to-Earth reality, one in which guns and fists are greater weapons than spells and curses, and monsters of the human variety spread evil across the land.

Though sometimes, all it takes is one mouthy son-of-a-bitch in a trenchcoat to put a stop to their fantasies of abuse and domination.

Opening the Trenchcoat

When all is said and done, Brian Azzarello and John Constantine are a match made in... *Hell*, actually. Azzarello's work was so successful that he and his version of Constantine were named Best Writer and Best Antihero by *Wizard* magazine in 2001. The individual arcs held up so well that *Paste* magazine, in 2013, named "Ashes & Dust" and "Hard Time" as two of the top ten *Hellblazer* stories.[9]

---

[9] Edgar, Sean. "The Top Ten *John Constantine: Hellblazer* Stories," *Paste*, 19 March 2013.

How could such difficult, disturbing material make such a positive, lasting impression on a mass readership? It's a legitimate question to ask, and the answer lies in the least sensational, most subtle facets of the work.

Viewed from start to finish, Azzarello's *Hellblazer* run stands out for its shocking subject matter, unflinching tour of American darkness, structural inventiveness, and tribute to crime fiction subgenres. Perhaps the most memorable and triumphant aspect of the work, however, is the way it reveals new insights into a long-lived and oft-observed character.

As *Hellblazer* readers, we know, going in, that Constantine can be cruel, not above sacrificing others for a greater good... but maybe we don't know how needlessly vicious he can be, willing to turn a prison into a true Hell on Earth or give Lucky Fermin back his gun when he knows his friend will use it to kill himself. We know, going in, that Constantine likes the gents as well as the ladies... but maybe we don't guess he'd become the lover of a man as warped and wicked as S.W. Manor.[10]

We know, going in, that Constantine has done some nasty things in his past... but maybe we don't suspect the full extent of the mayhem those prior bad acts might have unleashed, like the crimes committed by Manor after his condemnation by the Constantine-conjured ghosts of his parents. And we know, going in, that Constantine is a cold-blooded bastard with a heart of tarnished gold, but maybe we don't realize the true depths of his vulnerability – how he lives with secret burdens of pain and guilt and seeks atonement for his sins through self-sacrifice... how he struggles to heal and free those caught in his orbit, deserving and otherwise... and how much he secretly longs, just like the rest of us, for love and forgiveness, even as he sneers, lights a Silk Cut, and turns his trenchcoated back on them again and again.

---

[10] Check out James Wilkinson's essay, "'The Odd Boyfriend': John Constantine's Bisexuality in *Hellblazer* and Beyond," elsewhere in this volume, to learn about the history of John Constantine's bisexuality.

Silk Cut Smoke Breaks: Exploring the Themes of *Hellblazer* Fill-ins

by Draško Roganović

Throughout the course of its nearly three-decade tenure, *Hellblazer* was a comic book so reliant on capturing the voice of its appealing antihero that it was very much a writer's title, neatly divided into usually longer, self-sufficient runs. Such an approach made the rare fill-in issues stand out even more, but also set a much higher bar to clear for guest teams. For the sake of brevity and thematic unity, this text will focus solely on the issues of the main *Hellblazer* series that were written by guest writers, disregarding the occasional short story, issue, or arc by returning regular scribes, such as Jamie Delano, Garth Ennis, Brian Azzarello, and Mike Carey, as well as the various spinoff one-shots and miniseries.

The purpose of fill-in issues in ongoing comic titles is primarily to give the main creative team a small breather, but they also double as a testing ground for trying out new talents, or sometimes just as an opportunity to let acclaimed creators who wouldn't be able to commit to an ongoing gig, or a full arc, have a chance to work on a character. They can also serve as convenient jumping-on – or, at the very least, testing-out – points for new readers.

Still, it took precisely two years and 24 issues for Jamie Delano's seminal run on *Hellblazer* to resort to this trusty old staple of ongoing monthly comics, and the honor of playing substitute for Delano went to DC's golden boy, Grant Morrison, whose scripts were coupled with David Lloyd's moody chiaroscuro artwork. Morrison had by then already made a name for himself with his ongoing metatextual *Animal Man* run, as well as the incredibly popular Batman graphic novel *Arkham Asylum: A Serious House on Serious Earth*, and was well into his tenure on *Doom Patrol*.[1] Lloyd, on the other hand, was fresh off his work on the yet-to-be hit *V for Vendetta*,[2] and would, several years later, illustrate one of the best, if not *the* best, John Constantine stories outside of the regular title: the Delano-penned two-issue prestige miniseries *The Horrorist*.[3]

As can be glimpsed from the titles of *Hellblazer* #25-26 ("Early Warning" and "How I Learned to Love the Bomb," respectively), Morrison and Lloyd's two-parter dealt with the paranoia, fears, and tensions haunting the rural areas of the United Kingdom that host nuclear early-warning systems and various other military bases. The story follows Constantine's trip to the fictional northern village Thursdyke at the invitation of a psychic named Una, an old acquaintance of his from his stint as a patient at the Ravenscar Secure Facility for the Dangerously Deranged.

Una's ominous premonitions have been escalating in the days leading up to a big pagan festival, exacerbated by conflicts between anti-nuclear activists protesting the local army missile base and townsfolk defending the jobs that it brings. Things take a horrific and tragic turn once a scientist at the base seemingly tests experimental microwaves that bring unconscious desires and fears to the forefront of the crowds' minds. Morrison's staccato narration and Lloyd's heavily contrasted Dutch angles perfectly capture the grisly and horrific

---

[1] In fact, some three months later, Morrison would use *Doom Patrol* #31 to introduce Willoughby Kipling, his John Constantine analog – a character created solely because editorial decrees prohibited Constantine from interacting with superheroes. Morrison would eventually mock and eschew this rule simultaneously in *Doom Patrol* #53 by creating a superhero version of Constantine, this time actually called "The Hellblazer," in a dream-episode homage to Jack Kirby's Marvel cosmic comics. The Hellblazer would later return in the third *Books of Magic* annual.
[2] Written by John Constantine's creator himself, Alan Moore.
[3] He would later return to illustrate a single issue of Garth Ennis's run, "This Is the Diary of Danny Drake" in *Hellblazer* #56, as well as the short story "Christmas Cards" in *Hellblazer* #250, written by Delano.

atmosphere of "a town committing suicide,"[4] while also seamlessly blending in with the tone previously established by Delano.

Even though Delano had already broached the then-current subject of nuclear fears in the oneiric *Hellblazer* #13 ("On the Beach"), Morrison's story drew upon his own childhood experiences growing up with parents who were vehement anti-nuclear protesters, fearing nuclear missile bases in northern Britain, which he expanded upon decades later in his semi-autobiographical thesis on the need for superheroes, *Supergods: What Masked Vigilantes, Miraculous Mutants, and a Sun God from Smallville Can Teach Us About Being Human*:[5]

> Four miles across a placid stretch of water from where I live in Scotland is RNAD Coulport, home of the UK's Trident-missile-armed nuclear submarine force. Here, I've been told, enough firepower is stored in underground bunkers to annihilate the human population of our planet fifty times over. ... A couple of miles of winding road from here is where my dad was arrested during the anti-nuclear protest marches of the sixties. He was a working-class World War II veteran who'd swapped his bayonet for a Campaign for Nuclear Disarmament badge and became a pacifist "Spy for Peace" in the Committee of 100. Already the world of my childhood was one of proliferating Cold War acronyms and code names. And the Bomb, always the Bomb, a grim and looming, rain-coated lodger, liable to go off at any minute, killing everybody and everything.

It doesn't take a lot to connect this deeply embedded childhood fear to the Archbishop Bomb persona the local disenchanted pastor adopts once Thursdyke is consumed with the aforementioned frenzy. The townsfolk don giant papier-mâché heads symbolizing their unleashed ids[6] and start enacting their deeply suppressed macabre desires and impulses. Even John Constantine himself isn't immune to this collective mania: Una finds him with a giant head mask very much resembling the infamous Conservative Prime Minister

---

[4] Paraphrased from Una's dialogue in *Hellblazer* #26, page 13, first panel: "Do you believe a town can commit suicide, John? That's what's happening, John. Years of failure and neglect. It's destroying itself."

[5] From the Introduction to Grant Morrison's *Supergods: What Masked Vigilantes, Miraculous Mutants, and a Sun God from Smallville Can Teach Us About Being Human,* Spiegel & Grau, 2011.

[6] Freudian and Jungian themes were common in Morrison's work from this period, as seen in *Arkham Asylum: A Serious House on a Serious Earth*, while the small-town parable aspect of this story has its thematic follow-up in the 1994 original graphic novel, *The Mystery Play*.

Margaret Thatcher, leading a group of locals into the sea to drown, all the while chanting "Mummy knows best."

This scene illustrates John's well-established character traits: always having to be the one in charge, yet all too often merely leading innocents like lambs to slaughter. Una manages to snap him out of his trance, but his "flock" drowns while following the "Mummy" head mask after it is thrown into the sea. One might also argue that these personas – the scorned military man, the priest, the mother-who-knows-best – and the deaths that ensue merely take the idea of a depleted rural town which put its faith in weapons of mass destruction to its logical conclusion: in order to struggle on, these communities accepted warmongering as a way to survive the Thatcher-decimated Northern industry, but deep down they are aware of this deal with the Devil, thus developing a morbid, festering fixation with death.

Hellblazer had always been a series which wore its (or, rather, its writers') politics and worldviews firmly on its sleeve, and this story is no exception: after the catastrophic denouement in which the entire town is blown up when weapons in the base are detonated, John pops up to scorn the media that have already arrived on the scene, trying to spin the events as the work of a radical anti-nuclear group, while simultaneously relaying fake sympathy and support from the all-but-named Thatcher:[7] "Yeah, that's right, mate. Feed them all the old lies. You've got a posh accent, so it *must* be true."

Immediately following Morrison and Lloyd's two-parter was another fill-in issue, titled "Hold Me," this time by the acclaimed tandem of writer Neil Gaiman and artist Dave McKean. Gaiman would later single out *Hellblazer* #27 as "probably my favorite of all my short stories,"[8] and "one of the comics of which I am most proud,"[9] firmly cementing its status as the most sought-out single issue of the series. Gaiman's affinity for John Constantine is well recorded: his first-ever (unpublished) comic book script was a *Hellblazer* story

---

[7] Right around this time (late 1989 to early 1990), Morrison wrote a semi-autobiographical comic titled *St. Swithin's Day,* illustrated by Paul Grist and serialized in a *Trident Comics* anthology, about a teenager who seemingly plans to assassinate Thatcher. In the end, he simply points a finger-gun and says "Bang," thinking to himself as he is beaten by her bodyguards, "It was worth it, just to see her scared."

[8] From the foreword to "Hold Me" in *Neil Gaiman's Midnight Days.*

[9] Barnett, David. "The Creator of Constantine Reflects on His Epic *Hellblazer* Run, 30 Years Later." SyFy Wire, 24 January 2018: https://www.syfy.com/syfywire/the-creator-of-constantine-reflects-on-his-epic-hellblazer-run-30-years-later.

about the things that live in Constantine's fridge, titled "The Day My Pad Went Mad,"[10] and he featured Constantine in *The Sandman* #3, "Dream a Little Dream of Me," as well as making him one of the so-called Trenchcoat Brigade in his *Books of Magic* miniseries.

For this "a night in the life of John Constantine" tale, Gaiman brings John back to his familiar London haunting grounds for a low-key, bleak, and mundane horror story that deals with social issues such as LGBTQ marginalization, the HIV epidemic, and homelessness. McKean's wonderfully moody, scratchy artwork stands apart from his previously painterly work for DC on *Black Orchid, Arkham Asylum*, and, of course, *Hellblazer's* covers, and is a somewhat expressionistic take on the style he was using for his then-ongoing self-penned magnum opus *Cages*.

After a memorial party held in honor of John's gay friend Ray Monde, a year after his brutal and untimely death at the start of Delano's run in *Hellblazer* #7, Constantine meets a young woman by the name of Anthea, who manages a homeless shelter. She inquires if John has been tested for AIDS, then asks him to walk her home in a mostly abandoned block of council flats, where she offers him a drink and tries to seduce him. Meanwhile, a dead homeless man named Jocko, who is haunting the very same block of flats, pulls a young girl's unwilling mother into a hug, killing her with his freezing embrace. Sensing something's off with Anthea's advances, John remembers Ray talking about a lesbian couple named Anthea and Sarah. After he confronts her with that information, she admits she was merely trying to use him as an unknowing surrogate for the child she and her partner are trying to conceive. Angered by this revelation, Constantine leaves,[11] and on his way out, he encounters the little girl whose mother had been killed by Jocko.

Leaving the child in Anthea's care, Constantine breaks into the apartment to confront what the girl describes as "the smelly man." Jocko begs John to hold him, and – unlike the little girl's mother – Constantine willingly accepts. Having received this bare minimum of human warmth and comfort, the spirit passes on and vanishes, while the freezing mage is left to dwell on this tragic encounter:

---

[10] See "The Hell They Weren't: *Hellblazer's* Lost Lore," by Rich Handley, elsewhere in this anthology.

[11] John would later show that he has no qualms about inserting himself into lesbian relationships, in the infamous "Blimey. I'm shagging a lesbian. Do I win a prize?" scene from Garth Ennis's *Hellblazer* #131.

All he wanted. All he wanted was for someone to care about him. Someone to hold him. Someone to warm him. Nobody would. When we hold each other, in the darkness, it doesn't make the darkness go away. The bad things are still out there. The nightmares are still walking. When we hold each other, we feel — not safe, but better. 'It's all right,' we whisper. 'I'm here. I love you.' And we lie, 'I'll never leave you.' For just a moment or two the darkness doesn't seem so bad when we hold each other.

The comic ends with heartbroken John returning to Anthea, asking her to hold *him*.

Neil Gaiman's wonderfully written "Hold Me" shows off John's empathetic side.

As mentioned, Gaiman was a big fan of John Constantine as portrayed in both Delano's *Hellblazer* and Moore's *Swamp Thing* runs, so this story incorporates the then-established continuity of the two series by touching upon Ray Monde's death, and also by explaining John's aversion to being used as a "walking sperm bank" with the fact that he'd already been through something similar with Alec and Abby Holland in the pages of *Swamp Thing*.[12] This subplot deals with the hardships of the queer population that would become a staple of Gaiman's other work, especially his comic book magnum opus *The Sandman*. Of course, Gaiman had by then already started developing a work of fantasy fiction that would later become the BBC television series *Neverwhere,* in which he also tackled the problem of London's homeless and abandoned multitudes.

In a way, Anthea and Sarah can be viewed as a precursor to Hazel and Foxglove, the lesbian couple from *The Sandman: A Game of You* and *Death: The Time of Your Life,* whose character arcs culminated with the two having to bargain with Death for the life of their child. Staying true to this worldview in "Hold Me," Gaiman raises awareness of the problems plaguing disenfranchised groups like the homeless and members of the LGBTQ minorities, and presents us with a more tender and humane aspect of John's personality, while still not straying too far from the established characterization.

The next fill-in issue, *Hellblazer* #32 ("New Tricks"), written by Dick Foreman – *Black Orchid*'s ongoing scribe and a collaborator on Alan Moore's *Dodgem Logic* magazine[13] – with fittingly grisly and grotesque art by Steve Pugh, also slightly tackles the issue of homelessness. While investigating a series of shady disappearances of transients at a night shelter, John stumbles upon the soul of a retired policeman, Inspector W.S. Drummond, stuck inside the body of a monstrous bulldog[14] that now terrorizes London's East End.

Drummond's henchman, a "soft in the head" young man named Dougie, lures unsuspecting victims to a local junkyard, where Drummond the bulldog and his newly formed pack of people-eating hounds feast on them. Following the trail that leads to the junkyard, John finds Drummond's autobiography, penned by the borderline-illiterate Dougie, which reveals that the aging inspector had felt he'd received the short end of the stick, both in his career and in his life. Obsessed with being a "winner," he'd resorted to practicing magic, killing himself in a ritual that allowed his soul a brief period to find a new host.

---

[12] Swamp Thing possessed John's body to impregnate his human wife, Abigail Cable-Holland, in an inter-title crossover published in *Hellblazer* #9-10 and *Swamp Thing* #76-77.

[13] Even though the cover mistakenly co-credits Delano, this issue is written solely by Foreman – or "Forman," as his name is erroneously spelled.

[14] For a more uplifting take on the spectral hound trope, check out *Hellblazer* #98 ("Walking the Dog"), by Jenkins and Phillips.

Unfortunately, both grown men's and infants' bodies were protected from such incursions, and he'd ended up inhabiting the body of a dog. Soon enough, Drummond had mastered the dog-eat-dog politics of the canine world and had set his sights on overturning the human race from its pedestal, then replacing mankind with his own "dog empire." Forced into a deadly game of fetch, John outwits Drummond using the inspector's newly acquired canine instincts and heightened senses against him, and brutally demonstrates one of the main advantages of having opposable thumbs by delivering a lead pipe to Drummond's skull.

Foreman here tries to tap into the everyday urban horrors of roaming packs of dogs, though with a greater emphasis on humor punctuated by the visceral blood-and-guts visuals by Pugh. The almost obligatory social critique in this story is reserved for the people at the bottom rungs of society as the most vulnerable and easy fodder for all sorts of evils, with just the slightest hints of police brutality. Also, spirits unable to move on to the afterlife have been a staple of *Hellblazer,* from John's growing gallery of dead friends that haunt him, to Richie Simpson's digitized consciousness,[15] to Ennis's elderly spectral pub-owners,[16] to Richard "Lucky" Fermin in Azzarello's "Hard Time,"[17] all the way to the spectral audience at Constantine's wedding in *Hellblazer* #275.

Whereas Foreman went for the obvious and grisly carnage and horror, the next fill-in issue deals with nightmares that are merely implied. Penned by John Smith – a prolific *2000 AD* comic book writer who also wrote Vertigo's *Scarab* miniseries, illustrated by frequent guest artist and future regular artist Sean Phillips – *Hellblazer* #51 ("Counting to Ten") taps into John's rising paranoia during that most mundane of chores: a visit to the laundromat. After the exorcism of former schoolmate Jerry Monaghan quite literally goes to shit, John takes Jerry's soiled clothes for a wash. While he waits, he notices strange and unnerving omens all around him: a trio of old ladies waiting for their late friend who killed herself; a woman solving a newspaper puzzle filled with words such as "abattoir," "sodomite," "molest," "offal," "Satan," and "anal"; a child's drawing of a fatal car-crash titled "A Family Holiday"; and a suckling infant biting its mother's breast and drawing blood.

---

[15] *Hellblazer* #12 ("The Devil You Know...").
[16] *Hellblazer* #47-48 ("The Pub Where I Was Born"/"Love Kills").
[17] *Hellblazer* #146-150 ("Hard Time").

After receiving an unexpected and mysterious telephone call on the laundromat's payphone – possibly from Jerry himself – which poetically describes horrible and unsettling scenes and asks John what he's running away from, Constantine finally comes clean with himself. The reader finds out that Jerry was actually a pain junkie (or, rather, an exorcism addict) who, unbeknownst to John, had summoned "sixty or seventy" demons unto himself. After exorcising the first demon and learning about the others, Constantine, in his true bastard fashion, had left Jerry to deal with them himself, and instead had taken this little jaunt to the cleaners.

It's all about the coat.

Constantine is now haunted by guilt and unease, desperately trying to convince himself that his friend will be okay, while the bad juju from the unfinished exorcism is possibly seeping into the neighborhood. As John and the old ladies count down to the titular ten o'clock – the expected time for the undead granny's arrival – John loses his cool and runs out of the laundry place, shirking responsibility and refusing to deal with this unexpected supernatural problem so soon after his latest debacle. The elderly zombie is greeted by her friends, who plan to fix her up and then pay a visit to her negligent son, whom they blame for her death. The story ends with John unceremoniously vomiting in a dark passageway near the laundromat.

In the atypically low-key "Counting to Ten," Smith presents the banal and unglamorous aftermath that comes after the magic and the mayhem of Constantine's regular monthly adventures, as well as the rising emotional toll of his calling. However, leaning into his antihero status, John refuses to participate in yet another unwanted supernatural adventure. When your own friends and flat are a source of guilt and fear, and your life is so intertwined with the supernatural, there is no refuge even in the everyday and the ordinary. The story is perhaps evocative of *The Sandman* #6 ("24 Hours"), in which the villain, Doctor Destiny, uses a magical stone to turn an ordinary diner into a living nightmare for its unlucky patrons. Smith, however, leaves the situation unresolved, letting John give in to his basic survival instincts. The issue is serviceably gritty as illustrated by Phillips, who had yet to hit his stride by this point, though his painted cover shows promise of things to come.[18]

This story is also notable because it was the first to confirm John Constantine's bisexual history,[19] and is one of the rare instances in which a fill-in issue has changed the character's nature (albeit, significantly later), especially with such a throwaway line: "Girlfriends, the odd boyfriend... they all have a nasty habit of walking out on me." This was later picked up by Azzarello during his tenure on the title, as part of his larger arc with S.W. Manor. Constantine is now canonically and prominently depicted as bisexual, both in his various post-*Hellblazer* comic book series, as well as in his TV appearances in *Constantine*

---

[18] It is perhaps worth noting that most of the artists paired with the early fill-in scribes – Lloyd, McKean, Phillips – all got to paint the covers to their stories, instead of the regular cover artists.

[19] John's bisexuality had been slyly alluded to in prior issues. Check out James Wilkinson's essay, "'The Odd Boyfriend': John Constantine's Bisexuality in *Hellblazer* and Beyond," elsewhere in this volume, to learn more.

(implied) and *Legends of Tomorrow* (prominently depicted, with a male love interest who was a big part of a season-long character arc in season four).[20]

The next stretch of issues that qualify as fill-ins are *Hellblazer* #85-88 ("Warped Notions"), by Eddie Campbell, with significantly improved and much more self-assured artwork by new regular artist Sean Phillips. This four-part story is a bit of an outlier in this analysis, considering it was supposed to be the beginning of Campbell's run as the regular series writer. As such, the story seems a bit rushed and was perhaps supposed to set up supporting characters and plots who would've returned for many more issues to come.

The storyline follows Constantine as he teams up with the specter of Hellfire Club founder Sir Francis Dashwood, demonic cat Murnarr, ancient Roman fertility goddess Bona Dea,[21] the ghost of Ben Franklin, and other ethereal entities in order to stop the so-called "Everything Virus," a catastrophic threat to reality that is causing urban legends to come true. Notably, in the second half of his arc, Campbell moves the plot to his own stomping grounds, Australia, where he lived for three decades until 2018. There, he plays with native Aboriginal mythology, introducing the mythical Rainbow Serpent and the Aboriginal "witch doctor" Jeffo.[22] Campbell's story can be viewed as an extension of his interests of depicting ancient gods who exist in our contemporary world, which is the central motif of his seminal comics saga *Bacchus*.

It took five years for *Hellblazer* to publish another fill-in story, this time as a byproduct of Warren Ellis's sudden departure from the series after DC executive Paul Levitz decided to pull the controversial school-shooting issue "Shoot" in the wake of the Columbine massacre.[23] The two-part story "Ashes and Honey," appeared in *Hellblazer* #144-145. Written by Croatian[24] comic book author

---

[20] Both shows star Matt Ryan as John Constantine and essentially take place in the same continuity.

[21] The pseudonym for this ancient deity, meaning "The Good Goddess."

[22] Paul Jenkins, who stepped in after Campbell ended his run after only a single arc, chose to keep Constantine in Australia a bit longer, and to explore these characters and the local mythology of the Dreamtime, before returning John to the United Kingdom and setting up his own recurring cast and arcs.

[23] The issue was already drawn and inked, and subsequently leaked online, giving it a cult "bootleg" status among *Hellblazer* fans. A decade later, it was finally published in the *Vertigo Resurrected* edition of reprints and specials.

[24] Since *Hellblazer* was, due to its protagonist's nationality, always considered a U.K. title, written by Brits, Scots, and Irishmen, it's amusing to note that DC's editorial

Darko Macan[25] and illustrated by Gary Erskine, this tale – as Macan revealed when responding to inquiries for this essay – was originally pitched to then-Vertigo editor Axel Alonso as a 40-page one-shot, but was subsequently restructured as a two-issue arc after Ellis quit the title, since new writer Brian Azzarello wasn't ready to immediately take over the reins.

Macan tied his story in with the then recently concluded wars in former Yugoslavia, which he lived through, showing a family of Bosnian Muslim refugees in London who have brought their customs and ancestral magic to their new homeland. The ethnic wars that plagued the Balkans during the 1990s following the dissolution of Yugoslavia were also a common theme or subtext in Macan's other American comics from that period as well, such as *Star Wars: Jedi vs. Sith*, *Grendel Tales: Devils and Deaths*, and the short-lived Cable comic *Soldier X*.

Ashes and Honey starts off with John dropping by the funeral of a dead Bosnian mage by the name of Kemal, where he and the old man's grandson, Samir, reminisce about the recent events that led them there. Kemal could manipulate living creatures, such as his bees, and drew his powers from his native soil containing the ashes and remains of his ancestors. He's been making a special honey, which takes those who taste it to the time and place where they were happiest. However, Samir had used Kemal's old boots, filled with earth from "the Old Country," to resurrect a dead dog belonging to another child, for a fee. Eventually, the parents had discovered something amiss and had finally noticed tire tracks on the freshly zombified dog. As John puts it, "Same parents get suddenly upset and do their best to find the planetary authority on weird shit. Meaning, of course, me."

While Constantine tries to break through a bunch of teenage guards, Kemal discovers his magical boots are missing and reaches Samir as he attempts to use them to resurrect a rich kid's dead sister. The boy has been practicing magic and renting out his services in order to make money to go back to his homeland

---

staff let a non-native English speaker write John Constantine before they hired an American – Brian Azzarello – to take a turn.

[25] Macan's contribution to the Constantine mythos also includes the creation of Charles Constantine, the twin brother of John's paternal grandfather William, in the miniseries *The Sandman Presents: Corinthian – Death in Venice*. As one of the rare cases in which a Constantine twin doesn't kill his or her sibling in the womb, Charles is shown as weak-willed and lacking the Constantine killer instinct, until his fateful encounter with the Corinthian.

so he can resurrect his father, who'd had his head blown off during the war while trying to save Samir. To relieve his young grandson of his promise to resurrect the girl, the old man sacrifices his own life for hers, while Constantine helplessly watches.

Back at the funeral, Samir's mother Azra and pregnant sister Zana[26] arrive and start squabbling, while he spills the soil from the boots and tells John the story of the time his grandfather learned the cost of using magic for personal gain. John utilizes the boots to learn the horrific story of how Azra had bitten off her own finger while scrambling to feed her family during the war, then cooked it to make a broth for her children after losing to soldiers the potato she'd been planning to use.

While Samir scatters his grandfather's ashes, thereby making British earth the soil of his ancestors, John chooses not to employ the magical honeycomb he was gifted to relive his happiest memories, and instead uses it to get Zana's baby daddy to return to her. In the end, John muses about the refugee experience:

> We are so used to our creature comforts, our running water, our Silk Cuts... But what if, suddenly, we get transplanted elsewhere, strangers in a strange world? Only the strong survive, only those ready to conquer the new world. Grave by grave, baby by baby, word by word.

With that, he shows that he has learned a new multi-purpose swear-word: "Jeb'o."[27] As Zana puts it: "It means 'fuck it', but also other things. We say it when we are happy, surprised or down, when we fight the world and we lose. Or when we win. It helps when we don't know what to say, too."

It would take a hundred issues for the next fill-in slot to appear, featuring two newcomers with a lot of buzz: writer Jason Aaron, hot off his breakout Vietnam war miniseries *The Other Side* and the ongoing Vertigo crime series *Scalped,* and artist Sean Murphy, who would go on to illustrate Morrison's *Joe the Barbarian*, as well as his self-penned *Punk Rock Jesus* limited series.[28] The two-parter in *Hellblazer* #245-246 ("Newcastle Calling") is a short and grisly tale of a punk-rock documentary show crew trying to piece together the infamous

---

[26] Named after two popular Yugoslavian bands from the 1980s.
[27] Macan had put several lines of dialogue, incantations and, most importantly, swears in Serbo-Croatian / Bosnian as Easter eggs for any Balkan readers.
[28] Also worth noting is his stellar work on the *Hellblazer: City of Demons* miniseries with Si Spencer, which was originally intended to be a fill-in arc in the main series.

events that occurred at Newcastle's Casanova Club[29] and the ties they had to Constantine's band, Mucuous Membrane. The crewmembers all suffer horrible fates and, in a somewhat controversial retcon, it is revealed that John Constantine wasn't able to banish the terror elemental "Norfulthing" summoned by Astra Logue, and had merely spent the past three decades sacrificing one person a year to the creature in order to contain it.

Newcastle is also home to Sting, the real-life rock star on whom John's look was originally based.

After John contains the Norfulthing once again, he writes out a warning in blood – "BEWARE BIG FUCKING DOG!" – while singing out the lyrics from his band's single, "Venus of the Hardsell." Sadly, these references to Delano-era lore just act as reminders of much better and more thoughtful stories. Aaron was happy to dive into the familiar mythology of the series, re-examining and giving his own spin on one of the key moments in the character's life, but although appropriately bloody, nihilistic, and unsettling – and quite well-drawn – his edgy take seems more fitting to his work on *Punisher MAX*, the aforementioned *Scalped*, or his bleak biblical series *The Goddamned*, and

---

[29] As detailed in *Hellblazer* #11.

doesn't quite meld with the character other writers have spent several decades fleshing out.

Even if we disregard the geeky inter-continuity issues this annual deal with a demon raises – such as who would feed the Norfulthing during John's long and self-imposed stay in prison, or during his even longer pilgrimage across the United States, or what his plan for it would be after his own often likely demise – it is hard to reconcile this retconned borderline sociopathic Constantine with, say, the conflicted and broken man from Delano's "Family Man" arc, who is quite literally sickened when he finally kills the titular serial killer, and even that is presented as a mercy-killing, with the murderer personally begging him to do it. Meanwhile, "Newcastle Calling" pretty much turns Constantine himself into a serial killer; thus, by staying true to his own brand and worldview, Aaron failed to stay true to the character.[30]

The last fill-ins were a part of the all-star 250th-issue celebration, labelled as the "Hellblazer Holiday Special," which featured short stories from Azzarello and Delano, as well as then-upcoming regular writer Peter Milligan, with special guest-spots by Dave Gibbons and famed fantasist China Miéville. Art was provided by returning fan-favorite artists David Lloyd, Giuseppe Camuncoli, and Sean Phillips, while the guest artists were Rafael Grampà and – in a neat role-reversal – previous guest scribe Eddie Campbell.

Gibbons, with refreshingly familiar visuals by Sean Phillips, starts off the special with "Happy New Fucking Year," a sequel to his previous short Hellblazer story "Another Bloody Christmas" from issue #3 of Vertigo's short-lived Winter's Edge annual anthology series. The story is a playful take on the imagery of Baby New Year taking over from Father Time, wherein Constantine stops an Egyptologist obsessed with eternal life from sacrificing an infant to Osiris with "a good old-fashioned kick in the balls." It's a fine, fun, albeit forgettable little romp that fulfils the Christmas spirit of the annual, and it's practically analysis-proof.

Miéville, on the other hand, in his short tale "Snow Had Fallen," finds a surprisingly fresh angle for the long-running series. The story features Constantine investigating an alleged industrial accident in order to pay off a debt to a friend: a multinational plant with occult ties has blown up, filling the surrounding air with ash, and the children in the local slums, influenced by the

---

[30] For more on this point, see "A Nasty Piece of Work? The Mercurial Morality of John Constantine," by James Wilkinson, elsewhere in this volume.

Christmas picture-books donated to the local church, have mistaken the ash for snow, played around in it, and fallen ill. Worse, they have also been visited by "ash devils... without faces... with wings..."

Constantine's inquiries into the magical event flip the script – the explosion wasn't some sort of malicious magic by the evil corporations, designed to kill off the poor locals, but rather an accident, while the entities were newborn "snow" angels created by the children in the ashes, a manifestation of the spilled goodness the corporation was burning in order to create evil itself. As John says, "Magic goodness. Decency as an industrial byproduct." Constantine helps the children embrace their creations and send them to punish and eliminate the malicious mage who runs the factory. The story ends with John instructing them to keep up the good work:

> A company like that's got more than one wanker in a suit, you know that. But then... this lot were *marinated* in holy slag, and that's not just going to wash off. Who knows what they might do.
>
> Happy Christmas, angel-makers! You lot should go on *tour.* Think of all the powdery potential! Bad things happen in sugar mills and salt mines, cocaine plants and sand dunes and dust, and yeah, even in the *snow.*
>
> Lie down and wave your arms and legs wherever *injustice strikes,* eh? Call up a bit of *help.* I'll see you there.
>
> Fuck what you heard.
>
> I'm on the side of the angels.

In just eight pages, Miéville – a self-declared Marxist and socialist – manages to weave a socially aware story of the poor striking back at their capitalist exploiters that still has all the obligatory magic and mayhem of *Hellblazer*, but propels the character away from his selfish, self-serving persona as a more proactive force for good, without relinquishing or betraying his trademark edge.[31]

Hellblazer ran for a quarter of a century, and for the select club of fill-in writers who had the chance to contribute to it, writing John Constantine was almost a badge of honor, since a lot of them were fans of the character from way back in Moore's incredibly influential *Swamp Thing* run. Often, as in the stories by Foreman and Smith, they dealt with the horror of the mundane, most likely because fill-in issues traditionally mustn't interfere with the main series' planned longer plots and characters, or leave lasting repercussions in the world

---

[31] And in a much more believable way than the ending of the *Constantine* movie from 2005.

the character inhabits. With that in mind, slice-of-life snippets that find horror in laundromats and mean junkyard dogs fit the bill. Meanwhile, Gibbons was content to carve out his own little niche of tongue-in-cheek holiday-themed escapades.

Most of the time, though, the guest writers would try to punt the ball to their own side of the field, so to speak, and explore topics that aligned with personal interests that permeate their other works. Morrison leaned into fears of nuclear war and critiques of Margaret Thatcher; Gaiman explored the humanity of marginalized groups; Macan dealt with the Balkan wars of the 1990s, and Campbell explored myths and gods come to life in the modern world. Gaiman, Macan, and Miéville tried to bring out a more humane Constantine, while Aaron reverted the character to the incarnation he was most familiar with, or at least most fond of: the mysterious and conniving "I'm a nasty piece of work, chief" cutthroat character from his *Swamp Thing* beginnings.[32]

Still, sifting through the (often titular) ashes of these stories, there are gems to be found, containing some new or rarely seen facets of John Constantine's character that, even viewed separately and apart from the main runs, continue to shine brightly to this day.

---

[32] The same could be said about Brian Azzarello's tenure on the title, though the longer narrative provided opportunities for the occasional glimpse of humanity, such as the downtime drinking story in *Hellblazer* #169 ("Chasing Demons").

A Man You Don't Meet Every Day: Constantine's London

by Adrian Brown

The city of London is one of *Hellblazer*'s key supporting characters – always likely to play a part, though perhaps each writer brings a different version of the city to the story. The other places where John Constantine goes – Glastonbury, Newcastle, New York, Northampton, Thursdyke, his exotic global trips along "the synchronicity highway," even Liverpool, where he was born – may have plot points, but they usually contribute to the story geographically, both for artists and for writers. Constantine's chosen home of London, however, is a vital part of the series.

As Neil Gaiman has said, from its early days, *Hellblazer* broke the norm for British cities in U.S. comics to be "portrayed as an enormous English village."[1] Sometimes, it is slightly skewed with pseudonymous pubs and streets, but from Jamie Delano's introduction and Garth Ennis's London Irish vs. East End Mob, via the South London community of Paul Jenkins' run and the Inner London mythology of Warren Ellis, on through Mike Carey's A to Z, several episodes were based in real-world London. Andy Diggle's run built on these and, almost

---

[1] Barnett, David. "The Creator of Constantine Reflects on His Epic *Hellblazer* Run, 30 Years Later." SyFy Wire, 24 January 2018: https://www.syfy.com/syfywire/the-creator-of-constantine-reflects-on-his-epic-hellblazer-run-30-years-later.

at the end of *Hellblazer*, Peter Milligan took us to Suicide Bridge, a very real site in a North London borough. Even Denise Mina and Brian Azzarello told their London stories for *Hellblazer*.

London has always been a character in the tales of John Constantine.

Much of the Inner London area has changed in the past three decades, and some of this is addressed in the monthly comic. Here, I will try to draw a mental map of the streets where these writers took John Constantine.

> Let me take you by the hand and lead you through the streets of London
> — Ralph McTell, "Streets of London" (1974)

The debut issue opens in New York, but our first glimpse of Constantine is in London – red buses, black taxis, red phone box, all those simple signs that say "Olde London Towne." Constantine is home from his adventures in *Swamp Thing* #37, to which his internal monologue alludes: "The thin Sunday afternoon drizzle greases the tired streets. Ignoring the queasiness which quakes my stomach like an uneasy swamp... I turn up my collar against the gnawing of the early November wind... and merge into the welcome anonymity of the city. The streets are hardened arteries leading to the city's dead heart." And as his landlady asks where he's been, he replies, "It's good to get home, ennit?"

In his bath, Constantine finds an old friend from his punk days, Gary Lester, who is covered with insects and unaware of whether he's infested or hallucinating. The local community begins to be shown when John goes to the local shop to call Chas Chandler. That's how you sometimes had to do it in the days before mobile phones. Two racist skinheads abuse the shopkeeper. John calls them "pondlife," then buys 200 Silk Cut – maybe the synchronicity highway (the series of coincidences by which Constantine is said to travel) does not have duty-free? That first adventure spans London, Morocco, and New York. The two urban locations could be interchangeable, but artist John Ridgway captures the differences between high-rise modern and old-world clutter.

Constantine's love/hate relationship with London is at *Hellblazer*'s core.

Journalist Satchmo Hawkins, via Jamie Delano, attempts an interview at the end of this first story arc (in *Hellblazer* #4), which helps to introduce how Constantine fits into local folklore. They meet in a pub called The Butcher's Hook.[2] "Tremendous atmosphere: working class street cred" and "[The interior] is reminiscent, in atmosphere and colour, to the lungs of a forty-a-day man. The walls practically drip nicotine." That not only describes Constantine himself, but also any British pub of the day... before the smoking ban (which we will come back to later).

> Do you think you've made the right decision this time?
> — Morrissey, The Smiths, "London" (1987)

Many *Hellblazer* stories are very much rooted in Britain's current affairs and historical events. That manifesto is announced with "Going for It" (*Hellblazer* #3), set in the yuppie era – the "me first" politics of Margaret Thatcher's 1987

---

[2] This is cockney rhyming slang for "look," but it could also be taken literally.

election night. It's a contemporary political piece and resonates today, as the self-interests of Constantine's adversaries are at the fore again 30 years later. Delano gives a fairly downbeat noirish perspective of Inner London, but this story is mostly a political statement of intent – a character piece about Constantine and his author. This seems to be Camden, where Ray Monde's junk shop Serendipity is located. Camden is a locale visited several times throughout *Hellblazer* (a low-rise block of council flats called Ravenscar is located nearby, but has never been featured in the series[3]).

Ray sends John to Spitalfields, a very significant place for London's darker history, which is portrayed in the Inner London spectrum of greys, and Constantine is surprised to find yuppies living there. Nowadays, he'd expect them – the unthinking glass towers of wealth have rubbed up against the East End on the borders of The City, and many of the decaying buildings have been refurbished, replaced, or removed. Recently, I heard how the first Victorian charitable housing estates were founded here. It's always been at the interface of rich and poor, and John wonders, "What kind of rich wacko comes to a place like this to gloat...?" Also, beneath these streets lie the remains of thousands of Londoners, buried together due to mass deaths at times of plague and starvation – Peter Milligan will later refer to this toward the end of the original *Hellblazer*.[4]

Constantine returns to London from Bristol midway through the "Fear Machine" storyline (in *Hellblazer* #18) and there is a definite visual shift back to dour and dismal scenery. Artist Richard Piers Rayner shows a pastoral side to the previous rural, seaside, and smaller city, even as the threat gathers momentum. But with John surviving a train crash at this point, the scene shifts from green fields to blue-grey rain.

Constantine stays at the Hotel Oscar Wilde, in Islington, with guests "who have wives and reputations," and he visits a seedy Soho club, thinking, "Sometimes only the worst place will do." We're not here for the underbelly, however, but the good people who might come into it. The Soho community is often seen as dodgy, so we get to see a different side of it for a change. The

---

[3] Which is surprising, given Constantine's multiple stays at the Ravenscar Secure Facility for the Dangerously Deranged.

[4] McRobbieax, Linda Rodriguez. "The Dead Beneath London's Streets." Smithsonian.com, 25 September 2018: https://www.smithsonianmag.com/history/dead-beneath-londons-streets-180970385/.

hotel is run by a gay couple and doubles as a haven from the homophobic prejudices of the day, but people are still taking risks by being there. There is no judgement in this portrayal. Throughout the series, John has stayed in his share of hotels for the less well-off and vulnerable instead of using blackmail or magic to acquire more luxurious accommodations.

When Constantine, the policeman, and the journalist he saved from a hoax suicide hanging assemble to move against the threat, they go to The Hangman's Noose. As if often the case, the names of pubs and hotels in *Hellblazer* are subtle footnotes to the story (especially during Mike Carey's tenure).

As the Fear Machine is exposed, it's clear Constantine and friends are not concerned with an underbelly, but with the corruption above. As Constantine explores, he is led through Whitehall's corridors and ends up at Buckingham Palace. Follow the chain of command... any study of corruption in British politics will focus, by necessity, on this small area of London. Three palaces form a triangle around it: Westminster, Buckingham, and The Regent Palace Hotel, on the edge of Soho. The latter had fallen from its grander origins to a West End tourist's package, and has since closed and been converted to modern glass brutalism, in much the same way as the slums around Spitalfields.

In 1989's *Hellblazer Annual* #1, Constantine's narration tells us: "Crawling back into this ancient despotic threshing machine. This tormentor of the imagination, totem of oppressive civilization. Only a lunatic would escape one prison of the mind and then spurn liberty to burrow again in this contorted maze. This sweaty dungeon of the soul. London." This comes as a footnote to "Fear Machine," once more anchoring Constantine to the city after he leaves Ravenscar. John is dropped off by a former acquaintance from the punk scene, who is now a Porsche-driving yuppie.

> Good morning, Sodom and Gomorrah
> — Jack Rosenthal, *The Chain*[5]

Garth Ennis opens *Hellblazer* #41 with a focus on Constantine, who is dead on arrival, having been diagnosed with terminal lung cancer. John steps out to Ireland, and he'll return to London with a new set of friends... but first, we find more contacts in that triangle of palaces, the likely location of the Cambridge

---

[5] *The Chain*, a film written by Jack Rosenthal, addresses the housing "chain" in London and identifies the Seven Deadly Sins as personified by London Boroughs.

Club (in reality, the Oxford and Cambridge Club), and "The Snob" (a.k.a. the archangel Gabriel). Later, when John addresses the powers that be, he stands on Westminster Bridge and faces the clock tower of the Houses of Parliament. A building that has appeared perhaps too often in the series as a reference point in the background, it's an echo of Constantine's own DC Universe debut, when he introduced Swamp Thing to the Parliament of Trees.

Constantine returns to a room where he used to live when he first came to London, to conduct his most memorable magical sting on the three Lords of Hell. After John saves his own life, he loses a friend, and the final page quotes The Pogues' "Rainy Night in Soho," as Kit Ryan – the love of his life – embraces and consoles him. London's face is crying along with him.

"The Pub Where I Was Born" (*Hellblazer* #47) takes a look at one changing locale of London. Set in the Northampton Arms, a fictional Camden pub, the story is told through John's account of the couple who ran it. The name is a nod to the home town of Jamie Delano and Alan Moore – there is a real place that fits the description, The Oxford Arms on Camden High Street, and I have to wonder whether Garth Ennis had been there.

Ennis's London Irish background infuses his run, notably with issue and arc titles named after songs by The Pogues. "London Kills Me" (*Hellblazer* #65) takes its name from a 1991 independent London film with plot elements that have appeared in and around *Hellblazer* throughout its run – down-and-outs, drugs, deals, but no demons. There are no accounts of Constantine living in the punk homes of Ladbroke Grove and Notting Hill, although Peter Hogan's *The Sandman Presents: Love Street* and his unpublished *Marquee Moon* make that connection.[6]

> The Devil came and took me...
> — Chris Difford, Squeeze, "Up the Junction" (1979)

London football is referenced in more than passing terms three times in the series. In "Extreme Prejudice" (*Hellblazer* #6), there is more of John Ridgway's London, and the key moment is when a demon created from hooligans of opposing football teams rips itself apart after Constantine points out their conflicting tattoos. "The Crowd Goes Wild," from Garth Ennis and Peter

---

[6] See Rich Handley's essay "The Hell They Weren't: *Hellblazer*'s Lost Lore," elsewhere in this volume, to learn more about *Marquee Moon*.

Snejberg (*Hellblazer* #77) starts with Chas at a big local derby game. His friends have a fairly accurate depiction of the coarse banter that somehow normalizes the behavior of hooligans – a counterpoint to Constantine, with whom Chas was not on friendly terms in the stories leading up to this issue. "Funny Old Game" (*Hellblazer* #101), by Paul Jenkins, with art by Al Davidson, serves as a better study of crowd mentality and hooliganism, replacing the Grand Guignol grotesque with a consideration of what motivates the violence.

Later, Peter Milligan introduces a succubus who is also a soccer WAG.[7] A keen observer of London football might note that all four depictions of London football have Arsenal at the butt of their contempt. Jenkins writes of one of the lesser known football rivalries, Crystal Palace vs. Brighton, and it seems he writes from experience, because there is a fairly accurate representation of Selhurst Park, the South London club's home stadium. The artwork by Davidson echoes the British football comics of *Tiger* and *Roy of the Rovers*, but our eyes are drawn to the crowd throughout.

Hellblazer #116-117 comprise a two-part tale in which someone runs the wrong way around a burial ground and causes a supernatural disturbance. The title, "Widdershins," relates to an old Scottish folk warning that says one should only walk around hallowed ground in a clockwise direction. It takes place near Selhurst, most likely in Queens Road Cemetery, and it is in this part of London where Jenkins built the most robust and real supporting cast of *Hellblazer*'s 300-plus issues. At the same time, the location is recognizably South London, despite often being restricted to sparse backgrounds behind Sean Phillips's expressive characterizations, because where he draws detail, it is given depth and reference beyond the U.S. comics shorthand of a Royal Mail red post box and a friendly police officer in a tit-shaped helmet smiling in the background. Take out the magical history of Britain and these people would appear at home in a slice of London soap opera.

> London at the moment is somewhere with endless erasures and reinventions and disappearances and amnesia.
> — Iain Sinclair[8]

---

[7] An acronym that serves as a British slang term for high-profile sports personalities' wives and girlfriends.
[8] Chapman, Tim. "'When in doubt, quote Ballard': An interview with Iain Sinclair." *Ballardian*, 29 August 2006: http://www.ballardian.com/iain-sinclair-when-in-doubt-quote-ballard.

Warren Ellis's "Haunted" is based around Brixton, Camden, and Shoreditch, and visits Bank, Scotland Yard, and Soho. It's not just a tale of revenge for Constantine's lost love Isabel Bracknell, who has been murdered by Aleister Crowley wannabe Josh Wright, but a guided tour around Inner London's innards.

John muses, "I don't have the usual map of London in my head... London's got a different geography for me. Drying blood and the last shit before dying mark it all out, dark wet borders. And I see no one giving a toss about it. No one at all." In the fifth part of this story, we are led along the Thames via Chiswick and Hammersmith in the West to the Tower of London and Smithfield Meat Market – the old city. "My name is John Constantine, and here I stay," he says. "Haunted by London. And London, haunted by me."

"Telling Tales" (*Hellblazer* #143) explores another litany of London legends – fables and reconstructions, untruths and tall tales – but the real-world city is woven into the mix by the art of Warren Pleece, John Higgins, and Marcelo Frusin. This quick detour around the less-traveled streets of *Hellblazer*'s London presents four takes that are often overlooked, sometimes with good reason.

> A man can lose himself in London
> — Keith Waterhouse, *Billy Liar*[9]

John's trusted friend Chas (and his taxi) are the focus of Simon Oliver's and Goran Sudzuka's 2008 miniseries *Hellblazer Special: Chas – The Knowledge*. The titular "knowledge" is how taxi drivers learn the routes around London, and these pages are the real London – with annotations in the script as Chas teaches his trainee and the readers. Meanwhile, *Hellblazer: City of Demons*, by Si Spencer and Sean Murphy, has a jagged, sharp, and stylistic Constantine in terms of art and words, but when he's moving through the streets, they are shown in almost photorealistic detail.

When Brian Azzarello took on the monthly series, his stated intent was to remove Constantine from his home environment – and, of course, to write on familiar ground (rednecks, prisons, and porn). While his run is set in America, John visits London in flashback, when Stanley W. Manor – a Bruce Wayne analogue and wealthy collector of the arcane – hires him to search for Grigori

---

[9] *Billy Liar*, a 1959 novel by Keith Waterouse, later became a film starring Tom Courtney.

Rasputin's bloody clock. The story is so deeply immersed in the punk-rock scene that it is London by association, but we get glimpses of the city from Guy Davis's artwork... much less of a character, but a very atmospheric background.

Glasgow was surrogate London for most of Scottish crime writer Denise Mina's run, but there was one issue set in London (*Hellblazer* #223), and an *issue* it certainly was. "The Season of the Zealot" is probably the prime example of London as a *Hellblazer* character, with the city's bond to Map emphasized. Map is Ken Ondaate, which is probably a Sri Lankan name with Dutch origins. So like Constantine, he's one of London's immigrants – and he is targeted by racist thugs in his first appearance. The story sees Constantine and Map dealing with the impact of terrorism on London – like the hooligan allegories, the story wraps supernatural around a tricky subject.

More than half of London's population came from outside the city – like Constantine, who hailed from Liverpool. Introduced by Warren Ellis, Map is usually shown as a worker in the London Underground, often referred to as the city's arteries and veins. The buildings, trains, and passengers here are drawn with documentary realism by Cristiano Cucina. But Mina's treatment of terrorism, and the denouement of Map as a supernatural superhero protector of London – like Swamp Thing is to the Green – feels unsatisfactory, especially given the pre-New 52 Constantine's general disdain for "supers."[10]

> London is full of ghosts — ghost walks; a city's worth of cemeteries; ghost-advertising, scabs of paint on brick. The city invoked something, read a grimoire it shouldn't have.
> — China Miéville[11]

After bringing Constantine back home via Liverpool, Mike Carey latches onto Warren Ellis's version of London – even though Constantine travels the world much like he did in those early Delano issues. "This is my city," John tells readers in "A Game of Cat and Mouse" (*Hellblazer* #181). "I don't know what

---

[10] I really wish it had been tied in more with the terrorist attacks of 2005, and it appears that that was the intention (or is that just my Rorschach interpretation?). I like Denise Mina's interest in cities in her *Hellblazer* stories, but *my* city would not be threatened by one boy with a corpse fetish.

[11] Miéville, China. "Oh, London, You Drama Queen." *The New York Times Magazine*, 1 March 2012: https://www.nytimes.com/2012/03/04/magazine/china-mieville-london.html?smid=pl-share. Later reposted in abbreviated form at http://www.londonsoverthrow.org.

you've heard elsewhere, but it's mine. I found it mewling and covered in shit and I adopted it."

You can walk the route along which Constantine is pursued by the demonic Lukhavim, around the east of the city.[12] In fact, you could probably run it, as Constantine does, but as I am not a 50-something-year-old astral projection, I took my time when I followed John's path. New buildings have sprung up in the city, and it is now even more like an architectural historian's collage. But artist Jock does not pick the obvious, hackneyed Tower Bridge to set the scene. As Constantine approaches the alleyway where the Lukhavim first catch up with him, he passes near the mass burial grounds of Spitalfields[13] and what was once "the worst street in London," Dorset Street[14] (also connected to Alan Moore's *From Hell*, as the home of Mary Kelly). At the times of *From Hell* and this issue of *Hellblazer*, that street was buried beneath a car park. But here is evidence that even on a small scale, London is undergoing cosmetic surgery, as the street's line will soon be marked once again with a modern mall.

Later in Carey's arc, *Hellblazer*'s cast of Londoners is decimated by Constantine's demon-spawned children – three different versions of his personality, born from a succubus raiding his subconscious ("Happy Families," in *Hellblazer* #200). The horror that follows is often focused on splatter and gore, which is lovingly rendered by Leonardo Manco. For Carey's run, Manco uses the city sparingly to suit the mood and build suspense regarding whom the next victim will be. Three covers from this run see Tim Bradstreet drawing upon various London locations: Westminster Bridge (#202), The East End (#213), and the Streatham Lock-Up (#214). Surprisingly few of the series' covers feature London in this way, notably Glenn Fabry's joyful depiction of John and Kit emerging from Piccadilly on a rainy night in Soho (#82); and Lee Bermejo's celebration of the U.K. smoking ban (#238).

---

[12] See this writer's *Hellblazer* annotations from 2003, along with a map and notes from 2019, at
http://www.insanerantings.com/hell/comics/ongoing/hb181ann2.html. You can zoom in on the map at
https://drive.google.com/open?id=1kInaZlvQ6LUaM8LmgxMc-ywJZlU&usp=sharing.
[13] Hilts, Carly. "Reading the bones: Spitalfields' human remains." *Current Archaeology*, 6 August 2012:
https://www.archaeology.co.uk/articles/features/reading-the-bones-spitalfields-human-remains.htm.
[14] https://en.wikipedia.org/wiki/Dorset_Street_(Spitalfields)

In *Hellblazer*, London is connected to everything.

Carey's run ends with a scorched Earth policy, as Constantine gives up magic in much the same way addicts cut ties with their drug.[15] The long-established Streatham Lock-Up is razed to the ground, which is a catharsis but also symbolically removes ties to past continuity and Constantine's London.

> London calling to the underworld
> — Joe Strummer, The Clash, "London Calling" (1979)

Andy Diggle's run opens with Westminster, our old friend the Houses of Parliament (*Hellblazer* #230), and his tales take place around the suburbs that have been subsumed by the sprawl of Inner London. "Joyride" (#234-237) is laced with real places from around Greater London, and "The Smoke" (#238), even with Danijel Zezelj's abstract background, conjures up a quote from Londoner Alfred Hitchcock about his birthplace: "The sky was always grey, the rain was grey, the mud was grey and I was grey."[16] The term "The Smoke," of course, originally referred to London, back in the days when industrial pollution combined with fog off the Thames, so the double meaning carries here.

Diggle takes Constantine back to the fringes of London's mob scene created by John Higgins and Garth Ennis (in "Son of Man," *Hellblazer* #129-134), and features London's gangs as street hoodlums more than when gangland meant menacing men in smart suits, with repressions and perversions on a par with those civil servants who visit cheaper tailors. The final years of *Hellblazer* are played out here, between London's criminal underworld and its political elite.

> London loves the way people just fall apart
> — Damon Albarn, Blur, "London Loves" (1994)

Like Carey, Peter Milligan opens his time on *Hellblazer* in Liverpool and continues much more in the political vein of Delano's beginnings for the book. This sets the scene for the events that follow in "Scab" (*Hellblazer* #251-255), with links to the union battles that were happening during *Hellblazer*'s early years. There is not much to see of London's outdoors as the narrative focuses on Constantine's relationships (with Phoebe Clifton-Avery, Epiphany Greaves,

---

[15] He goes right back to using magic almost immediately, although this line of inquiry was briefly touched upon by later writers.

[16] https://www.timeout.com/london/film/a-tour-of-hitchcocks-london

and Chas Chandler), but we get a glimpse, courtesy of Simon Bisley, in the punks-versus-Tories tale "No Future" (#266).

Constantine contemplates Margaret Thatcher's 1979 election victory while standing on a canal bridge in Camden Lock – a hub for the second wave of punk rockers at that time, inspired by the Ramones' appearance at the nearby Roundhouse.[17] The Sex Pistols also played there during the genesis of the U.K. punk scene. Bisley's cover for the very next issue is one of those rarities that features London landmarks (*Hellblazer* #267), and this time offers an unusual perspective as Constantine falls from the London Eye. In this issue, you can see Christchurch at Spitalfields (page 9), a Nicholas Hawksmoor-designed church, also seen in *From Hell* and near the chase scene from "A Game of Cat and Mouse" (*Hellblazer* #181). Here, London's psychogeographers have a field day.

Every now and then, Bisley glances up from his story of the punk Constantine and shows London's Wormwood Scrubs prison (*Hellblazer* #273). Then, with "Suicide Bridge" (*Hellblazer Annual 2011*), Milligan and Bisley combine superbly to tell a slice of London life. This self-contained story says more about the people and the place than almost any of what came before and after. This is the *real* London Below – a melancholy, lonely place, as cities are for many isolated folks – in spite of them being apparently surrounded by others. For me, the BBC soap opera *EastEnders* comes to mind with the rest of this period. Then, after 300 monthly issues, plus specials and spinoffs, *Hellblazer* ends – or, rather, ends up back in the DC Universe. And there, Constantine sticks out like a sore arse until rescued by DC's Black Label[18] and his return to London four years later, courtesy of Simon Spurrier.

> We've a thirst like a gang of devils, we're the boys of the county hell.
> — Shane Mac Gowan, The Pogues, "The Boys from the Country Hell" (1984)

When you consider the way Constantine's narrators have remolded the book to their own identity, you can map the timeline against that of a London pub during the past 30 years. Simon Oliver said, at the time of his new *Hellblazer* series, "His life is shabby pubs and markets. Friends you bump into

---

[17] "In Pictures: Ramones at the Roundhouse." Roundhouse, 4 July 1976: https://50.roundhouse.org.uk/content-items/ramones-at-the-roundhouse.
[18] DC Comics' mature imprint, not to be confused with Johnnie Walker whisky or the Carling lager, although London pubs would sell those drinks.

down the pub, who you've known for twenty years but all you know them from is the pub."[19] Those old geezers sat and went on about the "good old days," then would go home for tea, and you'd listen to new-wave music on the jukebox until you were thrown out at closing time. It was refurbished several times since the 1990s, firstly in the style of an Irish pub, with Guinness at room temperature, a cracking atmosphere, and a great crowd. A new landlord stripped it back to the basics, and while the old guys had shuffled off, a new bunch of locals soon arrived. There was a short attempt at redecoration, and real ale ended when one of the new gang pulled a gun. Rebranded as an American bar, with sports screens, pizzas, and brash Pale Ales, it was barely recognizable to regulars. Then a British bar company (est. 2000 A.D.) gave the place a retro look; the owners knew the history, but the area had changed a lot and turnover diminished. A more mixed crowd was brought in when the final landlord gave the place a younger, louder vibe. But in the end, they didn't want a pub – they wanted a refrigerator at home.

Perhaps the bullet with which the retconned, vengeful Gemma ended the original *Hellblazer* contained liquid Multiverse, stolen from Grant Morrison during a boozy late night at the Tate Club, because the Constantines we have been sold since seem to be from a Crisis of Infinite Hellblazers. But it is true to form that the final puzzle, as *Hellblazer* #300 comes to a close, is left unanswered in a pub.

---

[19] Beat Staff. "Interview: Simon Oliver Reveals Why We Needed a British Writer on *The Hellblazer*." The Beat, 25 October 2016:
https://www.comicsbeat.com/interview-simon-oliver-reveals-why-we-needed-a-british-writer-on-the-hellblazer/.

Hell to Pay: How the 2005 Movie Changed the Theology of *Hellblazer* and Doomed John Constantine

by James Wilkinson

If ever there were an actor born to play blonde, blue-eyed, Liverpool-bred magus John Constantine, Keanu Reeves is most certainly not him. And sure enough, in the build-up to the release of *Constantine*, Hollywood's 2005 bastardization of *John Constantine: Hellblazer*, many a fan message board was cluttered up with complaints about DC Comics' most cunning Brit being played by one of the time-traveling halfwits from *Bill and Ted's Excellent Adventure*.

But while Reeves is a left-field choice to portray the character, this adaptation's problems run far deeper than the color of its star's hair. Writers Kevin Brodbin and Frank A. Cappello make a good fist of adapting the comic within Hollywood action-movie constraints, liberally borrowing from the comic's mythology and coming up with a suitably clever climactic con for their anti-hero. However, they also make a fundamental change to the theology of the comic – one that not only tosses away one of the key aspects of *Hellblazer*, but also castrates the character of John Constantine for good measure. Let's not get ahead of ourselves, though. To properly explain what I'm talking about, we're going to have to go back to the very beginning – which, in the case of Johnny-boy, is the Alan Moore-penned *Swamp Thing* #37.[1]

That issue, cover-dated June 1985 and titled "Growth Patterns," marks the beginning of the epic, 14-issue "American Gothic" storyline, in which Constantine sends Swampy off to battle all manner of classic horror monsters – including vampires, ghosts, zombies, and a particularly tragic werewolf – to prepare for an apocalyptic final encounter. But in this first issue, Swamp Thing isn't going anywhere: he's literally rooted to the spot, regrowing his body following a near-fatal encounter in the previous issue.[2]

One might expect such colorful language from such a colorful woman. Judith gives John a piece of her mind in *Swamp Thing* #37.

That gives Moore the opportunity to focus on Constantine, who is introduced to us in a psychedelically lit nightclub, wearing his iconic suit and trenchcoat as he consults a burned-out looking punk called Judith. Constantine tells her that "he" – the Primordial Shadow, a malevolent entity that Swamp Thing will confront 14 issues later – is "coming back." Judith disputes that

---

[1] A Constantine lookalike did appear in *Swamp Thing* #25, but let's not split hairs here.

[2] That encounter was with "Nukeface," a deranged, radioactive hobo addicted to drinking nuclear waste – proof that even a genius like Alan Moore has his off-days.

description, saying that the entity is not a "he," but "a massive extragalactic energy field that got drawn inside a black hole eight billion years ago." Later, another associate, a bookish young man named Benjamin Cox, tells Constantine that the force is Cthulhu, a horror character created by real-world author H.P. Lovecraft; a third friend, a scowling nun going by the name of Anne-Marie, claims "The name of our adversary is Satan."

As it happens, they're all wrong, but these atmospheric scenes do much to establish John's position inside the DC Universe's supernatural cosmos. Or, rather, his position outside of it: Constantine stands at the intersection between all worlds – religious, mythical, scientific, and magical – finding allies and enemies in all, and using each to his advantage. It's something that recurs throughout "American Gothic," as Constantine helps Swamp Thing explore the Green, the transcendental plane that connects all plant life; introduces him to the Parliament of Trees, his fellow plant elementals; takes him to a space station where he encounters DC's superhero population; and unites the super-scientist Mento with a team of occultists for the final push against the entity.

Now, to be fair, having to deal with multiple competing theologies, philosophies, and worlds is an inevitable part of living in the DC Universe – after all, it's a place where Amazon warriors, personifications of dreaming, and Judeo-Christian spirits of vengeance rub shoulders with heroic androids, shapeshifting Martians, and journalists from the planet Krypton.[3] But it's rare for a character to be defined by both his existence in these margins and his proficiency at manipulating these diverse worlds, as John is throughout "American Gothic." This is, to at least some degree, intentional. As Moore told *The Comics Journal*: "I just wanted this character who knows everything, and knows everybody – really charismatic. Who knows nuns, politicians and bikers, and who is never at a loss for what to do."[4]

When it came time to spin Constantine off into his own adventures in January 1988, Jamie Delano took the baton and ran with it. Although the newly minted comic was titled *Hellblazer*, the opening story gives Christian theology a wide berth, instead pitting Constantine against Mnemoth, a Sudanese hunger spirit that has been unleashed upon New York in the form of a swarm of deadly insects. The magus consults a witch doctor from Mnemoth's old stomping

---

[3] These would be Wonder Woman, Neil Gaiman's Morpheus (Dream of the Endless), the Spectre, Red Tornado, Martian Manhunter, and Superman, of course.
[4] "Alan Moore On (Just About) Everything," *The Comics Journal* #106, March 1986.

grounds, but in the end contrives a multitheistic solution to the problem, defeating the creature with the help of a voodoo priest called Papa Midnite and an electric chair from Sing Sing prison that has been rendered magically potent due to the souls that have passed through it.

John goes face to face with the Rainbow Serpent in *Hellblazer* #90.

These details will be familiar to anyone who has seen *Constantine*, which also features a bug monster, Papa Midnite, and the Sing Sing chair. But the film departs from the core of that story, and of *Hellblazer* itself, by making its universe a resolutely Christian one. In *Constantine*, Earth is the battleground for the armies of God and the Devil, although only half-breed angels and demons are allowed to actually set foot on the planet.[5] Aside from the notion of psychic powers, Midnite being an unspecified "witch doctor," and an ambiguous mention of "dragon's breath," there's no hint that anything exists outside of the usual biblical remit. Even Constantine – who is now exclusively an exorcist, because there's no magic in this world – comes armed with holy knuckledusters, shavings from the bullet used in the assassination attempt on Pope John Paul II, and a ludicrous crucifix-shaped shotgun.

Woah! Constantine has a crucifix-shaped shotgun? Who knew?

The most obvious effect of this change is the limitation it places on the writers. While *Hellblazer* was free to careen from religion to mythology to superstition, and even to dip into earthly threats such as serial killers and gangsters, *Constantine* is creatively hobbled by the need to hew close to some kind of biblical precedent. Oh, there's a bit of variety in the bad guys, sure: there are creepy, eyeless, emaciated things in Hell, and there's that bug-demon,[6] a spooky-looking woman on a bus, and green-skinned half-demons. But had *Constantine* succeeded in its ambition to become a continuing

---

[5] How you get a half-breed demon or angel when there's a ban on their full-blooded forebears remains unexplained.

[6] Similarly, how this guy managed to get to Earth when there's a ban in place is unclear.

franchise, it's hard to imagine how far it could really have gone.

From an adaptation perspective, however, there's a much, much more serious problem, and that's what it does to the character of John himself. A one-time punk rocker, comic book Constantine stridently opposes authority and frequently finds himself fighting for the rights of individuals, groups, and even humanity itself to make their own choices free from control and oppression. That's seen him going up against the police and even the monarchy,[7] of course. But some of his most notable adventures have seen him fending off even more powerful forces – not just those of Hell, but also Heaven, which in *Hellblazer* is portrayed as a force of order and control, rather than one of beneficence.

In *Hellblazer*'s first major story arc, which takes place across issues #4-12, John finds himself in the middle of a war between a fundamentalist Christian cult and a Hell-spawned army led by the demon Nergal,[8] both of which want to seize a woman who is predicted to give birth to a new messiah. Constantine, not liking the sound of either Hell on Earth or bowing to the yoke of Heaven, taints the would-be Madonna with his demon essence, making her an imperfect vessel and stopping her from being impregnated by an angel. Having tipped the scales in favor of Hell, he then rights things by helping Swamp Thing and his wife, Abigail Holland, to conceive their own messiah child[9] – a mix of human

---

[7] John battled a possessed Prince Charles in *Hellblazer* #52-55, by Garth Ennis and Will Simpson, and ended up mixed up with a bastard royal in the *Hellblazer* miniseries *Bad Blood (A Restoration Comedy)*, by Jamie Delano and Philip Bond. His fractious relationships with various police forces are too numerous to mention here; suffice it to say he's done prison and jail stints and has pissed off law-enforcement agencies around the world.

[8] Nergal's backstory is confusing. In his earliest appearances (setting aside his debut in 1941's *More Fun Comics* #67 as an enemy of Doctor Fate), he acts as a straight-up agent of Hell. In Garth Ennis's *Hellblazer* #60, he is revealed to have been a damned Babylonian human who subsequently attained demonhood. In Brian Azzarello's "The First Time," published in *Vertigo Secret Files: Hellblazer*, Nergal claims to have been "chucked out of Heaven" for excessive pride, implying he was an angel. And in Delano's 2010 graphic novel *Hellblazer: Pandemonium*, Nergal is both a demon of Hell *and* a Babylonian god – and, it would appear, an early adopter of the gig economy. Adding to this confusion, Mike Carey's *Hellblazer* #210 identifies Nergal's father as the demon Gurruth of the Twelve Mouths, while John Shirley's novel *War Lord* calls his demon dad N'Hept.

[9] In a crossover that takes place over the course of *Swamp Thing* #76, by Rick Veitch and Alfredo Alcala, and *Hellblazer* #10, by Jamie Delano, Richard Piers-Rayner, and Mark Buckingham.

and plant elemental, who will be named Tefé, and who fulfills the prophecy without letting either biblical side win the game.

This ability to turn figures from one pantheon against those of another is one of the most useful weapons in Constantine's arsenal, and comes up repeatedly in his comics – with predictably fatal results. He had a Celtic pagan god, the Lord of the Dance, confront Satan on his behalf.[10] He outwitted an Australian Aboriginal god, knowing that she had no power over non-believers.[11] He called on Aboriginal ghosts, Christian angels, Swamp Thing, a Benedictine werewolf, and several magicians to battle a creature from the dawn of Christian theology.[12] And he persuaded an Aztec god to take down a Hellspawn's sinister scheme in Los Angeles.[13] These are just a few of many examples; for *Hellblazer*'s Constantine, the trick to winning the game is to only play by the rules that benefit you *while* they benefit you – and the moment it looks like you might lose, switch them up for something else. Not only does it keep John ahead of the pack, it also allows him to remain independent from all sides – and to maintain his rebellious streak.

Not so for movie Constantine, who's tethered to a grimly Catholic universe in which Heaven vs. Hell is the only game in town, and so the choice is either a beneficent God and His (with a single notable exception) kindly angels, or an oily, reptilian Satan, played with relish by Peter Stormare, and his army of grisly underlings. (Or remaining neutral and opening a tacky nightclub like Papa Midnite, but that wouldn't make for a good film.)

So it is that Constantine finds himself doing the work of the Good Lord, trying to earn his passage into Heaven – a notion that his comic book counterpart would laugh out of town. Not only is he acting as an unbidden agent of God, in fact, but his work largely consists of performing flashy exorcisms on various spooky demons to send them back down to Hell – or, as the film's lingo has it, "deporting" them. Yes, John Constantine, the man who wouldn't let Heaven have him even if it wanted him, is turned into an unpaid

---

[10] *Hellblazer* #80, by Garth Ennis and Steve Dillon. It ended with the Lord of the Dance having part of his ribcage torn out. But the Lord's heart was in the right place – as any spectators could attest.

[11] *Hellblazer* #90, by Paul Jenkins and Sean Philips.

[12] *Hellblazer* #185, #186, and #189-193, by Mike Carey and Marcelo Frusin.

[13] *All His Engines* (2005), an original graphic novel by Mike Carey and Leonardo Manco.

immigration and customs official. Is any role more subservient and beholden to the status quo than that?

Then again, what choice does this version of John have? In *Hellblazer*, the afterlife holds near-endless possibilities for the nomad soul – the various paradises and punishments of the world's religions; the non-denominational good and bad places glimpsed by Swamp Thing in his own comic; and perhaps even the afterlives of other worlds. In *Constantine*, there's a stark choice: either you go to Heaven, complete with drifting, sunlit clouds, or you go to a Hell that looks like a circa-2003 nu-metal music video.

Of course, the Christian afterlife is the one featured most prominently in *Hellblazer*, but even there, comic book Constantine has, in theory at least, a get-out clause. One interesting rule of the DC Universe[14] is that the eventual destination of the human soul isn't decided by a higher power – unless it is sold or stolen by nefarious means, of course – but by each individual. As the rhyming demon Etrigan tells Swamp Thing, "God is no parent or policeman grim dispensing treats or punishments to all. Each soul climbs or descends by its own whim. He mourns, but he cannot prevent their fall. We suffer as we choose, nothing's amiss. All torments are deserved – none more than this."[15]

John knows this, of course, and theoretically that gives him incredible power. After all, it doesn't matter what horrible things he does in life. He can just forgive himself and spend eternity knocking back pints in the great big boozer in the sky – the old "saved by Jesus" ploy minus the middleman. But Constantine is defined as much as anything by his own guilty conscience. In the first issue of *Hellblazer*, he's confronted by the spectres of old friends and lovers who have died enacting his plans. In the second issue, after John has sacrificed his childhood pal Gary Lester to stop the rampaging hunger spirit, Papa Midnite tells him, "Grief, Constantine, is a luxury. A magician must separate himself from his humanity."

Constantine rejects that notion, of course, and spends a not inconsiderable chunk of the following 298 issues (plus specials, graphic novels, annuals, and

---

[14] At least, in *Swamp Thing* and *Hellblazer*; the rules vary from comic to comic, and the further into the DC Universe you go – even when you're in the *Hellblazer*-adjacent *The Sandman* and *Lucifer* – the less consistently this applies.

[15] *Swamp Thing Annual* #2, by Alan Moore, Stephen R. Bissette, and John Totleben. It should be noted that the "God" in Swamp Thing is not really the Judeo-Christian creator – rather, this is one facet of an unknowable being called the Presence that is perceived differently by everyone who glimpses it.

prose tales) getting drunk and wallowing in his own guilt and misery. Ultimately, he won't allow himself to go to Heaven because he doesn't feel he deserves it – and yet, he won't change his ways because he's too proud to do so. Those cigarettes forever hanging from his lips aren't just there to look cool, they're a metaphor for his entire existence.

But movie Constantine isn't blessed with even that option. The judgement of his God is absolute.[16] Attempt suicide and your soul is damned to Hell, even if you survive and spend the rest of your life licking the Creator's boots. John forgiving himself means nothing. Trying to find an out through another religion is a non-starter. The management's decision is final – and that, in turn, vastly diminishes the scope and complexity of John's character.

This Constantine is not a rebel against God, because to rebel in this world makes no damn sense at all – it guarantees damnation. He's not damned because he has confounded Heaven and done bad things in the name of good – he's doomed because he tried, and failed, to kill himself as a teenager. He doesn't get involved with the supernatural because he's an adrenaline junkie and restless explorer of the unknown – it's because he's trying to buy his way into Paradise. Even in the final twisty-turny climactic confrontation with Satan, which is actually rather splendidly written, John's ultimate victory comes because he sacrifices himself honestly and without guile, putting his fate in the hands of God. He gets a second chance *not* because he outmaneuvered everyone, but because of the purity of his intentions.

This is not John Constantine as the comic book readers know him – and yet, it couldn't be any other way, at least not with the universe we see here. The John Constantine of the comic could only exist in *Constantine* if he were the most catastrophically stupid person to have ever been born. Since a lead character so thunderously dim would probably just walk into traffic in the first moments of the film, he had to be given at least a handful of brain cells. And so we get this weird, bastardized non-Constantine (Nonstantine, if you will, which you probably shouldn't) rather than the whip-smart con man of the comics.

This, in turn, has a curious knock-on effect, destabilizing those parts of the comic that have been imported directly (and are possibly artefacts of earlier drafts). Constantine's bolshy demeanor comes across as petulant and unconvincing – he's essentially *The Simpsons*' Ned Flanders with a gun; why is

---

[16] Well, normally. John *does* get a second chance at the end of the film, but that's an unexpected turn for all involved. Except God, presumably. Omniscience and all that.

he such a dick? Satan deciding to pull John from Heaven's grasp by healing him in the hope that he will damn himself in the future makes no sense, since John was only Hellbound because he attempted suicide, something he's unlikely to do again. And the smoking... well, that works in the comic because it's symbolic of John's self-destructive streak, his pride in the face of oblivion. Movie Constantine has no pride, and has known his card was punched since he was 17 years old. Why would he risk developing fatal cancer before he can assure himself of passage to Heaven? Why wouldn't he be guzzling kale and celery like there's no tomorrow?

This neatly brings us to the final scene of the film – and the one that shows us quite how the theology of *Constantine* has destroyed the man himself. Gazing across Los Angeles, cured of cancer and saved by the grace of God, Constantine intones: "I guess there's a plan for all of us. I had to die twice just to figure that out. Like the Book says, He works His work in mysterious ways. Some people like it, some people don't."

Then, to compound the absolute mediocrity of that little speech (has there ever been a final line as underwhelming and noncommittal as "Some people like it, some people don't"?), he dramatically opens his mouth and... chomps some chewing gum. Within the universe of the film, of course, this makes sense – but could there possibly be a bigger betrayal of John's character?

For contrast, here's a little excerpt from a rant in *Hellblazer* #128,[17] in which Constantine meets Jesus Christ in the woods: "All this bloody allegory and metaphor, and d'you know what it's all for? 'Cause when push comes to shove, you've got fuck all to say ... It's all you can do to sit about being ineffable and smug, wittering on about how glorious this overcooked little world of clay is." Then John warns that if the Almighty doesn't do what he demands, John will die, take over Hell, organize its armies properly for the first time since Lucifer fell, and raze Creation. And Jesus, faced with stone cold blackmail from the craftiest man in the world, backs down and does his bidding.

That's how John Constantine works *his* work. Is it any wonder Hollywood wouldn't let *that* guy near their movie?

---

[17] By Paul Jenkins and Warren Pleece.

Constantine: Rhymes with Wine

by Lou Tambone

> **IGOR:** Dr. Frankenstein?
> **DR. FRANKENSTEIN:** "Fronkensteen."
> **IGOR:** You're putting me on.
> **FRANKENSTEIN:** No, it's pronounced "Fronkensteen."
> **IGOR:** Do you also say "Froaderick"?
> **FRANKENSTEIN:** No... "Frederick."
> **IGOR:** Well, why isn't it "Froaderick Fronkensteen"?
> **FRANKENSTEIN:** It isn't; it's "Frederick Fronkensteen."
> **IGOR:** I see.
> **FRANKENSTEIN:** You must be Igor.
> **IGOR:** No, it's pronounced "eye-gor."
> **FRANKENSTEIN:** But they told me it was "ee-gor."
> **IGOR:** Well, they were wrong, then, weren't they?
> — *Young Frankenstein* (1974)

Throughout the years, John Constantine, everyone's favorite pugnacious magus, has found himself at the center of many a crisis. Before he was even born, he strangled his twin in utero using the only weapon he had available at the time: an umbilical cord. He was the star of a punk-rock band (a crisis in and of itself, to be sure) and, after an occult mishap, found himself in and out of the Ravenscar Secure Facility for the Dangerously Deranged. He often bumps into an array of demons, and has also clashed with the Brujería cult, the King of the Vampires, the Lords of the Fallen, and other dangerous nemeses. And he's reluctantly been dragged into adventures with frenemies like Zatanna Zatara, Swamp Thing, and the Phantom Stranger. In fact, it was one of DC Comics' biggest and most famous crises that John was able to foresee: the *Crisis on Infinite Earths*.

Yet, after everything the man's been through, there still remains one ongoing crisis he can't seem to subvert: the pronunciation of his surname.

The name Constantine has Latin roots and is most famously associated with Constantine the Great, the Roman emperor who ruled from 306 to 337 AD.[1] He was famous not only for founding the city of Constantinople in 324, but for being the first emperor to convert to Christianity and, under the Edict of Milan, stopping Christians from being persecuted while letting anyone worship any deity they chose without fear. Not a bad guy to be named after, I suppose.

Traditional English elocution dictates that the name Constantine be pronounced /ˈkɒnstəntʌɪn/,[2] meaning the name rhymes with "fine" or "wine." It's hard to nail down when this happened, but at some point in time, people (most likely in North America, though it hasn't been proven) started pronouncing the name with a stronger "e," like "Constan-teen." This seems to be the popular explanation, but some folks, especially those in Europe, aren't all that keen about the change.

Until I began writing this essay, I hadn't realized that there exists a subtle, underground movement on the Internet that defends the original, European-style pronunciation of Constantine. Almost every search I conducted on the character's name ended in someone commenting about how the name's been incorrectly articulated for far too long. They perceive it as a small victory when someone on television or in a YouTube video rhymes the name with "wine." There's usually someone posting a link in a comments section to Garth Ennis — or just about anyone else from the United Kingdom — saying the name "correctly" in order to defend the blond magician's honor.

I'm convinced there must be a support group out there somewhere for *Hellblazer* fans which gathers weekly, its members sitting in circles, to expresss

---

[1] And may even have been an ancestor of John Constantine, per hints dropped in *Hellblazer* #40 and #49, as well as the *Destiny: A Chronicle of Deaths Foretold* miniseries.

[2] https://en.oxforddictionaries.com/definition/constantine

how difficult it is to deal with the reality of hearing their dearest friends and relatives mispronounce John's name in their presence, in spite of ongoing attempts to correct them. They break down into tears, sharing their feelings of shame and horror with each other. Perhaps they wind up at the pub afterward and raise a pint to the con man, proposing a toast to the day when all the good people of the world will join together and pronounce the name correctly. What a grand day that would be! But will it ever come?

Is it really so difficult?

The phenomenon of mispronouncing names in literary works is hardly anything new. Books or other written media are subject to name-mangling simply because there are often no accompanying audio or video dictionaries to establish the proper phonation. Think back to one of the first books you've ever read. If it contained names like Michelle or Mike, you probably didn't give those names a second thought. These are quite common names with which most people are familiar. If your name isn't Michelle or Mike, you probably knew someone with that name, especially if you grew up in North America.

If your first literary reads were works by J.R.R. Tolkien, however, you might have had to stop and think a moment before reading a name aloud, or even in your head. For example, I didn't know that the name Celeborn was pronounced with a harder K sound until I had watched the *Lord of the Rings* films. I was pronouncing the "c" the same way I would in the word "celebration." Names like Denethor threw me for a loop as well. Where did the accents sit? Was it

"DeNEEthor" or "DEHnethor" or "DEEnethor" or "DeneTHOR" – or something else entirely?

If you look closely, the clues to pronouncing John's surname correctly are there.

Comic books, as the well-respected literary media they are, are certainly no exception when it comes to mispronouncing words or names. While Marvel's Thor stories feature a plethora of Norse tongue-stumblers (Mjolnir comes immediately to mind), the DC Universe is rife with names and words that are easy to verbally distort. Wonder Woman's home of Themyscira is a bit tough to read the first time. Even her mother's name, Hippolyta, falls victim to the accent-placement dilemma. We could spend all day dissecting Mister Mxyzptlk, but the one that always perplexed me was the surname of Gotham City mob boss Carmine Falcone.

On the page, it always appeared plain as day to me, rhyming with "cone." Yet, in some visual adaptations, most noticeably Christopher Nolan's *Batman* films, the name is pronounced "Falconey," as in "Coney Island." Now, there could be a reasonable explanation for this since it's an Italian surname. Being Italian, I've had similar experiences growing up, as I was often called "Tamboney" instead of Tambone, pronounced as if you were referring to your femur or tibia. It still happens to this day, in fact. I often wonder why people have the ability to say the word "bone" correctly without effort, yet mispronounce my surname more often than I care to admit.[3]

---

[3] See how annoying it can be? Now imagine poor John's vexation.

One possible explanation is that in certain Italian dialects, that ending vowel found on words or names can act as an extra syllable. Think of *The Godfather* and its patriarch, Don Vito Corleone.[4] In the film, some characters call him "Corleone" (rhymes with "bone"), while others call him something like "Cor-le-OWN-eh." The little "eh" is barely there, but it makes a difference. It's not the same as "Cor-lee-OWN-ee," which I attribute to the Americanizing of Italian names and words, like bologna, which many people call "baloney." I believe the whole issue with Falcone lies somewhere lost in translation.

Another name with somewhat of a regional explanation for its pronunciation is Ra's al Ghul, which is Arabic for "the demon's head." In Arabic, you'd say "Rah-is" or "Raz," but in Hebrew it's pronounced "Raysh." The confusion about how the Hebrew pronunciation got involved is a long story.[5] Regardless, how you pronounce it will depend on what you're watching or reading, and whatever decision you make going forward. The television shows on The CW channel make great use of the "Raysh" pronunciation and have largely remained consistent throughout the years. The Nolan films took the "Raz" thing and ran with it.

Then there's Darkseid. For years, I pronounced it "Darkseed," because it just seemed right. Someone with the surname of Reid surely wouldn't (in my experience, anyhow) pronounce it as "Ride." My brain automatically kicked out the name as though it rhymed with "weed." Sure, it didn't sound as badass as "Dark Side," but that seemed a little too overt to me, even for a comic in which goofy names abound. Nonetheless, that's the proper way to say it, so who am I to argue? It's one I've since been able to mentally correct, which brings us back to our favorite occultist.

I often wonder what John Constantine would say about all this ado regarding his surname. Would he be offended that so many people have been mauling his name since his inception? We've already seen him correct people multiple times in the comics. The most notable example, and the most widely shared on the Internet, can be found in *Swamp Thing* #73. While walking with Chester Williams, who mistakenly refers to his companion as "Constanteen," John quickly corrects the well-meaning hippie. One blog describes the scene: "John Constantine shows up, to explain to Chester that he has become the centre of the synchronicity storm, and is due to become the next Swamp Thing.

---

[4] How did you just pronounce that? Exactly.
[5] https://www.youtube.com/watch?v=j8glOASNCU4

Chester calls John 'Constanteen,' but John corrects him, saying [that] it is ConstanTINE. So despite the TV shows and movie, please say it the proper way."[6] You'll find these kinds of snarky comments all over the Internet. Give it a try![7]

John corrects Chester Williams.

In *Hellblazer* #232, John once again leaves no ambiguity as to how to pronounce his surname. In the issue, written by Andy Diggle, John is decked out in a suit and gambling in a casino when he hits it big at roulette (with a little mystic assistance). He tells the observing employees to have the casino deeds drawn up in his name, "John Constantine. That's T-I-N-E. Rhymes with FINE." It seems as though the whole thing was a bit of in an in-joke at Vertigo. Every now and then, the writers considered it their duty to remind readers how to

---

[6] Dayton, Deejay. "*Swamp Thing* 73 - how to pronounce Constantine." Babbling About Comics, 2 March 2018: http://babblingsaboutdccomics.blogspot.com/2018/03/swamp-thing-73-how-to-pronounce.html.

[7] "That...doesn't rhyme (Hellblazer 39)." Reddit discussion, 2015: https://www.reddit.com/r/comicbooks/comments/2s1hr8/thatdoesnt_rhyme_hell blazer_39/.

properly pronounce the main character's name. It must have bugged them as much as anyone else to hear it said wrong on both the small and big screens.

Andy Diggle once again reminds readers of the proper pronunciation.

Here in the United States, the hints went over our collective heads, and it's hard to say whether such a change would even be possible without everyone getting on board. A single panel of a comic book every few years certainly hasn't proven to be enough. All the Internet comment sections out there loaded with pleas seem to be in vain. Whenever a new television appearance of John Constantine is imminent, I'm sure many fans wonder whether the producers will finally bite the bullet and use the correct pronunciation.

This has mostly resulted in one let-down after another, however. John has shown up on his own short-lived series, plus on other shows like *Arrow* and *Legends of Tomorrow*, which are all set in the same universe, dubbed the "Arrowverse" (named after the flagship show, *Arrow*). Matt Ryan does a phenomenal job of bringing the character to life in both live-action and animated roles, but as far as the name goes, the Americanized "Constanteen" pronunciation wins out time and time again.[8] The 2005 film *Constantine*, starring Keanu Reeves in the title role, was no exception – and may have set the template for all the later mispronunciations.

When are we going to get with the program, folks?

To enact change, I believe there needs to be a global effort. It's all up to us, because there are two camps. The first sticks with the traditional English pronunciation that rhymes with "wine." According to this crowd, John himself is on record correcting people in the books, so why shouldn't this be the official ruling? The second camp sides with the "teen" delivery, with the understanding that it really only matters to *you* in the end, so who cares? People mispronounce names all the time, they might say – so get over it, already.

I admit that I am guilty of having been a member of the second camp for a great many years. Growing up in the United States, whether Constantine was the name of a Pope, an emperor, or a comic book character, I always heard it pronounced as "Constanteen." Thus, it took hold and never let go. So when the first *Constantine* television show aired employing the "teen" pronunciation, it didn't faze me in the least. I had simply assumed it was correct.

Around that time, I began to read the collected *Hellblazer* books in earnest and in order, alongside another DC staple, *Swamp Thing*. I read the collected volumes in parallel, since I knew the two series crossed over at various points. It was fun, but I began to notice that I might have been wrong in my articulation of John's surname. After speaking to some experts, watching some videos on YouTube, and of course noting the various corrections by John in the comics themselves, I began to feel guilty for saying the poor sod's name wrong all those years.

As of this writing, I have firmly placed myself in the first camp for good. It's not easy, though. John would be the first to admit that old habits die hard – like smoking, for instance. It's a constant struggle, but it's a cause to which I'm now absolutely committed. I catch myself constantly Constanteening, but I make a conscious effort to correct myself and to get back on the "tine/wine/fine" track until it becomes second nature. I'll re-read the same bit of dialogue a few times as a mental punishment of sorts. The good news is that it's slowly working. I

---

[8] The CW's 2019-20 "Crisis on Infinite Earths" crossover event features a humorous scene in which Lucifer Morningstar pronounces John's surname as "ConstanTYNE." John corrects him with a hearty "ConstanTEEN," but the Devil laughs if off and says, "Is it? I don't care."

look forward to a day when I can relax and read through an issue of *Hellblazer* without being distracted by my own mangling of the main character's name.

I've fully accepted the fact that the correct way to say John's surname is to rhyme it with "fine," and I ask you, dear reader, to join me in my quest to right the wrongs of those who follow the lead of Chester Williams and his ilk. Don't be like Gene Wilder in *Young Frankenstein*. Be like Igor. It's not "Fronkensteen," for Pete's sake, it's "Frankenstein." Likewise, it's not "ConstanTEEN" — it's "ConstanTINE." Rhymes with "wine." Rhymes with "fine." Rhymes with "line."

The Constantine Creed

Those of you who are already using the proper pronunciation (wine, dine, fine, stein), don't change a thing. Keep on keepin' on. You're the bee's knees. To anyone else still pronouncing the name incorrectly (teen, ween, steen), please repeat after me:

> I hereby pledge, from this day forward, to respectfully pronounce the surname of John Constantine such that it rhymes with the word "wine" and not the word "teen." Whenever reading an issue of *Hellblazer*, or any other work containing the marvelous magus's name, I will recall this pledge and do my absolute best to adhere to it, thereby doing my part to make things right in the universe. I will make sure that the name Constantine is always shown the respect it deserves, forevermore.

And with that, we're off to the pub.

The Many Faces of Papa Midnite

by Frank Schildiner

> Ever have one of "those" friends? You know the kind. The kind of friend who always leaves you with the distinct impression that it was only a matter of time before they were going to take some time out of their busy schedule to finally getting around to killing you? Well, Papa Midnite was the poster child for one of those "friends."
> — John Constantine, *Hellblazer* #10 (July 2017)

Papa Midnite: enemy, ally, gangster, and trickster — a persistent, protean persona who has proved to be a fan favorite since *Hellblazer*'s start in 1988. Since issue #1, Midnite's place as a reluctant ally and recurring menace has provided some of John Constantine's most memorable tales.

One persistent feature of Midnite's story is the often-inexplicable set of changes surrounding the immortal voodoo master and organized criminal. As stressed at the outset, Midnite is a mutable character who presents faces that hide the truth behind his actions. Here are the known faces of the legendary antagonist who haunts John Constantine's universe.

We first meet Papa Midnite in New York, sought after by Constantine. There is a debt between them, stemming from John having conned the voodoo king out of fifty thousand dollars and a relic called the Ace of Winchesters. Despite that history, Constantine seeks out Midnite's help in regard to a tricky situation involving his friend Gary Lester and the hunger demon, Mnemoth.

Papa Midnite never forgets a face.

Papa Midnite in this incarnation is a huge, bloated man with a bald head, expensive suits, and a crude, borderline barbaric, speech pattern. He regularly threatens the living and risen dead and conducts conversations with the skull of his dead sister, Cedilla. However, readers soon learn this is a mere façade for a terrifying magus who casts off his thin veneer of civilization with apparent ease. A hint of horror lays hidden beneath the surface, as we learn that one of Midnite's sources of income is pit fighting using zombies, whom he animates via magic. Constantine expresses some understandable disregard for this brutal form of entertainment.

The true Papa Midnite, the mightiest houngan in the mystic world, later appears in a costume quite unforgettable to *Hellblazer* readers. Garbed in a white tuxedo jacket, a matching top hat, and a grass skirt, Midnite appears to be the embodiment of Baron Samedi, the legendary Loa (voodoo spirit) of the dead. This visual incarnation is perhaps best known to film lovers from Roger Moore's first appearance as James Bond in 1973's *Live and Let Die*. In that film, Trinidadian-American actor Geoffrey Holder plays Samedi. The Baron acts as henchman and assassin for the movie's main villain, Mr. Big, and, like his persona, appears unkillable. His costume, at several points throughout the film, matches that of Papa Midnite, as well as some modern images of the Loa.

This identity reappears in *Hellblazer* #72-75, when Papa Midnite plots revenge on John Constantine. This attempt fails, and the voodoo king receives retribution from the spirit of the woman he calls his sister – whom he had trapped in Hell as a means of gaining power. The result? Midnite throws himself off the Empire State Building, and Constantine hears a report of the man's death in graphic detail.

This first incarnation of Papa Midnite never returns, but the character does come back five years later in a different physical form, in 2005's *Hellblazer Special: Papa Midnite* miniseries, from writer Mat Johnson and artists Ronald Wimberly, Tony Akins, Dan Green, and Ronald Wimberly. This Midnite is slim, handsome, and well-dressed, possessing a zig-zag beard and a Trilby hat. He is the very image of a successful man, albeit one who fills police officers and criminals with respectful fear. He possesses unseen layers, which explain some of his latter-day deviltry toward Constantine. The *Papa Midnite* miniseries reveals his childhood, back in the 18th century, when he and his twin sister Luna used his slight magical skill to make their way as con-artists in New York City.[1]

In this story, young Linton Midnite is the quintessence of an arrogant grifter, using his skills to steal from sailors and slaves. His arrogance is evident in his every action, which ultimately causes a terrible downfall. After promising magical powder able to block bullets to an Ashanti warrior forced into slavery, Midnite brings about the deaths of dozens of slaves by giving them a mixture of pepper and other non-magical items that fail to protect anyone. The survivors force Midnite to cut off his sister's head, then curse him with immortality. This form of immortality is unique, condemning him to eternal life for as long as

---

[1] *Hellblazer* #72 reveals Midnite's fist name of Linton. That same issue calls his sister Cedella and places their birth in Trenchtown, Jamaica, in the 1960s, but the *Papa Midnite* miniseries implies that backstory to be a fabrication on his part, intended to scam his enemies. In the miniseries, her name is Luna, and she and Linton are born to slaves in Manhattan.

white men rule over black men in North America. The path of the man we know as Papa Midnite is forged by his arrogance, and in the blood of his many victims.

Later in this miniseries, we meet a different version of Papa Midnite. Now a trained practitioner of the mystic arts, he once again assists a slave rebellion against the American colonists. His idea, with help from the trickster god Anansi, is to aid another failing uprising in the hope that this will eventually lead to the end of slavery, and thus free him from his curse. Midnite's plan fails, however, and he ends up both burned at the stake and, thanks to his immortal nature, subsequently shipped off to the West Indies as a slave.

Thus ends another phase of Papa Midnite's existence, with the blood-soaked trickster brought low by Anansi and the son of one of his victims. No longer do we see the voodoo king seeking a cure for his curse, but rather a man who accepts that he shall exist throughout the centuries, so he may as well increase his power and position in society. We even gain a hint, in *Papa Midnite* #4, of why Midnite, in the monthly *Hellblazer* title, had looked like a bloated barbarian in a grass skirt and top hat, thanks to a conversation between him and Constantine:

> **John Constantine:** Look who's talking. I wasn't the one who used to wear a grass skirt and top hat.
>
> **Papa Midnite:** Maybe I chose to let you see me as you expected, white boy. Or maybe you could never see me any other way.

In 2011, the entire DC Comics universe was completely altered with the release of the company's *Flashpoint* crossover story arc, and the *Papa Midnite* miniseries marked the gangster's last true pre-*Flashpoint* appearance. However, he does appear in a non-speaking cameo at Constantine's wedding to Epiphany Greaves in *Hellblazer* #275, as a figure in a top hat.

The post-*Flashpoint* Papa Midnite, introduced in 2013's *Constantine* #4, appears as a combination of the brutal gangster of his *Hellblazer* debut and the suave, dangerous magus and organized crime boss from his solo miniseries. Here, Midnite is a bald, beardless, muscular man, dressed entirely in leathers decorated with fangs and teeth. This face of the protean magus is revealed after Constantine is captured by Midnite's thugs for stealing a speaking skull.

> This is Papa Midnite. Haitian voodoo sorcerer, sensualist, and slaver. Makes a plaything of the dead. Leads a brutally violent street gang. Styles himself as the meanest, bloodiest, most gruesome player in all of Manhattan. And that's exactly what he is.
>
> — *Constantine* #4 (2013)

"The meanest, bloodiest, most gruesome player in all of Manhattan."

This updated version of Papa Midnite has lost the debonair qualities of the past and now lives openly as a criminal boss. He is the voodoo king merged with the savage leaders of modern street gangs. Though Constantine considers him the "mystic godfather," this is a misnomer. The gangsters portrayed in Mario Puzo's *Godfather* novels possess a veneer of civility; a façade of respectability. This Papa Midnite, with his fang-covered leathers, bloody machete, and cadre of street criminals, more resembles brutal crime leaders like Mexican cartel boss Joaquín Guzmán (a.k.a. El Chapo) or narcotics mastermind Nicky Barnes.

Nonetheless, this new Midnite is a powerful presence – one who helps Constantine battle the evil Cult of the Cold Flame. He even rescues the protagonist from death in *Constantine* #6, despite his reluctance to do so. There is a level of respect here, with the two magicians acting as uneasy allies in conflicts against greater dangers.

This persona of Papa Midnite represents the modern age of comics – one in which heroes and villains share astonishing similarities. Midnite is a brutal, dangerous criminal; a mystic who uses his powers as a means of reinforcing his hold over the underworld. Nevertheless, he will fight against the forces of darkness when the need arises. Self-interest seems to be this Papa Midnite's greatest motivation, as well as a need for respect from anyone he encounters. This is the Midnite of the modern day, though it is uncertain, based on DC's ever-changing universe, how long this version shall endure.

Papa Midnite also exists in two alternate universes, demonstrating additional archetypes of the character. The first shows up in the 2005 film *Constantine*, starring Keanu Reeves as the title character. In this film, John Constantine is a dark-haired American exorcist residing in Los Angeles. He possesses some of the comic Constantine's cynical attitude, though his motivations are entirely different. While a poor adaptation of the *Hellblazer* universe, the film is an enjoyable story with some respectable writing and acting.

In this world, Papa Midnite exists as a well-dressed, Borsalino hat-wearing bar owner who once fought against the forces of darkness. Entry into the club can only be attained through the use of psychic powers: a bouncer holds up the back of a card, and an individual seeking entry must state what is on the hidden side. Constantine, of course, enters with ease. Meanwhile, his assistant Chas Kramer (played by Shia LaBeouf with zero similarities to his comic book analogue, not even in surname), is left outside due to a lack of skills and knowledge of the test.

The film and television representations of Papa Midnite.

Prior to the film's events, Midnite had made a pact of neutrality, protecting the balance between Above and Below. Played by Beninese American actor Djimon Hounsou, his presence is a standout in the story. The conversations between these versions of Constantine and Midnite provide some of the movie's most enjoyable moments, while also establishing their characters.

> **Constantine:** A demon just attacked me right out in the open on Figueroa.
>
> **Midnite:** They don't like you, John. How many have you deported back to Hell?
>
> **Constantine:** Not some angry half-breed, Midnite. A full-fledged demon, here on our plane.
>
> **Midnite:** Clearly, I do not have to remind you that is impossible.
>
> **Constantine:** And yesterday, I saw a soldier demon trying to chew its way out through a little girl.
>
> **Midnite:** Listen, John. Demons stay in Hell, angels in Heaven. The great détente of the original superpowers.

Later, when Constantine demands the use of Midnite's electric chair (introduced in 1988's *Hellblazer* #2), we see a hint of the gangster's true power. Tossing John across a room with a flick of his hands and some mystic might, he then burns the exorcist with a pair of glowing hands.

> **Midnite:** You dare? In my house?
>
> **Constantine:** Is this neutral? Bullshit! You're the only one still playing by the rules, Midnite, and while you've been imitating Switzerland, people are dying. Hennessy, Beeman – they were your friends once, too, remember? I need your help! Consider it a last request.
>
> **Midnite:** You play a dangerous game.

This Midnite possesses a genial personality when not doing business with angels and demons. He smiles at Chas's comments about demons and even provides the gear required for saving the world from Mammon.

The tie-in novelization by writer John Shirley provides further details about this iteration of Midnite. We learn that zombie pit fights do occur at the bar, and that the audience is not limited to Hell's denizens on Earth. The zombie gladiators also entertain Hollywood's most decadent wealthy residents. The fighters themselves are made up of failed actors, models, and reality stars – most of whom have lost too much money at Midnite's gambling tables. The criminal persona of Papa Midnite is quite present, though in a less obvious manner than most versions.

One of his most fascinating aspects is his vault. Shirley describes, in some detail, a fabulous hidden basement guarded by the stolen spirits of cult leader Charles Manson and serial killer Richard Ramirez. Among Midnite's collection are such items as the head of Blackbeard the Pirate, the dead body of an unknown saint, boxes of relics of Muslim saints, and several unique curios. The novel also contains the following detail:

> A set of Archie jam jar glasses. Constantine carefully lifted one up. "A full set?" he asked.
>
> "No," Midnite said, with regret. "No Jughead. I've tried eBay. All the stores. No luck."

Papa Midnite resurfaced on the *Constantine* television show, appearing three times as an antagonist played by American actor Michael James Shaw. In these appearances, Midnite is a criminal leader and a master of voodoo. He is again well-dressed and smooth-talking, though a feared gang boss and dark magus. Constantine, very ably played by English actor Matt Ryan, has a relationship with Midnite reminiscent of that portrayed in *Hellblazer*'s earliest issues, as illustrated in this dialogue from the episode "Waiting for the Man":

> **Constantine:** You finally did it. You traded your last thread of honor for a lousy, bloody bounty.
>
> **Midnite:** Your next words will be your last, Constantine. Choose them wisely.
>
> **Constantine:** There's a girl out there with a depraved killer. I'm her only chance of rescue. Can any bounty be worth that stain on your soul?
>
> **Midnite:** I gave up on my soul a long time ago. I'm sorry for the girl, but yes, the bounty is worth it. Your sacrifice will free my sister's soul from eternal damnation. A life for a life.
>
> **Constantine:** No one has that kind of power. Except the Brujería.
>
> **Midnite:** It seems that you angered them, John. Not your smartest move.

Constantine: Apparently not.

Midnite: If not me, someone else would've collected. Who would dare deny them?

They despise each other, yet briefly come together as a team when faced with a terrible menace. There is no chance of rapprochement between the two – and even when they are briefly allied, their differences are stark and hint at future battles. This Papa Midnite combines many of the previous incarnations' elements, though few positive characteristics emerge throughout all three episodes.

What does the future hold for Papa Midnite? That lies in the hands of DC Comics and its entertainment divisions. There are many archetypes available, and each possesses fascinating motivations and behaviors. I, for one, look forward to seeing which face of Papa Midnite shall appear next.

Ghosts, Grimoires, and Dealing with Demons: *Hellblazer*'s Real-World Magic

by Genevieve Williams

By any measure, *Hellblazer* is a work of remarkable creative imagination. The occult detective in his current form owes much to John Constantine, street-level wizard; it's doubtful we'd have Harry Dresden without *Hellblazer*.

Yet for all his novelty, in the outlines of his character, his magical praxis, and the world he inhabits, Constantine draws on a rich occult legacy. Throughout *Hellblazer*, we see him, his friends and allies, and his enemies engage in magical workings drawn from or based on humanity's centuries-old real-world attempts to make sense of and control our world, and the wealth of imaginative theory underlying those real-world formulae. Historical figures such as Johann Faust (a German magician during the Renaissance) and John Dee (court astrologer to Queen Elizabeth I) are among Constantine's antecedents, leavening our imaginative notions of the canonical magician.

Even when an aristocrat, the magician is a social outsider, viewed with suspicion even, or maybe especially, when her services are necessary. She exercises power based on knowledge not readily available to others (though Constantine points out more than once that *anyone* can do magic – his own life serving as ample reason, however, for why more people don't). Language is of critical importance, as is the power of names. The magician is often presented as seeking power for selfish reasons, and Constantine is no exception, though his idealistic notions of using magic for good persist for most of the series. Despite his best efforts, the magician is often described in the same terms once applied to Lord Byron: mad, bad, and dangerous to know.[1]

Replace Constantine's ever-present trenchcoat with a robe, and he'd be right at home in any number of wizardly tales (and that coat acquires some magical characteristics of its own, as in the arc "The Devil's Trench Coat," in *Hellblazer* #283-286). However, there's another stripe of magical practitioner aside from the likes of the demon-dealing Faust and courtly Dee. In his working-class origins and punk-rock attitude, Constantine has much in common with the cunning folk, historical practitioners of folk magic in Britain and elsewhere who provided such valuable public services as protection or love charms, finding lost or stolen property, and healing the sick. The cunning man (in Britain, about two-thirds of them were men) presents a stark contrast to the aristocratic Faustian sorcerer whose motives are both selfish and arcane, but he is every bit as much an heir to Europe's magical legacy.

What We Talk About When We Talk About Magic

Think of the word "magic" and you'll probably think of either stage trickery or the occult arts. Both carry connotations of deception, secrecy, and the uncanny, even if one is intended as entertainment and the other purports to call upon supernatural forces for the purpose of, as Aleister Crowley put it in *Magick in Theory and Practice*, "causing Change to occur in conformity with Will." But why does magic have such an unsavory reputation?

As with so much else, we can blame the ancient Greeks. The word "magic" is derived from a term for a Persian religious figure, from an era when religion, magic, and science (such as it was) were all basically the same thing: humanity's nascent attempts to make some sense of, and assert control over, our environment and lives. The Greeks did not mean anything complimentary by the word, Greece and Persia being historic enemies, and magic came to represent a practice with religious connotations that was foreign, contrary to

---

[1] A phrase originally used by Anglo-Irish aristocrat and novelist Lady Caroline Lamb to describe her lover, British poet and politician Lord Byron; also the title of John Trumble's essay, elsewhere in this anthology.

nature, possibly fraudulent, and certainly dangerous – connotations that magic has retained to the present day.

The advent and then dominance of Christianity in the Western world solidified and even calcified the distinction between magic and religion. Magic itself was increasingly defined as antisocial or deviant behavior; a religious ritual performed improperly, or in some way inverted from its legitimate operation, could be deemed magical, as could any operation seen to engage with unnatural forces. Today, the *Oxford Illustrated History of Witchcraft and Magic* defines magic as "a constellation of what are officially regarded as deviant ritualistic or ritualized ways of dealing with an individual's immediate problems by achieving access to sacred power which demands or compels the assistance of non-human entities."

During the Renaissance, however, magic accrued to itself some legitimacy as a branch of intellectual engagement and research, in part due to the rediscovery of classical texts. From this period date a number of canonical names, translations, and collections of magical treatises and spells, several of which appear in *Hellblazer*. But the Renaissance also marked the beginning of a great sorting-out of knowledge into the material, concrete, testable, and reproducible on the one hand, and the spiritual, aetheric, malleable, and unpredictable on the other. As understanding of the natural world increasingly became the domain of the scientist, religion was left to the exercise of social and moral authority.

Yet from its past, this evolving learned culture had inherited a belief in the supernatural, and especially supernatural beings. Christian monotheism would allow for only one god; thus, all other supernatural entities had to be either allies of God (angels and saints) or else in league with Satan (demons). Interestingly enough, the term "demon" is also Greek in origin, and originally meant a benign and even helpful spirit, less powerful than a god, but capable of aiding humans and interceding on their behalf. Hmm.

This paved the way for all magic to be considered derived from the Devil, and magical power to be achieved through satanic pacts. Lurid accounts of such pacts were a heady feature of witch trial accounts from the early modern period. Constantine deals frequently with demons, not to mention Satan himself, and was a recipient of a demonic blood transfusion early in *Hellblazer*'s run. On the one hand, long-standing folk practices acknowledged that there might be forces at work in the world that were natural in origin yet not understood. On the other hand, they also left a certain amount of wiggle room.

Cunning folk, for instance, were not typically viewed as demonic. The line between a prayer for assistance and an incantation to summon a familiar spirit could be a diffuse one indeed.

All of this makes for a rich history of real-world magical theory and practice, which the writers and artists of *Hellblazer* have incorporated into the story of John Constantine in a variety of ways, from a magical worldview that admits angels and demons, to mechanical techniques of achieving magical effects, to an emphasis on language and naming. Historical personages, grimoires, and uncanny places enrich *Hellblazer*'s setting, as well as entities drawn from real-world myth and legend. The cosmology of *Hellblazer* is a biblical one, and a Christian one at that, with God and the Devil as the goalposts in the endless contest for humanity's souls. Yet the reality of *Hellblazer* is malleable, and sometimes other mythologies assert themselves.

Riding the Synchronicity Freeway

Key to the magical worldview is the understanding that everything is fraught with potential significance. In the real world, manifestations of this belief range from the obnoxious (everything happens for a reason) to the plausible (there's a causality at work here, we just can't perceive all of it from this vantage), but in a setting in which magic unquestionably exists, it is necessary to question every apparent coincidence.

In *Hellblazer*, this is referred to as synchronicity, which Carl Jung defined as coincidental events that acquire meaning by their juxtaposition with one another, even though they have no causal connection. It tends to explicitly manifest in *Hellblazer* at those moments when Constantine most needs a convenient coincidence, such as in *Hellblazer* #102 ("The Single-Sided Coin"), when John is going through one of his periodic bouts of aimlessness and, as he puts it, "manipulates coincidence" to find where he needs to go – and ends up at the Ravenscar Secure Facility for the Dangerously Deranged, the aptly named institution that left serious wounds on his psyche following the Newcastle incident. In issue #103 ("The Trouble with Worms"), he describes it: "You move and stand still at the same time... you know where you're going without ever having traveled this way before." *Hellblazer* #119 ("Undertow"), fleshes synchronicity out further as something a magician can develop conscious awareness of and manipulate; events occur in patterns that, while coincidental, are predictable. And in issue #229 ("With a Little Help from My Friends"), Constantine describes it as "coincidence speaking to you with the voice of God."

With synchronicity, *Hellblazer* suggests that the magician has a special relationship with reality, an ability to affect events around her simply by existing.

Tools of the Trade

The association of the magician or wizard with a wand is so strong that it's one of the first things a young wizard receives in J. K. Rowling's Harry Potter novels, an occult relationship so special that each student is chosen by the wand she or he is to receive. But the idea of the magic wand can be traced back to the Middle Ages and *The Oathbound Book of Honorius*. From there, the concept of using a wand to summon and control spiritual entities passed into the *Key of Solomon*, an occult text from the 1500s that remained popular for centuries and was a foundational text in 19th-century occultism.

It's interesting, then, that Constantine uses wands so rarely – though he's been known to do so on occasion. In fact, his tools mostly seem to come out when the stakes are high, as in the "Critical Mass" story arc, in which John needs to rescue Syder and the other children's souls possessed by the demon Buer, while somehow contriving to avoid damnation himself. An illustration on page 21 of issue #94 ("The Devil and the Deep Blue Sea") shows quintessential magician's tools: a spellbook, a knife decorated with magical symbols, a cup, a box decorated with more symbols (which might contain anything), and an amulet – an object which has been imbued with protective or enhancing powers.

Magician's tools: knife, grimoire, chalice, amulet. And what's in that box?

Yet more than once, Constantine demonstrates that almost *anything* can be used as a tool, if the magician's will is strong enough. In "Wheels of Change" (issue #233), while performing a mirror-cage spell, Constantine lights a cigarette and pronounces it a flaming wand. Why not? As he says all the way back in issue #3 ("Going for It"), all you need is the right contacts and a bit of nerve – and it's a good thing, too, since he also admits that most of his magical kit is missing. On page 15, however, we do see him making use of a sword, incense, an amulet, and an altar on which various ritual objects have been arranged.

On some level, anything can be a magician's tool if the magician's will is strong enough. Hence, a cigarette becomes a flaming wand.

Another canonical magician's tool is the spellbook, or grimoire, the latter word having the same derivation as the word "grammar." Magic and language are inextricably associated; even today, we make reference to magic words in mundane contexts, like getting a small child to say "please" in order to get what she or he wants – the very definition of a magic word, really. The most cliché of magic words, "Abracadabra," dates to the third century CE, when it was prescribed for use on magical amulets to cure disease. Grimoires might contain such prescriptions, along with instructions for various magical operations, the names of demons and other entities, helpful illustrations, and so forth. Among the historically extant grimoires that make their appearances in *Hellblazer* is the *Grimorium Verum*, an 18th-century compendium for calling forth a range of powers for various purposes.

Grimoires are, in a sense, recipe books, specifying ingredients for workings that are often difficult or even dangerous to acquire; eye of newt and toe of frog don't even begin to cover it. It's a general rule of thumb that the bigger, more powerful, and more supernatural the effect you're trying to achieve, the stranger, rarer, and more expensive the ingredients will be. In *Hellblazer*, some of these stranger spell components include the electric chair from Sing Sing Prison (issue #2, "Feast of Friends"), the heart of the angel Gabriel (issue #66, "Down to Earth"), the head of Bran the Blessed (issue #113, "You're Just a..."), soil from Hell (issue #173, "In the City of Angels"), Constantine's sweat at the moment that he commits a murder (issue #291, "Dark Magic"), a cocktail of Constantine's blood, sweat, urine, semen, and tears (*Vertigo Secret Files: Hellblazer*, "The Gangster, The Whore and the Magician"), and more.

Grimoires can also be repositories of magical sigils, pictorial symbols of an entity or demon who might be summoned or bound to a particular task. The best-known magical symbol is the pentagram or five-pointed star, today primarily associated with Wicca but with a history of use stretching back to Babylonia. Stars with six or more points are used as well, along with any number of other signs and illustrations. In *Hellblazer*, these are most frequently seen when Constantine is trying to summon something, protect himself from something, or both.

Given magic's unsavory reputation, it's not surprising that grimoires themselves carry an aspect of the forbidden. In *Hellblazer* #243-244 ("The Mortification of the Flesh"), Constantine makes use of the Vatican's fabled Black Library. This seems to be something invented specifically for *Hellblazer*, but the notion of hidden archives and secret collections within famous repositories – the Vatican's library and archives are among the oldest and most extensive in the world – is a common one in discourses on magic, and the rediscovery of ancient tomes has historical precedent; see above regarding the Renaissance.[2] Much like spell components, the more obscure and harder a text is to obtain, the more powerful its contents are said to be.

Signs, Portents, and Divinations

There are more forms of divination in the world than we could possibly cover here, and more are being invented all the time (I used to know someone who came up with a method involving Skittles). All of them rely on the human propensity to perceive patterns in random phenomena (speaking of synchronicity...). The tarot deck, for example, is deliberately constructed around a cohesive set of symbols, but the order of the deck when shuffled becomes randomized, leaving the diviner to pick the pattern out of the resulting spread.

Tarot appears only occasionally in *Hellblazer*. Kit Ryan asks Constantine to explain the cards to her in issue #75 ("Act of Union"), and Sting's introduction to DC's *John Constantine: Hellblazer 30th Anniversary Celebration* mentions that

---

[2] This can and does happen in the real world: many of the books of John Dee, the Elizabethan era's most famous magician, wound up in the library at the Royal College of Physicians in London, which put together an exhibition of them in 2016. I was in London at the time and got to see them.

John has studied tarot. In *Hellblazer* #39 ("The Hanged Man"), Zed helps John with his Golden Boy problem by reading a tarot deck for him, while in *The Books of Magic* Book II, John has Madame Xanadu perform a reading to determine whether Timothy Hunter is in danger. In John Shirley's novel *War Lord*, Constantine even dates a tarot card reader named Tchalai Dermitzel, and he seems to respect her craft. However, he admits in issue #97 ("The Nature of the Beast") that he has little faith in card readings.

Typically, we don't see John reading the cards himself, other than in *The Sandman Presents: Love Street*, during his teenage years. This is possibly due to the truism that the cartomancer cannot read for herself, and when other people come to John it's not for tarot card readings. More likely, Constantine's propensity to wing it doesn't mix very well with the structure of tarot, with its set imagery and layouts of cards. Or perhaps John himself is too archetypal, resembling in his attitude and behavior the Fool of the canonical tarot deck; Book IV of *The Books of Magic* suggests as much, in the familiar figure Tim Hunter meets near the end of the universe. And in *Hellblazer* #36 ("The Undiscovered Country"), Marj does a spread that is obviously about John, and we get details of her interpretation, though not of what cards she's looking at (aside from the Devil).

Hellblazer #39's title, "The Hanged Man," references one of the cards of the tarot's Major Arcana, and is generally taken to signify being in a position of figurative as well as literal suspension. On page 14, a three-card spread is drawn for Constantine: the Hanged Man signifying his present position, the Tower indicating something he must pass through, and the Magus signifying where he wants to be. This is pretty easy to interpret, even if you don't know that the Tower signifies catastrophe; the spread can be read as the arc of the entire *Hellblazer* series, except that there ought to be multiple Towers. Then, in issue #97, John receives a card reading from God himself, in the guise of a fortune teller named Tom. He declines to look at the final card, and so doesn't know, although God (and the reader) does, that his journey will be iterative, not linear: both who John was, and who he will be, are represented by the Fox.

Constantine doesn't use divination himself all that often; one gets the impression that it's not his forte, and in *Swamp Thing* #70 ("The Secret Life of Plants"), he consults a number of divinatory specialists rather than perform any divination himself. However, one example occurs early on in *Hellblazer*, in issue #4 ("Waiting for the Man"), when he and Zed are looking for his vanished niece Gemma. Constantine makes a pendulum out of a toy crocodile that he gave

Gemma as a souvenir, dangling it over a map to triangulate the child's location. Pendulums have a long history of being used for this purpose, as well as answering yes/no questions (the pendulum's movement indicates the answer) and dowsing for water, as well as ley-lines – Mercury makes a reference to the latter in *Hellblazer* #15 ("Shepherd's Warning"). In the same scene, Zed engages in automatic writing – which, like the pendulum, purports to rely on outside agencies to determine the writing utensil's movement. Interestingly, while both divinations get Constantine and Zed to the right general location, they wind up having to ask a local child for directions once they arrive.

Another common form of divination is scrying, most canonically represented as crystal gazing. This can be done using the quintessential crystal ball, as well as mirrors, metal bowls filled with water, or even clear pools – anything is said to do, so long as it provides a reflective surface (the Mirror of Galadriel, from J.R.R. Tolkien's *The Lord of the Rings*, is another example). In *Hellblazer* #189-192 ("Staring at the Wall"), Constantine and his allies make use of a television screen as a kind of scrying crystal. They're even able to change the channels. And in issue #233 ("Wheels of Change"), John constructs a magical device called a mirror-cage to "reveal that which is hidden," specifically the madness that was taken from him at Ravenscar. "Mirror-cage" is a term that appears to be unique to *Hellblazer*, but the use of mirrors in magic is well established. In issue #242 ("The Laughing Magician"), we get the series' most dramatic example of a scrying mirror: Lord Calvin Burnham's window into Hell.

Illusions, Delusions, and Jedi Mind Tricks

Magic is often the craft of illusion – stage magic, to be sure, but there are also numerous examples in *Hellblazer* of causing people to see things that aren't there, or to perceive something that *is* there as something other than it is. The concept of the *glamour* is an old one, often associated with fairies and considered fundamental to fairy trickery. Constantine's use of illusion is often for the purpose of gaining access to places where he'd otherwise be denied entry; whether visiting Blathoxi in Hell or seeking audience with the angel Gabriel in an exclusive London club, it turns out that it's just a matter of wearing the right necktie – or appearing to do so, anyway.

In *Hellblazer* #52-55 ("Royal Blood"), Constantine makes use of illusion a few times, again to mess with the sort of upper-crust aristocrats for whom he has little respect. A more complex illusion, known in *Hellblazer*'s "Red Sepulchre" storyline (issues #177-180) as the Ward of Stolen Light, switches

A useful and terrifying scrying mirror: a window into Hell.

what's visible through two different windows in order to fool attackers. This one is interesting because it relies both on physics (the visual perception of reflected light) and the concept of the scrying crystal – a window, after all, can be a mirror under the right conditions.

More dramatically, Constantine's adventures with Marj, Mercury, and their friends involves a great deal of psychic manipulation, telepathy, and straight-up attempts at mind control. Much of this comes from Mercury, who is both unusually perceptive for her age and talented in ways that seem more psychic than psychological. Mercury's friends seem like refugees from the 1960s and early 1970s – they even refer to themselves as the Freedom Mob – when parapsychology enjoyed a brief period of mainstream vogue. Mercury's name is also interesting, being the name of a Roman god syncretized with Hermes – a deity of communication, trickery, and magic. Mercury's psychic skills increase steadily during her adventures with John, until she's able to use them to help thwart a plot to raise the ancient god Jallakuntilliokan (*Hellblazer* #14-22). Though Constantine himself is capable of this type of direct psychic manipulation, we rarely see him making use of it.

Ain't Afraid of No Ghosts

Ghosts occur frequently in *Hellblazer*, not the least of which are those haunting Constantine himself: the spirits of his friends, allies, and lovers whose deaths are laid to his account. Ghosts are typically considered to be the souls of the unquiet dead, those for whom the manner of their death prevents their moving on to the afterlife. This presupposes a reality in which the soul can continue to exist separately from the body, a duality that is key to *Hellblazer* in other respects. The ghost being such an entity, it can be interacted with and acted on in various ways. A number of real-world magical operations and techniques have evolved throughout the centuries for dealing with hauntings. Some of these have made their way into *Hellblazer*, where the presence and activities of ghosts is typically far more obvious and dramatic than what are taken to be their manifestations in the real world.

A tidy example is the Neil Gaiman-authored one-shot "Hold Me" (*Hellblazer* #27), in which the ghost of a man named Jacko, who froze to death, kills at least one other person in his quest for warmth. Constantine is able to satisfy the ghost with a hug. It's a simple little story, but it demonstrates one of the traditional methods for dealing with ghosts: figure out whatever it is they need, and provide it. This is easy in "Hold Me," since the ghost is capable of speech, but that isn't always the case.

Another example is issue #31 ("Mourning of the Magician"), in which the ghost of Constantine *père* haunts not his son John, but rather his granddaughter Gemma – even though John is the reason Thomas Constantine can't move on. John relates an adolescent attempt to cast a spell on his father, not really expecting it to work, and then invents a means to arrest the spell using formaldehyde that inadvertently tied his father's ghost to the mortal plane. The episode ends with the destruction of the spell's remnants by fire, a time-honored way of destroying haunted things. (Remember the Overlook Hotel from *The Shining*?)

Showing a ghost how to move on.

In *Hellblazer* #47-48 ("The Pub Where I Was Born" and "Love Kills"), fire is instead the catalyst. Though one of the owners of the Northampton Arms pub is already a ghost when the henchman for a corrupt developer destroys the building by arson, the death of the other owner in the blaze would be a textbook case for creating a ghost, if such a textbook existed. Constantine's solution to the ghosts' vengeful, murderous rampage is remarkably low-key: he talks to them, persuading the couple to abandon their course with an offer to rebuild the pub, using the resources of the developer they were about to kill. Though John's method here isn't magical at all – in fact, it's one of many occasions when he uses persuasion, not magic – it's another example of a ghost being assuaged by having some unmet need fulfilled.

In contrast, there's the story related by Constantine's overly loyal friend Chas Chandler in issue #77 ("And the Crowd Goes Wild"), in which John is called to deal with a haunting by a pair of Victorian-era ghosts. The trick here is that one ghost is the victim of the other, and Constantine wants to see the innocent headed safely to heaven while ensuring that the perpetrator goes to Hell. As is often the case, the spell goes wrong, and Chas never does find out how his friend survived the outcome. But the spell itself, with candles to light the path for the one ghost, to be knocked over and extinguished to trap the other, has precedent in real-world attempts to fascinate and trap spirits.[3]

Then there's the "Warped Notions" arc in *Hellblazer* #85-88, in which Constantine is enlisted by the ghost of Sir Francis Dashwood to help contend with the Everything Virus, which appears to be causing reality to come apart at the seams. Constantine eventually realizes that Dashwood is responsible for the whole affair and imprisons the ghost in a tree with the use of a binding spell. In addition to being an example of imprisoning a ghost whom John has found the cost of satisfying to be too high, this story is interesting for the inclusion of Dashwood, who was a real person and the founder of the Hellfire Club, the sort of secret society that shows up repeatedly in *Hellblazer*. Dashwood, in turn, repeatedly references Paracelsus, a 16th-century alchemist and astrologer who was also a noted physician and an influence on Rosicrucianism.

In short, Dashwood is exactly the sort of character to lend *Hellblazer* some depth of detail that has the advantage of being based to some extent on real-world events. Intriguingly, *The Sandman* #29 and *The Dreaming* #7 strongly imply that Dashwood is John Constantine's ancestor, since he is likely the illegitimate father of Lady Johanna Constantine.

A Demon-Haunted World

As we've seen above, magic hasn't always been considered demonic at all times and in all places, even when it did consistently receive social side-eye. But as examples like Faust show, some magicians do deal with demons at least some of the time, and the world of *Hellblazer* is rife with them. While Constantine also has dealings with nature spirits like Jack Green and non-Christian deities such as the Lord of the Dance, most of the time, when he encounters a supernatural entity, it has some connection to the infernal.

Hellblazer's very first story arc, in issues #1-2 ("Hunger" and "Feast of Friends"), involves such an entity, as Constantine must deal with the hunger

---

[3] Whether such attempts work is beyond the scope of this essay, but if you try it, make sure you have a reliable accomplice and a lot of salt. Just saying.

demon Mnemoth, first bound into a child's body by a Sudanese magician and later inadvertently released by Gary Lester, John's old mate from his Mucous Membrane days and the Newcastle debacle. This demon, which compels its victims to consume the objects of their deepest desire and devotion, is one of two general types that we encounter in *Hellblazer*: a creature of human appetites turned to obsessions. Another example is Buer, who has an obsession with children reminiscent of pedophilia, and whom John defeats in his rescue of his friends' son Syder from possession in *Hellblazer* #92-96 ("Critical Mass").

The other type emerges in *Hellblazer* #3 ("Going for It"). These demons also prey on human weaknesses, but in their stock-market trade in human souls, they remind one of the bureaucratic demons of C.S. Lewis's *The Screwtape Letters*. When Constantine contacts Blathoxi, a big player in the soul market, their subsequent conversation sounds like a pair of stockbrokers discussing insider trading. It's funny, but also highlights an important aspect of dealing with demons: there are rules to be followed, and equally important is knowing *which* rules to follow.

Contrast Constantine's summoning ritual here – when he freely admits that he's winging it, that "all you need are the right contacts and a bit of nerve" – with the attempted exorcism at Newcastle, in which he follows the ritual script exactly and triggers a disaster. We see both that his confidence has grown since the debacle, and that reproducibility, unlike in science, is not a sure characteristic of magic, which is dependent far more on belief than on technique (science, on the other hand, works whether you believe in it or not).

The Newcastle incident is both a canonical example of a ritual involving demons, and a great demonstration of how such a magical working can go horribly wrong. In issue #11 ("Newcastle: A Taste of Things to Come"), Constantine and company return to a seedy nightclub where his band, Mucous Membrane, recently played, because one of their magically inclined friends got an inkling of something going on there. They find the aftermath of a terror elemental summoned by the club owner's daughter, and John – who, one senses, has been *itching* to try something like this – insists on summoning a demon to deal with it.

Everyone who has read *Hellblazer* knows what happens next: they do the ritual, all right, but in not really understanding what they're doing, even though they follow the directions, Constantine unleashes one of *Hellblazer*'s more enduring recurring villains, the demon Nergal, and gets some of his friends killed. Not only are demons tricky to deal with, but this episode establishes something important about the power of names. In magic, they're more than something to put on a name tag; as the demon says, "The character you described was mine – but Sagatana's not the name that fits. And thus your invocation lacked the weight of magical imperative."

Constantine occasionally allies with demons – even Nergal – but *Hellblazer* never lets us forget that demons are not human, and they have priorities that humans would recognize as both selfish and twisted. This is in line with how demons are depicted in the discourses and grimoires that serve as some of *Hellblazer*'s source material. It still allows for complexity, such as in the recurring character of Chantinelle, a succubus John nicknames "Ellie," whom we first meet in issue #43 ("Friends in High Places") as John seeks a means of curing the cancer with which he's been afflicted. It's only later, in issue #60 ("Nativity Infernal"), that we learn why she's friendly to John and willing to help him at all; when he opines that she's all right, considering what she is, she reminds him that she's "just polite." Later, in "Fear and Loathing" (issues #64-66), she helps John facilitate the fall of the angel Gabriel, but it's clear that she's doing so to get revenge. Constantine's relationship with Chantinelle throughout the series is transactional in nature, which is presented as the closest to friendship that a demon can get.

Hellblazer isn't above a good demon-possession yarn, though, such as the one we get in issues #52-55 ("Royal Blood"). Constantine is called to an exclusive club for the rich and powerful, where one of the members participated in a demon summoning and wound up possessed. That individual, it turns out, is also a member of the royal family,[4] as writer Garth Ennis intersects the summoning of demons with a critique of power and privilege – a common theme for him, and one articulated in the argument that Constantine and his friend Nigel have as they discuss how to solve the problem.

"Royal Blood" is interesting for a few reasons, not the least of which is that Constantine has learned a thing or two since Newcastle and the séance he led in *Swamp Thing* #50 ("Crisis in Heaven: The End"). He's much more assertive here, both with the circle – three members of which are already dead – and with the demon Calibraxis. (In a nice shoutout to Alan Moore's *From Hell*, *Hellblazer* here posits that the tale of Jack the Ripper related there was, in fact, correct – with the added twist that Sir William Gull was possessed by

---

[4] It's clearly Prince Charles, though that's never explicitly stated (likely for legal reasons).

Calibraxis.) The power of names is important in magic, especially when dealing with entities who will try to cheat you at best, torture and kill you at worst. This is repeatedly emphasized in grimoires purporting to provide instructions to summon such entities: you have to get it right, and that doesn't just mean following the recipe.

A more inventive riff on the possession trope occurs in the "Son of Man" arc (*Hellblazer* #129-133), in which, early in his career, Constantine is charged with resurrecting a gangster's dead child. Knowing this to be impossible – resurrection of the body is established as a magical impossibility in *Hellblazer*[5] – John instead reanimates the body by summoning a fuckpig demon into it. Sixteen years later, he has to deal with the horrific results.

Fooling With the Devil

As mentioned earlier, the world of *Hellblazer* is an explicitly Christian one. Its notions of creation, evil, Heaven, and Hell are built out of a long and imaginative history and mythology that, in *Hellblazer*, springs to full supernatural life. Constantine's world is rife with angels and demons, and while he occasionally deals with non-Christian entities both at home (Jack Green, the Lord of the Dance, Mictlāntēcutli, Julian)[6] and abroad (the Rainbow Serpent, Anansi, Kali Yuga, djinn),[7] there is one supernatural entity who drives much of the events in *Hellblazer* and serves as Constantine's most powerful and challenging opponent. What better adversary than *the* Adversary?

The First of the Fallen, as he's titled in *Hellblazer* – to distinguish him from the character of Lucifer Morningstar, who originated in Gaiman's *The Sandman* – makes his first appearance in issue #42 ("A Drop of the Hard Stuff"), when he comes to claim the soul of Constantine's friend Brendan Finn. John, determined

---

[5] Even though Constantine himself does so during Peter Milligan's run, when he inadvertently reanimates many of Phoebe Clifton-Avery's ancestors while trying to bring her back to life.

[6] The fairy Jack Green appears throughout Paul Jenkins' *Hellblazer* run; Arcadian, Lord of the Dance, befriends John in Garth Ennis's stories; Aztec god Mictlāntēcutli is featured in Mike Carey's *All His Engines*; and Julian, a Sumerian spirit demon, shows up frequently during Peter Milligan's tenure.

[7] The Rainbow Serpent debuts in Eddie Campbell's *Hellblazer* four-parter; African trickster god Anansi causes havoc in Mat Johnson's *Papa Midnite* miniseries; and several djinn feature in Jamie Delano's *Pandemonium*. Kali Yuga, who appears in Milligan's "India" arc, is associated in Hinduism with the demon Kali, though the writer-artist team seems to have confused the entity with the Hindu goddess Kālī.

to save Brendan, tricks the First into drinking holy water, earning himself the Devil's specific and personal enmity. This leads to one of Constantine's cleverer gambits, though one that wouldn't have been possible were the Hell of *Hellblazer* not ruled by a triumvirate rather than the First solely, and were the Fallen not legalistic and bureaucratic by nature: in a fine twist on the trope of selling one's soul (which Faust, among others, was reputed to have done), he offers it to all three of the Lords of Hell, leading to a stalemate in *Hellblazer* #45 ("The Sting").

Of course, this isn't the end of it; after being warned by Chantinelle that the First has sent her to kill him, Constantine hatches a plot with her to kill the Devil, using a blade made from the remains of his former rivals (*Hellblazer* #83, "Rake at the Gates of Hell"). Talk about difficult magical ingredients to acquire. In freeing Syder and other children's souls from the demon Buer, Constantine tricks the First through a magical operation to split his soul in two, consigning all the bits he doesn't want to Hell (issue #96, "Hook, Line, and Sinker"). In terms of real-world analogues, this episode is mostly notable for involving the assistance (not entirely willingly) of Aleister Crowley, probably the individual most responsible for 20th-century popularization of the occult. Indeed, in most of his dealings with the First, whatever magical power John possesses avails him little – and he only gets out of the First claiming his soul with a little direct conversation with God (issue #128, "Sifting Through the Ashes").

The Last Laugh

In the second issue of *The Books of Magic*, John Constantine defines magic to Timothy Hunter thusly: "It's like stepping off the sidewalk into the street. The world still looks the same, on the surface, but you can be hit by a truck at any second. That's magic." Magic in *Hellblazer* is dangerous in a concrete sense, whereas in the real world, magic is often seen as dangerously delusional at best. Yet in its long history, its engagement with the uncanny, the inexplicable, and the strange, it shows itself as an exercise of humanity's creative imagination and ongoing attempt to make sense of human existence.

Magic lives in the interstices between the scientific and the religious, the intuitive and the rational, the things that go bump in the night and the stories we tell ourselves to rationalize them. In incorporating so much of our own occult history and practice, *Hellblazer* paradoxically feels more real.

The Hell They Weren't:
Hellblazer's Lost Lore

by Rich Handley

You've read all of *Swamp Thing*, *Hellblazer*, and *Books of Magic*, yet you're still hungry for more John Constantine. You've devoured the various *Hellblazer* one-shots, miniseries, and original graphic novels, as well as Constantine's guest appearances in other comics, and you've also poured through John Shirley's *Hellblazer* novels, *War Lord* and *Subterranean*. You've watched the movie and the TV shows, and yet you're still not satiated – you want to read everything Constantine, and you want to read it *now*.

Well... you can't. Sorry.

Unfortunately, not every Constantine tale has seen publication, so the sad fact is that you'll never be able to read *everything*. A surprising number of stories featuring John have been announced or conceived of throughout the years that have never seen the light of day, due either to their having been canceled or rejected by DC Comics, or to the writers themselves having walked off the projects. Either way, fans have missed out on a lot of *Hellblazer* lore, some of which sounds intriguing.

Here are some stories that never blazed their way out of development Hell.

Swamp Thing Volume 2 #89-91

Following Rick Veitch's sudden departure as the writer of DC Comics' monthly *Swamp Thing* title, due to a disagreement over the publisher's rejection of his script for issue #88 ("Morning of the Magician," the infamous "Swamp Thing meets Christ" story), these three issues — the concluding chapters of the author's long-spanning time-travel odyssey — were scrapped along with *Swamp Thing* #88, and were replaced with tales penned by newcomer Doug Wheeler.

The lost issues, plotted with help from *The Sandman*'s Neil Gaiman, would have culminated in the defeat and redemption of the evil wizard Anton Arcane. They never got past the treatment stage, however, and Wheeler plotted a new direction for the comic that was separate from Veitch's original plans... and not nearly as expertly crafted, to be sure. Veitch's issue #89 would have been titled "Retro"; the other titles are unknown. Some plot details about these missing chapters have emerged, most of which have been largely ignored by later writers, so they would no longer fit established continuity if published today. For *Hellblazer* fans, the cancelation of these issues tragically also meant the loss of a John Constantine and Swamp Thing team-up.

In Veitch's original story, the Claw of Aelkhünd, an ancient relic containing the amber-trapped soul of Swamp Thing, carries the elemental billions of years into the past, where he witnesses the dawn of life on Earth. Adopted by a civilization of plant beings, he obtains employment and starts a new family. In time, he forgets about his wife Abby, but memories begin to resurface and he struggles to recall who he is. Ultimately, Swamp Thing becomes trapped within the Claw, where he remains for billions of years.

Veitch had originally intended to conclude the saga by having John Constantine smash the relic in 1989, releasing Swamp Thing from his amber cage to battle Arcane via magic. Using lessons learned from Christ, the elemental causes Arcane's shots to pass through him harmlessly, until Arcane burns out his remaining hatred. Swamp Thing and Abby are reunited, their daughter Tefé is born (this also occurs in Wheeler's run, though under different circumstances), and Arcane becomes a normal human who, purged of hate, lives out his life as an ordinary country doctor. Writer Mark Millar would later revisit Arcane's redemption during his final story arc as *Swamp Thing* scribe, but it's intriguing to imagine what Veitch had in mind for Constantine and the bog god.

Twilight of the Superheroes

Alan Moore proposed this 12-issue miniseries to DC Comics sometime around 1986, but the company opted not to publish it. What's fascinating is that this proposal was submitted during pre-*Hellblazer* days, and that Moore himself – John Constantine's creator – actually suggested a spinoff title for John. It sounds phenomenal, too, akin to Mark Waid and Alex Ross's *Kingdom Come*. The story's loss to fans of *Hellblazer* and Alan Moore literature cannot be over-emphasized.[1]

So what was it about? In 1987, John Constantine receives a surprise visit from time-traveler Rip Hunter (no relation to *The Books of Magic*'s Tim Hunter, presumably), who knows personal details John has never told anyone. Hunter has come back from the year 2000 and says the Constantine of that era had helped him escape into the past so he could enlist the aid of John's younger self in alerting Earth's superheroes to a bleak future. In essence, Hunter plays Kyle Reese to Constantine's John Connor in a fascinating pastiche of *The Terminator* (John Connor... John Constantine... it works!). According to Hunter, this war-torn future, created by the Time Trapper's attempt to defeat the Legion of Super-Heroes, will end in the death or exile of every super-powered being on the planet.

Constantine agrees to help Hunter contact the metahuman community. Some heed his warning, while others ignore it. John worries that he might fail to avert disaster, yet he takes comfort in Rip's revelation that a woman in a bar will ask him for a light, and that they'll fall in love and become happily married. Only after John does as Hunter asks does the time-traveler reveal that the older Constantine has manipulated his younger self into setting into motion the very events about which Rip has warned him, in an attempt to rid the world of super-beings who have gone to war with each other and are thus endangering humanity. Furious at being conned – by himself, no less – Constantine gets even by letting the woman he's supposed to marry walk out of his life without meeting him.

Meanwhile, in the year 2000, the older Constantine plots to rid the world of super-beings, working alongside Batman, The Shadow, Doc Savage, and Tarzan – the latter three apparently visiting the DC Universe from the realm of the public domain. *Twilight of the Superheroes* thus serves as a prototype for Moore's later work, *The League of Extraordinary Gentlemen*, which (unlike *Twilight of the Superheroes*) was published.

---

[1] Check out John Trumbull's essay, "Mad, Bad, and Dangerous to Know: Alan Moore's John Constantine," elsewhere in this volume.

John manipulates the various groupings of superheroes and supervillains, promising to assist each of their respective campaigns. The magus, married in this alternate future to a woman called Fever – a character Moore had created for the DC series *Vigilante* – helps Rip Hunter escape to 1987. He asks the time-traveler to enlist the aid of his prior self in alerting the superheroes to the coming twilight, even though doing so will cause a chain of events leading to that very outcome.

Fever, from Alan Moore's *Vigilante* #17-18, might have been John Constantine's true love in another reality.

A war erupts among the metahumans, killing heroes and villains alike, including Superman. Batman's forces attack, along with Constantine's recruited army, creating a standoff with DC's extraterrestrial factions. Alien weaponeers, armed by Constantine in return for Earth's immunity, besiege Mars, Rann, and Oa, and all extraterrestrial beings leave the planet to defend their home worlds. With only Batman and other non-powered heroes remaining, Earth's society reorganizes, freed of super-dictatorship. In the end, Constantine looks forward to living quietly with his wife... unaware that his younger self has spitefully prevented him from ever marrying her.

It's simply tragic that Moore never received the greenlight to pursue this miniseries beyond the outline stage, as *Twilight of the Superheroes* could have been among the most poignant Constantine tales ever told, played out on what would certainly have been one of the most grandiose and bizarre landscapes. John's masterful manipulation of Earth's metahuman communities, and even himself, is pure Constantine – and it would have been penned by Alan Moore, so it would certainly have been beautifully scripted and authentic to the character. Given the description in his proposal, in fact, it might well have ranked among his best work. If there's any consolation, it's that the proposal made its way online and has long been distributed among fans.[2]

Hellblazer #141: "Shoot"

In *Hellblazer* circles, the counterpart to Veitch's aborted *Swamp Thing* #88 would be Warren Ellis's intended story for *Hellblazer* #141 ("Shoot"), which suffered a similar publication stall that resulted in the premature halt of his highly regarded run. In the wake of the Columbine High School mass shooting in April 1999, Vertigo opted not to publish this tale, even though it had already been illustrated by Phil Jimenez and Andy Lanning. The publisher deemed the subject-matter too sensitive, considering the tragedy that had left 14 students and a teacher dead, as well as 24 others wounded. Ellis disagreed and stepped down as *Hellblazer*'s monthly writer, rendering his all-too-brief tenure a lesson in missed opportunities and unfulfilled potential.

In the story, psychologist Penny Carnes, a specialist in mass and spree killings, becomes obsessed with determining the identity of a mysterious trenchcoated figure caught on tape and in photographs during multiple high-school shootings. Carnes hopes her research will reveal why many American high-school students have taken to killing themselves and their fellow classmates in recent years.

John Constantine (the trenchcoated man in question) is also investigating the trend, as a favor to a friend whose child was a recent shooting victim. Constantine provides Carnes with a key piece of the puzzle she has overlooked: the horror of the situation isn't merely that teenagers are killing their fellow students, but that the victims actually *want* to die. Examining the footage more closely, Carnes is horrified to see one victim facing his attacker calmly and uttering the word "Shoot," while others expectantly await death instead of running away, hiding, or defending themselves from slaughter.

DC over-compensated when, anticipating a public backlash, it canceled Ellis's story outright, mirroring what had happened with Veitch's Christ issue. Had the company simply delayed the issue's release for a few months out of consideration for the victims' families, Ellis would have had no reason to quit and "Shoot" would have debuted once a respectable span of time had passed.

---

[2] https://archive.org/stream/TwilightOfTheSuperheroes/TwilightOfTheSuperheroes_djvu.txt.

The writer's run mainly consisted of single-issue tales anyway, so the order of publication could have been adjusted to lessen the potential for causing offense.

After Ellis left *Hellblazer*, "Shoot" remained in comic book limbo for more than a decade. Unlike *Swamp Thing* #88, though, "Shoot" eventually *did* see publication – but not until 2010, when DC Comics corrected its error in judgment and at last presented this missing chapter to readers in a one-shot anthology titled *Vertigo Resurrected*. "Shoot" is a poignant tale ripped right out of news headlines – perhaps more so now than when it was written, given the horrific epidemic of gun violence in the United States and abroad in recent years, particularly involving mass shootings at schools.

Fans got lucky with Warren Ellis's "Shoot," which was eventually rescued from obscurity in the *Vertigo Resurrected* special.

Still, many have rightfully questioned the disturbingly misguided premise that shooting victims are somehow complicit in their own murders, which of course they are not. Ellis's stance on these tragedies is admittedly bizarre, and one would be hard-pressed to make a believable case for school-shooting victims actually *wanting* to be shot. That's the domain of conspiracy-theorist websites and tin-foil hat-wearers, and it's not backed up by reality. Regardless, it's gratifying that this once-lost Constantine tale is available to readers, so that they can judge for themselves whether Ellis was on to something... or was merely shooting blanks.

"The Day My Pad Went Mad"

Neil Gaiman penned a John Constantine story in 1985 after seeking Alan Moore's help in writing his first comic book script. Moore reportedly called the ending "a little wonky."[3] The story has never been published, though Gaiman described it in his introduction to his book *Neil Gaiman's Midnight Days*, a trade paperback presenting several previously published works, including *Swamp Thing Annual* #5 and *Hellblazer* #27, along with an original Swamp Thing tale titled "Jack-in-the-Green."

Andy Diggle's sly reference to Neil Gaiman's "The Day My Pad Went Mad" in *Hellblazer* #234.

---

[3] Wagner, Hank; Golden, Christopher; and Bissette, Stephen R. *Prince of Stories: The Many Worlds of Neil Gaiman*. St. Martin's Griffin, 2009.

"The Day My Pad Went Mad" was inspired by a same-named poem from English performance poet John Cooper Clarke, recorded in 1982. Little is known about Gaiman's story other than that it would have involved John Constantine returning to his flat in England following the events of Moore's "American Gothic" storyline, only to find something unusual growing in his refrigerator. Gaiman has not indicated what that was or why, though writer Andy Diggle would later reference the incident during his tenure on *Hellblazer*, in issue #234, revealing that it involved a reanimated chicken carcass.

Perhaps Gaiman and DC Comics will one day reopen the fridge and serve up this undercooked and overlooked meal. Even if it's just leftovers at this point, Gaiman is among the comic book industry's best chefs, so it's sure to be delectable.

The Sandman Presents: Marquee Moon

British writer Peter Hogan, of *2000 A.D.* fame, penned this follow-up to *The Sandman Presents: Love Street* in 1997. *Marquee Moon*, illustrated by Peter Doherty and Matt "D'israeli" Brooker, remains unpublished, though Hogan granted permission to share it online when I interviewed him in 2010.[4]

Love Street had offered insight into Constantine's youth in the 1960s, setting the stage for the cynical magician he would become. *Marquee Moon* would have revisited John's early years, showcasing his time with punk band Mucous Membrane in 1977 and revealing his encounter with an American woman with a secret. Had this one-shot seen publication, punk-rock band The Clash would have made their comic book debut.

On New Year's Day, Mucous Membrane attends a performance by The Clash at London's Roxy Club, where a pair of record label executives seek new bands to sign. Unable to interest The Clash, they search for a second-division lineup and discover Mucous Membrane. After the duo promise to attend the band's next gig, John Constantine rushes home to write some songs. Meanwhile, backup band The Uninvited adds a new lead singer: a sexy, naïve werewolf named Tammy, who senses the presence of another wolf among her bandmates.

---

[4] The fully lettered artwork can be downloaded at http://www.hassleinbooks.com/pdfs/MarqueeMoon.pdf, while the script is available at http://www.hassleinbooks.com/pdfs/MarqueeMoonScript.pdf.

Constantine and Mucous Membrane get their first big chance at fame in Peter Hogan's *The Sandman Presents: Marquee Moon*.

When Mucous Membrane and The Uninvited perform at London's Marquee Club, John senses the two werewolves thanks to his latent psychic abilities. The record execs offer Mucous Membrane a recording deal at the show, but another company, KGB, has already offered a five-figure advance. As the two men leave, John reads William Peter Blatty's novel *The Exorcist*. Fully aware that his music career won't last forever, he decides to study exorcism, setting the stage for the mage whom fans will come to know in *Swamp Thing* and *Hellblazer*.

Hogan's writing displays a firm handle on the comedic side of Constantine's personality, and on how it contrasts with his darker occultist aspects – which is no surprise, of course, considering the high quality of *Love Street*. The audience at the club gets out of control, repeatedly spitting at both bands, and John stops singing halfway through performing Mucous Membrane's hit single "Venus of the Hardsell," threatening to beat up the next person who dares to spit at him. A wave of saliva immediately hits Constantine in response, and he dives angrily at the crowd, causing a riot that nearly destroys both groups' instruments. The scene is played for laughs, but it's pure John.[5]

The Sandman Presents: Marquee Moon is a great read. The story is well-paced, wonderfully illustrated, and darkly amusing. It gets John's character just right, and it represents a lost chapter in not only *Hellblazer*'s history, but also *The Sandman*'s. The reason for its cancelation remains a mystery even to Hogan himself, but the writer holds out hope (as does this essayist) that DC might someday reverse its decision. Let's hope so. Like "Shoot," *Marquee Moon* deserves its day on stage – especially since DC Comics has already legitimized it by allowing its inclusion in an official *Hellblazer* timeline[6] published in 2018's *John Constantine, Hellblazer: 30th Anniversary Celebration*.

"Notes Towards a Vegetable Theology"

In 1989, Gaiman penned the essay "Notes Towards a Vegetable Theology" to serve as a bible for DC's supernatural comics line. The essay tied in with his plans for the Swamp Thing character, as he and Jamie Delano had been hired to succeed Rick Veitch as *Swamp Thing*'s co-writers. But when Veitch quit the series in protest of issue #88's cancelation, Delano and Gaiman supported their friend by declining the gig. "Vegetable Theology" was slated to appear in an issue of *Black Orchid*, but this never came to pass.

Reproductions of the essay were later auctioned by the Comic Book Legal Defense Fund, and it was finally made publicly available in 2008 in *Prince of Stories: The Many Worlds of Neil Gaiman*. In an interview that year with Brian Hibbs,[7] Gaiman discussed his and Delano's plans for their intended *Swamp Thing* run:

> I didn't really have any [specific plans for the Swamp Thing character]. We never quite really got that far. I had a few ideas about what I was going to do. It was going to be me and Jamie Delano. We were going to split it, and do sort of three issues each on a turnabout basis. Neither of us could have

---

[5] Sting (John Constantine's real-life inspiration) once erupted in anger after having mud thrown at him by an audience member, then spat on this individual in retaliation, during a concert recorded for the video *Police Around the World* (https://www.youtube.com/watch?v=YDs3flO6FSs). *Marquee Moon*, meanwhile, is the title of the debut album of rock band Television, a seminal release of the post-punk era. These may be intentional homages, or they could just be happy coincidences.

[6] Full disclosure: I wrote the timeline, along with other materials for that collection.

[7] Fulgham, Joe. "Gaiman Interview with Brian Hibbs." The Dreaming, 5 August 2008: https://thedreaming.moteofdust.com/2008/08/05/gaiman-interview-with-brian-hibbs/.

done another monthly book at twelve issues a year, but we could have done it on that basis. It really hadn't even got to the plotting stages. Having said that, there was a lot of stuff that I did, back when I was originally creating *Black Orchid*, in terms of working out a unified vegetable theology in the DC world. So there is a lot of stuff in the background that I know about the Swamp Thing world that we never used. Some of that was hinted at in [*Swamp Thing Annual* #5].

Gaiman told Hibbs he'd planned to bring back recurring *Swamp Thing* cast member Jason Woodrue (the Floronic Man) as a villain, explaining, "He was getting back to being Woodrue, the Rue of the Wood, and probably on a much bigger scale, a much nastier scale. It would have been fun, but again it didn't happen." The writer also intended to add Black Orchid to the mix, as well as a certain trenchcoated magus with an addiction to Silk Cuts. As he recounted to Hibbs:

> I talked to Rick, we sort of co-plotted Rick's last few episodes, which never saw print. When I say co-plotted, I mean that we had long bull sessions about them when I stayed up in Vermont for a couple days last winter. I spent a day with Steve Bissette, a day with Rick, and the evening I spent with Rick we were plotting out Rick's final sequence. Rick had the end of the time-travel sequence, and some Arcane stuff. We talked through what we would have done during the "birth of the baby" story. We would have done a whole "Gifts of the Magi" number, with various characters coming up, and bestowing the newborn child a gift. What John Constantine would have done, and so forth.

Gaiman and Delano's decision not to pursue their *Swamp Thing* plans is understandable, given the circumstances, and standing in solidarity with a respected colleague is certainly laudable. Unfortunately, it was the fans who truly paid the price, as the duo would surely have hit the ball out of the bayou. Delano, as *Hellblazer*'s first ongoing scribe, created one of DC/Vertigo's most beloved supernatural titles, so the thought of his contributing monthly adventures to *Swamp Thing* delights the imagination. Gaiman's intention to utilize Constantine in the storyline makes the decision even more heartbreaking, as the writer's work on *Hellblazer* #27 ("Hold Me"), *Books of Magic*, and *The Sandman* #3 ("Dream a Little Dream of Me") proved without a doubt that Gaiman possessed a solid grasp of how to write John Constantine.

Arcane Blood

Nancy A. Collins stepped down as *Swamp Thing*'s regular writer near the end of 1993. A few years later, Collins pitched a miniseries to editor Axel Alonso that would have tied in with both *Swamp Thing* and *Hellblazer*. Collins' idea was to utilize supernatural characters from various DC and Vertigo Comics titles, including Swamp Thing, his wife Abby, their daughter Tefé, and their nemesis, Anton Arcane, along with the Phantom Stranger, Madame Xanadu, Etrigan the Demon, Kid Eternity, *Animal Man*'s Maxine Baker, and *The Sandman*'s Thessaly and the Three Witches. From *Hellblazer*'s corner, she intended to borrow not only John Constantine, but also his ancestor Lady Johanna Constantine and the First, Second, and Third of the Fallen.

During a 2013 interview conducted for the Hasslein Books blog,[8] Collins recalled, "It was called *Arcane Blood*, and it was about the consequences of crossing a Constantine with an Arcane." Previously, in 1998, Collins had described the combining of the Arcane and Constantine bloodlines as being "like mixing nitroglycerin in a bumpy truck,"[9] and *Arcane Blood* would have explored why this was so. The story would have put Tefé in a starring role, just as Brian K. Vaughan's short-lived *Swamp Thing* run would later do.

Still angry about her elemental father (Alec Holland) having denied Tefé her birthright during Mark Millar's *Swamp Thing* storyline, the hybrid would have sought out John Constantine, her biological dad, in order to learn about her magical heritage. Constantine would have initially rebuffed his daughter's outreach, but eventually would have relented in an effort to get to know her better.

In exploring the Arcane genealogy, John would have learned a great deal about not only Tefé's family history, but his own as well. According to Collins' proposal, "a mating between an Arcane and a Constantine would produce a child of immense occult potential. And if the child happens to be female, then she would possess the innate power & wisdom to one day become the Strega Regina: the Queen of the Witches." As Collins noted during the Hasslein Books interview:

> Swamp Thing and the others travel to the Parliament of Trees to find his daughter. Swampy discovers Tefé is now known as Rima the Jungle Girl. He also discovers that Lady Jane has born him a "son," known as the Page. As the Page is the first elemental born of elemental cross-pollination, they

---

[8] Handley, Rich. "Nancy Collins on Exploring Cajun Culture and Breaking Up Swamp Thing's Family." Hasslein Blog, 3 February 2013: http://hassleinbooks.blogspot.com/2013/02/nancy-collins-on-channeling-cajun.html.

[9] Yarbrough, Beau. "Nancy Collins: Hard-headed horror with a Southern accent." LBY3, 1 June 1998: https://www.lby3.com/1998/06/01/nancy-collinshard-headed-horror-with-a-southern-accent/.

decide to transfer the "Sprout" energy from Tefé/Rima to her half-brother. Of course, Anton Arcane tries to fuck with things from beyond the grave, as he has formed an alliance with Nergal, the demon who contaminated Constantine's blood and now claims Tefé/Rima as his "grandchild."

Abby is revealed to be descended from a long line of witches and necromancers, and uses her nascent occult abilities to battle her dead uncle. At the end, the Page becomes the new Sprout, Tefé becomes Rima (and retains certain occult abilities, such as an ability to talk to birds), and Abby goes off with the Phantom Stranger and Madame Xanadu to learn how to use her new powers, and she takes the name 'Arcana.'

Collins' story would have offered an unexpected twist on Abby's lineage, revealing her to have been the product of incest. Unexpected... yet hardly shocking for this family, since Abby's Uncle Anton had molested her in the guise of her husband Matt Cable (during Alan Moore's *Swamp Thing* run) and had repeatedly raped his sister Aniela when she was a child (per Rick Veitch's *Swamp Thing* #83). But the proposal would have dropped an even bigger bomb on *Swamp Thing* fans, for according to Collins' proposal: "The [spirit] of Astra warns Constantine to watch the child for signs of the tell-tale Arcane instability. She confirms that she and her husband were first-cousins, although admitting the possibility Anton Arcane was actually Abby's biological father."

This would explain why Anton had so badly mistreated his brother Gregori (Abby's father), turning him into the Patchwork Man – and the roots of this had been planted in Collins' *Swamp Thing* #125, which revealed that Anton had loved her and had never forgiven Gregori after she chose him instead. To punish them, Anton had convinced villagers to burn his sister-in-law at the stake for witchcraft, while Gregori, holding baby Abby, watched helplessly. Collins' proposal would have given this mysterious woman a name: Astra Arcane (the story "Lady Arcane," published in *Vertigo Secret Files & Origins: Swamp Thing*, would later christen her Anise). *Hellblazer* fans know well the name Astra, as it was the damnation of Astra Logue, during the Newcastle debacle in issue #11, that resulted in Constantine spending years in an insane asylum.

Sadly, Collins never had a chance to pursue these intriguing concepts. "Of course, no one at Vertigo was interested in the proposal," Collins explained during the Hasslein Blog discussion, "and it has since been rendered a moot point, as that universe no longer exists." *Arcane Blood*, it seemed, was dead in the water. Still, as *Hellblazer* and *Swamp Thing* have demonstrated time and again, things that are dead have a tendency not to stay that way – and in the case of *Arcane Blood*, that has proven true. In March 2019, Collins offered a tantalizing post at The Parliament of Trees,[10] a *Swamp Thing*-based Facebook group: "Now it can be told! My run on *Swamp Thing* is being collected! It will feature an original introduction by me, plus the proposal for *Arcane Blood*, and previously unseen artwork by Russ Braun, Kim DeMulder, Scott Eaton and more!" The collection, titled *Swamp Thing by Nancy A. Collins Omnibus*, was published in April 2020, making this lost *Hellblazer* tie-in available to readers at long last.

In 2020, DC Comics' *Swamp Thing by Nancy A. Collins Omnibus* finally published Collins' *Arcane Blood* proposal, featuring John Constantine.

---

[10] https://www.facebook.com/groups/theparliamentoftrees/permalink/2277790799105966/

Swamp Thing Volume 3

When Vertigo Comics relaunched *Swamp Thing* in 1999, Darko Macan (the writer of *Hellblazer* #144-145) was among those invited to submit a proposal regarding Tefé Holland's future in the wake of Mark Millar's *Swamp Thing* run. Vertigo ultimately hired Brian K. Vaughan, but Macan shared his proposal with this essayist years ago, granting permission for it to be disseminated among fans.[11] It's fascinating to compare what Macan had in mind with Vaughan's published comics, as there is some overlap in how Tefé is characterized in both writers' work.

In Macan's version, Tefé forms a new body after being betrayed by her father at the end of Millar's saga, and discovers that her death in that concluding storyline caused her to miss the moment when every person on Earth shared in Swamp Thing's planetwide mind-merging revelation. She grows bitter and desperate for her parents' love, but her dad, elevated to near-godhood and disconnected from Alec Holland's soul, is too busy with affairs of the world to have time for her.

As an act of rebellion, Tefé grows an adult body, has sex with an industrialist, throws all plants out of his house, and manipulates the man into damaging the Green. This hurts her as well, but she endures it to punish her father. Swamp Thing, of course, repairs the damage and fights the monsters she creates, convinced she'll come around eventually. Unable to hurt her father, Tefé punishes the industrialist instead, then turns her attention to her mother Abby, who has found a new live-in partner and is raising a second baby girl. Abby is unhappy to see her.

Enraged, Tefé uses her flesh-molding ability to turn the baby into a series of creatures, then flees after restoring the infant's human form. Tefé travels to London to visit her human birth-father, John Constantine, who tries to be a parent but is unsuited to the role. She leaves him as well, but acknowledges that he, unlike Alec and Abby, at least tried to be a dad. Tefé then explores her inherited demon blood by seeking out Nergal in Hell, and travels to the Balkans to connect with her sorcerer great-uncle, Anton Arcane.

With both Constantine and Nergal in the mix, Macan's storyline would have had strong connections with *Hellblazer* lore, and it sounds like it would have been quite the emotional roller-coaster for John's elemental daughter. As it happens, Vaughan also explored Tefé's estranged relationship with her human

---

[11] You can read it at http://www.hassleinbooks.com/rich/SwampThing_Macan.pdf.

father, though their interactions in the writer's hands were more adversarial than in Macan's proposal.

The Brave and the Bold

At Emerald City Comic Con 2008, *Babylon 5* creator J. Michael Straczynski revealed plans for a relaunch of DC's long-running title *The Brave and the Bold*. The series' focus has varied throughout the decades, but it has frequently featured team-ups of popular DC characters. Straczynski announced his hopeful team-ups at the event, including Lex Luthor and Swamp Thing, as well as John Constantine and Eclipso, among others.

For reasons never made public, neither team-up ever came to fruition – but just imagine how exciting the latter story could have been. In DC lore, the supervillain Eclipso (introduced in 1963's *House of Secrets* #61) is a former incarnation of the Wrath of God and the Angel of Vengeance, who was replaced by the Spectre after growing megalomaniacal and evil. Setting aside the "supervillain" label for a moment and focusing more on the character's religious and supernatural aspects, Eclipso seems like a snug fit for a Constantine-centric tale.

Whatever Happened to the Thing from the Swamp?

Writer Martin Conaghan submitted a proposal to DC/Vertigo in the early 2000s regarding a *Swamp Thing* miniseries spanning five issues, each 24 pages in length. The individual issue titles would have been "The Strange Case of Doctor Alec Holland," "The Heart of Darkness," "Out of the Blue," "Into the Fire," and "Journey to the Centre of the Universe" (alternate title: "The Parliament of Stories"). Had DC opted to publish it, the miniseries would have tied in with not only *Swamp Thing*, but *Hellblazer* as well.

Conaghan has shared his intriguing proposal with me, asking that I not provide extensive details regarding its content, other than that it would have incorporated characters from throughout *Swamp Thing*'s publishing history. Among the intended lineup were Alex Olsen, Linda Olsen, and Damian Ridge, from the very first *Swamp Thing* story, published in *House of Secrets* #92; Swamp Thing's nemesis Anton Arcane and allies Matt Cable, Chester Williams, and Jordan Schiller; former earth elementals Aaron Hayley, Albert Höllerer, and Allan Hallman; and, of course, John Constantine.

Going by the proposal, it's clear that *Whatever Happened to the Thing from the Swamp?* (named as an homage to "Whatever Happened to the Man of

Tomorrow?", a 1986 comic storyline by Alan Moore, published in *Superman* #423 and *Action Comics* #583) had great promise and would have thrilled *Swamp Thing* and *Hellblazer* fans alike. The concept would have mined DC Comics' pre-New 52 continuity, exploring many facets of *Swamp Thing*'s macabre history, and it would have reunited the earth elemental and the British mage, which is usually a recipe for success.

But Wait – There's More

At least three other unpublished comics would have featured appearances by Constantine, though few details are known about them. In 1988, Roy Thomas submitted a "Mature Readers" HELIX proposal featuring villains from *Infinity Inc.*, guest-starring Swamp Thing, John Constantine, Black Orchid, Animal Man, Green Arrow, the Question, and other DC characters. Steven Grant, a decade later, pitched a story for the third iteration of *Challengers of the Unknown*, featuring Constantine and Swamp Thing, which would have unfolded beginning with issue #19. Neither submission resulted in a published story.

In addition, Vertigo had been considering a one-shot in 1999 that would have teamed up Swamp Thing, Constantine, and Zatanna Zatara. This story would have led into *V2K: Totems*, from writer Tom Peyer and artists Duncan Fegredo and Richard Case, which had been released that same year as part of the publisher's millennium celebration. The creators slated for the unpublished one-shot are unknown, but given the decidedly lukewarm reception *Totems* received from readers, it's probably just as well that the lead-in story was rejected.

Justice League Dark Film

Director Guillermo del Toro, in 2012, announced a *Justice League Dark* film titled *Dark Universe*, to the great excitement of comic book and horror fans everywhere. The movie was reportedly slated to star John Constantine and Swamp Thing, along with many fellow supernatural denizens, including Deadman, the Spectre, Madame Xanadu, the Phantom Stranger, Sargon the Sorcerer, Etrigan the Demon, Jason Woodrue, and the father-daughter team of Giovanni "John" Zatara and Zatanna Zatara. Quite a lineup, eh? A story bible was completed, and the movie would have seen Constantine recruiting Swamp Thing and others to face a supernatural danger – a callback to how John first met the elemental in Moore's "American Gothic" saga.

Dark Universe was intended to be part of the same DC cinematic continuity that began with the movie *Man of Steel*. Intriguingly, Del Toro hinted that his film could coexist with the *Constantine* television series starring Matt Ryan,[12] though the director later clarified that while the movie would not actually synch up with Ryan's TV series, he was considering the possibility of hiring Ryan to play Constantine on the big screen, and of incorporating elements from the show.

A script for the movie was completed and submitted to Warner Bros. in 2014, and then... nothing happened. The project faced one delay after another as DC Comics and Warner Bros. hashed out how to approach the material. Updates and rumors continued to show up on comic news sites, but the movie eventually stalled, and del Toro had moved on to other projects by 2015. Doug Liman was hired to replace him as director, but he, too, ultimately departed. At press time, a *Justice League Dark* TV series is reportedly in the works from J.J. Abrams, without the involvement of del Toro or Liman, and will air on WarnerMedia's HBO Max streaming service.

Down in a Blaze of Gory

Other than "Shoot" and *Arcane Blood*, the above John Constantine stories have never been officially presented to fans, and several remain unavailable in any form, official or otherwise. If it weren't for the industrious nature of fandom, much of this material would still be collecting dust in desks or filling up computer folders, unread by anyone and unheard of by most. But thanks to the efforts of those determined to overturn every stone and learn all that can be learned, many a quaint and curious volume of forgotten *Hellblazer* (and *Swamp Thing*) lore has been unearthed and shared.

It's a good bet there are other rejected, canceled, or otherwise unpublished John Constantine stories out there, just waiting to be uncovered and recovered. In fact, the above list may be just the tip of the hellish iceberg. Perhaps we'll be lucky, and more of these lost gems will eventually see the light of day. If "Shoot" has proven anything, it's that long-lost lore need not remain forever forgotten.

---

[12] Collura, Scott. "Guillermo del Toro Says *Justice League Dark* and the John Constantine TV Show Can Coexist." IGN, 15 October 2013: https://www.ign.com/articles/2013/10/15/guillermo-del-toro-says-justice-league-dark-and-the-john-constantine-tv-show-can-coexist.

Cursing the *Waverider*: John Constantine in the Arrowverse and in Animation

by Sabrina Fried

John Constantine's first appearance in *Swamp Thing* #37 dates back to 1985, making him a fairly young character in the DC Comics pantheon. His formative years in the Vertigo comics line allowed him to develop into a character who mostly stuck to his own universe, played by his own rules, and just sort of did his own thing, for his own reasons. He wasn't exactly the kind of character one expected to see movies and TV shows made about.

By design, Constantine was about as far as any character could get from the likes of Batman or Superman. But as DC sought to cash in on its stable of characters, it was only a matter of time before Constantine, too, would make his debut on both the big and small screens. There was just one problem with that plan: John Constantine. In its unaltered state, much of his story is unfilmable in any way that would attract a mainstream audience. It was tried in the 2005 *Constantine* film starring Keanu Reeves, but even then, substantial changes were needed to make the character fit the actor cast to portray him. In the end, the less said about that movie, the better.

Then the success of the Marvel Cinematic Universe made shared universes with huge superhero teams all the rage for multimedia properties, so if ol'

Johnny Boy was going to adapt to this new world, he had to undergo a few more changes. Like so many other DC characters, Constantine seems to be faring better on television than he ever did on the big screen. But in a strong parallel to the magic of Constantine's world, that success came with a pretty hefty price.

The original *Hellblazer* comics established Constantine as a loner mage. Although not entirely separated from the mundane world, he kept his associations few and carefully chosen. This is largely attributed to the fact that, although jaded and cynical, John does appear to care about the well-being of humanity as a whole. He keeps his distance, even from people he cares about, knowing that misfortune has a way of finding them, as most brutally demonstrated by the plight of long-suffering sidekick Chas Chandler. This depiction of John Constantine largely holds through the New 52 reboot of the character, in which, among other things, he is transported to Earth 2 and forced to sacrifice his own doppelgänger to survive.

The New 52 relaunch of most DC characters also brought with it a series devoted to a new superhero team, known as Justice League Dark. Despite his aversion to working in "teams," especially superhero teams, Constantine not only is convinced to work with this group, but leads it for a time. After John's departure from the team, he confronts – and is bested by – Doctor Fate, leaving his current, well, fate, unknown.

As the New 52 line began to breathe new life into Constantine as a character, with a new self-titled comic and a key role in *Justice League Dark*, Constantine was finally adapted for television in 2014. Portrayed by Matt Ryan, this John Constantine, like his comic book counterparts, is a well-accomplished mage. The comparison pretty much stops there. TV's Constantine becomes a magical detective of sorts in a supernatural procedural, in which he defends the mortal realm from the Rising Darkness. However, low ratings canceled the show after 13 episodes without truly revealing what the Rising Darkness was. While the show itself may have missed the mark with Nielsen families, a strong fan base developed around Matt Ryan's depiction of the mage. Ryan not only went on to shepherd the character through his live-action appearances, but he has since become the go-to voice actor for John Constantine in his animated outings.

Building on the popularity of the *Justice League Dark* comic series, an animated film of the same name was released, direct to video, in 2017. Intended as a continuation of the comics, the animated feature had the JLD team formed as sort of an unofficial offshoot of the main Justice League, created to handle threats that the "capes," as Constantine calls them, were ill-equipped to deal with on their own. Like the comic series, the fact that the team is collectively some of the most powerful magic- and supernatural-based characters in the DC Universe seems to be enough for Constantine to overcome his usual aversion to playing with others long enough to save the world.

John Constantine is featured on the cover of *Justice League Dark*, Volume 5.

In true Constantine fashion, it also helps that, in investigating the magical mystery, John can slay (literally) a demon from his past, crossing paths again with Ritchie Simpson – a key character both from the original *Hellblazer* comic series and the short-lived *Constantine* TV show. Also in true Constantine fashion, crossing paths with Ritchie again exacts a powerful toll on both of them: Ritchie is dragged off to Hell as the price John pays to ensure that the demon Destiny cannot return to the mortal plane.

Matt Ryan reprised the role of Constantine in the *Justice League Dark* animated film, as well as in *City of Demons*.

The animated *Justice League Dark* also spawned its own spinoff title in the form of the Web series *Constantine: City of Demons*. The Web series, later released as a feature-length video, brings Constantine back to his solitary roots and takes place in the same storytelling universe as the animated *Justice League Dark*. It is a somewhat faithful adaptation of Mike Carey's *All His Engines* graphic novel from the original *Hellblazer* run, save for an interesting, but not really necessary, insertion of the Nightmare Nurse[1] into the story.

City of Demons delves deeply into Constantine's past as he works to help save Chas's daughter from the demon Beroul. This Constantine is dark, brooding, and world-weary, and although he is willing to help his friend Chas, his past traumas make him worry about getting close to anyone, knowing that there is usually a dark price to be paid for that. As with the original graphic novel, John's fears turn out to be valid, as the cost of freeing Chas's daughter is not only the love Chas has for his family, but the long and loyal friendship he and John have for each other.

Although the *Constantine* show did not go over as well as expected, in hindsight, it turned out to be only the beginning of the Hellblazer's new life on television. In addition to *Constantine*, DC had a full slate of TV shows airing on The CW featuring more traditional superhero characters, such as Green Arrow and The Flash. These superhero shows exist in a shared universe known colloquially as the Arrowverse. Not long after the cancellation of his own show, Constantine appeared in an episode of *Arrow* during the show's fourth season, in which he helps Team Arrow restore Sara Lance's soul after her resurrection in the Lazarus Pit.[2] It's not entirely clear whether this John Constantine is the same one who had his own show, or exactly what his connection might be to the many incarnations of Constantine in the comic books. Multiverses are funny like that.

After his appearance on *Arrow*, the TV incarnation of Constantine went dormant for a while, returning a few years later on another Arroverse show, *Legends of Tomorrow,* during its third season, as part of an effort to shift the show to a completely new realm of storytelling. In previous seasons, the show had focused primarily on the Legends hunting down people who, in one way or another, had become unstuck in time. With the introduction of the demon

---

[1] A character created by Dan Didio and J.M. DeMatteis for 2013's *Phantom Stranger* #8.

[2] *Arrow*, season 4 episode 5, "Haunted."

Mallus to the series, the team would now face more supernatural threats as well.

John joins the cast of CW's *Legends of Tomorrow.*

But the recurring Legends had collectively very little experience with the supernatural, and were thus out of their league when dealing with these new threats. Constantine, realizing that Mallus was not the only demon released unto the world, approaches the Legends and asks for their help. Without knowing his true motivations for the move (yet[3]), it seems a bit out of character for him – but, hey, it's their show, and if you are going to be on *Legends of Tomorrow*, the Legends are going to be on the show with you.

The shift of *Legends* toward the supernatural was an intentional move, and not just as a way to justify Constantine's presence on the team's mobile base of operations, the timeship *Waverider*. In an interview with *TV Line*, co-showrunner and executive producer Phil Klemmer confirmed that he wanted to play around with the idea that Earth hadn't always belonged to humanity, and that the old beings who had shared the world with us in the past not only were still around, but were confused by the efforts of humans to keep it all to themselves.[4] The Rising Darkness was mentioned offhand a few times as a sort-of Arrowverse in-joke, but was then politely tucked away to keep the focus on

---

[3] As of this essays's writing, the full season had not yet aired on television.

[4] Mitovich, Matt Webb. "*Legends of Tomorrow* Boss Tees Up Finale's Showdown With Mallus (and Beebo?), Annual Team Shake-Up." *TV Line*, 7 April 2018: https://tvline.com/2018/04/07/legends-of-tomorrow-season-3-finale-preview-mallus-showdown-team-exit/.

the show at hand. By the start of season four, not only were the Legends hunting anachronisms of both time and magic, but Constantine was upgraded to series regular.

Constantine's addition to the Legends seemed to be an odd placement at first. At best, he provides comic relief as an inexperienced time traveler who refuses to wear period-appropriate clothing if he can help it, the timeline be damned. He also serves as a magical MacGuffin with a name familiar to DC fans. He chants in strange tongues and throws beams of magic from his hands in a way that is not at all dissimilar from what was seen in the *Doctor Strange* film, and is more typical of that character than most of Constantine's own magical history in the comics. As with his other outings aimed at a broader audience, the showrunners preserve as much of the character as they can get away with on a network series. Before his debut as a regular character on the show, Klemmer confirmed that their version of Constantine is still "an alienated, chain-smoking, bisexual, world-weary demonologist," and that he would feel right at home among the Legends.[5]

In typical Constantine fashion, he joins the Legends, but remains aloof, wary of what could happen to the other team members if he were to get too close. As such, while he is quick to voice his opinions on how the Legends are handling their mystical adversaries, he pays little heed to their advice regarding time travel. The episode "Hell No, Dolly!" features a very loose adaptation of the 2015 "Art of the Deal" storyline from the *Constantine: The Hellblazer* comic series, in which John resists an effort by the demon Neron to use him to stage a hostile takeover of Hell, ultimately costing him his boyfriend's body and soul. In the mid-season cliffhanger, Constantine commits the classic novice *Legends* faux pas: breaking the cardinal rule of time travel by making multiple attempts to change his past, and even trying to prevent his own birth.

The Arrowverse version of John Constantine starts off with a backstory largely unknown to any fan not already familiar with *Hellblazer* history. *Legends of Tomorrow* has made an attempt to flesh the character out a bit more than he had been on *Constantine*, but somewhere in the process, he has lost a great deal of what set him apart from other comic book mages. He's simply a magical

---

[5] Bucksbaum, Sydney. "Matt Ryan to Reprise *Constantine* Role for 2-Part *Legends of Tomorrow* Arc." *The Hollywood Reporter*, 9 October 2017: https://www.hollywoodreporter.com/live-feed/matt-ryan-constantine-legends-tomorrow-2-part-arc-1047123.

know-it-all who is conveniently interrupted from smoking every time he tries to light up, thanks to modern guidelines concerning the depiction of smoking on network television. And although it is made clear that his knowledge is vast, the use of his magic seems largely limited to the spells needed to banish magical anomalies back to where they came from.

A new *Swamp Thing* television series aired in May 2019. It was canceled before the showrunners had a chance to work in Constantine, though Matt Ryan had expressed interest in appearing.[6] Broadcast via DC Universe, the show retained the adult themes of the original comics.[7] Hopes were high, but creative differences and budget cuts did the series in. The *Justice League Dark* animated film received a sequel, *Apokolips War*, in which John proved he hadn't learned his lesson when it came to time travel. As for the Legends, well...

The major crossover for all Arrowverse shows in the 2019-2020 season was an adaptation of DC's *Crisis on Infinite Earths*, and Constantine's role was largely a side-plot. In the aftermath, John was reimagined once more. Though he was still a Legend, his home away from ship was now a mansion that may or may not be the House of Mysteries – and in a most un-Constantine-like fashion, he took Gary Green on as an apprentice. The focus of season five shifted, with Astra Logue seeking revenge on John for his having sent her to Hell. At press time, *Legends of Tomorrow*'s current season is nearly done, but no matter how it ends, it would be a perfect opportunity for John to experience another rebirth and return to being the iconic antihero mage we know and love.

---

[6] Burlingame, Russ. "*Legends of Tomorrow* Star Matt Ryan Wants to Play Constantine on *Swamp Thing*." Comicbook.com, 31 March 2019: https://comicbook.com/dc/2019/03/15/legends-of-tomorrow-matt-ryan-constantine-swamp-thing/.
[7] Topel, Fred. "*The Nun* Screenwriter Gary Dauberman Talks *Conjuring* Spin-offs, *It: Chapter 2* and DC Universe's *Swamp Thing*." *Slash Film*, 7 September 2018: https://www.slashfilm.com/the-nun-screenwriter-interview/2/.

John Constantine's Banishment from the DC Universe

by Brian Cronin

> There is violence in everyday life, there is sexuality, often violent sexuality intruding into the child's world, and in my opinion, the only way that we can possibly help our children is to give them the information that they need to deal with that.
> — Alan Moore, *Comics Journal* #118 (December 1987)

If you were to walk into a comic book store in June 2020 to pick up a DC Comics title, you would find yourself with a variety of choices, and each book would have a different rating on it to tell you the age group for which that title was intended. *Batman* #92 had a T rating, which is the most common rating for DC, meaning that the book is meant for a 13-year-old or older. *Young Justice* #17 had a 13+ rating, which means that you should be an older teen to read that comic. *Looney Tunes* #256 had an E, meaning the comic was appropriate for everyone. Finally, *The Dreaming* #21, a Black Label-branded comic book, was termed "Mature Readers," which is generally understood as being appropriate for an 18-year-old or older.

These ratings are common sights for comic book readers and have been for decades. Thirty years ago, however, they were the cause of great debate among creators and comic companies, and the institution of them at DC led to the departure of John Constantine's creator, Alan Moore – and it also led to Constantine's disappearance from mainstream DC comic books for more than two decades!

When Moore began writing *The Saga of Swamp Thing* at the end of 1983, there were two types of comic books produced by DC: those that were released through general distribution methods (convenience stores, newsstands, drug stores), as well as through the direct market (comic book specialty stores), and those that were released only via the direct market. The former titles were all approved by the Comic Code Authority, an independent agency that the major comic book companies had formed in 1954 to quiet down fears from the public regarding the content of comic books by demonstrating that each publisher was voluntarily getting its books approved by a fairly restrictive "Comics Code." The latter titles were typically released without Code approval, like Mike W. Barr's and Brian Bolland's riff on the King Arthur mythos, called *Camelot 3000*, and Frank Miller's futuristic ninja series, *Ronin*. Since *The Saga of the Swamp Thing* was sold through both distribution methods, it had to be approved by the Comics Code.

The Comics Code had been modernized in 1971, so Moore had more freedom on *Swamp Thing* than he would have once had writing under the Code, but even that new level of freedom was not enough to keep up with Moore's approach to the title. In just his tenth issue, Moore wrote a story involving Abby Cable being terrorized by her villainous uncle, Anton Arcane, that featured such disturbing imagery from artists Stephen R. Bissette and John Totleben that there was no way the Comics Code would approve it. DC, therefore, decided to release the comic without Code approval. After all, the Code was a voluntary process, and so DC simply wouldn't submit Moore's *Swamp Thing* issues for Code approval anymore. However, DC determined that it would be a problem to release these comics without some sort of warning to readers about the content, so the phrase "Sophisticated Suspense" was featured on the book's cover.

The phrase, though, was essentially meaningless when it came to how DC treated the series. It was still firmly ingrained in the overall DC Universe despite it not being Comics Code-approved. In fact, when John Constantine made his official debut in *Swamp Thing* #37 (he had made a couple of earlier cameo appearances), it was just a week or two before he also appeared in *Crisis on Infinite Earths* #4. Therefore, right from the start, Constantine was a part of the overall DC Universe.

That became even clearer in *Swamp Thing* #50, when Constantine put together a collection of magicians from DC's long history, including Zatanna, her father Giovanni "John" Zatara, Sargon the Sorcerer, Doctor Fate, Baron Winters, and the Phantom Stranger. Steve Dayton, formerly known as Mento of the Doom Patrol, was also involved in the story. Marv Wolfman actually had Constantine guest-star in an issue of *New Teen Titans* that set up Dayton's role in *Swamp Thing*, since Dayton was a recurring character in *New Teen Titans* at the time (Dayton's adopted son, Changeling, was a member of the Titans). Constantine's status in the DC Universe, though, was about to go through a dramatic change.

The year 1986 is considered an iconic one in comic book history, primarily because it saw the release of both Frank Miller's *Batman: The Dark Knight* (now best known by the title of the first book in the series, *Batman: The Dark Knight Returns*) and Alan Moore's and Dave Gibbons' *Watchmen*. Both series were released only to the direct market and neither was Comics Code-approved. They were both classics of the comic book medium and likely were the two greatest influences on the next three decades' worth of comics. In addition, though, 1986 ended up being a key turning point in the so-called "warning labels" movement.

Alan Moore was also writing *Miracleman* for Eclipse Comics that year, while still writing *Swamp Thing* and *Watchmen* for DC. In 1986's *Miracleman* #9, the eponymous hero's wife, Liz, gave birth to their child. Artist Rick Veitch made sure to depict the childbirth as accurately as possible, which caused a great deal of consternation from comic book retailers and distributors. Steve Geppi, the owner of Diamond Comics Distributors, wrote a stern rebuke of the issue in 1987, arguing, "Diamond values its retailers too much to take chances on such a dangerous situation... We are not censors. We no more want someone deciding for us than you do. We cannot, however, stand by and watch the marketplace become a dumping ground for every sort of graphic fantasy that someone wants to live out. We have an industry to protect; we have leases to abide by; we have a community image to maintain."[1] Amusingly enough, that issue of *Miracleman* actually *had* a label on the cover noting, "ATTENTION PARENTS: This issue contains graphic scenes of childbirth."

---

[1] Duin, Steve and Richardson, Mike (ed.s) "Direct Distribution" in *Comics Between the Panels* (Dark Horse Publishing, 1998) ISBN 1-56971-344-8, p. 126-130.

Still, the dual threats from distributors like Geppi and major comic book store owners like Buddy Saunders of Lone Star Comics made publishers rethink their approach regarding warning labels on their comics. Marvel, which had already abandoned the Comics Code on any product shipped in the direct market, agreed to start including the Code on its direct-market books as well. *Swamp Thing* had already begun to have "For Mature Readers" replace "Sophisticated Suspense" on the cover with late 1986's *Swamp Thing* #57. However, DC decided to go one step further and put labels on *all* of its comics – "For Universal Readership" or "Suggested for Mature Readers."

A group of creators, including Alan Moore, Frank Miller, Marv Wolfman, and Howard Chaykin, vowed to no longer work for DC if the company implemented the system. DC partially backed down, eliminating "For Universal Readership" but keeping "Suggested for Mature Readers" on certain titles, like *Swamp Thing*, which was re-formatted in early 1987 with issue #60 to be released only in the direct market and with the "Mature Readers" label on the cover. The other creators were satisfied with that compromise, but Moore was not. He quit writing *Swamp Thing* for DC, finishing his run with May 1987's *Swamp Thing* #64.

Rick Veitch, the artist under Moore (with inker Alfredo Alcala), took over writing the series as well. Around this same time that Moore was leaving *Swamp Thing*, John Constantine, while continuing as a supporting character in *Swamp Thing*, received his own spinoff solo series, *John Constantine: Hellblazer*, by writer Jamie Delano. That new title was also labeled "Suggested for Mature Readers."

While *Hellblazer* was clearly committed right away to keeping Constantine in his own little world (save for the occasional *Swamp Thing* appearance), Veitch's *Swamp Thing* continued to be a part of the DC Universe despite its "Suggested for Mature Readers" labeling. In fact, Swamp Thing even participated in the 1988 crossover event *Invasion!*, with aliens invading Earth. Once Veitch left the book in August 1989 due to DC reneging on its approval of a story for issue #88, in which Swamp Thing would have travelled back in time to witness the death of Jesus Christ, new writer Doug Wheeler effectively removed Swamp Thing from the DC Universe to match the similar development with Constantine over in *Hellblazer*.

The first blatant example of this new status quo for Constantine and Swamp Thing occurred in early 1990, when Grant Morrison wanted to use John for a story in his and Richard Case's run on *Doom Patrol*. The series was a direct

Willoughby Kipling, one of Constantine's many other analogues.

market-only title and was not Comics Code-approved, but it did not have a "Suggested for Mature Readers" label either. Morrison was denied the use of Constantine, since John was now only a "Mature Readers" character. Instead, Morrison had to invent a new character to substitute for Constantine. He came up with Willoughby Kipling, a Knights Templar member who would assist the Doom Patrol on magical missions. Since the character's visuals could not be based on the rock star Sting, like Constantine had been, Morrison chose to have Case base Kipling's look on Richard E. Grant, from the cult classic film *Whitnail and I*. Kipling made 12 appearances during Morrison's run on *Doom Patrol*.[2]

Ambrose Bierce, a hilarious John Constantine analogue, from DC humor title *Stanley and His Monster*.

While that was all well and good, things were even trickier when Phil Foglio created a rebooted version of the classic DC humor title *Stanley and His*

---

[2] Remarkably, Kipling made a comeback on the *Doom Patrol* TV series on DC Universe's streaming service.

Monster in 1992. "Stanley and His Monster" was originally a back-up feature by writer Arnold Drake and artist Winslow Mortimer about a young boy who has a pet monster, which ran in the funny animal title *Fox and the Crow* in the late 1960s. Eventually, "Stanley and His Monster" took over the series from *Fox and the Crow*, and the last four issues were titled *Stanley and His Monster*.

Foglio did his own take on the concept in a miniseries that was direct market-only and not Comics Code-approved, but it was also not "Suggested for Mature Readers." Foglio wanted to use John Constantine in the series, but he too was turned down. He then asked to use Willoughby Kipling, but in the ensuing two years since Kipling had been introduced, *Doom Patrol* had also become a "Suggested for Mature Readers" title, so Kipling was now off-limits as well! Foglio thus had to invent *another* John Constantine replacement. He took the name of the real-life 19th-century satirist Ambrose Bierce and simply retained Constantine's look for the character.

In 1993, DC officially established a "Suggested for Mature Readers" imprint of comic books called Vertigo, and *Swamp Thing*, *Doom Patrol*, and *Hellblazer* all became part of this new imprint. The titles had an infrequently used shared universe that made it clearer that these characters were nominally "off-limits." Ironically enough, once Constantine was firmly planted in his own "Mature Readers" universe, DC became more open about sharing him with the DC Universe. He only had small appearances, of course, but John began to make somewhat regular cameo appearances in other titles. He showed up in 1993's *Spectre* #15 (by John Ostrander and Tom Mandrake) when Doctor Fate was looking for other magicians to help on a mission. Then in 1995, he made two separate, shocking cameo appearances in, of all places, *Guy Gardner: Warrior*!

The first was at the opening of Guy Gardner's superhero-themed bar and restaurant, Warriors, in *Guy Gardner: Warrior* #29 (by Beau Smith, Phil Jimenez, Dan Davis, and John Stokes) and the second was at the Warriors Christmas party in issue #39 (by Smith, Marc Campos, Dan Davis, and Nick Napolitano). The Guy Gardner appearances, though, seemed to play to the "off-limits" nature of Constantine's character, as he was not named in either cameo and only appeared in one panel in each story (spiking the holiday punch in the Christmas issue).

This made it all the more shocking when DC made a notable exception to its Vertigo "off-limits" policy by allowing both Swamp Thing and John Constantine to appear at Hal Jordan's funeral in 1996's *Green Lantern* #81 (by Ron Marz, Darryl Banks, and Romeo Tanghal). Swamp Thing even played a major role in the issue, transforming Hal Jordan's old hometown of Coast City (which had been destroyed in an alien attack that had driven Jordan into villainy in response) into a giant grassy park. Constantine's cameo in 1998's *Challengers of the Unknown* #15 (by Steven Grant, Ryan Sook, and Bill Reinhold) was a more typical appearance, as he gave assistance to one of the characters in a library without his name being used.

Swamp Thing and Constantine attend Hal Jordan's funeral in 1996's *Green Lantern* #81.

Those cameos, though, were the exception, and Constantine largely remained a Vertigo-only character for the next decade. As the years went by, *Hellblazer* emerged as the dean of the Vertigo imprint, as *Swamp Thing* and *Doom Patrol* both eventually ended and *Hellblazer* became, by far, the longest-running Vertigo series. In January 2011, DC belatedly decided to follow Marvel's lead and stop submitting its books to the Comics Code Authority, thereby putting the Comics Code out of business. Marvel had stopped using the Comics Code in 2001, leaving Archie Comics and DC as the only two companies still using the Code. Archie dropped it along with DC in 2011. With DC now using its own labels for its comics, the company re-introduced Swamp Thing and John Constantine into the DC Universe in *Brightest Day* #24 (by writers Geoff Johns and Peter Tomasi and artist Ardian Syaf), which led to a miniseries about Constantine and Swamp Thing in the DC Universe called *Brightest Day Aftermath: The Search for Swamp Thing* (by Jonathan Vankin, Marco Castiello, and Vincenzo Acunzo).

In September 2011, DC relaunched the DC Universe with the New 52, which comprised 52 new ongoing titles, all set within the DC Universe. One of the titles, *Justice League Dark*, featured a team of magic-based characters, including John Constantine. The title was labeled "Teen." Constantine's "Mature Readers" adventures, meanwhile, continued in *Hellblazer*. This, though, came to a close in January 2013, when *Hellblazer* ended its long run with issue #300. Two months later, Constantine officially became "only" a DC Universe character with the launch of *Constantine*, a "Teen Plus" ongoing series set in the mainstream DC Universe. Essentially, the rest of the DC Universe had caught up to the sort of stories Alan Moore was telling 30 years earlier, so DC no longer felt like there was a need to keep Constantine split off from the rest of its characters.

Amusingly, in 2018, DC launched a new imprint called Black Label, which would once again be used to tell superhero stories for "Mature Readers"; in 2019, Vertigo was retired after 26 years, with its titles folded into the Black Label imprint. The first comic in the line was a book titled *Batman: Damned*, by former *Hellblazer* writer Brian Azzarello and artist Lee Bermejo, that involved Batman teaming up with... John Constantine. The issue pushed things a bit *too* far, though, as there was a sequence in which Batman's penis was visible in silhouette. This made national news (much to DC's chagrin), and the publisher pulled the scene from any online version of the comic book. Not even a "Mature Readers" label protected DC from outrage over *Batman: Damned*'s content.

It makes sense that John Constantine would be mixed up in all of this trouble. Alan Moore would be proud.

A Nasty Piece of Work? The Mercurial Morality of John Constantine

by James Wilkinson

In 1993, *Hellblazer* – along with a string of other "Mature Readers" comics, including *The Sandman*, *Doom Patrol*, and *Swamp Thing* – was partitioned off from *Superman*, *Batman*, and the wider DC Universe and shunted into the company's adults-only Vertigo Comics imprint. While some characters, such as the Doom Patrol, managed to bleed back through during the years that followed, John Constantine remained tethered to Vertigo, save for a scant few cameos.[1]

That changed in 2011, when the release of the miniseries *Brightest Day Aftermath: The Search for Swamp Thing*[2] saw the mainstream DC Universe being given its own version of John Constantine, one whose adventures were to

---

[1] Although Garth Ennis did continue a couple of his *Hellblazer* storylines in DC's mainstream *Hitman* comic, which he made with John McCrea from 1996 to 2001. In *Hitman* #15, Catwoman and titular hitman Tommy Monaghan hunt the Ace of Winchesters, a magical rifle from *Hellblazer* #76. Then, in #37-38, Tommy goes up against Darius and Mary, two vampires introduced in *Hellblazer* #68.

[2] Written by former *Hellblazer* editor Jonathan Vankin; art by Marco Castiello and Vincenzo Acunzo.

run parallel to, but separate from, those depicted in the ongoing *Hellblazer* comic. In May 2013 – the month after *Hellblazer* folded with #300 – this new John bounced into *Constantine*, a new, superhero-friendly title firmly embedded in DC's New 52 relaunch.[3]

But while John Constantine was back in a world of capes and tights, authors Ray Fawkes and Jeff Lemire were quick to establish his gritty credentials. In the first issue, John browbeats a pliable young psychic named Chris into following him to a church housing a mystical MacGuffin. When the villainous daughter of Sargon the Sorcerer[4] arrives and holds the psychic hostage in exchange for the item, John flees, leaving the lad behind to be magically shredded by the villain,[5] who also appears to blow up John's nameless taxi driver. John offers a quiet "Sorry" to Chris as he plods away. The taxi driver's apparent death isn't acknowledged.

Constantine seems to have shaken it off by the next issue, when the Spectre – an agent of God's wrath – arrives to judge John for casting "the ones who would befriend you into the furnace of war." John doesn't even realize he's being judged at first, and while he admits to the ghostly figure that he deserves to be executed, nothing in his internal monologue suggests he actually means it. In fact, a few pages earlier, he was telling the reader that being a magician "feels fantastic."

> Imagine the rush, you're the clever bastard who gets to outwit the universe itself. All the guilt and regret in the world can't hold a candle to it. You just can't give it up. And when you've lost everyone you've ever loved, and everything you've ever valued? When you've turned bitter and twisted, rotting from the hurt and the shame... that's when you get really powerful.

Is John talking about himself here, or his enemies? In most of *Hellblazer*, it wouldn't have been so ambiguous.

---

[3] The "52" in question being the 52 parallel universes of the wider DC Universe (and, initially, the number of monthly titles); "New" because the DCU had just undergone one of its periodic continuity reboots. In 2016, it went through yet another, slightly less severe, continuity shuffle called Rebirth.

[4] Sargon was inadvertently killed during Constantine's séance back in *Swamp Thing* volume 2 #50, before returning from the dead in volume 2 #148, and again in volume 4 #4. It's unclear exactly how or if these events occurred in the New 52 timeline, however.

[5] In *Constantine* #6, John tells the psychic's ghost that he was going to die of a terminal magical illness anyway, but this comes as cold comfort to the victim – and seems rather like a retcon to soften the blow to the reader.

Constantine idly watches as Philip's magical eyes are removed from his head after they were sold to a demon.

In the third issue of *Constantine*, John discovers that another MacGuffin, a magical lens, has been created by a powerful sorcerer who then hid it in his own son's eyes. The son, now a harmless old man named Philip, is oblivious to this. Nevertheless, Constantine – in order to both save his own life and keep the lens out of the hands of the villains – "sells" Philip's eyes to a demon. It duly gouges them out of the man's head and leaves him bleeding and prone on the floor. John departs as Sargon's daughter battles the demon in Philip's shop, which quickly catches fire. Constantine doesn't comment on Philip's fate, and the hapless man is never seen again.

If that seems cold, then another scene from this era is outright chilling. In *Earth 2: World's End* #8,[6] itself part of one of DC's interminable line-wide crossovers, Constantine attempts to recruit some cryogenically frozen super-criminals to help save the planet, but finds his would-be band of merry men fracturing from the beginning because one of them is a racist and another is black. So John shoots the racist dead. Then he announces, with a shrug: "Had to be done though, right? I can already tell... we are all of us feeling very team-worky!" John as a stone-cold, gun-toting murderous psychopath is horrendously wrong – and that poor man's Joss Whedon dialogue is somehow even worse.

The Whedon overtones didn't end there, though. *Constantine* lasted for 23 issues before DC pulled the plug and relaunched it in June 2015 as *Constantine: The Hellblazer*, with new writers Ming Doyle and James Tynion IV, and a wackier, *Buffy the Vampire Slayer*-inflected tone. This time, John Constantine's bastardly credentials are on full display on page one – as are his underpants. That's because Doyle and Tynion begin his adventures with him half-naked, smeared in blood, and standing in a clothes store. He quickly hypnotizes the shop girl into giving him clothing for free, while his childhood friend-turned-impotent spirit Gary Lester[7] lambasts him for likely losing the girl her job. John doesn't care, though – he's too busy getting dolled up.

In issue #4, we flash back to a young Constantine on the punk scene in New York, treating his then-girlfriend Veronica so badly that it causes a magical chain reaction that makes her start to slip out of reality. When she first confronts him about this, he pushes her away, apparently unconcerned about her fear. Then, when she returns to beg for help – this time partially transparent – he does nothing, not even shed a tear. He later checks to see if she's with her best friend, but slopes off when he finds out she's not.

The narrative alternates between these moments and those of modern-day

---

[6] Cover-dated January 2015. Written by Daniel H Wilson, Marguerite Bennett, and Mike Johnson; art by a small army of people too numerous to name here.
[7] Who died in *Hellblazer* #2, back in 1988; we'll go into more detail on that soon. Bits and pieces of *Swamp Thing* and *Hellblazer* lore keep cropping up in the *New 52* John's stories, but exactly how it all fits together is anyone's guess. *Constantine: The Hellblazer* #4 sets the events of issue #1 of *Hellblazer* proper at "five years ago." John's passport in that same issue of *Constantine: The Hellblazer* still puts his year of birth at 1953, but he's not drawn to look 61 years old.

John in a drunken, self-pitying stupor after finding out that Veronica is now dead, though why he's bothered by this now when he wasn't before is unclear. He's also being begged by a young female ghost to stop a tentacled monster that is obliterating spirits. Sick of her moaning, John barges onstage at a David Copperfield-style magic show, summons the monster – thereby putting the audience at risk – and watches unmoved as it destroys the ghost and all of her undead pals. Constantine later realizes the creature is actually a mutated Veronica, and in the next issue he persuades her best friend, now a powerful magician, to unwittingly kill her because he doesn't want to have the guilt of doing it himself. The issue after *that*, he hooks up with someone else.

These scenes – which come early in both series – are there to establish what kind of a man John Constantine is. The conclusions drawn are grim: he's a coward; he's amoral; he's an oppressive borderline sociopath; he doesn't care about the poor; his sense of responsibility and guilt is fleeting and whimsical; he's only in it for himself; everyone is just a tool to be used for his pleasure; and he kills without compunction – unless it's a "friend" who needs putting down, and then he gets someone else to do the dirty work.

And this is all great, right? This is the kind of thing that John Constantine does – killing people or getting them killed, fucking people over, not giving a toss about innocents and quipping all the while. This is classic Constantine, right? Right? *Right?*

Well, you're a savvy reader and you can see we're only about 1,000 words into this essay, so it will come as little surprise to you that the answer to that question is a resounding *no*.

Sure, in his first real speaking appearance in comics,[8] Constantine might have introduced himself to Swamp Thing with the immortal line, "I'm a nasty piece of work, chief. Ask anybody." Sure, he has a pitch-black sense of humor. And sure, his time in both *Swamp Thing* and *Hellblazer* was regularly punctuated by the deaths of friends, allies, and acquaintances alike. However, despite the image that seems to have pervaded modern-day DC stories of Constantine as a dead-inside, snarky asshole,[9] the character portrayed in classic

---

[8] In *Swamp Thing* #37, by Alan Moore, Rick Veitch, and John Totleben.
[9] It's worth pointing out that both *Constantine* and *Constantine: The Hellblazer* contain scenes in which John acts more recognizably human and less awful, but it's not enough to counteract the moments described in this essay, which are so egregiously out of step with the Constantine developed in the original *Hellblazer* comic that he might as well be someone else entirely.

Swamp Thing and original-flavor *Hellblazer* does, in fact, have both a conscience and an actual (if somewhat flexible) moral and ethical code.[10] In fact, early *Hellblazer* establishes a character who is, in some cases, precisely the opposite of the man seen in the New 52.[11]

To be fair, Constantine's earliest appearances are hardly warm and fuzzy. In those issues of *Swamp Thing*, he cajoles and taunts the frustrated bog god into manifesting at sites of paranormal activity with little indication of what to do once he gets there. Following a battle with vampires in the sunken town of Rosewood,[12] Constantine reprimands Swamp Thing for helping a family escape the carnage, with John telling him: "The whole point was to stop that happening... Before you know where you are, everybody within fifty miles believes in vampires a little bit more." That, in turn, will help the sinister Brujería cult achieve their goal of bringing back an ancient force of destruction.

Sure, allowing a child and his parents to die for the greater good might sound pretty rough, but this isn't moral cowardice posing as tough decision-making; *this* John Constantine is willing to sacrifice himself for the cause. In *Swamp Thing* #48, Swamp Thing is torn between rescuing John – who is being drowned by the Brujería – and stopping a magician, Judith, from being transformed into the messenger that will awaken the destructive entity. Of

---

[10] In between the writing of this essay and this anthology's publication, *John Constantine: Hellblazer* was relaunched yet again, this time under *The Sandman Universe* imprint, a sort of Vertigo-lite gathering place for "mature readers" DC Universe titles such as *Lucifer* and *The Dreaming*. As of January 2020, three issues and a special had been published, and all were far more recognizably Constantine than the more recent iterations, with him only committing dreadful acts when his back is against the wall. Still, the points about the other New 52 titles stand.

[11] There's another criticism to be made of the New 52 Constantine, which is that he spends too much time having flashy magical battles with supervillains like a grubby Doctor Strange, but that's another essay. For an entertaining takedown of this trend, check out 2016's *Six Pack & Dogwelder: Hard-Travelin' Heroez*, by Ennis and Russ Braun. A spinoff of *Hitman*, it features a maudlin Constantine who wears a space helmet, rides a flying surfboard, and packs a "Hellblazer .45" laser pistol. John helps the motley heroes while constantly moaning about what DC Comics has done to him in the name of sales. "There wasn't no peril [in the Vertigo days]," he says in issue #4. "No derrin' do! No ******* one-liners an' plays on words like summink outta bloody *Die Hard*!"

[12] In *Swamp Thing* #39, by Moore, Totleben, and Stephen R. Bissette. Rosewood and its undead denizens first appeared in *Saga of the Swamp Thing* #3, by Martin Pasko and Tom Yeats.

course, Swamp Thing rescues Constantine, who thinks to himself: "The idiot. The big, stupid idiot. He saved me. He let them change Judith and saved me."

That context is useful for the final act of the storyline,[13] in which John persuades reluctant former superhero Mento to use his psychic power – boosted by a team of sorcerers including Sargon, Baron Winters, and Zatara – to oversee Swamp Thing's confrontation with the entity. The supernatural shockwaves drive Mento insane, but Moore makes a point of contrasting John's regret over that with Winters' glee at their "victory," and by having both Sargon and Zatara willingly sacrifice themselves during the ritual, recognizing that their own lives are insignificant in the face of reality-wide oblivion.

Swamp Thing rescues Constantine from the Brujería.

Even in these early issues, and despite operating with cool pragmatism, Constantine is clearly not amoral or sociopathic. However, it's in *Hellblazer* proper that he is able to flourish into the complex, cunning, and – yes – compassionate man who sustained 300 monthly issues and a multitude of

---

[13] In *Swamp Thing* #49-50, by Moore, Bissette, Veitch, Stan Woch, and Alfredo Alcala.

miniseries, graphic novels, and prose stories.[14] The comic launched three months after Moore departed *Swamp Thing*, and author Jamie Delano immediately made it clear that despite his cool, collected exterior, John is haunted by his past. Literally: in the first issue, Delano brings back John's slain *Swamp Thing* supporting cast as an entourage of ghosts, stalking him in silent judgement. Whether they are truly ghosts or personifications of his guilt remains ambiguous; Delano also makes it clear that John is not of the soundest mind, turning a brief mention in *Swamp Thing* of time spent in a madhouse[15] into an ongoing struggle with mental illness.

Definitely *not* a figment of Constantine's imagination, though, is Gary Lester, his childhood pal and the bumbling magician responsible for releasing the African hunger spirit Mnemoth upon New York. Lester is set up as a mirror of Constantine, a fellow working-class boy from Liverpool who looked to punk music and the occult for an escape. While John became a mover and shaker on the magical scene, Lester became a dropout, eventually bumming around the back alleys of Morocco looking for heroin. There, he found a Sudanese child with Mnemoth bound inside him, and − unable to resist the demon's call − freed the creature before binding it in a bottle. This is the first contrast Delano creates for us: while Constantine's pursuit of magic is likened to a drug several times throughout *Hellblazer* and the subsequent New 52 series,[16] he rarely uses it purely for his own satisfaction. Lester, meanwhile, draws Mnemoth from the boy's body because he cannot resist the temptation it represents.

John, upon hearing this story, asks Gary what happened to the child. Gary is so enraptured by the memory of the conjuring that he doesn't even hear the question until Constantine asks again, at which point he impassively remarks:

---

[14] *War Lord* and *Subterranean*, two *Hellblazer* novels by John Shirley, were released in 2006, one year after the *Constantine* film. In addition, short *Hellblazer* prose stories were published in the seasonal anthology comic *Vertigo Winter's Edge* #3 and the special *Vertigo Secret Files: Hellblazer*, and John features prominently in a prose tale included in the DC Heroes Role-Playing Game's *Swamp Thing Sourcebook / Adventure*.

[15] In *Swamp Thing* #46 by Moore, Bissette, and Totleben. This is the first mention of the "Newcastle incident" that Delano would later explore in *Hellblazer* #11. The *Swamp Thing* story dates the event as happening in the summer of 1985; *Hellblazer* #10 puts it in 1978, but there was one of those big DC continuity resets in between, so let's chalk it up to that and move on.

[16] Including, to be fair, the *Constantine* quote from Ray Fawkes and Jeff Lemire that I included earlier in this essay.

"The kid? The kid is dead. Looks like he's been flayed. Flesh hangs in bloody tatters." This is the second contrast Delano presents us with: Lester as a conscienceless magus, Constantine as someone who is naturally empathetic toward others. John may be fallible, but he's not a callous lunatic or a careless magic junkie, and Delano makes that quite clear here.[17]

So it's pretty startling to remember how Doyle and Tynion presented these two characters in the opening pages of *Constantine: The Hellblazer*: John as the self-absorbed asshole willing to have a shop girl fired because he wants free clothes, and Gary as the angel on his shoulder telling him to not to be so selfish. It's precisely the opposite of what *Hellblazer* set up, a Bizarro affair, inverse and perverse – and it's hard to imagine how Doyle and Tynion could have gotten the relationship so very wrong.

Not that John's an angel in that first *Hellblazer* story, of course – his plan to save New York from destruction hinges on offering up Lester as a new vessel for Mnemoth, which will consume first the man, then itself. But this is preceded by pages of guilty monologuing from Constantine. At one point, he buries his head in his pillow so that his ghostly retinue can't hear him cry. He also flees Mnemoth as it consumes a priest, knowing that he isn't powerful enough to confront it alone. It's a scene that would later be echoed in the Fawkes-Lemire *Constantine* run, when John flees Sargon's daughter at the expense of Chris's life, but here John's feelings of guilt are made absolutely clear in his narration, and he recalls the incident with regret later in the story.

Lester isn't the only mirror Delano creates in this story: John is also contrasted with Papa Midnite, the voodoo crime boss who is called in to help bolster Constantine's power and ensnare Mnemoth. Whereas Constantine lives in a run-down flat in London, Midnite resides in a penthouse apartment in his own soaring Manhattan skyscraper;[18] and while John spends his relatively humble life among friends, Midnite lives alone save for a collection of skulls[19] and a gaggle of zombified humans who beat one another to death for paying

---

[17] Contrast Gary's lack of empathy for the boy with the way Constantine went insane with grief after sending young Astra Logue to Hell in *Hellblazer* #11.

[18] A sure sign of villainy.

[19] One of which belonged to his sister, whom Constantine refers to as "an amazing woman." In a minor continuity fluff, *Hellblazer* #74 (by Garth Ennis and Steve Dillon) has John apparently meeting her for the first time as a spirit. She reveals Midnite killed her decades prior, when he was a child, raising the question of when John was supposed to have met her before issue #1.

crowds. Toward the end of *Hellblazer* #2, after Gary has been sacrificed and John is in the middle of his first on-panel booze-addled meltdown, Midnite looms over him and says: "Hmm, for a man of power, you leave yourself vulnerable. Grief, Constantine, is a luxury. A magician must separate himself from his humanity." John, of course, does not, and instead steps outside to meet his ghostly followers – with Gary now among them.

David Lloyd's acclaimed portrayal of John Constantine in Jamie Delano's *The Horrorist.*

In fact, despite the New 52 depiction of Constantine as irresponsible and largely unburdened by regret, guilt is John's overriding emotion through much of *Hellblazer*, and is a key factor in not just John's present, but his past. Later in his run, Delano establishes two key moments in Constantine's history that hang over him for much of the rest of the series: his guilt at accidentally having condemned an innocent girl to Hell,[20] and at having caused his mother to die during childbirth.[21] The one time Delano wrote him as recognizably sociopathic was in the prestige miniseries *The Horrorist*, with artist David Lloyd, and the whole point of that story was to show John regaining his lost humanity.

Issue #24 saw Delano introducing one of his most chilling villains: the Family Man, a serial killer who targets loving families. After discovering that his friend Jerry O'Flynn has been aiding the killer, Constantine vows to stop the madness, but initially gets cold feet – until nightmares about the dead families spur him into action. The resulting game of cat and mouse sees Constantine's own father slain by the murderer, with John taking revenge by shooting the man dead.[22] Unlike the cold-blooded shooting portrayed in *Earth 2: World's End* #8, however, John doesn't just shrug off his first hands-on murder[23] with a quip. Instead, he reels, vomits, and staggers away, and by *Hellblazer* #34 he's undergoing a full-on breakdown and descent into alcoholic misery, from which he is saved only by the intervention of child psychic Mercury.

John's angst over the damage he's done became an endlessly renewable resource for subsequent writers, with the next permanent author, Garth Ennis, stacking the weights heavily onto John's conscience. In his opening storyline, "Dangerous Habits,"[24] Constantine, dying of terminal lung cancer, sells his soul separately to each of the three Lords of Hell – knowing that they'll go to war over its ownership, which would weaken their forces so much that Heaven would be able to take control of Earth. Realizing their stalemate, the three elect to cure his condition instead. Constantine is initially elated, but soon slips into a pit of alcoholic self-loathing for having the temerity "to condemn everything

---

[20] In *Hellblazer* #11, by Delano, Richard Piers Rayner, and Mark Buckingham.

[21] First mentioned in *Hellblazer* #28, by Delano, Ron Tiner, and Kevin Walker; it is revealed in issue #100, by Paul Jenkins and Sean Philips, that his father had a hand in this, too, having weakened her body by forcing her to undergo back-alley abortions.

[22] In *Hellblazer* #30, art by Tiner and Buckingham.

[23] Delano would retcon this in *Hellblazer* #84, in which John saves his pal Chas, who is under the thumb of his occultist mother Queenie, by drowning her chimpanzee familiar, Slag. He does so fully aware that Queenie will die due to her psychic connection with the animal. But she's miles away at the time, which provides perhaps a little moral wiggle-room.

[24] *Hellblazer* #41-46, art by Will Simpson and others. This remains one of the definitive *Hellblazer* arcs and was drawn on heavily for the 2005 movie adaptation *Constantine*.

that's ever lived to the slavery of the angels,"[25] and calling himself a "selfish, stupid, arrogant little shit," to boot.

Ennis continued to revisit the theme right up to his final storyline, "Rake at the Gates of Hell,"[26] which ends with Constantine advising an acquaintance: "You let that little twinge of guilt stay with you and slide up close to you on long winter nights, and maybe you'll get some good out of it." Sure enough, John's twinges of guilt are there for all to see under most of the other *Hellblazer* writers, whether he's reflecting on the damage done during Paul Jenkins' run,[27] blaming himself for an ex-girlfriend's grisly death in Warren Ellis's opening arc,[28] letting himself go to prison because he let a pal kill himself in Brian Azzarello's issues,[29] or burning up his life in a fit of self-loathing after getting his sister killed in Mike Carey's finale.[30]

Another key characteristic of Constantine is his hatred of authority. If anything can be said to motivate John, it's the desire to undermine and tear down the powers that be when they overstep their bounds, whether that's Heaven or Hell,[31] politicians or royals,[32] police or gangland bosses.[33] He is, after all, a Sex Pistols-era anarchist punk from a conservative English city. And for the majority of *Hellblazer*'s run, the writers are usually careful to show him not using his abilities to screw over the little man – well, unless the little man *really* pisses him off.

Still, there is a tension between John the anarchist and John the manipulator. In *Hellblazer* #81, Constantine has a pimp beaten up and chased

---

[25] The notion of the forces of Heaven as oppressive monsters was introduced in Delano's *Hellblazer* #10, as John foiled their plan to create a new messiah. It was revisited in Jenkins' issue #105, in which one of John's ancestors stopped another scheme by the angels, this time involving the poet Samuel Taylor Coleridge.

[26] *Hellblazer* #78-87, art by Steve Dillon.

[27] *Hellblazer* #114, art by Sean Phillips.

[28] *Hellblazer* #139, art by John Higgins, although Ellis smartly points out that John is also using her death as an excuse to get involved in something nasty.

[29] *Hellblazer* #150, art by Richard Corbin.

[30] *Hellblazer* #215, art Leonardo Manco.

[31] Particularly in Delano's "Damnation's Army" plotline in *Hellblazer* #4-12, art by various.

[32] Both in *Hellblazer* #52-55 by Ennis and Simpson.

[33] For the former, see long-suffering DCI Watford, who makes his first appearance in *Hellblazer* #134, by Ellis and Higgins. For the latter, see the eerie fate John visits upon a gang boss in issue #201 as punishment for exploiting a group of young junkies.

out of London; then he gets blind drunk and rants to a priest: "They could have killed the tosser for all I know. And now I'm just like all the bastards I've hated all me life. Kill him! Fire him! Close them down! Piss all over him! ... I'm in charge!" A subtler exploration of that tension comes in the Grant Morrison-penned *Hellblazer* #25-26, in which Constantine is affected by psychic waves that bring his darkest urges to the surface. He promptly puts on a mask of Conservative Prime Minister Margaret Thatcher and leads a parade of similarly affected townsfolk, saying: "Follow me! Mummy knows best! In your hearts, you know it's right!"[34]

Thatcher, of course, was symbolic of oppression, repression, and authoritarian control to the left-wing comic book writers of the 1980s – as *Hellblazer* demonstrated when demons cheered her election in issue #3, and when police attacked a band of harmless hippies utilizing her government's new anti-traveler law[35] in issue #16. John's complex relationship with authority is ironed out in the relaunched *Constantine* series to an elevator-pitch-friendly: "[Constantine] fights to maintain balance and stop anyone from becoming too powerful." This, of course, turns him into a man on a quest rather than a drifting figure with a chip on his shoulder – much like the Keanu Reeves film adaptation, *Constantine*, did by making him someone bent on exorcising demons to earn a spot in Heaven.

None of this is to say that he's a terribly *nice* man, of course. In fact, he's capable of dreadful things. But *Hellblazer*'s writers are usually careful to establish first that John has no other recourse, and at least make him feel bad afterwards. In issue #10, he uses his demonic essence to taint Zed, who is supposed to be the new Virgin Mary (emphasis on the Mary, not the virgin), leading to her rejection by Heaven and her apparent death,[36] but says there

---

[34] Echoing Thatcher's speech to a Conservative Rally in Cardiff in April 1979: "I think that many traditional Labour supporters want the same things we want ... You know in your hearts that Britain must take a different road."
(https://www.margaretthatcher.org/document/104011)
[35] The Public Order Act of 1986, which placed restrictions on public processions and assemblies with the intention of limiting gatherings by New Age sorts. It was preceded by the 1 June 1985 "Battle of the Beanfield," when more than 1,000 police officers and Ministry of Defence officials violently rousted hundreds of hippies and travelers who had congregated for a festival near Stonehenge.
[36] Zed survives the ordeal, returns during Delano's "Fear Machine" storyline as a member of the ill-fated Freedom Mob hippie group, and is later mentioned in John

was no other way to stop humanity's enslavement by Heaven. In issue #67, he backs out on a promise to help President John F. Kennedy's spirit in Hell when he realizes it would mean a fatal confrontation with the First of the Fallen. In issue #104, he seduces and betrays Chantinelle, a succubus ally better known as "Ellie," to retain the demonic taint he previously lost, saving his own life but leaving her exposed to the Devil.[37] The list goes on.

Whenever Constantine *does* dish out something truly dreadful, his subjects are usually worthy of his ire: the cruel angel Gabriel having his wings chainsawed off,[38] bastard magician Aleister Crowley being tricked into giving up his soul,[39] psychopathic killer Joshua Wright being trapped in a mortuary cabinet with the decaying body of one of his victims,[40] murderous gangster Domine Fredericks being killed by one of his possessed employees,[41] and sadistic mages Lord Calvin Burnham and Mako being trapped in their own private, tiny Hell for eternity.[42] Even when writer Eddie Campbell has John mug a man to steal his passport in *Hellblazer* #87, it's made clear the man in question is a yuppie.

Come on, a *yuppie*. You know he had it coming.

All of this, however, is balanced out by occasional bouts of – well, if not heroism, then at least some sense of justice. In *Hellblazer* #6, John follows some skinheads into a public toilet, thinking they're about to beat up a gay man, and muses, "You can't pretend it isn't happening, can you?"[43] In fact, John's inability to look away from the grim horror of what's going on around him spurs him into acts of selfless risk-taking. Unlike the John of the *Constantine* comic, he's not on a mission to maintain balance,[44] and unlike the John of *Constantine: The*

Shirley's *Hellblazer* novels as working alongside Mercury with the Peace Corpses, ghosts of soldiers who seek to end war on Earth.

[37] And creating something of a bootstrap paradox – John needs the taint to regain his dark side, but if he can screw Chantinelle over like that, both figuratively and literally, surely he already *has* his dark side?

[38] *Hellblazer* #66, by Ennis and Dillon.

[39] *Hellblazer* #95 and 96, by Jenkins and Phillips.

[40] *Hellblazer* #139, by Ellis and Higgins.

[41] *Hellblazer* #180, by Carey and Marcelo Frusin.

[42] *Hellblazer* #248, by Andy Diggle and Manco.

[43] As it happens, the "victim" is a demon who swiftly dismembers the thugs, but points for effort.

[44] Something that's traditionally been the Phantom Stranger's beat anyway.

Hellblazer, he's not trying to make some cash as a freelance occult troubleshooter. He's just getting involved, because if he doesn't, who will?

Remarkably, these core characteristics – John's conscience, anarchist spirit, and vicious streak tempered by a genuinely noble impulse to help the doomed – remain solid for the vast majority of *Hellblazer*'s run. He becomes a little harder, a little more inured to the horror, from Warren Ellis's run onward – as Ellis himself has John say, in issue #139, "I'm not the milkman of human kindness I used to be" – but the character remains more or less the same.

It's not quite flawless, mind you. Brian Azzarello has a couple of wobbles in his run, as his hard-boiled noir sensibilities prove an awkward fit with Constantine as written up to that point. In *Hellblazer* #151, a hitch-hiking John unnerves his drivers so much that they lose control of their car and careen fatally into a tree. With the men dead, John opens the car's trunk and releases a bound woman whom they had kidnapped. So far, so Constantine. However, it goes rather off-piste in the final moments, as John leaves the half-naked woman to walk alone up the secluded road from which she'd just been snatched. In issue #161, John persuades a mentally disabled man to become a serial murderer in order to dispatch some hostage-takers, which seems rather like overkill. And in issue #168, John verbally abuses a bunch of old women for looking at him funny, saying they're just jealous of his youthful vitality, which is a bit much coming from a guy who's just about to turn 50.

The next three writers – Mike Carey, Denise Mina, and Andy Diggle – get things more or less on track, and it's not until a catastrophically misguided two-parter by Jason Aaron[45] that things *really* go wrong. Aaron's story concerns a group of people putting together a documentary about John's old punk band, Mucous Membrane, who go to the site of the ill-fated exorcism that cost a girl her soul and John his sanity[46] and end up waking a slumbering horror elemental, the Norfulthing. At the end of the story, John reveals that he's had to feed the demon one nasty person a year for decades – basically, making him a serial killer – and does almost nothing to help the documentary crew, who are fatally succumbing to its influence, even egging on one man who is pulling his own veins out of his hand to keep going until he dies.

---

[45] *Hellblazer* #245-246, with fantastic art by Sean Murphy.
[46] The so-called "Newcastle incident," as revealed in *Hellblazer* #11, by Delano, Rayner, and Buckingham.

Sure, it's just a short fill-in story, but it was sadly a harbinger of things to come. Peter Milligan took over regular writing duties in March 2009 with *Hellblazer* #251, and while the first part of his run was more or less in tune with what had come before, things began to get a little wild with issue #266, as familiar characterization was jettisoned. In that issue, which concludes a two-part story involving old punks and even older spirits, John remarks: "I'm just too tired and cynical to care much anymore. I tried... fighting the Conservatives. Fuck me, I really tried."

To some extent, this might seem fair enough. Why not push John in new directions? And why wouldn't he feel just a wee bit weary of fighting authority at age 57? The answer to that question is that it shatters the very core of Constantine's character. It might make sense from a real-world perspective, but if you take the class struggle, the drive for autonomy, and the desire to overthrow the rich and powerful away from John Constantine, you don't have a lot left.

Well, you *do* have the conscience, the compassion, and the bastardry. Unfortunately, two of those take major hits in Milligan's run as well. In *Hellblazer* #276, John discovers that his Brixton apartment building has been bought up by Marcus Molloy, a finance whiz who plans to evict him and all the other tenants. So John does what any deranged lunatic would do: tricks him into using an ancient Celtic spell that causes his body to become horribly deformed. Molloy begs John for help, but Constantine shoves him out into the street, where he collapses before turning into a whirling, frothing mass of tentacles and disappearing from reality altogether.

It's too late, Molloy.

Now, Molloy is by no means a great guy; he's a sexist, arrogant prick who's happy to turf poor Londoners out of their homes to make a bit of cash that he doesn't even need. Still, basically killing him – or at least ending his life as he knows it – is way out of character for Constantine. Destroy the guy's business empire? Sure. Terrify him into signing over the property to you? Fine. This, though? Yuppies might deserve the odd punch in the stomach and a pilfered passport, but this is going too far.

In the next issue, John replaces his severed thumb[47] by figuring out when a car accident is fated to occur. After it has happened, he then snips one off the crash victim – who is apparently still alive at the time.[48] The issue after *that*, John finds himself fending off his niece, Gemma, who thinks he raped her at his wedding.[49] In fact, the perpetrator turns out to have been Constantine's demonic double, whom John had made out of the worst parts of his soul way back in issue #94. Think about that, though – doesn't that mean John was harboring incestuous urges toward his then-15-year-old niece when the demon was created?

Actually, no – it's best not to think about that at all.

Of course, these examples are cherry-picked, to an extent; there are scenes in Milligan's run in which John acts like a recognizable human being, just as there are scenes in prior writers' tenures in which he acts horribly. As with those moments from *Constantine* and *Constantine: The Hellblazer*, however, pulling John to such extremes – even if it's just for a moment – critically damages the character established by the preceding 17 *Hellblazer* writers. By the end of Milligan's run, it feels less like the closing part of Vertigo Comics' longest-running series and more like a preview of what was to come. The New 52, it seems, was already here.

---

[47] Lost following magically induced madness in *Hellblazer* #268, by Milligan, Giuseppe Camuncoli, and Stefano Landini.

[48] Mitigating factors: the crash was destined to happen, and John scares off a demon that's come for the driver's soul, but it's still three shades darker than Constantine should be.

[49] Which occurred in *Hellblazer* #275, an issue that also transformed Mike Carey's tough-as-nails heroine Angie Spatchcock into a bitter, obese crybaby. But that's a whole other rant.

A Total Wanker in London: The Poison Truth and the Hellblazer's Rebirth

by Richard Gray

A black hole. The biggest tosser. Magical rogue and gadfly. Scouser. Magician. Wanker. A nasty piece of work. Londoner. That bastard John Constantine.

In the course of DC Comics' Rebirth era, the long-suffering antihero has had these names thrown at him like weaponry. After all, in the realms of magic, there's a lot of power in words. Despite the negativity swirling around them, the trenchcoated con man gets to wear them as badges of honor as the publisher returned to a version of the character not seen in years. Indeed, in the first issue of writer Simon Oliver's run, an airborne John Constantine answers his accusers up front: "Is that all you've got?" Yet it's the most innocuous of those names ("Londoner") that Oliver focuses on in a back-to-basics approach that features his old pal Swamp Thing, a tenure in the United Kingdom, a political undercurrent, and an overt reference to Sting lyrics in the text.

A few years earlier, Constantine was having something of an extended lost weekend. In 2011, DC Comics launched the New 52, "a historic renumbering of the entire DC Universe (DCU) line of comic books with 52 first issues."[1] New versions of classic titles and characters were launched, from *Action Comics* to *Zatanna*. The marketing strategy was, at least initially, a massive financial success. However, not all fans were pleased. Iconic characters were altered beyond recognition or were simply omitted entirely. Constantine left the darker Vertigo imprint to join the mainstream DCU in *Justice League Dark*, then eventually got his own title, simply titled *Constantine*. Yet it was only a matter of time before this reboot would also meet its end, and 2015's *Convergence* event wrapped up the New 52 branding with a crossover that briefly restored the old guard by pitting characters from various continuities against each other.

Coming out the other side of this was DC You, a rebranded set of titles bridging the New 52 world and something closer to the original DC Universe. *Constantine: The Hellblazer* (2015-2016), written by Ming Doyle and James Tynion IV, was a bit of a curiosity in this mix. Stylishly rendered by artist Riley Rossmo – and later by the likes of Vanessa Del Rey, Travel Foreman, Joseph Silver, and Ivan Plascencia – the short-lived series only ran for 13 issues. Yet in that time, Doyle and Tynion set up so much. Like Mike Grell's run on *Green Arrow*,[2] Constantine is shifted to a real U.S. city (in this case, New York), consciously kept away from other superheroes until the very end, with a focus on his inner demons as much as his outer ones. The comic introduced the character of Oliver, a bartender with whom John falls in love and inevitably damns – a theme that the writers of television's *Legends of Tomorrow* would pick up for the show's fourth season. This story cycle solidified the mood for Constantine's overarching narrative, ending with John's admission that he knows he will always be alone. Bummer.

---

[1] Hyde, David. "DC Comics Announces Historic Renumbering of All Superhero Titles and Landmark Day-and-Date Digital Distribution." 31 May 2011: https://www.dccomics.com/blog/2011/05/31/dc-comics-announces-historic-renumbering-of-all-superhero-titles-and-landmark-day-and-date-digital-distribution.

[2] In the wake of one of DC's earlier reboots, the infamous *Crisis on Infinite Earths*, Grell was hired to reboot the then second-stringer character of Green Arrow. Starting with *Green Arrow: The Longbow Hunters* miniseries, he started an 80-issue run in which the character aged in real time and stood apart from the rest of the DCU. (Read more about this era in 2017's *Moving Target: The History and Evolution of Green Arrow*, by Richard Gray, published by Sequart Organization.) By way of cosmic coincidence, the contemporaneous *Hellblazer* (1988-2013) also saw Constantine age in real time, right up until the final issue. It was all about gritty realism back then.

DC ultimately decided to stop messing about and have an each-way bet on what the fans wanted. In 2016, the Rebirth event rebooted and renumbered many of the comics line (again), kept the New 52 continuity intact, but brought back characters and stories that had long been dormant. For our pal Constantine, this meant a new writer and a new title: *The Hellblazer.* The series was written by Simon Oliver, a name familiar to Constantine fans from previous iterations, such as the 2008 miniseries *Hellblazer: Chas – The Knowledge*, with artists Goran Sudžuka and Matt Hollingsworth. While many were still lamenting the rounding of the edge that got sanded off when John left the Vertigo line, Oliver authentically told a story that ran Constantine down the rabbit hole and rebirthed the rogue with his most essential qualities. Of course, as we quickly learned, that didn't necessarily make him a nice guy.

Making London Great Again

Oliver's first order of business was to bring Constantine home, or at least to his mostly permanent abode of London. After all, Oliver was the first British writer to tackle the character since Peter Milligan finished his run just prior to the launch of the New 52. In a special *Rebirth* preview issue,[3] John returns home to finally rid himself of a curse that had made him physically sick upon entering London. Oliver wastes no time in reintroducing us to old allies Chas Chandler, Mercury, and Swamp Thing, each of whom fill a vital role in the ongoing series. In the midst of some demon swindling, artist Moritat's seductively underlit fetishization of John's cigarettes leaves us with no doubt that this is a return as much as it is a rebirth.

The plot opens with a basic Constantine move: he cheats a demon by gambling the souls of the entire city of London, betting on Mercury's knowledge of the demon's name. It pays off, of course, and the curse is lifted. At this point, the issue is nothing more than a teaser of things to come, a restorative gesture for Constantine's loyal fans. So it's somewhat appropriate to see him breaking the fourth wall in the final panels. After contemplating whether he would have damned eight million souls in London if Mercury hadn't shown up, he turns to the readers and challenges them: "Well, that's something you're gonna stick around and find out for yourselves. Or not. Because, quite frankly, at the end of the day – do I strike you as the kind of guy who gives a fuck?"

---

[3] Collected with the first six issues of the run in *The Hellblazer: Rebirth Vol. 1 – The Poison Truth*.

John Constantine is so happy to be home that he breaks the fourth wall in *The Hellblazer: Rebirth* #1.

In fact, it's the answer to this question that dominates "The Poison Truth" arc, from Oliver and his art team, Moritat and Andre Symanowicz.[4] After a potted and sepia-toned history of humanity's violent 20th century – from Sarajevo in 1914 to the death of Adolf Hitler – we are brought to the cold, blue tones of South London in the present day. As is the case in many of the issues, Constantine is introduced hungover, naked, and in someone else's home. Swamp Thing soon turns up in Chas's greenhouse and needs help finding his old flame, Abby. Constantine subsequently seeks out his former companion Mercury, completing his band of merry freaks and geeks. As Mercury learns to explore the "eleven dimensions of time and space," it becomes evident that

---

[4] Originally published as *The Hellblazer: Rebirth* #1-6 (2016-2017). Other artists on this run include Pia Guerra, José Marzan Jr, and Carrie Strachan.

there is an ancient cabal of djinn who are reasonably pissed at no longer being in control of the Earth.

By the second issue, every London pub, club, and seedy establishment to which we are introduced leads us deeper down the rabbit hole. One of the dominant textual and visual themes in this first arc is establishing a sense of place around London. While there are countless Easter eggs and references to Constantine's past – John tells Swamp Thing he won't be his "kinky booty-call, body-swap sex object," for instance[5] – this arc is designed as a jumping-on point for pretty much any reader.

To achieve this, Oliver firmly establishes London and its surroundings as a character that is as equally necessary to the plot as Chas or Mercury. Moritat's and Symanowicz's London is positively Victorian, shrouded in shadows and Gothic architecture, and dwarfing the would-be hero. With Constantine pursued by a couple of djinn, Oliver and his art team tick off a series of London icons, which naturally includes a pub called The Blind Mick. After all, as Constantine reminds the reader in another fourth-wall-breaking moment, "Us English don't trust anyone who isn't at least a closet alcoholic."

The increasingly grainy shadows give way to the red glow of the Tate Club, a tea room introduced all the way back in Warren Ellis's "Haunted" arc.[6] A meeting place for magic-users in England, it not only serves as a focal point for the broader plot, but Oliver wields it as a means of reminding us that this book is London to the core. In a single-page graffiti montage, one that culminates in (what else) one of London's tube stations, Mortiat and Symanowicz slip in a visual reference to Orbital Comics.[7] As readers caught in this spiral running through London, we are one step behind the eight ball perpetually, which is exactly where the typically astute Constantine remains for much of this arc.

More than anything, Oliver is setting up the Hellblazer for a massive comeuppance, especially after several cocky victories he's experienced in the

---

[5] A reference to Jamie Delano's "Sex and Death" story in *Hellblazer* #9 (October 1988).

[6] In *Hellblazer* #134 (February 1999). The issue also introduced Clarice Sackville, who plays a large part in Oliver's first two *Rebirth* arcs. In "The Poison Truth," she is introduced as one of the most powerful magicians in London, possibly immortal, and has the ability to make herself appear much younger than the two centuries she has spent on the planet.

[7] The bright yellow signage of the Eisner Award-winning shop, founded in 2002, has quickly made it one of the destination comic shops/galleries for discerning comic book fans visiting Central London.

previous year or so.[8] Yet at that moment, he is content to let us bask in this return home, even describing the djinn's relentless pursuit of the magician with a sampling of the early 1980s stalker ballad "Every Breath You Take." As any fan will tell you, songwriter Gordon Matthew Thomas Sumner, better known as Sting, was the main inspiration for Constantine's iconic look.

This arc is so London that it Stings (from *The Hellblazer* #2).

The 12 issues that make up "The Poison Truth" and its companion arc, "The Smokeless Fire," take us across the United Kingdom, over to Paris, and even to the Arabia of 1936 (thanks to Phillip Tan's and Elmer Santos' gorgeously painted art). Writer Richard Kadrey also briefly takes Constantine back to the United States with a San Francisco jaunt that leads him to vow "I'm never coming back." Oliver creates such an anchor in London that his successor, Tim Seeley, continues to use it as a backdrop across the remaining dozen issues of the *Rebirth* run. Whether we are witnessing flashbacks to his punk days or seeing

---

[8] An expanded examination of the issue, written by this essayist, can be found at https://www.newsarama.com/31319-best-shots-reviews-star-wars-23-hellblazer-2-josie-the-pussycats-1.html.

Constantine battle a "new wave Ronnie Kray," Oliver re-establishes London as a kind of teacher, brother, and maybe even secret lover.[9] Constantine may have gambled with the eight million souls that make up the capital of England, but he did it so he could ultimately walk its streets again. Or, as Constantine quips at the start of Oliver's run, "London was still a pus-filled boil on the face of humanity. But at least it was *my* pus-filled boil again."

Queen, Country, and Racial Purity Bullcrap

Early on in "The Poison Truth," Constantine visits the powerful Clarice Sackville at the Tate Club, fully expecting a verbal (and possibly physical) bollocksing for playing fast and loose with the souls of his beloved London. "How refreshingly English of you," she purrs. "Enjoying the punishment more than the crime. You should have taken my advice and got into politics, Constantine." John's reply is completely on brand: "Even I have my limits." Oliver does not seem to share this limitation, placing Constantine against the backdrop of a political omnishambles that is still in a state of arrested development at the time of this essay's writing. While Oliver never sets out to be a political commentator, at least not in the way that Vertigo's writers were back in the day, topical references pepper the scripts and leave no doubt as to which side of the political divide Constantine ultimately falls into.

Returning a street-level character to contemporary Britain naturally brings with it the massive elephant in the room of Brexit.[10] In the first pages of the *Rebirth* issue, Constantine remarks that "When a racist, short-fingered, failed meat salesman began circling the White House," it was time to get out. Oliver's none-too-subtle middle finger pointed at Donald Trump is stated as the reason that Constantine left the United States. However, returning him to the U.K. came with its own set of problems, according to the writer. "[B]y the time the issue came out Brexit had happened so we were all like, hold on a minute? He's run from Trump to a country that just passed Brexit?!"[11] In the same interview

---

[9] For more about Constantine's strong personal connection to the city, read "A Man You Don't Meet Every Day: Constantine's London," by Adrian Brown, elsewhere in this volume.

[10] In case you've been exiled to one of the various levels of Hell for the last few years, Brexit is a portmanteau of "British" and "exit" commonly used to describe the United Kingdom's withdrawal from the European Union.

[11] Lu, Alex. "Interview: Simon Oliver Reveals Why We Needed a British Writer on *The Hellblazer*." The Beat, 25 October 2016:

with *The Beat*, Oliver contends that the rapid pace of contemporary political discourse made it difficult to make *The Hellblazer: Rebirth* a truly political book.

> I think when [Jamie] Delano was doing the book when it first started and Thatcher was in, things were moving much slower then, and we kind of settled into it. A lot of what we're dealing with now, particularly with the Trumps and the election, it's the threat of something that hasn't been realized yet.

Nevertheless, Constantine and the characters that surround him can't help but comment on the world as it's happening, and like the best forms of speculative fiction, they hold up a mirror to the stories occurring around the reader – even if that mirror is filled with otherworldly demons.

Brexit doesn't feature heavily as a plot point, but the tensions underlying it are present at every turn. With the comic depicting London and its underbelly, Chas's misguided attempts at gambling lead him to run afoul of White Boy and his group of shaved-headed minions, who are labelled as followers, in the words of Constantine, of "Queen, country and racial purity bullcrap." *The Hellblazer: Rebirth* #4 (January 2017) declares its unapologetic approach on John Cassaday's and Paul Mounts' glorious cover art. Constantine stands in the foreground, with trademark smoke billowing out of his mouth and his head ablaze. The backdrop is the looming head of Swamp Thing, an army of identical djinn, and a massive, stylized, all-white Union Jack dominating the one-sheet.

With Chas and Constantine tied up, White Boy brings John's "sorry puckered left arse" up to speed with a monologue worthy of a supervillain:

> You bloody do-gooders, with your marches, and protests and endless, never-ending bloody petitions to ban this, boycott bleedin' that, free some bloody sooty... Then comes the nineties... Deep down you all thought you'd bloody won, didn't you? Squeezing poor Maggie out, God rest her soul, and getting Blair in. What a con that turned out to be... Now, look around you... The real Englanders are rising up to cast the illegals, the inbreds and the subraces from our shores....

While the references to former Prime Ministers Margaret "Maggie" Thatcher and Tony Blair may put us right back in the thick of Constantine's adventures, White Boy's call for a return to the glory days is a super topical viewpoint. Putting aside the racist rhetoric, the character neatly summarizes contemporary British politics, articulating how the perceived disenfranchisement of the "real" Britons led to a resurgence of conservative

https://www.comicsbeat.com/interview-simon-oliver-reveals-why-we-needed-a-british-writer-on-the-hellblazer/.

nationalism. Constantine ultimately gets under White Boy's skin by guessing that his anger comes not just from England's current levels of migration, but also his relationship with his mother. It might be a super-simple way of explaining it, but in a single page of this comic book – published only weeks after the 2016 U.S. Presidential elections – it taps into the same mindset that swung to the (alt) right.

In the follow-up arc, "The Smokeless Fire," John and Mercury chase a shoe across Paris. (It's got an enchantment on it, OK?) Meanwhile, the Majority Party Chambers of the Houses of Parliament meet in an opulent room. Oliver depicts a group of squabbling power brokers, led by Mr. Carver, a man so powerful he allegedly tells the Prime Minister "whatever I want her to bleeding think." Marid, a djinn and the chief antagonist of the arc, refers to Carver as "the man who sold the voting public the shit sandwich that is Brexit." (It seems that even the immortal villains find something abhorrent in modern conservative politics.) Later in the same issue, Constantine mockingly insults unwitting American tourists with a litany of virulent French: "I hope you drown facedown in your matcha lattes... Over here spending tax breaks stolen from those less fortunate... while your country burns at the hands of a demented orange psychopath."

So, while Oliver may not have consciously set out to write a political book, he certainly found himself working against the backdrop of one. Constantine is not the outspoken mouthpiece for the left that one of Denny O'Neil's characters was in the 1960s and 1970s, but he wears the mantle – as well as that trenchcoat he seems to be so fond of.

If You're Going to Be a Bastard, Be Like a Dolphin

This brings us to the depiction of Constantine himself across the first two arcs of The Hellblazer: Rebirth. Unlike the strict moral codes of Superman or Batman, Constantine has always existed in the shadowy grey areas of morality. He brushes up against pure evil, beds it, and would just as readily skip out on it before it has a chance to make breakfast. Oliver's two arcs hammer this home repeatedly: as we are often reminded, John did gamble with the souls of eight million Londoners for personal gain.

Constantine's self-interest is the basis of a poignant conversation between Mercury and Swamp Thing. The latter contends that Constantine is the man who must live in a confusing and messy world, make painful choices, and "carry the burden of those choices." Mercury is skeptical, pondering whether John has anything other than self-interest in his heart. "I believe you are correct in referring to him as a 'total wanker,'" muses Swamp Thing. "But I also believe that you underestimate his intentions at your own peril."[12] It's no surprise Mercury feels the way she does: aside from the big green hero, virtually everyone she encounters is happy to offer their two cents about Constantine's untrustworthiness. Indeed, at the start of the *Rebirth* run, John is swindling a demon and, by the end, he is selling out a former girlfriend. Constantine doesn't experience a character arc so much as a smoky full circle.

Despite Swamp Thing's endorsement, heroism is a mantle that Constantine denies on multiple occasions throughout this run of books. The superhero community is just as happy to distance themselves from him as well. During Constantine's London soul gambit, Shazam makes his feelings clear to Wonder Woman and Swamp Thing. "Take my word for it," he declares. "John Constantine has no place amongst us." As he will later with Mercury, the enigmatic Swamp Thing restates his trust in Constantine. As a reader, we may start to wonder why such a powerful entity continues to put his faith in a man who has sold out or caused chaos to almost everyone he has ever been close to. Indeed, by the conclusion of the *Rebirth* run, Constantine uses deceit against both friends and foes to justify his own actions. In order to understand his ethics, we are asked to turn to the gentle wisdom of the dolphins.

Tumbling through a void somewhere in the London underground, Constantine contemplates how everyone loves dolphins. Citing the positive images from ancient times to modern days, he claims that nobody ever talks about those nasty dolphins who just let sailors drown to watch them die. "See, the moral is, if you're gonna be a bastard, be like the dolphin – think big picture, protect your image and above all, leave no trace." Getting a little bit more self-reflective, he adds: "Because in the bloodshot, bleary eyes of the world, once you're a bastard, you're always a bastard."[13]

It might be more of Constantine's self-justifying bullshit, but it's a moment of awareness that reveals the protective spell that John has cast around himself. Unbeknownst to Constantine, this actually makes him closer to his fellow heroes than he might ever be willing to admit. How many heroes put on the tights and masks as a means of giving them the agency and armor needed to fight the literal and figurative demons in their past? Constantine's costume

---

[12] *The Hellblazer: Rebirth* #2 (November 2016).
[13] *The Hellblazer: Rebirth* #3 (December 2016).

may not be as colorful or flashy as those of his fellow fellow DCU citizens, but it serves the same purpose. It's all about image.

Nevertheless, Constantine is constantly shown evidence of his own mortality, and occasionally he shows signs of some of the chinks in his carefully crafted armor. A few issues after his revelation about dolphins, Mercury calls Constantine out on his coping mechanisms by forcing him to revisit some of his regretful past.[14] "It's taken the best part of a lifetime to develop the bad habits and dodgy moral fortitude that has got me this far... I ain't about to go changing now," he says in his defense. Mercury's not having it, claiming, "There's a truth in there, under all your crap." She concludes:

> You believe that – abhorrent and terrible as we are... that one day we'd find our own way. And eventually we – us stupid, crappy humans – would finally do the right thing and make the world a better place. John Constantine, I believe *that* is what gets you out of bed.

Mercury isn't the only one who holds a moral mirror up to the Hellblazer. Ambiguous ally and ofttimes antagonist Papa Midnite comes to Constantine's rescue, but questions whether the old-school Constantine would have ever left himself that vulnerable. Echoing earlier warnings to Mercury, he doesn't repeat his lack of trust for the hustler. "With John Constantine," he declares, "there never were any good old days." John shrugs it off as usual, but later the comments seem to have gotten to him. "Maybe under the veneer of blagging and bragging, I was afraid to admit that Midnite was right?[...] But it still came as a shock when I stared into the mirror and didn't recognize the old man staring back." Later still, Mercury puts it even more succinctly: "You ever afraid that you might have just turned into that sad wanker in the pub?"

Yet even after the self-analysis, Constantine still manages to prove that he remains a right bastard. In the *Rebirth* finale, specifically Tim Seeley's conclusion to "The Good Old Days" arc,[15] Constantine has managed to stop the resurrection of the tortured souls of a duo who bear a remarkable resemblance to the notorious Kray Brothers.[16] With one of the brothers inhabiting Margaret

---

[14] *The Hellblazer: Rebirth* #5 (February 2017).

[15] *The Hellblazer: Rebirth* #24 (September 2018).

[16] Twin brothers Ronald "Ronnie" Kray and Reginald "Reggie" Kray notoriously led a variety of criminal enterprises across London in the 1950s and 1960s. As nightclub owners, they had connections with celebrities in the United Kingdom and from the United States. The subject of multiple television series and films, they have been parodied by everyone from Monty Python to Alexei Sayles, and they were even name-checked in issues #1 and #134 of the original *Hellblazer* comic. In *The*

Ames, Constantine (kind of) saves his ex-girlfriend and "current *daemonium ostium*" by turning her into a vampire, thus trapping the evil soul in a body that can never see the sunlight.

Constantine, not done using the women surrounding him, convinces the Kray wannabe to inhabit costumed crusader the Huntress. Of course, this plays right into John's hands: this action summons Franco Bertinelli, a former mobster, former priest, and the Huntress's father. He banishes the tormented soul back to the hellscape he came from, leaving the Huntress aggrieved and contemptuous toward Constantine. Now a vampire, the furious Ames claims John deliberately cursed her because he couldn't take her finally being free. "You knew I finally realized what a bastard you are." The Huntress is even less kind with her damning words: "You are as deceitful and manipulative as the demons you battle."

Constantine remains a complex character, both tortured by the mistakes of his past and seemingly unrepentant for the lives and loves he often ruins along the way. In some cases, they are people or demons who have crossed him in the past, thereby deserving whatever punishment the Hellblazer deems fit to dole out at his chosen time. It's a twisted morality that's not as clear-cut as the truth and justice of the Man of Steel, but it's a personal echo chamber that John has worked hard to maintain.

Commenting on the biblical notion of eternal torment in the Pit, the Huntress remarks, "Extended exposure to most anything makes one inured to it."[17] She's talking about demons, but she could just as easily be talking about John Constantine. He's a total wanker, but wouldn't anybody be after a lifetime spent in the darkness? Perhaps it is as Swamp Thing suggested, and Constantine simply has to make the tough choices others find distasteful so that the world can keep spinning.

Like the greatest magic tricks, the truth is undoubtedly in plain sight, and maybe Constantine keeps just enough familiar people and locations in his life to stop him from crossing a line that only he can see the edge of. As John says in a typically unguarded moment, "You'd be surprised how far being an asshole has got me."

Hellblazer: Rebirth, a third brother – who is now a priest – is actively trying to resurrect the souls of his departed brethren by having them inhabit a series of people.

[17] *The Hellblazer: Rebirth* #23 (August 2018).

Prime Time and Vertigo Do Not Mix Well

by Robert Greenberger

Prime-time television is always an iffy landscape in which to produce a horror TV show. First of all, there are those pesky commercial breaks, and we have gone from a teaser and four acts to a teaser and five or six acts, so viewers barely have a chance for goosebumps to rise on their flesh before the story pauses to sell products. Sustaining the tension and creating a truly horrific scenario is incredibly challenging. Producers then need to contend with a network's standards and practices department, ensuring viewers are not exposed to excessive gore or blasphemous language – and definitely no naughty bits.

The last truly interesting show to manage a spooky edge was probably Fox's *The X-Files*. As a result, NBC's willingness to fill Friday nights not only with its homegrown *Grimm,* which successfully launched in 2011, but with an adaptation of Vertigo's *John Constantine: Hellblazer*, was a bold move. The *Constantine* TV series arrived at the dawn of the 2014-15 television season, then vanished after just one half-season. It did launch to a promising start, though, with *Variety* writing:

> For starters, *Constantine*, the TV show derived from DC's *Hellblazer* comics, is better than *Constantine*, the 2005 movie starring Keanu Reeves, which amounts to damnation with faint praise. Matt Ryan is certainly appealing

as the doomed-to-hell exorcist/demonologist, and the concept is perfectly positioned as a companion to NBC's *Grimm*, premiering right before Halloween, no less. That said, the series – adapted by Daniel Cerone with an assist from genre specialist David S. Goyer – nearly chokes on its mythological mumbo-jumbo, and frankly, yelling at demons in foreign tongues seemed a whole lot scarier back when *The Exorcist* first turned heads.[1]

There had been immediate talk of reviving the series, thanks to the #SaveConstantine movement, or perhaps translocating it to another venue, such as The CW, where other DC Comics properties were thriving. It made sense for one of the major networks to try a comics property, given how hot they were on the big screen at the time, and how The CW was making noise with *Arrow*. Whereas CBS tried its hand not long after with *Supergirl,* that, too, failed to find a sizeable enough audience, and it was quickly snatched up by The CW, where the show prospered.

Poor John Constantine. He would find life anew, but in bits and pieces – first with a guest appearance on *Arrow*, then in the animated miniseries *Constantine: City of Demons*, in which the title character was voiced by Matt Ryan, and finally, joining *Legends of Tomorrow*, with its occult-themed 2018-2019 season. By then, however, any resemblance between television's Constantine and the character introduced in *Swamp Thing* was merely coincidental. Everything else had been sandpapered smooth.

That had not been the intent when the show was first pitched to NBC in 2013. Whereas the lead-in show, *Grimm,* featured square-jawed David Giuntoli as Nick Burkhardt, inheriting the ancestral mantle of being a Grimm (a monster-hunter), *Constantine* was its opposite. John Constantine was a punk rocker turned shabby adult – a chain-smoking, psychologically scarred man who walked the razor's edge between the mortal world and the supernatural realm. Together, Burkhardt and Constantine made an occult odd couple for those looking for escapist fare on the cusp of the weekend.

Daniel Cerone conceived of the adaptation, partnering with David S. Goyer to develop the series. Cerone had cut his teeth on similar shows, including the sisterly witches of *Charmed* and the psychologically complex *Dexter*. It's interesting to note that he segued from *Constantine*'s failure to working on the network's *The Blacklist*, which was more horrifying than the former. Goyer was

---

[1] Lowry, Brian. "TV Review: *Constantine*." Variety, 22 October 2014: https://variety.com/2014/tv/reviews/tv-review-constantine-1201331412.

a comics fan who had adapted various properties as writer and/or producer, including *Blade, The Dark Knight, Godzilla*, and similar fare. Together, they had all the right pedigrees to make the show work, and NBC snatched it up.

In the comics, John had little in the way of a long-term supporting cast, given the tragic outcomes of anyone befriending or daring to love him. He had Chas Chandler and his disapproving wife Renee, and over time, his niece Gemma Masters and a handful of others who came and went with each writer, but that wasn't enough for a television series. So, they used Chas (portrayed by Charles Halford), dropped the wife character, and added original character Liv Aberdine, who could see supernatural entities walking among us.

Poor Liv never had a chance to develop on NBC's *Constantine*.

The pilot was shot, but it was ultimately decided that Liv, portrayed by Lucy Griffiths, wasn't working out. She was soon replaced with Zed (Angélica Celaya), a character who'd originated in the comics. Once the show was picked up for series, the writers also decided to use Papa Midnite (Michael James Shaw) as a recurring foe, and created an original character named Manny, an angel (Harold Perrineau).

In the pilot, Constantine says, "I'm a nasty piece of work, chief. Ask anybody." This is a direct lift from Alan Moore's script for *Swamp Thing* #37, showing that the writers were doing their homework. As they geared up to begin weekly production, Mark Verheiden joined the team. Verheiden had begun writing comic books with the acclaimed *The American* for Dark Horse Comics, before tackling *The Phantom* at DC and parlaying his connections to become a screenwriter and showrunner. His credits include *Timecop* (based on his own comic), *Falling Skies, Ash vs Evil Dead, Heroes, Battlestar Galactica, Daredevil, Smallville*, and *Hemlock Grove*. More recently, he was the showrunner on the short-lived *Swamp Thing* TV series.

When new character Liv didn't work out with viewers, she was quickly replaced with Zed (Angélica Celaya), who originated in the comics.

Verheiden was just coming off work on the latter when he received a fortuitous phone call. "I got a call from David Goyer, who I had known many, many years earlier," he said. "We had been acquainted, and I guess sort of stayed in touch but not super in touch. Anyway, he gave me a call and said, 'Would you like to do something?'" Verheiden was writing a pilot at the time, which ended up not being picked up. "The timing worked out, and I felt like, well, 'David Goyer. Constantine. Cool.' So that's essentially it."[2]

A longtime comics reader, Verheiden was intrigued. As he explained:

> I knew [*Hellblazer*] pretty well. I was a fan of the book – I think probably the earlier versions, rather than the later. I hadn't kept up with the later stuff, but the Jamie Delano stuff from the beginning – yeah, the early stuff I was familiar with. I went back and [reread] a bunch of the earlier *Constantine* [stories] and the *Swamp Thing* issues Alan Moore wrote. I think I had sort of the institutional memory of Constantine in my head anyway, just from being around comics. The whole sort of gestalt of who he was and the dark character that he was – the dark hero, I guess you'd

---

[2] All quotes from Verheiden come from an interview conducted for this essay.

call him. Once I got the job, I went back and reread it. I would say those books sort of became our inspiration for a lot of what we did on the show.

As a result, Verheiden recalled, the first collected editions – primarily Jamie Delano's run – formed the TV series' bible. Sharp-eyed readers will recognize asides, callbacks, and moments pulled from these stories and incorporated into *Constantine*'s 13 episodes.

"Obviously, there's characters in the show that weren't in the comic, but definitely some storylines came out of the books, like the Gary Lester story," Verheiden said. "The prison story was inspired by a Brian Azzarello-written run where he ended up in a prison. The stories are completely different, but I just like the idea of Constantine in prison."

Lester, a former bandmate with Constantine in the punk band Mucous Membrane, was introduced in the first issue of *Hellblazer* as a strung-out junkie occultist. He later wound up dying and going to Hell, only to have his spirit come back and haunt John. On the series, he was the focal point of episode four, "A Feast of Friends," and was played by Jonjo O'Neill.

Constantine's old friend Gary Lester, on the page and on the screen.

Verheiden joined the TV show as an executive producer and wrote two episodes as well. "For *Constantine*, my job was to be in the room and to write scripts and to be out on set when we were shooting," he told me. "Essentially, you know, the titles are sort of more of a function of the hierarchy of things. Just like a military rank, almost. I've never really gotten used to that in the TV business, but sure, you know executive producers – one of the higher sort of titles. I'd worked my way up to that on other shows, and I didn't want to take a step back."

As he arrived, NBC and Cerone were discussing replacing Griffiths. As it turned out, the show hewed closer to the comics by introducing Mary "Zed" Martin, who'd debuted in *Hellblazer* #4.[3] The switch to a Mexican-American character was a benefit of the casting process, keeping the show from being impenetrably British.

According to Verheiden, "Celaya is a very sweet, very nice lady. I thought she was fun on the show. So, yeah, we cast her while we were shooting." As a result, her introductory episode aired out of production order, so the second one filmed aired sixth, without Zed. As they went from pilot to weekly series, Cerone and Verheiden were feeling their way through how to make things work tonally. "Remember that, again, when you're trying to find the show at the beginning, there were questions about how scary we should be – or not scary – which is kind of what I want to talk about, which was: Vertigo was very edgy, so we were finding ways to be palatable."

In the comics, Constantine is often a bastard. He does whatever is most expedient to resolve the current problem, knowing full well there will be another right behind it. He burns relationships, watches others become collateral damage, and just trudges ahead, a Silk Cut dangling from a trembling lip. The nastiness of his persona is something that was hinted at in Ryan's performance, but was never fully explored. As Verheiden recalled:

> I don't recall anyone saying 'Here's a limit.' I think we didn't want him just willy nilly. Well, actually, he did willy nilly murder people occasionally. You know, he's the antihero of the show. So, in that sense, we did want him to have some sort of moral grounding, even though Constantine himself doesn't really have that in the comics. It feels like we made him a much darker character on the show.
>
> But if you're asking how far we could take him in terms of double-crossing people or hurting others, I just don't know that we ever pushed the envelope that far. Again, in the prison episode, he murders like eight or nine people, maybe more, and he was being possessed by a demon at the time. So you could kind of blame it on the demon, but he murdered guys left and right. No, I don't recall anybody really laying down on us about him, 'He needs to be a better guy' or 'He can't do that because he's our hero' or anything like that.

Whereas *Grimm* retold classic fairy tales and monster stories in the context of that show, the threats on John Constantine came from all manner of the occult and supernatural worlds. The writing staff was free to explore different

---

[3] Zed's birth name was never provided in the comics, though a religious cult did call her "Mary" since she'd been chosen to birth a new messiah.

cultures and their beliefs, Verheiden explained, including the dark undersides:

> I think we were able to do quite a bit of just horror, per se, but it was within broadcast standards. You know, the craziest thing was the prohibition on him smoking – even though I don't like cigarettes either, [so] I'm fine with the prohibition. We shouldn't promote smoking; however, that's just his character. And so, this thing we had where he's constantly almost lighting up or we never showed him actually taking a puff until later in the series.
>
> I think when we knew we were being canceled and we just didn't care and [NBC] didn't care, I think he actually did smoke in one of the last episodes. But that's just one of those odd network things, where you go, 'Really, *that's* where you draw the line?' It would crack me up about that. We did an episode I wrote where, to get out of a jam because he's been possessed by a demon, Constantine shoots himself up with a bunch of heroin and it works. Okay, so the guy can, like, do tons of heroin, but we can't show him smoking a cigarette?

Another issue that had fans and LGBTQ groups up in arms was NBC's refusal to explore Constantine's sexuality. While his great romances in the comics were with women, notably Irish beauty Katherine "Kit" Ryan, he had been known to fancy a man or two, an element introduced a few years after his 1985 introduction.[4] Despite increasing rainbow representation on television, the network just wasn't interested in exposing this aspect of the character. "I do recall that coming up," Verheiden stated, adding, "I don't recall there being a whole lot of discussion about it. It may have been something we would have tried later. You know, it's one of those things. I don't recall anyone saying, 'You absolutely can't do that side of Constantine's personality and his life.'"

Goyer, though, at New York Comic Con 2014, said, "We never said he *wasn't* bisexual."[5] Cerone went further to defend the move, saying, "In those comic books, John Constantine aged in real time. Within this tome of three decades [of comics], there might have been one or two issues where he's seen getting out of bed with a man. So [maybe] 20 years from now? But there are no immediate plans."[6]

---

[4] See James Wilkinson's essay, "'The Odd Boyfriend': John Constantine's Bisexuality in *Hellblazer* and Beyond," elsewhere in this volume.

[5] Wilson, Angel. "Constantine's Bisexuality Acknowledged by Executive Producer." The Geekiary, 12 October 2014: https://thegeekiary.com/constantines-bisexuality-acknowledged-by-executive-producer/17725.

[6] Roncero-Menendez, Sara. "NBC Says Title Character of *Constantine* Is Straight. Fans Disagree." Huffpost, Queer Voices, 2 February 2016:

Constantine was, therefore, reshaped for the mass millions NBC anticipated would tune in. He was a man of contradictions, some self-inflicted, others network-dictated. It certainly proved a challenge for the production team. Atop his personal habits, Verheiden recalled, the format also became an issue:

> So that dichotomy was there. [The] thing that just made it difficult to do the show was that I think the network was looking at it as sort of a supernatural procedural, where every week Constantine would go out and solve some sort of supernatural crime, and to accomplish that in 42 minutes every week, it required a lot of 'What is supernatural?'. He's up against 'What can we get into the story really quickly?', because you've only got 42 minutes and, you know, [you have to] create a problem and then have them solve it.

Grimm was already a procedural with an over-arching mythos, so you would think the network would have wanted something different. This is emblematic of how prime-time network drama executives think. What works for one series can be endlessly replicated, such as how so many 1970s series were forced to imitate the premise of *The Fugitive*. Even ABC's *The Night Stalker* was reduced to being a monster-of-the-week show, a premise repeated in the flawed Frank Spotnitz 2005 remake. As Verheiden said:

> I think we sort of chafed against that a little bit. You always felt it would have been more interesting to have done multipart episodes. You could have one grand or supernatural threat so there's something to fight, but I think that was sort of one of the bigger issues for us, just trying to walk that line. NBC wanted more of a supernatural procedural and less sort of the character-based stuff that I think attracted all of the writers on the show to *Constantine*. NBC wasn't in favor of character-based, but they wanted that engine, they wanted that procedural engine, and those two things proved to be difficult to do both of.

It was a lot easier for simplified, easily digestible threats, given the episode running time. The more complex demons and occult figures and mythologies proved a challenge to the writers, turning them into easy-to-follow threats. Here's where the multi-episode arc would have allowed for that, but it wasn't what NBC wanted at all. The writers were allowed a single two-parter, "The Saint of Last Resorts," in which a nun, Anne Marie (Claire van der Boom), one of Constantine's many exes,[7] asks for his help in Mexico City in dealing with a demon that has been taking babies.

---

https://www.huffingtonpost.com/2014/07/17/constantine-nbc-bisexual_n_5591483.html.

[7] The nun, called Sister Anne-Marie (hyphenated) in the comics, was never John's lover in that medium, though she *was* secretly in love with him.

The show certainly didn't shy away from the eternal struggle between Heaven and Hell, with Manny and Papa Midnite as surrogates for the two sides (a big departure from Midnite's typical role in *Hellblazer*, in which he was a self-serving gangster, not an agent of evil). Given the fear-adverse nature of network television, it's interesting to note there were few religious qualms expressed.

Manny was an invention of Cerone and Goyer, designed to give the series more of that dichotomy between Constantine's darkness and the angelic side of things. "I don't recall any particular notes or issues from the network on that," Verheiden said. "You know, that is sort of baked in the cake when you're doing *Constantine*. So, I would assume that if there were issues with that, they were discussed at the pilot stage. But, you know, we had our angel, Manny. I think, had we gone on further, the plan was to strip away his powers at the end of season one and have him be sort of mortal, who would be helping Constantine on a sort of less lofty plane."

Similar threads would wind up in another Vertigo adaptation, Fox's *Lucifer*, which debuted in 2016, soon after *Constantine*'s cancellation. The difference between the two series is telling, as Fox allowed the show — which centered on Lucifer Morningstar, who'd abandoned his rulership over Hell in favor of living life on the mortal plane, running a nightclub, and helping to solve crimes — to neatly blend horror and humor.[8] After being canceled in 2018, *Lucifer* quickly made a soft landing at Netflix.

"I think we had discussed [that] Manny turned out to be a bit of a fraud at some point," Verheiden recalled. "And Manny is like a fallen angel with a kind of mystique. Toward the end of the run, when we thought maybe we'd be picked up for a few more episodes, at the very end they didn't give us an order for three more scripts after #13." As it stands, Verheiden wrote what would have been episode #16, an unproduced tale.

While Manny was unique to the show, Papa Midnite was elevated from small-time voodoo priest/gangster to recurring player, and he even fronted his own tie-in Vertigo miniseries in 2005, Mat Johnson's *Hellblazer Special: Papa*

---

[8] Lucifer's abdication of Hell's throne occurred in Neil Gaiman's acclaimed comic series *The Sandman*, with the Morningstar then having his own long-running spinoff comic, Mike Carey's *Lucifer*. In the source material, Lucifer does not solve crimes since he has no interest in the affairs of mankind. In the comics, as well as on the *Constantine* TV series, the Devil is known as the First of the Fallen. Lucifer and the First of the Fallen are separate individuals (DC's version of Hell is rather complex).

Midnite. Like Lester, he was introduced in *Hellblazer* #1. The sharply dressed, charismatic criminal was a natural for the television series. "We loved Papa Midnite," Verheiden said, "and I will say some of the choices we made in terms of guest stars were dictated by who DC would allow us to use. Midnite was someone who we were allowed to use, and that made him immediately more attractive than the ones we were not. So I'm surprised DC had limits."

During production, the film studio was working with director Guillermo Del Toro on a later-aborted *Justice League Dark* movie. As a result, characters that were a natural fit for Constantine, such as Madame Xanadu, Zatanna Zatara, Deadman, and the Phantom Stranger, were forbidden fruit. Of course, the one the writers most wanted to feature was Swamp Thing, whose eponymous comic first introduced the world to John Constantine. However, *Justice League Dark* went from being a Del Toro-directed feature film to a J.J. Abrams-produced TV series intended for HBO Max in 2021.

"So, it was basically Papa Midnite, who was someone we wanted because we like the sort of voodoo-ish world that he came from, and there was just a different feel to that character," Verheiden stated. "But again, he was someone DC would allow us to use, so that dictated sort of who we could play with. It was the same with Jim Corrigan [Emmett J Scanlan], who was someone they said [we could play with]." Had there been a second season, Corrigan would most certainly have returned, to be killed and resurrected as the Spectre, a long-running DC Comics character who served as God's Agent of Wrath.[9]

There was some discussion about bringing the Lord of Order, Doctor Fate, onto the show, but that never went beyond conversation. Eagle-eyed viewers, though, would have noticed other Easter eggs from the comics beyond Nabu's helm of Fate, including Ibis the Invincible's Ibisstick, a shard of Eclipso's Black Diamond, Pandora's Box, and Psycho-Pirate's Medusa mask. On the other hand, Liv's father was named Jasper Winters, and fans were convinced he was the comics' Baron Winters, who was a colleague and rival of John Constantine and, like Jasper, lived in a mysterious mansion. That, however, was more coincidence than plan, according to Verheiden.

Nightmaster's sword appeared in "The Rage of Caliban," in which Chas reminisced about using the weapon to save a family from being destroyed by

---

[9] This would eventually happen elsewhere in the Arrowverse – in episodes of *The Flash* and *Arrow* – but with a different actor, Stephen Lobo, in the role of a different Jim Corrigan.

the Monkey King, a character from Alan Moore's *Swamp Thing*. And when the show brought in Felix Faust, the Justice League of America's most major mystical nemesis, he bore little resemblance to the four-color source material, which Verheiden admits:

> Yeah, it was that just something that didn't work. You know, it's funny, episodic television. Some things work, some things don't. Sure, for some people that may be their favorite episode. I think, for me, the guy playing Felix [Mark Margolis] was an incredible actor who was on *Breaking Bad*. A very talented guy, but he played it in a way that sort of leaned into the Mandrake of it all. That was a choice that, for me, just didn't work. But I'm always reticent to criticize the show, because I'm criticizing someone else's work and they can rip me one if they want. But on that one, I think we all saw the dailies and were like, 'Wow, *that's* a choice.' So, it's unfortunate, I think, that for whatever reason, the portrayal of Faust wasn't my favorite on the show.

After years away from John Constantine and his world, Verheiden refreshed himself by watching several episodes, after which he declared:

> The production values were very high. I thought Matt Ryan was just perfect as Constantine. I just thought he nailed it. Aside from being an incredibly good guy and a very talented actor, he just, to me, nailed it. I tried to imagine anyone else playing the part – you know, Keanu Reeves. I don't dislike the movie, but I don't think he was Constantine. No, he wasn't. I thought Matt really captured as much of that sort of hollowed-out soul that Constantine would have.
>
> I do know we had really talked a lot about doing the [Garth Ennis-written] 'he gets cancer' story and 'has to make deals with the Devil'-type episodes. We really wanted to go down that road of showing how his lifestyle choices – not just about consorting with demons, but also the smoking and drugs and stuff – basically destroyed him. I think those would have been very interesting places to go with him, and I think Matt would have knocked him out of the park.
>
> I think they hold up surprisingly well. I think if there's any one sort of overworking... I just thought it is probably that that's a show that would have better been a better fit maybe on cable or on a premium channel or something, where you really could just go to the botched side of Constantine, as well as the antihero. You know, the part of him that wants to try to help him do good, you know, and also that might have opened up sort of the character to being less of the procedural aspects and exploring more sort of just that world he inhabited. But, you know, NBC was gracious enough to pick it up and pay me, so I can never, you know... [They're] heroes in my book.
>
> But I'm just not sure it was a great fit on NBC, for a variety of reasons.

NBC president Robert Greenblatt has suggested that the show failed because there was too much comic-inspired programming on television.[10] It was that season The CW introduced *The Flash* and Fox invited people to visit *Gotham*, and both found audiences. The appetite for such fare has only increased exponentially since the series' November 2014 cancellation. Verheiden disagreed with Greenblatt, however, noting:

> I think he was wrong. Yeah. No, he was not exactly prescient on that one. I think it was NBC tried a show called *The Cape*. It was an original superhero show, which I don't think was particularly successful coming from... Yeah, I think they did 13 of those. You know, they obviously did *Heroes*, which worked like gangbusters for a while.[11]

"But clearly, it wasn't that there were too many comic book characters," Verheiden maintained, adding:

> [*Constantine*] was just kind of in the wrong place to flourish. That said, NBC and Warners gave the show a pretty lavish budget, so there was money for production and to make it look good, and it wasn't like anybody was stinting on it. I think, just creatively, it became off, as often happens. There was a lot of discussion about, you know, the week to week of it, and the week to week of just sort of trying to come up with a procedural element was difficult.

Fittingly, Verheiden returned to Constantine's world in 2018, when he joined DC Entertainment's *Swamp Thing* series as executive producer. The production proved troubled, with DC cutting its order to ten episodes, then canceling it, despite critical acclaim. Although a clip was used in the Arrowverse's "Crisis on Infinite Earths" crossover, showing *Swamp Thing*'s world as a parallel universe, Matt Ryan's Constantine seems unlikely to meet up with the plant elemental there or in future works.

---

[10] Nededog, Jethro. "NBC Brass Talk Giving Up on Bill Cosby: Allegations Reached 'Critical Mass'." The Wrap, 16 January 2015: https://www.thewrap.com/nbc-brass-talk-giving-up-on-bill-cosby-allegations-reached-critical-mass/.

[11] *Heroes* was a short-lived phenomenon from Tim Kring, which aired from 2006 to 2010, with accompanying comics, then was briefly revisited in 2015 as *Heroes Reborn*. Despite his having claimed to know nothing about superhero comics, Kring wisely surrounded himself with comics professionals: Verheiden, as well as Jeph Loeb, Chuck Kim, and Michael Green. *The Cape*, meanwhile, was an original show which debuted in January 2011 and was so poorly rated, the network cut the order from 13 episodes down to only 10. It may be best remembered for its appealing cast, which included genre veterans Keith David, Summer Glau, and James Frain.

The Constant Serpentine: Anti-Savior Resurrected

by Tony Simmons

Though he shares initials with an arguably more famous J.C. – no, not Jack Carter of *Get Carter* – John Constantine was never intended to be a Christ figure. Nor, despite his obvious distaste for heavenly authority, is he an Antichrist figure. He's just a working-class bloke, perhaps more well-read than most others in a particular specialty – which actually gives him something in common with Jesus, who, according to the Bible, was the son of a working carpenter and who studied the scriptures well enough to confound the religious leaders of the day by the age of 12.[1]

But that's not the point.

Having come up on those grittier byways, Constantine's not above mixing with those whom the authorities might consider rabble, as well as those the rabble might consider undesirable: prostitutes, loan sharks, gangsters, and the like. Jesus, too, surprised his followers by showing love and mercy to the lowest of society, a kinship that again gives them parallels. Jesus wasn't above asking a strange woman for a drink,[2] or defending an adulterous woman against the

---

[1] The Bible, Luke 2: 41-52.
[2] The Samaritan woman at the well, John 4: 4-42.

holier-than-thou.[3] Looking even at Jesus's personality traits and how they align to John's, there is as much similarity as difference. Both have a playfulness, such as Jesus deciding to walk to the boat in the midst of the lake rather than waiting for the storm to pass – and righteous anger, such as when He cast the moneylenders from the temple grounds.

But while Jesus turned his other cheek, Constantine's a fighter, more than willing to knock heads to set things closer to right. John's not beyond sacrificing himself to win the day for others, but he's more likely to sacrifice others so that he can live to fight another day. You won't see John offer himself for crucifixion if there's another who's willing (or dumb enough) to do it. Whereas Jesus was submissive (both to the will of his Father and to the authorities of the time), John is not. He'd rather give God a piece of his mind,[4] and you can bet he'd have pissed on the high priest's servant who came to arrest him in the Garden of Gethsemane before he'd have healed the bastard's ear.[5] John is neither patient nor always truthful, and when he has a message to deliver, he's generally more direct and less about the parables.

What they do have in common goes back to a sense of mercy toward the weak and downtrodden, and a responsibility to protect those who can't protect themselves. I imagine John in Gethsemane saying something in line with his questions in *Hellblazer* #10: "Am I insane to care what happens to these stupid sheep? Is it some psychotic arrogance that drives me to save my species from itself?" The Gospels took another view of the mindset, calling it compassion when Jesus blessed the multitudes who came to Him, as they were "helpless, like sheep without a shepherd" in Matthew 9:36. So while John has saved the species more times than he could count, he's no hero, as such. He's what the snobs like to call an antihero – one who will save the world. An anti-savior.

To be clear, that is not the same as an Antichrist, as those things are defined. He's got no interest in ruling the world. No one must bear his mark in order to buy or sell. And while he might be tempted to shag the Whore of Babylon (he's not above bedding a demon succubus, after all), Constantine would be the last to declare himself the Alpha and Omega when it comes to all knowledge and ultimate authority.

---

[3] The Bible, John 8: 2-11.
[4] And has, in fact, in *Hellblazer* #97 and #128.
[5] The Bible, Matthew 26: 51-52.

"Love 'em and leave 'em" is John's game in *Hellblazer* #9.

Constantine hates and distrusts authority. It's kind of his default. He's even stopped a nascent Antichrist on at least three occasions – deflowering the intended mother in one case,[6] taking an ax to the newborn in another,[7] and offering his own body for Swamp Thing's energy matrix to possess in order to father a child with Abigail Holland,[8] in order to keep the Green from birthing its own version of the Beast. That same offspring, Tefé Holland, would later experience a vision of tricking John – her biological father – into siring the Antichrist himself by impregnating her.[9]

Throughout history, many have been accused of being an Antichrist, and if the "beloved Apostle" is to be believed, even in his era there had already been many such beings.[10] The definition of such is that a person would put himself in the place of worship, declaring himself the savior of the human race and equal to (if not one and the same as) God. The great Beast of the Book of Revelations is considered by many scholars to be *the* Antichrist, as embodied in modern fiction by the character of Damien Thorn in writer David Seltzer's and director Richard Donner's 1976 film *The Omen*, or by the Romanian Secretary General of the United Nations, one Nicolae Jetty Carpathia, in the 1995-2007 *Left Behind* series of novels by Tim LeHaye and Larry B. Jenkins. But the title has also been bestowed upon others throughout history, including Adolph Hitler, the Pope, and the Holy Roman Emperor Constantine "the Great" Augustus.[11]

Bunch of snobs, John Constantine might say. Not just authority figures. Glory hounds. Fascists. He'd give them a two-finger salute and keep walking.

When Alan Moore created John Constantine, he had little in mind for him beyond the artists' desire to draw a character who resembled the rock star Sting and a vague concept of a working-class magician who might act as a guide to Moore's new version of Swamp Thing (or so he says in an oft-repeated interview in *Wizard* magazine in 1993[12]). As with any good mystery character,

---

[6] *Hellblazer* #9 ("Shot to Hell," September 1988).
[7] *Hellblazer* #133 ("Son of Man, Part Five," November 1998).
[8] *Swamp Thing* Vol. 2 #76 ("L'Adoration de la Terre," September 1988).
[9] *Swamp Thing* vol. 3 #20 ("Saga," December 2001).
[10] The Bible, 1 John 2:18.
[11] No relation... or is there? *Hellblazer* #40 and #49 slyly imply the two may, in fact, be related, as does *Destiny: A Chronicle of Deaths Foretold* miniseries, though they never comes out and say so.
[12] Christensen, William A. and Seifert, Mark. "The Unexplored Medium: Alan Moore speaks on what makes working as a comic writer so appealing." *Wizard*, November 1993: http://www.qusoor.com/hellblazer/Sting.htm.

hints of a shady back-story can carry weight in a reader's imagination, and Moore gave John those to spare. It was writer Jamie Delano who set about nailing down the details of Constantine's history in his 40-issue run as the initial scribe of *Hellblazer*. It's in those pages that we begin to learn about John's family, the tragic details of his birth, and the fact that he descends from a bloodline of mages.

"The Constant One" and "The Laughing Magician" are two more ways to describe Constantine, according to *Hellblazer* #240 by Andy Diggle.

It's through later writers that we delve into and drive out the mystery. Under the pen of Andy Diggle, we get the concept of Constantine as "The Constant One" from a line of Laughing Magicians, who maintain the mystic balance of power in the earthly realm. There's no virgin birth, but there is a tendency toward miracles – and more than one resurrection from the dead. Because that's a biggie: The Antichrist, like Jesus, is foretold to come back from the dead, according to some scholars who say Revelation 13 describes the Beast suffering a head wound, dying, and descending to Hell, then returning from the Pit to seat himself in the Holy of Holies and declare himself God. (Others say it's a description of a nation's fall and rise. Your mileage may vary.)

Likewise, our John has kipped off the mortal coil and returned again – in more ways than one. In-story, John's deaths and returns have been aplenty: He avoids his first death (by cancer) via a con, outsmarting the triumvirate Lords of Hell, who heal him rather than go to war over his soul.[13] He's dragged to Hell and gets back in time for his own funeral.[14] Finally, he gives his niece the choice of whether he lives or dies, and she pulls the trigger, only to discover he's vanished – and thus ends his original solo series, *Hellblazer*, at issue #300.

But if we take the meta-fictional view, the *Hellblazer* series was canceled to make way for a new series featuring a 30-years-younger John. *Constantine* was part of the hard reboot of the New 52 era, but was killed off and revived again as *Constantine: The Hellblazer* with DC's soft reset, Rebirth. Likewise, the *Constantine* NBC television series of 2014-2015, starring Matt Ryan, was canceled, only for Ryan to play John again and again – first on The CW's shows *Arrow* and *Legends of Tomorrow*, then in the 2017 DC animated film *Justice League Dark*, and then in the streaming CW Seed animated serial *Constantine: City of Demons*.

So John Constantine, though many times the savior of the world, having gathered a ragged coven or a handful of super-folks and pointed them at the enemy, has defeated any number of demonic incursions, possessions, and hauntings – not to mention the Great Darkness from the chaoplasm. But he's no Christ figure. A mad prophet with supernatural abilities, wrapped in his own ersatz shroud, wandering the wilderness of the Earth to drive out evil, yes, but no moral guidepost for others. John's friends, followers, and loved ones inevitably die horrible deaths – some of them even end up in Hell, while others hang on as ghosts.

Meanwhile, the Constant One carries on.

---

[13] *Hellblazer* #42 ("Dangerous Habits, Part II: A Drop of the Hard Stuff," June 1991).
[14] Hellblazer #77 ("And the Crowd Goes Wild," May 1994).

Still Blazin' After All These Years: An Afterword

by Lou Tambone

Hellblazer isn't something you read; it's something you experience.

As Rich Handley alluded to in his introduction, it's addictive, like a bag of chips or a bowl of M&Ms. It's like starting that series on Netflix that everyone's talking about and finding out that they were right. Once you start, it's hard to stop. Like Rich, who followed our friend Joe's advice and blew through *Hellblazer* some time after it began its long and successful run, I began my journey into the mystical world of John Constantine after that initial run had concluded, three hundred issues later. I may regret not having read these wondrous stories sooner, but I no longer have to say that I regret never having read them at all.

As you know, reading comics requires a certain suspension of disbelief. You have to be able to accept that beings with special abilities can fight off enemies of all kinds while simultaneously delivering gallant speeches. You're asked to trust that the world can be saved time and time again. And you need to believe that once-dead characters can return to life in order to fight the good fight once more. It's all part of the fun.

Comics like *Hellblazer*, and its no-so-distant cousin *Swamp Thing*, ask you to take your suspension of disbelief up a notch or two. You stare at the pages and ask yourself, "What the Hell am I looking at?" You aren't simply moving your eyes from panel to panel, ingesting a generic fight scene, and going through the motions. When you let go and become immersed in the overall narrative, the outcome is a different kind of fun.

It's not the kind of fun you'd have, say, playing a sport or enjoying a pint of Guinness on a Friday night. It's that guilty pleasure you feel when rooting for the bad guy in a book, film, or television show. It's that feeling of excitement you get whenever Darth Vader rears his obsidian, helmeted head in a *Star Wars* movie. When that happens, you aren't simply reading – you're *experiencing*. That's what makes Vader a pop-culture force to be reckoned with, and it explains why he's still relevant after all this time.

It's important to note, however, that character longevity is historically hit or miss in the comic book world. Some of the longest-lasting characters hail from the Golden Age and are still around today. Others have fallen by the wayside, mostly due to the inability to move issues, I assume. John Constantine might not be as popular a character as Batman or Superman, yet he endures.

When it was all said and done, the original *Hellblazer* had taken readers to Hell and back throughout its quarter-century of publication. That's no small feat for any comic, but it does make one wonder what magical formula DC Comics used to keep the character and his adventures fresh and selling well.

It's almost as though John reached beyond the page (or screen) and mystically influenced the various creative minds who guided his journey throughout the years. He aged in real time while most other characters did not, but when it appeared he had gotten too old, he was rebooted as a younger version of himself. How many of us wish we could do that? He had his own short-lived television show, a film, and animated appearances, and he was inserted into several of The CW's DC-based series. DC could have easily dropped the character at any time. Instead, they kept him around and he became more popular than ever.

Constantine, you cheeky devil, you.

While I'd like to believe that John himself is responsible for his lasting popularity, we need to face facts. People just like the guy, even though he's a nasty piece of work – at least on the outside. Well, maybe a little on the inside, too. It depends on his intake of nicotine and ale on any given day, I suppose.

If you've ever had a friend or family member who is, for lack of a better term, a jerk (and who hasn't?), then you know what I'm talking about. They're intrusive, obnoxious, needy, and they usually have horrific timing. When they

Lovable to the core.

show up at your door, it's almost never for a good reason. The core of John Constantine's friends and family members seem to tolerate him. Perhaps they feel that they *have* to, but do they really *want* to? Just like that weird uncle who shows up every holiday and insists on talking politics at the dinner table, they're stuck with him, and so they make the best of it.

Unfortunately for them, John's a user, a taker, and a one-sided, toxic friend. Yet, he's as keenly aware of his faults as he is his strengths. He knows what a right bastard he is and he knows he'll never change. He's his own worst enemy, as well as yours. So why does everyone like him so much? Do they feel sorry for him? Do they owe him favors? Are they rebelling against their own good natures? Are they succumbing to their dark ambitions? Do they like being tortured? Are they unknowing victims of his enchantment?

I can only speak for myself, of course. I know he's a dirty, rotten scoundrel, but I enjoy his swagger and his ability to react to just about any situation by lighting up a Silk Cut and calmly proclaiming, "Sod it all." There's something endearing about that kind of self-imposed carelessness, but there's more to love about Constantine than that. He's witty as Hell, has some musical ability, bathes in the occult, and sometimes does good things, even though people around him seem to pay the ultimate price as a result.

Funny thing, that. Folks like to insinuate that he gets off scot-free for the deaths of the innocents who have crossed his path. They assume he gets away with what he does because he's a coward, and that he'll throw anyone under a bus or into a fiery abyss in order to save his own hide. I disagree. I don't think he is getting away with anything. The way I see it, John Constantine has to live with his decisions the next day – and all the days afterward. His scars aren't necessarily visible. He has to try to reconcile everything internally – and that, in itself, is a heavy price, innit?

Perhaps that's why he's still blazin' after all these years. He's *still* paying that price.

Since you're reading this book, I assume you've already experienced *Hellblazer* and John Constantine in some fashion. If you haven't had the pleasure, then what are you waiting for? You might regret the lack of sleep once you get started, but you certainly won't regret experiencing these highly creative and haunting stories. They are truly like no others.

Just make sure you pronounce John's surname correctly. It rhymes with "wine."

Appendix: From Liverpool to Swamp Thing's Fool

by Rich Handley

When John Constantine first appeared in DC Comics' second *Swamp Thing* series, writer Alan Moore and artists John Totleben, Stephen Bissette, and Rick Veitch could not have known how popular their creation would be with readers. That was more than 30 years ago, and the character has since enjoyed a marvelous longevity, not only in *Swamp Thing*, but also in *The Books of Magic* and, more importantly, in John's own spinoff title, *John Constantine: Hellblazer*.

Thanks to Matt Ryan's portrayal on television, the mage has emerged as a household name among fans of comic-based TV shows in recent years – something that certainly hadn't happened following the 2005 Keanu Reeves film. But even from his initial comic book appearance, Constantine stole the show. The chain-smoking, wise-cracking, thirty-something Brit showed up mysteriously in the United States one day, barking orders and talking down to Swamp Thing as though the latter were a dimwitted child. It was unheard of for anyone to treat Alec Holland with such disdain, yet here was this rude, slightly built, trenchcoat-clad Sting wannabe, puffing away on a cigarette and showing him as much respect as one might allot to a pile of rotting cabbage – and getting away with it.

John knew more about Swamp Thing's true nature than he was telling, which made him immediately intriguing, yet he would only portion out information like bread crumbs. For 14 issues, this ill-tempered man of mystery led Swamp Thing around on a metaphorical, mossy leash, bribing the muck-encrusted mockery of a man to do his bidding, on the promise of new clues about his heritage and abilities. By the end of that story arc (Alan Moore's "American Gothic" saga), Swamp Thing – the character and the comic book – had been forever changed, and John Constantine had become a bona fide fan favorite with a long future ahead of him.

What was Constantine's life like before his swampy debut? As it happens, a great deal has been established regarding John's early years and his family history, going back millions of years before his birth. John descends from a long line of disreputable individuals – criminals, sorcerers, con-men, and killers – with a few uncharacteristically decent types sprinkled here and there along the way. His bloodline includes:

- A distant ancestor who mocked other early humans for striking fire from stone and trying to conjure gods from shadows (*Hellblazer* #240).
- Konz of the Tin Mound, who, during the Bronze Age, allowed a demon (Nergal's father) to possess him so Konz could avenge his murdered parents (*Hellblazer: War Lord*).
- Possibly Roman Emperor Constantine, who converted the pagan tradition of Saturnalia into Christmas, thus frustrating Arcadian, Lord of the Dance (*Hellblazer* #49).
- A second emperor (this one African), a psychic assassin born on the Moon, and a priest in Clapham (*Hellblazer* #40).
- A magician called Constantine, in the court of Constantinople's Justinian the Great, who seduced the emperor's wife Theodora and cured the ruler of bubonic plague by summoning a demon into his body (*Destiny: A Chronicle of Deaths Foretold* #1).
- Kon-sten-tyn, a powerful mage who assumed the throne of Britain and ruled from the castle Ravenscar, but grew corrupted by magic (*Hellblazer* #113, Annual #1).
- The author of the Bible's heretical Gospel of Constantine, which allowed a room in the Vatican's Apostolic Palace to remain unconsecrated so Pope Alexander VI could rape young boys without God finding out (*Hellblazer* #243).
- Jack Constantine, who was killed by night-walkers in an Essex churchyard during the reign of Queen Elizabeth I (*The Sandman* #13).
- Harry Constantine, who joined Oliver Cromwell's Drogheda Massacre in order to steal loot but angered the Ribbon Queen, who cursed him with

immortality and buried him alive (*Hellblazer* #62).

- Several individuals whom the Atlanteans found annoying (*War Lord*).

- Pub owner Hugh Constantine, who schemed with Linton Midnite to magically turn East River sludge into Mancunian ale. After leading revolutionaries against British officer Daniel Horsmanden, Hugh was burnt at the stake and hanged, then came back from the dead via sorcery (*Papa Midnite* #1-5).

- Johanna Constantine, born to Lord George and Lady Harriet Constantine, and possibly the illegitimate daughter of Sir Francis Dashwood. Johanna's twin sister died soon after birth. Johanna became a street magician, then a powerful noblewoman, and had a daughter called Mouse (*The Dreaming* #5, 7, 29; *The Sandman* #7, 41, 47; *Lady Constantine* #1-4).

- Opium-dealing apothecary James Constantine, who prevented angels Justinian and Faziel from telling Samuel Taylor Coleridge how to end his poem "Kubla Khan" (*Hellblazer* #105).

- English nobleman Conrad Constantine, who studied the *Necronomicon*, joined occult brotherhood The Brimstone Circle, and allied with the demonic Old Ones, becoming the undead pirate Dark Conrad (*Swamp Thing* #111, 114-115).

- Another John Constantine who was hanged at Tyburn (*Books of Magic* Book II).

- British infantryman Aloysius Quinn, on John's mother's side, who fought the Phansigar cult in Jabalpur, India. Thuggees attacked Quinn with the mystical Red Sepulchre, trapping part of his soul inside the weapon (*Hellblazer* #179, 201).

- William "Bill" Constantine (John's grandfather) and his twin brother Charles. William lacked his family's penchant for magic and failed to kill his twin in the womb, and Charles then grew up feeling inferior to Bill (*Hellblazer* #69; *The Sandman Presents: The Corinthian* #1-3).

- A Gotham City occultist named Constantine, who, in an alternate timeline, helped Bruce Wayne and Harry Houdini determine whether a string of child kidnappings were supernatural in nature (*Batman/Houdini*).

- Thomas Constantine (John's father), born to William and Alice Constantine. Alice and William had six other sons (including Roy and Jack) and a daughter, Dolly (*Hellblazer* #28, 35, 100, 253; *Vertigo Secret Files: Hellblazer*; *The Dreaming* #32).

- John's mother, Mary Anne Quinn (*Hellblazer* #31, 44, 179).

- John's Aunt Jean, with whom he was close (*Hellblazer* #253).

- John's Uncle Nobby, who sported a large beer gut (*Hellblazer* #90).

- John's Aunt Beatt, who lived near Clacton Pier (*Hellblazer* #13).

- A Scotland Yard Inspector, Frank Constantine, who worked with Batman in another reality to solve a murder (*Batman: The Order of Beasts*).

- John's older sister Cheryl and her offspring, daughter Gemma Masters and son Finnbar Brady (*Hellblazer* #4, 288, 293-297).

Then along came John. The following timeline[1] details all we know about the mage's life prior to *Swamp Thing* #37, as chronicled in comic books, graphic novels, short stories, prose novels, and role-playing game sourcebooks published up to 2011. Why 2011? Well, DC Comics revamped its entire universe that year under its New 52 banner, following the *Flashpoint* crossover arc. Since this altered *Constantine*'s history and de-aged him in the process, all stories published thereafter have formed a separate continuity outside this chronology's parameters. Television shows, movies, and video games are likewise ignored. There's much to enjoy about these other versions of John Constantine, but they're simply not the same guy as the one in the original *Hellblazer*.

It all started on a typically dismal note, not long after John's conception...

1952 or 1953: Mary Anne Constantine gets drunk while pregnant with John and tries unsuccessfully to self-abort in a bathtub (*Shade the Changing Man* #44).

10 May 1953: Thomas Constantine forces Mary Anne to have a coat-hanger abortion with four months left of her pregnancy. Mary Anne carries twins, and one sickly fetus strangles his brother with the umbilical cord, then ruptures his placenta and pushes him into the hanger's path. Mary Anne and the strangled twin die, but John, the weaker child, survives. Thomas shuns him as evil and ugly (*Hellblazer* #31, 39, 63, 100, 288).

> Note: In *Hellblazer* #40, John's birth seems to take place in a hospital setting involving doctors and nurses. Issue #100, however, negates this.

Between 1953 and 1957: Thomas takes young John and his sister Cheryl to a Liverpool sporting arena, but it rains and their team loses (*Hellblazer* #100).

1953 to Late 1960s: Thomas raises Cheryl and John in Liverpool, keeping the dead twin's existence a secret (*Hellblazer* #28).

Mid-1950s: Thomas gets drunk and acts abusively toward his children. Cheryl hides in fear behind her toddler brother's high chair (*Hellblazer* #96).

1957: Four-year-old John often breaks his toys. Thomas finds it difficult to keep up with his chaotic son (*Hellblazer* #100).

1957 or 1958: At age four or five, John visits his mother's gravesite with his father and sees the glowing form of his aborted twin's soul. He wonders if the child is Jesus and nicknames him the Golden Boy. The spirit leaves without a word, and John throws a tantrum until Thomas smacks him for disrespecting the dead (*Hellblazer* #39).

1957 to Late 1960s: John continues to see the Golden Boy whenever he feels sad, but the other child refuses to be his friend, so John grows to despise him (*Hellblazer* #39, 40).

---

[1] Excerpted from a larger work compiled for DC Comics' *John Constantine, Hellblazer: 30th Anniversary Celebration*, published in November 2018.

John Constantine's misery began at the moment of birth, as depicted in *Hellblazer* #40. Is it any wonder his life turned out the way it did?

1959: When John is six years old, Thomas lies that the boy's head size killed his mother, then throws hot coffee at him and leaves the stain on the wall as a reminder. (*Hellblazer*/*Books of Magic*) John visits the London Zoo and is frightened by lions (*Hellblazer: Pandemonium*).

1950s to 1960s: John and his playmates bully Gerald "Gerry" McCann, comparing the dimwitted boy to a turnip. When Gerald's brother Billy claims John's mother went to Hell for trying to self-abort, John blacks out and wets his pants – for which Thomas beats him (*Shade* #43-44). The women in John's neighborhood deem him a sneak because he is sickly and shabbily dressed (*Hellblazer* #39).

John and Gary "Gaz" Lester become friends, though Gaz's mother considers John a bad influence on her son (*Hellblazer* #2). John spends hours climbing rocks at the beach. He loses his balance one day and falls into a pool of crabs, sand-ticks, and jellyfish (*Hellblazer* #34). He hears about the United States and fancies it to be a magic land full of superheroes, extraterrestrials, and pizzas (*Books of Magic* Book II).

John wakes up screaming one night from a precognitive nightmare of fairy Jack Green building a coffin to contain the leprosy-infected denizens of Faerie (*Hellblazer* #110). He punches Jamie Ellis in the face for urinating on his new shoes (*War Lord*), learns not to believe in coincidences (*House of Mystery* Annual #2), and gets to know his beer-gutted Uncle Nobby (*Hellblazer* #90).

1961: When Thomas Constantine is jailed for six months for stealing clothes, John and Cheryl stay with their Aunt Dolly and wife-abusing Uncle Harry in Northampton. Other boys make John steal dirty books from a hermit called the Bogeyman. He finds a buried animal corpse, mistakes it for a murdered child, and keeps its petrified heart, hoping its magic can help Dolly. After a time, she and Harry send John and Cheryl to stay with their Aunt Jean and Uncle Roy (*Hellblazer* #35, 253, 100; *Secret Files*).

When John is eight years old, Mictlāntēcutli, the Aztec god of death, appears in his bedroom. John screams until his father threatens to beat him (*Hellblazer: All His Engines*).

In or After 1961: Mary Anne's ghost tells John that he has the ethics of a Sunday joint, and that she worries he'll end up in jail like his father (*Hellblazer* #66; *Hellblazer: Subterranean*).

> Note: John's mother dies during childbirth, so these interactions must involve ghostly visitations – which makes sense, given his ability as an adult to see the spirits of the dead. Her concerns prove well-founded, for John serves several prison, jail, and asylum stints during his lifetime.

1960s: John becomes familiar with the works of an occultist named Fraser (*Hellblazer* #143). He looks inside a truck transporting offal and cow heads, then suffers a week of sleepless nights, unable to stop thinking about the contents (*Hellblazer* #11).

Each summer, John visits his Aunt Beatt for two weeks with Thomas and Cheryl at her home near Clacton Pier, where he reads comics, eats beans on toast, watches *Rawhide* on television, and visits the Fun Fair. He fears the Chamber of Horrors, which makes him feel sick, but always goes in anyway (*Hellblazer* #11, 13, 28). John builds a shanty hut out of bricks and old doors at a Liverpool bombsite, intending to run away and live there – which he never does (*Hellblazer* #14).

John and other children torment Robert/Roger Huntoon, whom they nickname "Piggy." Huntoon holds a grudge on into adulthood (*Swamp Thing* #66; *Magic Sourcebook*). Cheryl and John often seal their oaths to each other with the phrase "Cross my heart and hope to die. Stick a needle in my eye" (*Hellblazer* #288).

The demon Nergal observes John's early behavior, deems him an insolent child, and decides to teach him a lesson in manners (*Hellblazer* #8). Nergal meets John while posing as another child on a beach. He jokes that John's first name means "loo" (bathroom), so John decides to simply call himself "Constantine." Nergal convinces him to try his first cigarette, and John steals the whole pack (*Secret Files*).

1963: At age 10, John has few friends other than Gary, since children find him weird. John talks Gaz into taking honey from a wasp nest, claiming Cheryl will let him feel up her skirt if he does. He also convinces Gaz to wipe his rear end with nettles, and to call the school's headmaster "arse-bandit" to his face (*Vertigo Winter's Edge* #2). Thomas builds John a slingshot to shoot birds, then mocks him for failing to hit anything (*Hellblazer* #31).

In or After 1963: John becomes an ardent fan of *Doctor Who*, but despises The Beatles' music – which Cheryl adores (*Hellblazer* #7, 31, 169).

In or Before the Mid-1960s: John's Aunt Jean teaches him how to perform a séance (*Hellblazer* #213).

Mid-1960s: Constantine develops incestuous thoughts regarding his sister Cheryl and watches her change clothes after work (*Hellblazer* #7). During detention, he memorizes "The Charge of the Light Brigade," by Alfred, Lord Tennyson (*Books of Magic* Book IV).

Bullied by Kenny Nelson, John bribes Kenny's sister Anita to reveal details about their late mother Lizzie Seddon, then stages a fake séance to make Kenny think she is accusing him of smothering her with a cushion. Kenny runs into the street and is hit by a truck, resulting in his legs being amputated. John realizes he has a gift for lying (*Hellblazer* #213).

1966: At age 13, John befriends Katie Morgan, whom he walks home on Guy Fawkes Night after a bonfire reminds her of her father's death. The two date until a disapproving teacher, Mister Watson, threatens to have John thrown into a borstal unless he keeps his distance. John thus ignores her thereafter (*House of Mystery* Annual #2).

Between 1966 and 1981: John collects *Silver Surfer* comics (*The Sandman* #3).

Late 1960s: John develops a crush on schoolmate Karen Laing and often stares at her breasts. He receives multiple detentions from a teacher called Brownlee (*Hellblazer* #51). While growing up in Liverpool, John spends a lot of time with Tim "Timmy" McCabe, whose sister Dora becomes his occasional sex partner (*Hellblazer Annual 2011*).

In or Before 1967: By age 14, John develops strong resentment and fear regarding his father, who frequently gets drunk and threatens to beat him (*Hellblazer* #100). He befriends schoolmate Jerry Monaghan, a masochist drawn to the occult (*Hellblazer* #51).

1967: John's anger erupts after Thomas berates him for not finishing an essay. He asks his father for help, but Thomas slaps his face, causing John to strike back and threaten his dad's life (*Hellblazer* #100). When his high school class creates time capsules, John uses magic to hide his own innocence, vulnerability, and childhood naïveté in a house-shaped locket, which he buries in the capsule (*Hellblazer/ Books of Magic*). John avidly pursues the "Hidden World" of magic and the occult, but purely for laughs and sex (*Hellblazer* #9,

31; *War Lord*). He works as a newsboy, selling papers in the street (*Love Street*).

Summer 1967: In the "summer of love," John is expelled for organizing an "Out demons out" chant during assembly. Thomas burns his son's magic books, but John rescues an article about practical magic, then shoots a cat, curses it with slow death, and binds his dad's spirit to the animal, causing his father to grow old and weak. Terrified that Thomas will die, John preserves the cat in formaldehyde and buries it near his mother's grave. His father thus spends his later years feeble and sickly (*Hellblazer* #31).

Late 1967: Constantine convinces musician John Lennon to change the title of The Beatles' next song to something "far out." He suggests "I Am the Walrus" (*The Sandman Presents: Love Street*).

> Note: This may be a fabrication on John's part, given his age and the fact that he hates the band's music. Or maybe he was trying to sabotage them with a ridiculous title.

In or Before 1968: John reads a book about Roderick "the Magus" Burgess describing "freaky" rituals. He longs to obtain a tarot deck made by the occultist (*Love Street*).

1968: At age 15, after fighting with his father, John receives an unsigned letter containing a photo of Suicide Bridge, causing him to consider killing himself. His friend Tim McCabe looks at the picture and becomes suicidal. John lets Tim keep the photo, and the youth jumps to his death (*Hellblazer Annual 2011*). He befriends a music producer named Rick, exorcises a noisy spirit preventing Suzi Quatro from recording her second single, and makes out with the singer (*Hellblazer* #285).

Summer 1968: Gary Lester rents a London flat and invites Constantine to move in. John promises to do so before Christmas if he can raise the cash (*Hellblazer Special* #1). John runs away and rents a room on Notting Hill's Portobello Road. He spends a lot of time with his housemates – occultist Nancy "Estella" Weston (who teaches him how to read tarot cards), immortal yoga practitioner Ravi, and ballet student Pamela. John befriends fellow runaway Oliver and arranges for the boy to live with them (*Love Street*).

> Note: Although a caption in *Love Street* sets the story in July 1968, Constantine's age in that miniseries (16) would seem to push it to 1969 since John was born in 1953. It could be that John is lying about his age, however, in which case the 1968 placement stands.

August 1968: John and his housemates attend a free concert in Hyde Park, as well as a festival at the Wych Cross home of Alex Burgess – Fawney Rig, the former estate of John's ancestor, Johanna Constantine. John witnesses magic and tantric sex demonstrations (*Love Street*).

1969: When John is 16, the rift between him and his father grows quite deep (*Hellblazer* #28). He and Francis "Chas" Chandler become friends (*Hellblazer* #84; *Subterranean*).

Summer 1969: Gary Lester rents a London flat and invites Constantine to move in. John promises to do so before Christmas if he can raise the cash (*Hellblazer Special* #1).

September 1969: Two U.C.L.A. dropouts, Alice and Lynn, pick up Constantine in their van. He convinces them he's Paul McCartney's cousin, culminating in a ménage à trois. The trio gets high together and he promises them an autograph (*Hellblazer Special* #1).

While visiting former family estate Fawney Rig in *The Sandman Presents: Love Street*, teenage John notices a painting of a like-minded ancestor, the Lady Johanna.

October 1969: Father Phillip Tolly gives Constantine a ride and pressures him into oral sex. As Tolly bends toward the teen's crotch, John slams him in the head, causing the priest – who'd hidden a razor blade in his mouth, intending to castrate John – to cut up his own face (*Hellblazer Special* #1).

1969 to 1989: John and his father refuse to speak to each other for 20 years, though John occasionally sends Thomas money out of guilt (*Hellblazer* #28).

1960s or 1970s: During a Vietnam protest at London's Grosvenor Square, Constantine hypnotizes Chief Inspector "Basher" Babbadge to smoke marijuana in front of the American Embassy, resulting in the officer's forced resignation (*Hellblazer* #1).

In or Before 1970: John befriends fellow magic user Paul, who is heavily into voodoo, amphetamines, and breaking-and-entering (*9-11* #2).

1970: John and friend Dave Coombs ingest hallucinogenic mushrooms, causing Dave to chase John with an onion (*Hellblazer* #89). His smoking habit reaches 30 cigarettes a day (*Hellblazer* #43).

Constantine moves to London at age 17 and rents a room in Chas Chandler's home, where Chas lives with his mother Queenie, a bedridden witch, and her vile chimpanzee familiar, Slag. John helps Chas kill the ape, causing Queenie to die as well. He lives with Chas for a year, then leverages the incident to gain free rides and other favors for decades (*Hellblazer* #44, 84).

In or After 1970: John and Chas find the latter's Uncle Dave conversing with a garden gnome, a hat rack, and other items. Constantine decides the house must be haunted, until Chas realizes his uncle is merely a ventriloquist. John works at a Mafia-run casino, befriends magician Archie Fein, and has an affair with a possibly underage woman named Kim. He magically convinces winners they've lost, then pockets their earnings. Casino owner Ronnie Watson orders him beaten, but John utters magic words that leave the mobsters dead or insane [*Hellblazer* #120].

| Note: The casino story may be a fabrication on Archie's part.

Between 1970 and 1978: A man named Wong teaches Constantine about the *I Ching*, an ancient Chinese divination text [*Hellblazer* #102].

1970s: John experiments with LSD and has colorful hallucinations [*Hellblazer* #89]. He discovers communal living in a Brixton squat filled with rotten carpets and boarded windows, and the situation ends in tears [*Hellblazer* #14].

1972: John gets heavily into magic after a friend plays up its positives, then asks Brendan Finn to help him research occultists in his family tree. Brendan learns about Harry Constantine, who was buried alive after being cursed with immortality. John partially digs up his ancestor to chat, then reburies him [*Hellblazer* #243].

| Note: *Hellblazer* #75 claims John met Brendan while in Mucous
| Membrane, but the band didn't yet exist in 1972.

Constantine becomes a ritualistic magician and learns how to access the disciplines of communication and control, and to reach across the mana stream to contact potent otherworldly and extraterrestrial entities [*Magic Sourcebook*]. At age 19, he steals Piggy Huntoon's girlfriend Diane and gets her caught up in the world of magic and sexual depravity [*Swamp Thing* #66].

Before January 1973: Looking to fund free rock festivals, Constantine hustles bookies by wagering on the date on which U.S. President Lyndon B. Johnson will suffer a fatal heart attack – which he accurately predicts [*Hellblazer* #1].

Mid-1970s: John briefly attends college and dates Zatanna Zatara while studying occult practices. The two join a tantric studies group in San Francisco. Her father, Giovanni "John" Zatara, does not approve. John teaches Zatanna how to lock her house via a protection spell [*Swamp Thing* #49; *Secret Origins* #27; *Magic Sourcebook, Zatanna: Everyday Magic, Who's Who: The Definitive Directory of the DC Universe*].

Early 1970s: Constantine has sex a few times with a rotund woman named Renee, who fancies his friend Chas and begins dating him instead. Renee grows to dislike John intensely, whom she considers scary and a bad influence on Chas [*Hellblazer* #84].

1975: John befriends Bill Greenwood, an irascible older man, while frequenting the King's Head bar. John deems Bill's wife Nellie a national treasure [*Hellblazer* #106].

Late 1975: Snobby magician Sir Norman invites John to join a magic lodge, which orders him to defile a Christian crucifix. For six months, he works to impress the "wine bar wankers," and even meets a well-dressed werewolf. John earns a reputation as a middle-class black-arts master, quickly rises through the ranks, and is predicted to be named grandmaster by age 25. When the lodge orders him to sever his past by killing Chas, however, he refuses and is expelled [*Swamp Thing* #169; *Hellblazer* #109].

1975 to 1995: John frequents the King's Head bar on and off for 20 years, often stopping by Bill and Nellie Greenwood's house for tea [*Hellblazer* #106].

1976: Constantine witnesses a senior Freemason having sex with a corpse in a graveyard. He photographs the incident, then uses the pictures as leverage to obtain information about the secretive fraternity [*Hellblazer* #54].

20 September 1976: John attends a Sex Pistols concert at London's 100 Club. Ten minutes later, he cuts off his hippie locks and adopts a punk rock haircut [*Love Street*].

1977: John grows fascinated with summoning demons after arcana expert

Benjamin "Ben" Cox obtains a copy of the dark-arts book *Grimorium Verum*. He spends months assembling the items required for a ritual, just in case (*Hellblazer* #11). His niece Gemma Masters is born to Cheryl and her ultra-religious husband, Tony Masters (*Hellblazer* #4).

Summer 1977: Constantine forms the punk rock band Mucous Membrane, with John providing lead vocals. Members include Gary "Gaz" Lester on guitar, Benjamin "Beano" Digby on drums, and a revolving cast of bassists, including Stu and Les (*Hellblazer* #1, 77, 153, 162, 245; *The Sandman Presents: Marquee Moon* [unpublished]).

> Note: Mucous Membrane has typically been drawn with four members, but five bandmates have been named: Constantine, Lester, Beano, Les, and Stu. Les could be short for Lester, or he could be one of the bassists.

Fall 1977: Mucous Membrane debuts at Newcastle's Casanova Club. During a rendition of Chuck Berry's "Johnny B. Goode," the crowd grows abusive and John ends the show abruptly. Club owner Alex Logue invites the band to party with his friends, but John declines after noticing Logue inappropriately touching his daughter Astra (*Hellblazer* #11, 245, 246).

Between Fall 1977 and 1978: Constantine writes the song "Lies of My Own," which Mucous Membrane releases as a 45 single. He gets drunk with Sid Vicious one night, and they bring two women back to his flat; Sid passes out, leaving both women for John (*Subterranean*). John also befriends Patrick McDonell, a.k.a Destructo Vermin Gobsmack of the punk band The Hopeless Heroins (*Hellblazer Annual* #1; *Pandemonium*).

John finds fellow punk Angie White annoying, despite their shared interest in the occult (*Hellblazer* #162). Punk rocker Sadie takes a liking to Constantine, but drives into a tree before they can hook up (*Hellblazer* #99). At a Mucous Membrane performance, John meets Rose, a spelling bee semifinalist from Doglick, West Virginia, who sticks a pin in his abdomen when he asks her to spell "fellatio." The two have sex, but his inability to commit drives her to marry Richard "Dickie" Fermin. EMI Records executives attend the band's next gig (*Hellblazer* #153-155).

Chas works as a roadie at nearly all of Mucous Membrane's performances, but Constantine fails to pay him. Chas never admits he thinks the group sounds awful (*Hellblazer* #77, Annual #1). Mucous Membrane often performs Marvin Gaye's "I Heard It Through the Grapevine," which John considers his theme song (*The Sandman* #3).

> Note: Oddly, Chas doesn't know Gary in *Hellblazer* #1, despite Gaz having been in the band.

John becomes close with Brendan Finn while the latter manages the band The Squitters (*Hellblazer* #75, 295). At a Sex Pistols concert in Camden, the two friends create the illusion of a haunted amplifier, then convince band manager Malcolm McLaren to let them perform an exorcism (*Hellblazer* #42).

Late 1977: Constantine joins a group of master mages, including Clarice Sackville and Gordon Alfred Haine. Though decades his elder, Clarice performs oral sex on John in Highgate Cemetery (*Hellblazer* #134, 137, Annual 2011).

In or Before 1978: Constantine befriends Ray Monde, an older gay man. Their relationship remains platonic, despite Constantine being bisexual, since Ray already has a lover. In addition, John dates a woman named Judith while studying tantric yoga at the Borth Beach Ashram and befriends American ex-soldier Frank North (*Hellblazer* #7, 11).

While visiting South America, Constantine learns how to cast a holding spell to subdue a man possessed by wild demons (*Shade* #42). He comes to fear the Arab, a pointy-toothed savage who eats live animals and can appear in two places at once (*Hellblazer* #163).

January 1978: Mucous Membrane attends a performance by The Clash at London's Roxy Club. Two music executives, Les and Maurice, seek bands to sign for their label. They approach Constantine, who rushes home to write songs. Mucous Membrane performs in Ayelsbury, where producer KGB signs the group for a record deal, then at the Marquee Club, on London's Wardour Street, where John senses two werewolves in the backup band, The Uninvited (*Marquee Moon*).

1978: Thomas Constantine travels to London to check on his son, but John slams the door in his face (*Hellblazer* #100). Mucous Membrane books gigs at the Electric Banana, where he meets Richard "Rich the Punk" Eldridge, the lead singer of Fatal Gift. After Rich borrows his instruments, John fights him to get them back, and they become close mates. Rich dubs him "Johnny Con-job" and introduces him to his friend Muppet (*Hellblazer* #91; *Secret Files*).

John meets Robert William "Straff" Strathern and his mother Betty, both of whom are epileptics. On weekends, John, Straff, Muppet, and Rich frequent a Romford chip shop, where Muppet often picks fights with football hooligans (*Hellblazer* #98). Every woman in the crowd longs to take John home during a Mucous Membrane gig at Dingwalls (*Hellblazer* #245, 246).

Before Early 1978: Constantine balks at how magic users like the Phantom Stranger, Baron Winters, Doctor Fate, and Jason Blood become lost in the part (*Hellblazer* #50). He meets Belfast conman Francie Fallis, who sells replica guns to the Provos, and dates Karen, who develops an unhealthy fascination with "whore magick" (*Hellblazer* #75). Constantine sets up a scam operation with fake psychic Neville Sharp, who pretends to be a reverend able to speak to the deceased. John dons a dress during one performance (*Hellblazer* #120).

John dates several girlfriends and occasional boyfriends, but few of his love affairs last (*Hellblazer* #51). He convinces Sharon Grant that he has his own coven, then has sex with her at the Fifth Form Disco when she asks to join (*Hellblazer* #72). He befriends Header, a violent Scotsman; Header's friend Terry Butcher; Mange, a grumpy magician trapped in a rabbit's body; and drug dealer Jehosaphat P. "Jerry the Dealer" O'Flynn, who becomes like a brother to him (*Hellblazer* #24, 63). Brendan and John guest-write *News of the World*'s horoscope column and make up ludicrous predictions filled with rectal puns (*Hellblazer* #75).

Early 1978: "Venus of the Hardsell," a hit single from Mucous Membrane, is published by 'Snot Music. Dean Motter records a music video for the song filled with violent imagery (*Hellblazer Annual* #1). *NME* magazine interviews Constantine and the band (*Hellblazer* #62). John and Jerry get into trouble with police for walking along the side rail of a bridge while intoxicated (*Hellblazer* #24). John grows marijuana in a window box (*Hellblazer* #48).

Constantine returns to Newcastle's Casanova Club with Gary Lester, Ben Cox, Judith, Frank North, psychic nun Anne-Marie, and quantum magic pioneer Ritchie Simpson. They find a basement filled with corpses shredded by a demonic creature known as the Norfulthing. John tries to summon a demon, Sagatana, to fight the terror elemental, but accidentally conjures Nergal, who takes Astra Logue to Hell, leaving John holding her severed arm. John suffers a mental breakdown and is committed to the Ravenscar Secure Facility for the Dangerously Deranged. Many, including the Phantom Stranger, erroneously believe him dead [*Hellblazer* #11; *Swamp Thing* #46; *The Sandman* #3; *Who's Who in the DC Universe* #15].

Early 1978 to Early 1980: Constantine spends two years at Ravenscar under the treatment of Doctor Huntoon (whom 'John had bullied as a child) and administrator Dalton-Brewer. Cheryl never visits, though Clarice Sackville does [*Hellblazer* #7, 102, 202]. Medication prevents John from dreaming for several months [*Hellblazer* #7], and he coerces Huntoon to wipe his rear end for him [*Swamp Thing* #66]. John befriends a psychic patient named Una, who hears voices in her head [*Hellblazer* #25].

Mistreated by Huntoon, Constantine is subjected to electroshock therapy to eliminate delusions of demons. Guards break his fingers and knock out his teeth [*Hellblazer* #8, 50, 114]. John cuts himself and draws magic sigils on the walls, terrified that something will get in to kill him otherwise. Interns move him to a padded cell and fit him with a straitjacket, but he creates more wards from his own blood. Unable to sleep, he hallucinates [*Hellblazer* #233].

Before 6 July 1978: Constantine temporarily leaves Ravenscar, reunites with Mucous Membrane, and resumes his typical lifestyle [*Hellblazer* #91, 162, 163, 271].

> Note: John is depicted as having adventures as a free man during this period of his Ravenscar stay, which means he must have left the asylum.

After 6 July 1978: American industrialist Stanley "S.W." Manor hires Constantine to find a clock once owned by Grigori Rasputin, capable of foretelling the future. John scams Manor with a fake clock and a staged murder scene [*Hellblazer* #162, 163, 173, 174].

6 August 1978: Mucous Membrane performs at The Hope and Anchor [*Hellblazer* #271].

Late 1978: John, Rich the Punk, and their friend Deanie ride bikes to see the Plasmatics at Stratford Poly. Deanie vanishes and is transported to the year 1642 [*Hellblazer* #91].

Between 1978 and Early 1979: Constantine returns to Ravenscar but fails to respond to treatment. Dalton-Brewer electrocutes his testicles as punishment and tries to draw out John's madness by channeling the Golden Boy's power. This forms an "insanity-thing" that leeches off John for years, causing him to make bad decisions [*Hellblazer* #102, 233, 249].

Between 1978 and 1982: John reads Doctor Terrence "Terry" Thirteen's book debunking the occult [*Books of Magic* Book II].

Early 1979: Constantine temporarily leaves Ravenscar again, then struts along Carnaby Street in punk regalia, telling the old "swinging London" types to sod off [*War Lord*]. He dates self-harming drama student Mandy, then breaks up with her two hours before one of her performances [*Hellblazer* #142].

> Note: Once again, John is shown having adventures during his Ravenscar stay, implying another departure from the hospital.

4 May 1979: John checks out of Ravenscar again so he can vote against Margaret Thatcher, but is swept back in time by Rac Shade (the Changing Man), first to 1973 and then to 1692. Upon returning to the present, he has a premonition of Thatcher's government damaging England, then tries to jump from the Camden High Street road bridge. Faeces McCartney, a member of the punk band No Future, stops him from killing himself, and the two remain friends. John soon returns to the asylum [*Hellblazer* #266; *Shade* #42-44].

Constantine is heartbroken to hear, in *Shade the Changing Man* #42, that Margaret Thatcher has been named the new U.K. Prime Minister.

Mid- to Late 1979: Constantine escapes from Ravenscar. While he's out, he and Faeces get their bands together for several gigs in Camden, attend warehouse parties in Fulham, and share a bondage girl in Bromley (*Hellblazer* #266, 274).

July 1979: Constantine casts a spell to create a living woman, which fails. Reggae singer Malcolm Campbell asks John to put him in touch with his roots, so John arranges for an old African demon to possess Malcolm – which then refuses to leave. He has sex with Epiphany "Piffy" Greaves, his own future wife, after she travels back in time (*Hellblazer* #271, 272).

13 August 1979: Mucous Membrane and No Future perform at the Hope and Anchor, located in Camden (*Hellblazer* #265).

In or After August 1979: Cheryl asks John to let her and Gemma stay with him when her husband Tony begins acting odd, but he turns them away. Older John arrives from the future to retrieve Epiphany and punches his younger self in the face. A physician brings young John back to Ravenscar yet again (*Hellblazer* #273, 274).

Eventually, Constantine's fascination with magic outweighs his interest in punk music. Therefore, he disbands Mucous Membrane so he can fully pursue the occult (*Hellblazer* #162; *Magic Sourcebook*).

Late 1970s: A thug named Victor nearly kills Constantine for hinting that he'd molested Jenny Singleton. Mictlāntēcutli, the Aztec god of death, kills everyone in the room except for John and Chas (*All His Engines*).

1970s or 1980s: Constantine has sex with Chas's cousin Norma (*Hellblazer* #214).

In or Before the 1980s: Constantine, Doctor Fate, and the Phantom Stranger all join the Magi Guild (*Swamp Thing* #137).

> Note: It's unclear when this occurs in relation to John's various Ravenscar stays.

Early 1980: John is deemed cured and released from Ravenscar, though his friends' ghosts haunt him thereafter (*Hellblazer* #7, Annual #1). He hires Patrick McDonell to promote a Mucous Membrane music video, but McDonell fails to share the profits. John considers burning down the man's house (*Hellblazer* #33). Brendan invites John to meet his girlfriend, Katherine "Kit" Ryan. Kit and Brendan marry, though John secretly falls in love with her as well (*Hellblazer* #42, 70, 75).

After Early 1980: John spends a month working for an undertaker, but finds the smells of flesh and formaldehyde disturbing (*The Sandman* #3). He reads *The Old Straight Track* and books by John Michel, and he dates a geomancer (*Hellblazer* #14), as well as acupuncturist Nancy Ming, who can glean information by reading his body's electromagnetism. On one occasion, Nancy "accidentally" hits the wrong nerve, causing pain (*Swamp Thing* #89). For three weeks, John seeks to learn about Baron Winters' past, but he turns up no information about the magician (*Books of Magic* Book II).

Late 1980: Constantine suffers a mental relapse within six months of his release from Ravenscar and is re-admitted to the asylum (*Hellblazer Annual* #1).

1980 or 1981: John lives in an East Croydon high-rise with his junkie girlfriend Rachel (*The Sandman* #3).

> Note: It's unclear when this occurs in relation to John's various Ravenscar stays.

1980 to 1982: Constantine is released from Ravenscar, then is re-admitted three more times due to other relapses. Each time, he contemplates committing suicide at a mountain cliff (*Hellblazer Annual* #1).

1980 to 1983: Kit Ryan and Brendan Finn become Constantine's closest friends, offering refuge whenever John can't handle life. During summers, he smokes opium and drinks whiskey with them on the edge of the Dublin Mountains (*Hellblazer* #42, 46, 50).

1980 to 1988: Ritchie Simpson sometimes hacks into electronic reality for John, placing his consciousness in computers to track down information (*Hellblazer* #7).

1981: Constantine buys a sand pouch at a San Francisco garage sale, unaware that it belongs to Lord Morpheus (Dream of the Endless). He spends six months in Alaska handling the "Lupus affair," during which he consults with Jason Blood. While he's gone, John's girlfriend Rachel steals the pouch, along with his stereo, television, and *Silver Surfer* comics, and sells them all for drug money (*The Sandman* #2, 3; *Books of Magic* Book II).

> Note: The nature of the Lupus affair is unspecified.

In or Before October 1981: Constantine again returns to Ravenscar (*Hellblazer Annual* #1).

October 1981: John is released from the asylum, vowing never to return. Doctors give him drugs to deal with anger and recommend journaling (*Hellblazer* #102, Annual #1).

> Note: This occurs six months before the British Navy leaves Portsmouth for the Falkland Islands in April 1982. It is said to be his fourth release, but evidence in other tales indicates the number is quite higher.

Between 1981 and 1983: John and Brendan obtain compromising Polaroid photos of Sir Peter Marston, a member of Britain's House of Lords, with which they blackmail him (*Hellblazer* #52).

Between 1981 and 1984: Constantine lives in a flat in Notting Hill (*The Sandman* #3).

Early 1982: Constantine and an acquaintance, Kipling, pull a con in Bangkok, angering several lapsed martyrs (*Hellblazer* #51). He befriends Reverend Richard "Rick the Vic" Nilsen, who has a penchant for sacrilege and obtains taboo items for him (*Hellblazer* #130; *Secret Files*).

> Note: Kipling likely refers to Knights Templar member Willoughby Kipling, a character whom Grant Morrison had introduced in Doom Patrol – and, in fact, had based on John Constantine.

Constantine finds Patrick McDonell selling "Nuke Buenos Aires" sweatshirts. Once again, his friend fails to pay him royalties owed from the old Mucous Membrane music video (*Hellblazer* #33). John goes on a drinking binge, has sex with a mysterious woman, and dreams of his evil ancestor Konsten-tyn (*Hellblazer Annual* #1). Unable to put Newcastle behind him, he has himself committed to Ravenscar one final time (*Hellblazer* #130).

June 1982: Gangsters Harry and Norman Cooper arrange for John to be released from the asylum against his will, then force him to bring Harry's five-year-old son Ronnie back from the dead. John performs a summoning with help from Brendan, Rick, and Header. After inadvertently conjuring Sid Vicious, they bind a fuckpig demon to young Ronnie, which takes over the mob but remains childlike in appearance. John begs to be let back into Ravenscar, but the staff refuses and he considers suicide (*Hellblazer* #129-133).

Mid- or Late 1982: John pulls a con in Scunthorpe with grifters Neville Sharp, Boz, and Tony. Sharp acts as a faith healer, while John poses as paraplegic Falklands War hero Harry Tyler. An actual man by that name is in the audience, however – whom Sharp somehow heals, despite being a fraud (*Hellblazer* #120).

After 1982: John realizes the Norfulthing, as an elemental, cannot truly be destroyed. He thus returns to Newcastle and makes a deal: if the creature stays out of trouble, he'll allow it to feast once a year on someone who deserves it (*Hellblazer* #246).

In or Before 1983: Constantine begins dating Emma, an American artist, who squeezes his hand supportively whenever he has flashbacks to Newcastle. She playfully sketches him, labeling one drawing "Bastard" (*Hellblazer* #142). John introduces her to Kit Ryan and his sister Cheryl, both of whom like her. Emma's father, however, warns his daughter to leave the mage (*Swamp Thing* #37; *Hellblazer* #62).

1983: Benjamin "Beano" Digby becomes strung out on heroin. John finds Beano's flat haunted by Victorian-era ghosts, then dies during a spell gone awry. He returns during his own funeral, never revealing how he escaped from Hell (*Hellblazer* #77).

Tommy Cox introduces John to New York City lowlife Zeerke, who offers him the Ace of Winchesters for half a million dollars. After Zeerke doubles the price, John steals the demon-killing rifle with help from Brendan, Rick the Vic, and Jerry the Dealer, then hides it at the home of Scurve the Elephant Handler. John and Brendan cheat on Emma and Kit with two young women in New York (*Hellblazer* #72, 76; *Hitman* #16). Soon thereafter, Constantine loses touch with Kit and Brendan (*Hellblazer* #42).

John's ill-fated girlfriend Emma, as depicted in *Hellblazer* #142, before her tragic death in *Swamp Thing* #37.

Gary gives Constantine chalk containing virgin blood, useful for summoning demons (*Hellblazer* #44). John works with fellow magician Ghant and police detective Roger Bentham to solve the murder of his friend Carl in Scotland. They discover starving vampire-succubus hybrid children living on Gruinard Island, then cast a binding spell to prevent the creatures from reaching the mainland (*Hellblazer* #187, 188).

October 1983 to Autumn 1985: Constantine discovers that the Brujería, a male witch cult, plans to awaken a great evil in the aftermath of an impending crisis. With help from Ben Cox, Frank North, Anne-Marie, and Judith, John spends two years preparing to stop them, while plotting how to elicit help from the reigning Earth elemental, Alec Holland, who is not yet up for the fight (*Swamp Thing* #49).

26 November 1983: Robbers break into the Brink's-Mat warehouse at London's Heathrow International Trading Estate in the so-called "crime of the century." John Constantine is among the suspects (*Hellblazer* #107).

1980s: Chas's daughter Geraldine grows up calling Constantine "Uncle John," but sees him infrequently since her mother Renee dislikes him (*Hellblazer* #84). The mage befriends mobster John "Pearly" Grey (*Hellblazer* #1, 230, 231), as well as magic user and prognosticator Lenny. In Nigeria, John manipulates Lenny into summoning a pair of demons. Lenny loses his mind in the process, then withdraws from society and thereafter begs for money on the streets (*Hellblazer* #122).

Gemma Masters sometimes pretends to be scared of monsters just so her Uncle John will comfort her. He tells her not to worry – and to remember, if ever she encounters a monster, not to let it scare her since she's a Constantine (*Hellblazer* #280). John begins wearing white gloves as a fashion statement (*Hellblazer* #230, 231).

Mid-1980s: Constantine forms a low opinion of Doctor Lawrence Polygon, whose slipshod research causes a woman's death when the mystic taps into repressed psychic powers, causing her to combust (*Swamp Thing* #128, 137).

John saves Bartholomew "Binky" Carter-Browne, Britain's future parliamentary undersecretary, after a Haitian envoy's daughter turns into a crocodile (*Hellblazer* #21). He works on a student-union haunting with psychic journalist Nigel Archer/Engels, but the ghost turns out to be non-menacing, so John merely tells it to piss off instead of bothering with an exorcism (*Hellblazer* #53, 63; *Secret Files*).

> Note: Nigel's surname changes from Archer to Engels from one story to the next.

Late Summer 1984: Prior to his first contact with Swamp Thing, John observes Abby Arcane-Cable from afar (*Swamp Thing* #25).

In or Before December 1984: Constantine obtains the files of Doctor Hindley, from the Whitechapel Hospital for the Criminally Insane, which prove she treated patients with thalidomide for two years after the drug was banned. He then blackmails the physician for years (*Hellblazer* #60). John rents a flat in Paddington from Brenda McGuire, above the apartment of a Rastafarian known as Mighty Mouse (*Hellblazer* #1, 44, 245).

December 1984: The succubus Chantinelle (Ellie) and her angel lover Tali seek John's assistance after she becomes pregnant. He hides them from Heaven and Hell using pentangles, but smears his own blood into the sigil mix in case the demon ever becomes a danger to him. Chantinelle owes him a debt of gratitude thereafter (*Hellblazer* #60, 104).

In or Before 1985: Constantine and his friend Seth meet two women, Barbara and Martha, at a pub. Seth challenges John to see who can bed Martha first (*Vertigo Jam: Louder Than Noise* #1). John finally meets Baron Winters. The two fail to get along, though each respects the other's skills. He does a prison stint and shares a cell with a man arrested for raping and torturing old women (*Swamp Thing* #48-49).

1985: Constantine extorts money from the Cooper crime family to pay Brendan, Rick, and Header for their help in binding the fuckpig demon to Ronnie Cooper (*Hellblazer* #133).

Summer 1985: With the Primordial Shadow intent on destroying the world, Constantine teaches Swamp Thing about his true nature so the elemental can prevent the apocalypse. John guides Swamp Thing in defeating the Brujería, introduces him to the Parliament of Trees, and awakens extraordinary powers in his friend Steve Dayton (Doom Patrol's Mento) for the battle ahead. He and Dayton hold a séance with Baron Winters, Doctor Fate, Doctor Occult, Sargon the Sorcerer, and Zatanna. The crisis is averted, but John's friends Judith, Anne-Marie, Frank North, and Ben Cox, as well as Dayton, Sargon, Fate, and John's girlfriend Emma, all perish during the struggle (*Swamp Thing* #37-50; *Crisis on Infinite Earths* #4; *New Teen Titans* #22).

Bayou-Bound

So there you go: John Constantine's shady and pain-filled life up to the point when we first meet him in Alan Moore's *Swamp Thing*. As this chronology makes abundantly clear, Constantine is not a typical protagonist. His associates have included criminals, demons, and perverts, plus he's been jailed for a wide range of disturbing crimes – and, mind you, this is just in the period prior to his *Swamp Thing* debut. During the decades that followed, his life would take even darker turns and he would commit even more appalling acts, including the murder of innocents.

Given Con-job's narcotics abuse, serial womanizing, criminal history, selfish lifestyle, and basic lack of ethics, it's sometimes difficult to view him as a good person, even when he's reluctantly saving the world for the umpteenth time. Yet despite his many flaws and all the horrible things he has done, John Constantine remains one of DC Comics' most beloved characters. It's easy to see why: from the moment of his birth – indeed, even *before* his birth – John's story was already immersed in magic, tainted by the occult, and submerged in endless pain, depression, and death. As the magus has blazed his self-destructive path through Hell, Heaven, and everywhere in between, the *Swamp Thing* mythos and the DC/Vertigo Universe have been immeasurably enriched by his presence.

It's been one Hell of a journey our John has taken – and it all began long before that fateful day in the bayou.

About the Contributors

Leah Battle works and lives in California's Coachella Valley. She's been a professional artist since 1982 but has been an artist nearly all her life. Leah studied under Tony Askew and Cynthia Martin (not the *Star Wars* comics illustrator) in Santa Barbara, and was a student of fine arts and art history at Santa Barbara Community College. Her passion for animals turned professional when she started a business illustrating pets. The business was eventually featured in a *KEYT News* segment series called *Businesses That Work*. After 20 years of pet illustration, she was invited to participate in creating sketch cards for licensed properties (*Star Wars* and *The Lord of the Rings*, among many others), and she was chosen as an artist for *Star Wars* Celebration in 2010. Since then, Leah has worked on personal commissions, has dipped a toe into the basics of photography, and has more recently looked to different avenues of creativity. Her preferred mediums are colored pencils, markers, and digitally created works. She recently completed her second cover for Sequart (for an anthology about classic monsters), and is currently working on several personal projects.

Adrian Brown is a Londoner like John Constantine – i.e., not born there but lived there most of his life. His career as a psychiatric nurse has mostly been in addictions, with two dozen publications on hospital interventions. In his spare time, Ade contributed to a football fanzine and then comics fanzines, including a charity comic called *Just 1 Page*. He got back into comics in the mid-1980s, just in time to make *Hellblazer* his favorite book.

John Boylan is an illustrator, graphic designer, and lifelong comic book enthusiast. He holds the Guinness World Record for Largest Collection of *Swamp Thing* Memorabilia and publishes the annual, international *Swamp Thing* fanzine, *Holland Files*. John curates his collection at rootsoftheswampthing.com, the most comprehensive *Swamp Thing* database, where he has catalogued more than 3,500 *Swamp Thing* appearances and collectibles to date. The site celebrates and documents *Swamp Thing*'s history, housing comprehensive lists of *Swamp Thing* appearances and collectibles to serve as a reference tool for fans and collectors. He promises he's not obsessed with John Constantine's rear end.

James Chambers is the Bram Stoker Award-winning author of the original graphic novel *Kolchak the Night Stalker: The Forgotten Lore of Edgar Allan Poe*, as well as the Lovecraftian novella collection *The Engines of Sacrifice*, described in a *Publisher's Weekly* starred-review as "...chillingly evocative...." He has also written the story collections *Resurrection House* and *On the Night Border*, and the dark, urban fantasy novella *Three Chords of Chaos*. His story "A Song Left Behind in the Aztakea Hills," published in *Shadows Over Main Street 2*, was nominated for a Bram Stoker Award. His tales of crime, fantasy, horror, pulp, science fiction, steampunk, and more have appeared in numerous anthologies and magazines. James has also edited anthologies – most recently *A New York State of Fright* – as well as comics and graphic novels such as *Leonard Nimoy's Primortals*, *Gene Roddenberry's Lost Universe*, and *Shadow House*. His website is www.jameschambersonline.com.

Julianne Clancy is a book marketer, copywriter, amateur chef, Tar Heel alum, Nintendo aficionado, distance runner, and certified Master of Horror, having received her M.Phil degree in popular literature from Trinity College Dublin, with a thesis on Satanic horror. She fell in love with John Constantine a few years back, an affair of which her husband thankfully acknowledges and approves. She just hopes her daughter grows up to be as accepting and supportive of her mother's devilish obsessions as the rest of her family and friends have always been.

Nancy A. Collins is the award-winning author of numerous weird and creepy stories, but is perhaps best known for the punk vampire slayer Sonja Blue, and for being one of the founders of the urban fantasy genre. She is the only woman to have written *Swamp Thing*, and the first woman to have written *Vampirella*. She also wrote a miniseries called *Jason vs. Leatherface*, back in the day. Nancy's most recent works are the weird fantasy novel *Absalom's Wake*, from Macabre Ink/Crossroad Press, and the *Army of Darkness: Furious Road* limited series. She is currently working on an original *Vampirella* prose novel for Dynamite Entertainment, as well as the seventh book in her Sonja Blue series, and looks forward to the release of DC Comics' collected omnibus edition of her entire *Swamp Thing* run in 2020. Nancy currently resides in the Atlanta Metro Area with a cat that won't stop walking across her lap.

Brian Cronin has been writing professionally about comic books for more than a dozen years as a senior writer at CBR.com (primarily with his "Comics Should Be Good" series of columns, including "Comic Book Legends Revealed"). He has written two books about comics for Penguin-Random House – *Was Superman a Spy? And Other Comic Book Legends Revealed* and *Why Does Batman Carry Shark Repellent? And Other Amazing Comic Book Trivia!*, as well as one book, *100 Things X-Men Fans Should Know & Do Before They Die*, from Triumph Books, published in April 2018. Brian's writing has been featured at ESPN.com, the *Los Angeles Times*, About.com, the Huffington Post, and Gizmodo. He features legends about entertainment and sports at his website, Legends Revealed (legendsrevealed.com). Follow him on Twitter at @Brian_Cronin and feel free to e-mail him suggestions at brianc@cbr.com for stories about comic books that you'd like to see featured!

Jamie Delano, the first regular writer on *John Constantine: Hellblazer*, also wrote two *Hellblazer* miniseries, *Bad Blood—A Restoration Comedy* and *The Horrorist*, as well as an original *Hellblazer* graphic novel, *Pandemonium*. Since the publication of his first professional work in the early 1980s, Jamie has made a diverse contribution to the comic book medium, scripting both original works (*World Without End, Tainted, Ghostdancing, Hell Eternal, Cruel and Unusual, Territory, Outlaw Nation, Narcopolis*, and *Rawbone*) and publisher-owned properties such as *Captain Britain, Doctor Who, Night Raven, Animal Man, The Batman, Shadowman*, and *Crossed*. These days, he mainly writes and publishes novels via his micro indie imprint, Lepus Books (lepusbooks.co.uk).

Joseph Dilworth, Jr., was born at a very young age in a small hospital the day before episode six of the *Doctor Who* serial "The War Games" aired. He's been hooked ever since. A lifelong writer, he served for six years as the founder, editor, and lead writer of Pop Culture Zoo. At PCZ, Joe wrote numerous reviews, conducted many highly acclaimed interviews, and offered fair and balanced opinions about numerous topics. He is currently a co-host of The Flickcast's weekly podcast, writes a regular column about TV for *Long Island Pulse Magazine*, and has contributed to other Sequart essay anthologies discussing

Planet of the Apes, *Star Wars*, *Blade Runner*, and *Battlestar Galactica*. Joe firmly believes that *Doctor Who* is the greatest show ever created, period, and *Cinema Paradiso* is his favorite film. He resides in the Pacific Northwest, where he spends time with his family, brews beer, writes, reads, and expresses his opinion to whoever will listen. Just be warned: He has little regard for the laws of space and time.

Sabrina Fried has been a contributor to the many worlds of fandom for more than twenty years as a writer, editor, blogger, and all-around creative person. Her previous publications include contributions to *A More Civilized Age: Exploring the Star Wars Expanded Universe*, *The Cyberpunk Nexus: Exploring the Blade Runner Universe*, and *Somewhere Beyond the Heavens: Exploring Battlestar Galactica,* available now from Sequart. She currently lives in British Columbia, Canada.

Alex Galer, honestly, could not have been happier to see Blockbuster get what it had coming. When his mom and pop's VHS rental shop got put under by the chain, it became his mission to watch every single film in the store before they all got sold off or thrown out. Forgoing an education, Alex learned how to live by the media he consumed. Making a small mark in the indie comic scene under a pen name in the early 1990s, Alex later retreated to working at his local library and writing angry rants on the movie and comic forums he frequented. He spent a time editing funny books for BOOM! Studios and DC Comics, but now searches for purpose as physical media dies and streaming services forget to offer anything made before the mid-'80s. He used to have a cat, but they parted amicably. Now he makes do with a roommate named Bullwhip.

Richard Gray is a writer of things about film and pop culture. Since 2010, he has been the editor of The Reel Bits (thereelbits.com). His first book, *Moving Target: The History and Evolution of Green Arrow*, was published by Sequart in 2017. As the host of Behind the Panels (behindthepanels.net) and several other pop-culture podcasts from 2011 to 2018, he has been talking at length about comics, whether you wanted him to or not. Since 2013, Richard has been a regular columnist at Newsarama's "Best Shots Reviews." He has been heard on the wireless radio devices talking about film for ABC Radio. Follow him on Twitter and Instagram at @DVDBits. He is in Australia and is in your future.

Robert Greenberger is a writer, editor, and teacher. He began his career working at Starlog Press before joining DC Comics in 1984. He has since worked for Gist Communications, Marvel Comics, and *Weekly World News* in various editorial and management capacities. Robert is also a freelance writer with a wide range of genres and audiences, from media tie-in fiction to young-adult nonfiction. His novelization of *Hellboy II: The Golden Army* won the 2009 Scribe Award. He cofounded the digital imprint Crazy 8 Press and continues to write. He reviews for ComicMix and has a twice-monthly column at Westfield Comics. Currently, Robert teaches English and journalism in Maryland, where he lives with his wife Deb. For more, visit bobgreenberger.com.

Rich Handley edits Eaglemoss's *Star Trek Graphic Novel Collection* and has written the introductions to more than a hundred volumes of that series. He has written books about *Planet of the Apes*, *Back to the Future*, and *Watchmen*, as well as licensed *Star Wars* and *Planet of the Apes* fiction. Rich co-edited Titan's Scribe Award-nominated *Planet of the Apes: Tales from the Forbidden Zone* with Jim Beard, plus eight Sequart anthologies to date discussing *Planet of the Apes*, *Star Wars*, *Battlestar Galactica*, *Hellblazer*, and classic monsters. He has written essays and introductions for DC's *Hellblazer: 30th Anniversary Celebration*; IDW's five *Star Trek* and three Eisner Award-nominated *Star Wars* comic-strip reprint hardcovers; BOOM! Studios' four-volume *Planet of the Apes Archive* series; Sequart anthologies about *Star Trek*, *Blade Runner*, and *Back to the Future*; and ATB Publishing's *Outside In* series focused on *Star Trek*, *Star Trek: The Next Generation*, *Buffy the Vampire Slayer*, *Angel*, and *The X-Files*. In addition, Rich is a columnist for HeroCollector.com and the managing editor of RFIDJournal.com.

Robert Jeschonek is an award-winning author who has written for DC and AHOY Comics, composed essays on *Battlestar Galactica* for Sequart, and crafted official *Star Trek* and *Doctor Who* fiction. You can find his envelope-pushing prose stories in *Pulphouse, Fiction River, Galaxy's Edge, Escape Pod,* and many other publications. An Amazon bestseller, Robert has won an International Book Award, a Scribe Award from the International Association of Media Tie-In Writers, and the grand prize in Pocket Books' *Strange New Worlds* contest. He's explored plenty of unique characters, but John Constantine will always hold a special place in his black little heart. (Now you know why he wore trenchcoats and smoked too many ciggies in college.) Hugo and Nebula Award winner Mike Resnick (*Santiago* and the *Starship* series) calls him "a towering talent." Join his continuing twisted adventures on Patreon, Facebook, and Twitter, as well as at www.robertjeschonek.com.

Ross Johnson lives in snowy upstate New York with his husband and two wonderful, but unnecessarily large, dogs. He co-hosts the long-running current affairs radio show *The Sound of Tomorrow* (soundoftomorrow.com), where he discusses trends in politics and pop culture, with a focus on queer and women's issues. Ross writes and performs for several regional comedy television shows, and occasionally shows up onstage. The big, grown-up-looking book he's reading is very often concealing a few comics.

Martín A. Pérez (a.k.a. MaGnUs) hails from Montevideo, Uruguay, and is a writer, letterer, and radio host/producer who lives with his wife, son, and two cats. He has published in print and online; writes articles and columns about roleplaying games, comics and sci-fi; and hosts a radio show (Perdidos En El Eter, perdidoseneleterstudiorobota.blogspot.com) about the same nerdy subjects. His main focus is on writing and lettering comic books, for his own imprint (GAS Comics has published nine anthology magazines, four books, two ongoing webcomics, and numerous short stories), as part of other collectives, and for customers. He also writes narrative and flavor text for video games, and he translates (English-Spanish-English) comics, articles, and short stories, among other things. In his father's words: "So unconventional, and yet so traditionalist...." You could say that kind of describes Martín – longing for more civilized times, yet a passionate futurist.

Draško "Rogan" Roganović is a Serbian comic book translator, essayist, and general busybody. One of his greatest achievements in life was having his nickname immortalized in the background graffiti of a trademark Tim Bradstreet brick wall cover for *Hellblazer* #214, along with his compatriots from the Straight to Hell *Hellbazer* message boards (hellblazer.ipbhost.com).

Frank Schildiner is a martial arts instructor at Amorosi's Mixed Martial Arts in New Jersey. He is the writer of the novels *The Quest of Frankenstein, The Triumph of Frankenstein, Napoleon's Vampire Hunters, The Devil Plague of Naples*, and *Irma Vep and the Great Brain of Mars*. Frank is a regular contributor to the fictional series *Tales of the Shadowmen* and has also been published in *The Lone Ranger and Tonto: Frontier Justice, The Joy of Joe, The New Adventures of Thunder Jim Wade, Secret Agent X* Volumes 3, 4, 5, 6, and *The Avenger: The Justice Files*. He resides in New Jersey with his wife Gail, who is his top supporter, and two cats who are indifferent on the subject.

Tony Simmons is an award-winning journalist based in northwest Florida, and the author of several novels and short-story collections. His latest is the pulp pastiche *Capt. Gideon Argo and the Flying Zombies vs. The Lost Lemurians*, and his next will be the third volume in his urban fantasy series *The Caliban*

Cycle, titled *Sins of the Fathers*. He was a contributor to *Somewhere Beyond the Heavens: Exploring Battlestar Galactica*, also edited by Rich Handley and Lou Tambone. You can find him at Facebook.com/WriterTonySimmons and in his capacity as a founding member of The Syndicate creative group at TheSyndicateStudio.com. He's not Herbert.

Lou Tambone is a freelance writer, editor, independent musician, and UX designer from New Jersey. A lifelong fan of pop culture, he was an early HTML adopter, creating and maintaining some of the first *Star Wars* fan sites under the Starwarz.com banner. As well as the occasional magazine and Web piece, he's been published in anthologies from Sequart covering the *Planet of the Apes, Battlestar Galactica,* and *Star Wars* franchises. His editing credits include *The Cyberpunk Nexus: Exploring the Blade Runner Universe* and *Somewhere Beyond the Heavens: Exploring Battlestar Galactica*, both for Sequart. When he's not reading or writing, Lou is usually making music or rehearsing with one of his many bands. During his "spare time," he tries to remember to eat and breathe.

John Trumbull has been called both "an aging fanboy who hates everything" and "a curmudgeonly Kermit the Frog." (He agrees with the second one.) He's written for TwoMorrows' Eisner-Award-winning *Back Issue* magazine since 2013 and the Atomic Junk Shop website since 2016. A graduate of the Kubert School, John has drawn coloring books for DC Comics' licensing department. As a stand-up comic, he has performed at Carolines on Broadway and the Broadway Comedy Club. He co-hosts *SNL Nerds*, a podcast about *Saturday Night Live*, with his friend and fellow comic Darin Patterson. John is currently writing a book about the DC Animated Universe. You can follow him on Twitter at @TrumbullComic and @SNLNerdsShow.

James Wilkinson is a New York-based journalist and editor whose credits include *Time Out, Metro*, the *South China Morning Post* and – to the horror of his parents – *The Daily Mail*. Occasionally, he gets paid to ramble on about pop culture. He is too tall.

Genevieve Williams has published short fiction in *Asimov's Science Fiction, Analog Science Fiction and Fact, Strange Horizons*, and other publications. She has an MFA degree in popular fiction from Stonecoast and is a Clarion West Writers Workshop graduate. Genevieve lives in Seattle.

ALSO FROM **SEQUART**

SOMEWHERE BEYOND THE HEAVENS: EXPLORING BATTLESTAR GALACTICA
THE CYBERPUNK NEXUS: EXPLORING THE BLADE RUNNER UNIVERSE
BRIGHT LIGHTS, APE CITY: EXAMINING THE PLANET OF THE APES MYTHOS

A LONG TIME AGO: EXPLORING THE STAR WARS CINEMATIC UNIVERSE
A GALAXY FAR, FAR AWAY: EXPLORING STAR WARS COMICS
A MORE CIVILIZED AGE: EXPLORING THE STAR WARS EXPANDED UNIVERSE

OTHER BOOKS ON SCI-FI FRANCHISES:

BOOKS ON GRANT MORRISON:

BOOKS ON WARREN ELLIS:

ON TV AND MOVIES:

OTHER BOOKS:

DOCUMENTARY FILMS:

For more information and for exclusive content, visit Sequart.org.

Made in the USA
Middletown, DE
09 January 2021

31210086R00215